THE KURDS
OF IRAQ

THE KURDS OF IRAQ

Building a State Within a State

Ofra Bengio

LYNNE
RIENNER
PUBLISHERS

BOULDER
LONDON

Published in the United States of America in 2012 by
Lynne Rienner Publishers, Inc.
1800 30th Street, Boulder, Colorado 80301
www.rienner.com

and in the United Kingdom by
Lynne Rienner Publishers, Inc.
3 Henrietta Street, Covent Garden, London WC2E 8LU

Library of Congress Cataloging-in-Publication Data
Bengio, Ofra.
The Kurds of Iraq : building a state within a state / Ofra Bengio.
      p. cm.
  Includes bibliographical references and index.
  ISBN 978-1-58826-836-5 (alk. paper)
  1. Kurds—Iraq—History. 2. Kurds—Iraq—Government relations.
3. Kurds—Iraq—Politics and government—20th century. 4. Kurds—Iraq—
Politics and government—21st century. 5. Kurds—Iraq—History—Autonomy
and independence movements. 6. Kurdistan (Iraq)—Politics and government—
20th century. 7. Kurdistan (Iraq)—Politics and government—21st century.
8. Nationalism—Iraq—Kurdistan. 9. Iraq—Ethnic relations. I. Title.
  DS70.8.K8B458 2012
  956.7'20443—dc23

                                                2011034887

British Cataloguing in Publication Data
A Cataloguing in Publication record for this book
is available from the British Library.

Printed and bound in the United States of America

The paper used in this publication meets the requirements
of the American National Standard for Permanence of
Paper for Printed Library Materials Z39.48-1992.

5 4 3 2 1

To Shmuel, Lavi, and Adi

Contents

Part 3: A Kurdish Entity in the Making, 1998–2010

Part 4: Conclusion

Preface

This book tells the story of the Kurds of Iraq, who, like the phoenix, rose out of the ashes of the wars and civil strife of the twentieth century to establish a self-governing Kurdish entity. Observers, analysts, and many Kurds themselves could hardly believe that such an outcome was possible, particularly in light of Saddam Hussein's brutal campaign against them that verged on genocide. Yet, whereas the Kurds had long been branded as the losers of the twentieth century, by the beginning of the twenty-first century they had cast off this sorry image. This book is the story of that profound transformation.

Treating a half-century of Kurd-state relations in Iraq, the book addresses the following questions: How did Kurd-state dynamics shape the ultimate outcome—the collapse of the Baathi centralized state and the rise of an autonomous Kurdistan? What were the internal and external obstacles to Kurdish nation building? To what extent did the Kurds succeed in overcoming those obstacles? What has been the impact on the geostrategic map of the region?

The study is based on a variety of rich source materials, ranging from British archival documents to Baathi ones acquired following the 1991 and 2003 wars. Other primary sources include Iraqi and Kurdish newspapers, Baathi and Kurdish documents, speeches by public figures, and official declarations. In addition, I draw on a broad swath of secondary sources in Arabic, English, French, German, and Hebrew, as well as on interviews with Kurdish activists and officials in Iraqi Kurdistan and the Kurdish diaspora.

Writing a historical study is an endeavor to which many people contribute, whether knowingly or unknowingly. I was fortunate to become acquainted with many Kurdish friends, whose generosity in sharing with me their experiences, feelings, and insights contributed immensely to my understanding of Kurdish society and politics. My heartfelt thanks to Sherko Kirmanj, Mirza Dinayi, Barzan Faraj, Muhammad Sabir Isma'il, Musa Kaval, Mirza Dimmayi, and many others who prefer to remain anonymous.

ix

I am deeply grateful to my friends and colleagues at the Moshe Dayan Center for Middle Eastern and African Studies, whose assistance and advice were invaluable for bringing the book to completion. Uzi Rabi, the Dayan Center's director, provided moral and professional support. Bruce Maddy-Weitzman was part of the project from its very beginning, was extremely generous with his time, and provided numerous insights throughout the process.

I owe a great debt to Hayim Gal, of blessed memory. Until his untimely passing, he served as the indispensable pillar of the Dayan Center's Documentation Unit. Generations of researchers have benefited from his devotion and dedication to unearthing whatever materials they needed. Without him, I simply would have not been able to successfully carry out my research. His absence is felt keenly by all who knew him.

Marion Gliksberg, the Dayan Center's librarian, was helpful in providing me with research material. Ilana Greenberg assisted in administrative matters and Elena Kuznetsov drew the maps for the book. Guy Bracha, Yair Hoch, and Dotan Halevy provided indispensable assistance in tracing research material and solving technical problems. I also benefited greatly from the linguistic editing and styling of Belina Neuberger, as well as from the feedback of two anonymous readers. Finally, my thanks to Lynne Rienner and her entire team for their help in bringing the manuscript to publication.

Acronyms

CIA	Central Intelligence Agency
ICP	Iraqi Communist Party
IMK	al-Haraka al-Islamiyya fi Kurdistan (Islamic Movement of [Iraqi] Kurdistan)
INC	Iraqi National Congress
IUMK	Islamic Unity Movement of Kurdistan
KDP	Kurdistan Democratic Party (in Iraq)
KDPI	Kurdistan Democratic Party of Iran
KNC	Kurdistan National Congress
KRG	Kurdistan Regional Government
KRP	Kurdistan Revolutionary Party
NGO	nongovernmental organization
OPEC	Organization of Petroleum Exporting Countries
PKK	Partiya Karkerên Kurdistan (Kurdistan Workers' Party) (in Turkey)
PLO	Palestine Liberation Organization
PUK	Patriotic Union of Kurdistan
RCC	Revolutionary Command Council (Iraqi)
UNESCO	United Nations Educational, Scientific, and Cultural Organization

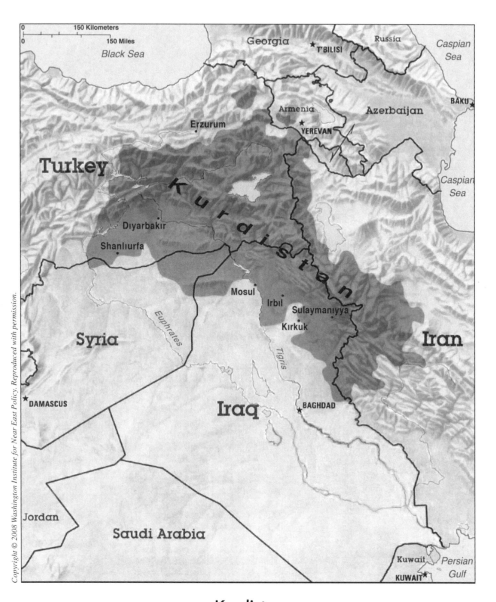

Kurdistan

1

The Evolution of
Kurdish Nationalism

*I met her in a Parisian café in October 1993. She had fled sometime
before from Saddam's Iraq, where she had worked as a scientist. She
was very friendly but, at the same time, extremely frightened. She disclosed neither her name nor any personal details, except for the fact
that she was a Kurd and had lived a nightmarish existence in Iraqi
Kurdistan. The next time I met her was in May 2009, in the Iraqi Kurdistan city of Sulaymaniyya. No longer in need to protect her identity,
Dr. Akhtar Najmaddin had until 2006 served as minister for higher
education in the Sulaymaniyya-based Kurdistan government. These
two meetings epitomize the profound vicissitudes of Kurdish fortunes
over the last half-century. This book is an account of that story.*

Who Are the Kurds?

Kurds began writing their own history only in the late sixteenth century, and
very timidly at that. Hence, scholars and interested parties alike must rely on
non-Kurdish sources for tracing Kurdish historical roots, which causes no end
of controversy. Many researchers and a broad range of Kurdish nationalists
trace the origin of the Kurds to an "Iranian" migration in the first millennium
B.C.E. from an unknown eastern territory into the area where the Kurds now reside.[1] Referring to two Sumerian inscriptions from about 2000 B.C.E., which
mentioned a country called Kar-da-ka, Vladimir Minorsky suggests that the
Kurds are "an Iranian people of Nearer Asia."[2] C. J. Edmonds, too, opines that
"the Kurds constitute a single nation which has occupied its present habitat for
at least three thousand years. They have outlived the rise and fall of many imperial races."[3] Not surprisingly, Kurdish historians, scholars, and politicians
have wholeheartedly embraced such theses.[4]

1

There are, however, more measured and qualified approaches to the question of Kurdish origins. Maria O'Shea says, "It is impossible with the information available to achieve a reasonable understanding of either the precise origins of the Kurds, when they coalesced into such an identifiable group, or their early history, much before the Arab/Islamic invasion."[5] To be sure, in the sixth century C.E., the Talmud repeatedly referred to Kardu and Karduyyim.[6] However, the earliest known document that mentioned the word *Kurds* as a group appeared at the beginning of the Islamic era, in an exchange of letters between the imam 'Ali bin Abi Talib (d. 661) and the governor of Basra.[7] The term became more widespread in the tenth century among leading Muslim historians such as Abu Ja'far Muhammad bin Jarir al-Tabari and Abu al-Hasan 'Ali bin al-Husayn bin 'Ali al-Mas'udi.[8] Both refer to the Kurdish revolt circa 840 in the Mosul region. As to the term *Kurdistan* ("the land of the Kurds"), it was mentioned at the beginning of the twelfth century by Seljuk Turks in reference to an area extending from Azarbaijan to Luristan.[9] Nowadays *Kurdistan* refers to a larger region extending from the Taurus Mountains in the west to the western heights of Iran in the east, and from the Ararat Mountains in the north to the plain of Mesopotamia in the south. Apart from these bare facts, a wealth of controversy remains.

Differences over terminology reflect the larger issues of identity and sovereignty. On the whole, in modern times, official parlance in the so-called host countries in which the Kurds reside shied away from using the term *Kurdistan*. Official Turkish discourse, for example, tended to use the label *southeast Turkey* when referring to the Kurdish-populated region while successive Iraqi regimes mentioned only *northern Iraq*.[10] For their part, Kurdish nationalists determined to represent Kurdistan as a single ethnonational territory spoke of *Northern Kurdistan* for the Turkish, *Southern Kurdistan* for the Iraqi, *Eastern Kurdistan* for the Iranian, and *Western Kurdistan* for the Syrian part.[11] Jalal Talabani, head of the Patriotic Union of Kurdistan (PUK) and president of Iraq since 2005, used the term *Kurdistan al-'Iraq* (Kurdistan of Iraq), pointing to a territory that is found in Iraq, and not *Kurdistan al-'Iraqi* (Iraqi Kurdistan), indicating a territory that belongs to Iraq. In fact, Kurdish independence of mind and power were thus foregrounded.[12] The Kurdish historian Mehrdad Izadi uses a different, Kurdish-centered terminology; namely, "the five sovereign states that share Kurdish land."[13] In that same vein, Kurds in the diaspora do not like to be referred to as Iraqi Kurds or Turkish Kurds, preferring such terms as *Kurds from Iraq* or *Kurds from Turkey*.[14] Nor do the Kurds accept the qualification of "ethnic minority." Asked by Osten Wahlbeck whether he felt that he belonged to such a minority, a Kurdish informant from Turkey answered, "I get really angry when they say Kurdish minority . . . how they call 20 million people a minority is just amazing."[15]

This more assertive language harks back to the representation of the seventeenth-century poet Ahmadi Khani, who writes in his epic *Mem û Zîn:*

Look, from the Arabs to the Georgians,
The Kurds have become like towers.
The Turks and Persians are surrounded by them
The Kurds are on all four corners.[16]

In modern times, however, the very term *Kurd* was at risk of being obliterated by governmental policies. For example, on 3 March 1924, the same day that the caliphate was abolished in Turkey, Mustafa Kemal decreed that all Kurdish schools, associations, and publications would be banned, and that the use of the words *Kurdish* or *Kurdistan* would become a legal offense.[17] Henceforth, the Kurds were officially referred to as "mountain Turks" because, according to folk etymology, the snow made sounds like "kart" and "kurt" when they plodded through the mountain snow.[18] The use of Kurdish place names was also forbidden. The Kurdish name for Diyarbakir, for example, was "Amed." Its use was prohibited, to the extent that one man was even prosecuted for having written it in a letter of invitation.[19] In Iraq, too, such policies of name suppression and replacement were recurrent. Thus, in 1999 the Iraqi minister of interior for security affairs issued instructions for preventing the use of Kurdish names on identity cards.[20] In Iran, a circular was issued in 1923 prohibiting the use of Kurdish in schools. At the beginning of the 1980s, the Islamic regime lifted the ban on Kurdish publications, but the teaching of Kurdish in schools remained prohibited.[21] Even when it was used, it could be problematic because of the social stigma attached to Kurdishness. A member of the Kurdistan Parliament in Exile complains, "Our oppressors have described us, unjustly and successively, as primitive mountain people to civilization, lawless, nomadic, tribes without any national consciousness."[22] In Syria, the infamous 1963 Baathi study by Muhammad Talab Hilal calls for a "policy of making [the Kurds] ignorant" (*siyasat al-tajhil*) by preventing the establishment of schools and educational institutions in their region. Hilal justifies this approach by the failure of an earlier policy, which had been built on the premise "teach them, to Arabize them" (*'allimuhum yasta'ribun*).[23]

The questions as to who is a Kurd and what is the size of the Kurdish population are no less controversial. While governments seek to play down the numbers, Kurdish nationalists tend to inflate them. As the governments do not publish statistics on this matter, we must rely on estimates; in 2006 the number of Kurdish people in the world was considered to be 30 million, thus constituting "the largest stateless nation in the contemporary world."[24]

What, and where, is Kurdistan? For maximalist Kurds, mainly those in the diaspora, the "imagined" map of Greater Kurdistan stretches "from the Caucasus to the Mediterranean and from there to the [Persian] Gulf."[25] However, practically speaking, the historical record is incontestable on at least one point; namely, that the Kurds, who have populated this area from time immemorial, have never succeeded in establishing their own independent state.[26] Even in what is considered their golden era of autonomous principalities (from the sixteenth to the mid-nineteenth century) the Kurdistan region was divided into two areas of influence: one under the Persian Empire and the other under the Ottoman Empire.

Whereas the question of what constitutes Greater Kurdistan is primarily academic, delineating the contours of Iraqi Kurdistan in post-Saddam Iraq has become a real bone of contention between Arabs, Turkmen, and Kurds, with the Kurds aspiring to include the Kirkuk region within its confines. For Iraqi Arabs, this is utterly unacceptable. As one commentator states:

> Have you ever heard of a region that swallowed the original homeland, trampled its identity and changed it into that of the region? The answer is no, we have not heard nor have we read that a region and a small nation could become so domineering as to obliterate the unique history of the big homeland and nation, except in Iraq. . . . Arab Iraq, whose civilization is seven thousand years old, has become the Kurdish region's tail, while the Arab nation has turned into a mere servant of the Kurdish nation.[27]

The Kurds were also variously accused of implementing the "imperialist project for splitting Iraq";[28] of attempting to deny the Islamic identity of the state; of refusing "to consider Kurdistan as part of the Arab nation";[29] and, worst of all, as Israel's agents, of seeking to establish a "second Israel."[30]

What about the nature of Kurdish nationalism? Here, too, there is much controversy, stemming from the fact that there are several distinct Kurdish dialects so that speakers of different dialects do not always understand one another. Some scholars say that they are, in fact, separate languages. Those who emphasize the distinctiveness of the different dialects infer from this that the Kurds do not constitute one nation, but rather different ethnolinguistic groups.[31] Middle Eastern leaders say the same thing, albeit for political reasons.[32]

Kurdish nationalist movements, of course, reject these views and their implications. They are, "like all other nationalisms . . . eager to construct a common Kurdish history, identity, culture and language."[33] Still, as Fred Halliday points out, "there is no single Kurdish nationalist movement, ideology or politics; the history of modern Kurdish nationalism is that of three distinct movements, corresponding to the different contexts of Iran, Turkey and Iraq."[34] In fact, one should also include Syria in this list.

Concerning Kurdish nationalism, the Kurdish linguist Amir Hassanpour advances two notions: feudal nationalism and middle-class nationalism.[35] According to his thesis, feudal nationalism developed in the seventeenth century as a direct result of the wars between the Ottoman and Persian empires, amidst which the Kurds were sandwiched. Thus,

> the enormous destruction and suffering caused by foreign domination resulted in the genesis of national awakening in a feudally organized society. . . . The

idea of nation and nationalism, an apparent anachronism in this part of the world in the seventeenth century, did in fact develop in the particular circumstances of Kurdistan at this time.

Hassanpour bases his thesis on sayings by poets, princes, and "the masses of the people."[36]

According to Hassanpour, the second wave of middle-class nationalism began to take shape in the aftermath of World War I so that "by the 1960s, the modern nationalist ideas had developed into a coherent system of thought that was named *Kurdayeti*," which was, he says, basically secular nationalism.[37]

Abbas Vali puts forward an important distinctive trait between classical nationalism in Europe and Kurdish nationalism. He explains that while classical nationalism in Europe was introduced by modernity, bringing with it democratic citizenship and a civil society, Kurdish nationalism was a response to the denial of Kurdish identity and rested on the suppression of civil society and democratic citizenship in Kurdistan.[38]

To examine Kurdish nationalism through a state-ethnic minority prism, other theoretical writings might be useful. Thus, the *Kurds* could be defined as "a nonstate nation with all the peculiarities of such nation."[39] They may also represent what Miroslav Hroch terms a "non-dominant" ethnic group, which operated within the realm of a territorial nation-state dominated by a different ethnic group, and which was historically hostile toward alternative conceptions of political and social order. The Kurds might thus fit into Anthony D. Smith's definition of a modern *ethnie*—a "named unit of population with common ancestry myths and historical memories, elements of shared culture, some link with a historical territory and some measure of solidarity, at least among [its] elites."[40]

In trying to understand the nature of Kurdish ethnic self-assertion, I apply Frederic Barth's notion of ethnic boundaries; that is, the perception that the major constituent of ethnicity is the maintenance of boundaries between different ethnic groups in polyethnic social systems, and that ethnicity is not simply determined by "objective" cultural determinants. According to Barth, "ethnic groups only persist as significant units if they imply marked difference in behavior, i.e., persisting cultural differences."[41] This appears to complement Hroch's notion that the "nation-forming process is a distinctively older phenomenon than the modern nation and nationalism and that any interpretation of modern national identity cannot ignore the peculiarities of pre-modern national development, or degrade it to the level of a mere myth."[42]

State vs. Ethnicity: The Historiographical Debate

Even a superficial comparison of the literature on the Kurds at the beginning and at the end of the twentieth century points toward dramatic changes, both quantitative and qualitative. Throughout most of the century, few books about the Kurds per se were written in Western languages.[43] As the land of the Kurds was divided up between five states (Turkey, Iran, Iraq, Syria, and the Soviet Union) in the aftermath of World War I, scholars mainly treated the Kurds as an integral part of those nation-states. At times, the Kurds were ignored altogether. In fact, this was part of a larger phenomenon; namely, that "the traditional focus of international relations tended to obscure or ignore the role of nonstate actors."[44] To illustrate this trend the Kurds of Iraq, who in fact represent the most active, tragic, and successful of all Kurdish nonstate actors, serve as a case study.

Until the mid-1960s reference to the Kurds of Iraq was mostly part of the general discourse on Iraq itself, as exemplified by the seminal books of Stephen H. Longrigg, Uriel Dann, and Hanna Batatu.[45] Although all three authors discuss various aspects of their situation in depth, they do so only in the context of the larger issues facing the state. Most startling is Majid Khadduri's book *Independent Iraq*, which almost totally ignores the Kurds while pursuing a pure "nation-state narrative." Covering the period from the time of independence to the overthrow of the monarchy (1932–1958), Khadduri devotes less than 1 out of 368 pages to a discussion of the Kurds.[46] He writes:

> The Kurds, who are racially different from the Arab majority, had long complained of discrimination against them and had agitated for decentralization; but their complaint could hardly be justified, for the southern Arab areas, which were as poor and backward as the Kurdish, had been just as badly neglected and misgoverned by the central Government.

As for the Barzani clan, who led the various revolts in those years, he describes them as mere adventurers.[47]

The Kurdish National Movement, the work of another contemporary Iraqi historian, Wadie Jwaideh, proves that the general neglect of the Kurds in historical writings was due neither to a lack of developments nor to a dearth of material. Interestingly, Jwaideh completed his doctoral thesis in 1960, concurrently with the publication of Khadduri's book, but Jwaideh's dissertation, which epitomizes an "ethnic narrative" counterpoint to that of the nation-state, was published posthumously forty-six years later.[48]

Indeed, there has been a hidden debate or competition between the ethnic narrative and the nation-state narrative. This debate has colored the works of most scholars writing about the Kurds and Iraq. Both approaches are heavily influenced by political developments and personal preferences. As one scholar puts it, "Much of the literature about Kurds seems to be written by uncritical lovers or unloving critics."[49] Needless to say, Kurdish writers have adopted the first approach, although many non-Kurdish scholars have done so as well.

As demonstrated by the "classic" books on modern Iraq, the nation-state narrative was the dominant one until the early 1960s. This was due to a number of factors: Iraqi Kurds, and Kurds in general, were far from the limelight of scholarship, which was focused on postcolonial state-building efforts. Their own inhibitions, caused by political or cultural shackles, prevented them from contributing significantly to the field. There was a dearth of printing presses in the Kurdish region, which remained quite acute until the late 1950s.[50] And, perhaps most importantly, a widely held perception prevailed among scholars and analysts that Iraq was a nation-state of which the Kurds were an integral part, and not a state in which two national movements (the Arab and the Kurdish) were vying for influence.

However, the ethnic narrative began to gain ground little by little in the aftermath of the war between the Kurds and the Iraqi ruler, Colonel 'Abd al-Karim Qasim (1961–1963). Journalists David Adamson and Dana Adams Schmidt, intrigued by the Kurdish war in the Qasim era, each wrote a book on the subject.[51] This trend was subsequently reinforced, especially with the Baath rise to power in 1968. But the main boost to the ethnic-centered narrative came at the turn of the twenty-first century. The shift in focus from the state to the Kurds of Iraq reflects the changing focus of attention among scholars, which in turn reflects the sea changes in the regional and international arena that took place at the end of the twentieth century.

The end of the Cold War and the collapse of the Soviet Union brought about the rise of new states in Central Asia and in Europe, reminiscent of the collapse of the Ottoman Empire in 1918 and the rise of the new states in the Middle East. The demise of the Soviet Union granted increased legitimacy to ethnic voices in the region, empowering Kurdish aspirations for self-assertion and even self-determination. Political developments in Iraq itself, which coincided with those in the international arena, contributed significantly to the new outlook. Most important of all, of course, were the 1991 Gulf War and the resulting establishment of a semiautonomous Kurdistan Regional Government (KRG) in 1992.

Concurrent with these developments in Iraqi Kurdistan were a number of major socioeconomic changes: an improved economic situation, the rise of educational levels, the revival of the Kurdish language, and an active role played by the Kurdish diaspora. Increasingly, Iraqi Kurdistan seemed to be on a track distinct from the rest of the country, thus warranting new research. The growing involvement of the United States in Iraqi affairs also influenced a new generation of scholars. In essence, the voice of the Kurds is being heard more clearly thanks to the studies of a number of scholars and writers throughout the world.[52] One of them, Peter Galbraith, gives expression to what the Kurds themselves did not dare convey; namely, a call for the establishment of a Kurdish state in Iraq.[53]

Not all scholars, however, favor the ethnic narrative. In a book published in 2005 Eric Davis criticizes the ethnic narrative, which in his view is represented by Elie Kedourie, Uriel Dann, and Waldemar Gallman. He maintains that they "all possess a hidden text"; that is, that they are politically motivated. In his idealized conception of Iraq as a nation-state, Davis altogether ignores Kurdish ethnonationalism. He asserts,

> the war effort [of the 1980–1988 Iran-Iraq War] which was not hampered by ethnic or sectarian tensions demonstrated once and for all the shortcomings of viewing Iraq through the conceptual prism of ethnic cleavages. *Iraqis of all ethnicities worked together under duress to successfully prosecute what was by all accounts the largest and most brutal war of the twentieth century.* (emphasis added)

Davis further asserts that the commitment of all ethnic groups to Iraqi nationalism "should dispel the idea that Iraq is an artificial nation-state."[54]

Where do the Kurds of Iraq themselves stand in terms of Kurdish historiography and their contribution to it? As mentioned earlier, due to political and cultural shackles the Kurds were quite late in presenting their own version of Kurdish history in modern times.[55] An important exception to this is Muhammad Amin Zaki, who served as minister in various governments in Baghdad between the years 1925 and 1936. In the two books that he published in 1931 and 1939, Zaki lays the foundations for the study of the Kurds by a Kurd and in the Kurdish language.[56] In his vanguard study, he explains the rationale for writing in Kurdish; namely, that the history of the Kurdish people should be written in their own language and not in Arabic or Turkish. He even goes as far as to criticize Emir Sharif Khan al Bidlisi, the author of *Sharafnameh* (1597) the first account of Kurdish history, for writing in Persian and not in Kurdish.[57] In fact, the first to use Kurdish in their creative work were poets in the sixteenth and seventeenth centuries.[58]

As a Kurdish nationalist, Zaki challenges some of the theories about how far back the Kurds can be traced. While some scholars claim that the Kurds were newcomers to the region, Zaki suggests that they had lived in the region from time immemorial and that they arrived in their present homeland in the seventh century B.C.E.,[59] but had gone by different names and appellations. Zaki rejects the notion presented by some Arab and Muslim historians, like al-Mas'udi, who claims that the Kurds were of Arab origin.[60] He also challenges the common estimates of the Kurdish population. Thus, for example, while the number of Kurds in Iraq in the 1920s is commonly estimated at 494,000, his own estimate is higher; namely, 600,000 or one-fifth of the Iraqi population[61] and the same percentage is claimed today by the Kurds of Iraq.

On the whole, there is a correlation between the political achievements on the ground of the Iraqi Kurds and their ability to present their own narrative. It is clearly demonstrated by the fact that, of all the Kurdish communities, the Kurds of Iraq have produced the most prolific historical and literary writings. By way of comparison, 2,265 Kurdish titles were published in Iraq, but only 10 in Turkey, 31 in Syria, 150 in Iran, and 377 in the Soviet Union between 1920 and 1985.[62] There is no doubt that this was also due to the fact that, relatively speaking, Iraqi Kurds enjoyed much greater freedom of expression. After the establishment of the KRG, the trickle became an avalanche and by 2011 printing houses in major cities in the KRG published abundantly in Kurdish.[63]

Among Kurdish writers themselves, a gradual change became apparent—from a tendency to glorify Kurdish history or portray the Kurds as mere victims, to a more critical approach that examines the Kurds' role in history, the causes for their failure to establish a state of their own, and the most effective ways to improve their lot in the present circumstances.[64] Some Kurdish writers criticize their Kurdish colleagues for overstating the role of the Kurds in history by trying to appropriate certain governments and periods so as to prove the grandeur or antiquity of their nation. Kamal Fu'ad, for example, contends that the fact that a ruler was of Kurdish origin, such as the legendary, twelfth-century sultan Salah al-Din al-Ayyubi, does not mean that the state he governed was Kurdish. "The national belonging of a certain ruler is secondary in importance to such factors as the land, the people, the language and culture," he argues.[65]

Another critical voice is that of Nezan Kendal. In his essay "The Kurds Under the Ottoman Empire," he puts the blame for the Kurds' failure to establish a state of their own on the Kurds themselves: "Following the fall and the dismemberment of the Ottoman Empire all its subject peoples were able to set up their own states. The only exception was the Kurdish people, largely because of the political incompetence and historical backwardness of its leaders."[66]

The debate over who is to blame, the Kurds' own weakness or outside factors, continues to reverberate. Nevertheless, it seems that, at least in the Iraqi case, the Kurds increasingly have taken responsibility for their own fate. Similarly, the quite pervasive way of thinking that one has no friends but the mountains also has changed drastically.

An interesting phenomenon that developed over the years is the crystallization of what can be called local "Kurdish Iraqi" national identity, which distinguishes it from Kurdish communities in the other states. This development mirrored the crystallization of distinct territorial-national identities in the Arab, Iranian, and Turkish states. The delineation of five different states cutting across the Kurdish-speaking lands impacted their situation in two ways. First, the dynamics of politics, culture, language, and social norms of each state left a particular, distinct imprint on each of the five Kurdish communities. Second, the interests of a particular Kurdish community collided at times with the interests of other communities, occasionally resulting in conflict between them; for example, the skirmishes between the Kurdistan Democratic Party (KDP) of Iraq and the Kurdistan Workers' Party or Partiya Karkerên Kurdistan (PKK) of Turkey, particularly in the 1990s.

However, this is not to say that there was no mutual influence. In fact, from the 1960s onward Iraqi Kurdish activism served as a model for Kurds in other countries. Additionally, in recent decades, pan-Kurdish tendencies or movements similar to those of pan-Arabism began to develop among Kurds in the growing diasporas in the West. One of its most important expressions is the Kurdistan Parliament in Exile, established in The Hague in 1995 and now based in Brussels. Other important organizations include the Kurdistan National Congress (KNC), which was formed in London in 1989; student associations established in France; the National Union of Kurdish Students in Europe founded in Munich in 1965; and the Kurdish Academy of Science and Arts established in 1985 in Stockholm.[67]

The Kurds of Iraq and the State: Anatomy of a Changing Relationship

Ever since its establishment, the Iraqi state has had to contend with the Kurdish issue, which has impacted all areas of its socioeconomic and political life as well as its foreign relations. The Kurds of Iraq, for their part, have fashioned a national movement whose achievements far outstrip those of all other Kurdish communities.

Several historical, geopolitical, and demographic factors may explain this phenomenon. In the immediate aftermath of World War I, the Kurds began to make rather inadequately formulated demands for Kurdish independence. They even gained a measure of international approval in the Treaty of Sèvres of 10 August 1920, which promised autonomy and the option of an independent Kurdish state in large areas of Kurdistan that were formerly under Ottoman control while excluding Kurdish Persian areas. It left an opening for the Kurds in the province (*vilayet*) of Mosul (mostly in present-day Iraqi Kurdistan) to join such an autonomy arrangement. However, the Treaty of Sèvres was rendered null and void by the 1923 Treaty of Lausanne, which offered the Kurds nothing.

For Turkey, and in fact for the rest of the world, the Treaty of Sèvres was for all intents and purposes dead and buried. However, this has not been the case for the Kurds. Lacking any current international agreement or resolution to support their cause, Kurdish nationalists have continued to cling to this treaty as providing international legitimacy for their struggle for self-determination. According to a British official in 1943, "although the policy of Mustapha Kemal shattered their immediate hopes, the leaders of the Kurdish national movement regarded these clauses of the Treaty of Sèvres as a recognition by the Western European powers of the Kurdish question and they never ceased to work for Kurdish autonomy."[68]

The fact that the province of Mosul was incorporated into the Iraqi state only in 1926 and that Iraq was ruled by a mandatory power, Great Britain, until 1932 was crucial in creating the unique character of the Kurdish region in Iraq. While post–World War I Iran and Turkey emerged as fully sovereign states and were thus able to impose their will on the Kurdish minority, in Iraq matters were decided by Britain, whose considerations were alien to both Iraqi and Kurdish interests. In addition, Britain itself vacillated for a long time between encouraging Kurdish aspirations for autonomy—and even for the establishment of an independent state in part of the province of Mosul—and incorporating the province into Iraq. This British wavering served as a fertile ground for the development of a Kurdish national movement in Iraq. It also formed the basis for granting special rights to the Kurds there such as the Local Languages Law described later. When Iraq became an independent state, Iraqi regimes were too weak to discard this precedent. At the same time, Kurdish national sentiments grew stronger. An indirect testimony to the burgeoning Kurdish nationalism in the 1940s can be found in the correspondence of British officials. Thus, for example, a British Mandate representative in Iraq derogatorily refers to "those [Kurds] infected by the impracticable idea of Kurdish nationalism." A more tempered British official states, "Whatever their origin, the Kurds, like the Jews, possess a national tenacity which resists any attempts to absorb them." Others describe the developments in Iraqi Kurdistan as "Kurdish nationalism."[69]

According to different estimates, the percentage of Kurds in Iraq ranged from 15.9 percent to 28.0 percent.[70] Such a high percentage, even if one recognizes only the lower figure, was bound to impact the balance of power between the Kurds and the central government. Equally important for the Kurds' relative success in Iraq was the tradition of foreign involvement in the Kurdish issue in Iraq, including that of Great Britain, Iran, Israel, Syria, the Soviet Union, and the United States. In the early 1970s, the dynamics of the Kurdish issue were considerably affected by the power struggles between the United States and the Soviet Union, which sought to advance their interests in an area that did not clearly fall in either's sphere of influence. Another unique feature of the Kurds of Iraq was the fact that they produced a charismatic leader, Mulla Mustafa Barzani, who headed the national movement for over thirty years and contributed greatly to the formation of a Kurdish national consciousness.[71]

The Kurdish case in Iraq basically entailed a clash between two national movements—the Iraqi Arab and the Kurdish—which made coexistence difficult since they were struggling over the same piece of land and the same economic and human resources. Accordingly, two visions developed. While Baghdad sought a centralized government, the Kurds strove for self-government inside Iraq. Iraq's governments were willing to recognize the Kurds as a "national minority" entitled, at the very most, to limited linguistic or cultural rights, but the Kurds demanded that they be recognized as a national movement that shares the right to the state of Iraq with its Arab population. It should be noted that the Arabs and the Kurds who lived in this area were in a similar position in that both were ruled by the Ottoman Empire until the establishment of Iraq. Moreover, until the mid-nineteenth century the Kurds had maintained three semiautonomous principalities in the area that would eventually make up Iraqi Kurdistan. In other words, Kurdish nationalists felt that as the Arab and Kurdish national movements had emerged at the same point in time, they should have equal standing in Iraq.[72] The fact that Iraq was composed of different communal and ethnic groups, which the central government failed to weld into a new Iraqi national entity, exacerbated the conflict even further and made it more difficult to resolve.[73] The sensitivity of the central government was compounded by the fear that any concession to the Kurds would be interpreted as a sign of weakness and result in additional claims, not only on the part of the Kurds, but also by other groups that felt discriminated against such as the Shiʻa. The greatest fear of any Iraqi government was that the Kurds' demands would endanger Iraq's territorial integrity and ultimately lead to the division of Iraq into three "small states" (*duwaylat*): a Kurdish state, an Arab-Sunni state, and a Shiʻi state.[74]

These fears were not expressions of paranoia or demagoguery on the part of the central government, but had their roots in a fractured Iraqi social reality whose different components were held together by particularly weak connecting links. This was especially salient regarding the nature of the bonds between Iraqi Kurdistan and other parts of Iraq. The impregnable mountains of Kurdistan, alongside linguistic and ethnonational differences, determined the exclusive, closed nature of Iraqi Kurdistan and made it more difficult to control from the center. Difficult as such control was, conceding it was inconceivable from the authorities' viewpoint. This resolute approach was not only a function of a natural political instinct seeking to preserve the status quo. It also reflected the supreme strategic and economic importance of Kurdistan given that many valuable resources were concentrated within its territory, including oil wells—indeed, some of Iraq's and the world's largest oil reserves—dams and power stations, and rich agricultural lands that transformed the region into the state's granary. As early as 1925, King Faysal I speaks of the region's importance: "I consider that [the province of] Mosul is to Iraq as the head is to the rest of the body."[75]

What were the historical, geopolitical, and structural constraints under which the Kurds operated? The most salient one was geopolitical. The location of Kurdistan in a landlocked region and on a chain of rugged mountains resulted, first and foremost, in the Kurds' chronic fragmentation on the sociolinguistic, political, and economic levels. Another sociopolitical phenomenon stemmed from the fact that the Kurds maintained tribal-religious alongside national loyalties. Each of these loyalties stood in an ambiguous relationship with the others. On the one hand, the original Kurdish nationalists had arisen from a traditional leadership of agas and shaikhs, who succeeded in bringing the Kurdish masses into the movement because of their special status in Kurdish society. On the other hand, chronic conflicts between these leaders prevented the Kurds from uniting. Usually, a tribal leader's position determined whether his tribe would oppose, join, or remain neutral toward the national movement.[76] In fact, Hussein Tahiri for one puts all of the blame for the Kurds' difficulties and failures on the prevalence of tribalism among the Kurds, which, he maintains, "undermined both the spirit of nationalism and the prodigal emergence of a coherent and unified national movement."[77]

Geographical isolation and the lack of access to the sea delayed the penetration of foreign influences and modern ideas into Kurdistan. The Kurds frequently were one step behind their neighbors, and found it difficult to catch up with political developments. This factor constrained their freedom of action and ability to exist independently. Indeed, the Kurds' dependency on foreign elements became a closed circuit from which they could not escape. Moreover, until the late twentieth century, theirs was for the most part a one-way relationship, from the outside to the inside. The Kurds were thus unable to position themselves in the international arena as an influential power capable of exerting pressure to advance Kurdish interests.

The other side of the coin was that, despite being too weak to achieve independence, the Kurds were strong enough to pose a constant threat to the central government and to force it to grant them various concessions. The Kurds' repute for being courageous and experienced fighters was put across by the nickname they gave their guerrilla army, Peshmerga (i.e., ready to die). Moreover, despite the massive resources at the disposal of the central government, the Kurds had the advantage of being in control of natural fortresses, which enabled them to fight a guerrilla war with a minimum of resources.

Roughly speaking, until the advent of the Baath to power in 1968, three main periods in the history of the Kurdish struggle in Iraq can be distinguished. The first period (1918–1946) was marked by a slow transition from uncoordinated tribal revolts, lacking a defined political direction, to more focused ones led by one accepted leader, Barzani. In 1945, the short-lived Hiva Party acted as a liaison between the political elite and the tribes that this party attempted to unite.[78] The second period (1946–1961) was marked by the establishment in 1946 of the KDP,[79] which henceforth provided the Kurds with an organizational framework, an ideological direction, and a political center. The third period (1961–1968) witnessed the emergence of a strong Kurdish national movement, which overcame—albeit temporarily—chronic divisions, and managed to merge, for the first time in modern Kurdish history, the combative element with the ideological-political one. At the same time, the politicization of Kurdish society moved the Kurds to mobilize for an all-out armed struggle. The Kurds took advantage of different transitional periods characterized by a political vacuum and of the central government's weakness to press their claims. Hence, the Kurdish struggle has been closely linked with the vicissitudes of Iraqi political life ever since its establishment.

The Kurds' demands pertained to both the national and regional spheres. Nationally, the Kurds made repeated demands for proportional representation in all state institutions (including parliament, government, and army) and the proportional division of resources in the state.[80] However, no regime acceded to this demand until 2003. Over a period of eighty years, only two Kurds served as prime ministers and then only for brief periods (Nur-al-Din Mahmud, from November 1952 to January 1953, and Ahmad Mukhtar Baban, from May to July 1958). Similarly, since the early 1940s, there was a growing tendency to reduce the number of Kurds in the staff officer colleges, the air force, and the police—to the extent that by the 1970s Kurds represented only 2 percent of these units.[81] The reason for this was that, in times of trial, many Kurds chose loyalty to the Kurdish nation over loyalty to the state. In the rebellion of the 1940s, and later in the 1960s, 1970s, and 1991 rebellions, Kurdish officers deserted from the army and joined the Kurdish camp.

Another demand on the national level, which also went unanswered, concerned the establishment of a democratic system in Iraq. The Kurds regarded the satisfaction of this demand as a guarantee of fair Kurdish representation and the fulfillment of the regime's commitments to them.

What's in a Name? Kurdish Autonomy

Kurdish demands regarding the status of the Kurdistan region were ambivalent. At times this ambivalence was tactical while at other times it reflected mere confusion and indecisiveness.[82] In theory, the Kurds had three options: full independence, a federation between the Arab and Kurdish parts of Iraq, or Kurdish autonomy in the framework of the Iraqi state. In actuality, the most practical alternative, which was adopted as the movement's primary objective, was autonomy. Nonetheless, independence slogans were occasionally voiced. For example, Shaikh Mahmud Barzanji, the spearhead of the Kurdish rebellions between 1918 and 1931, established a Kurdish government in the district of Sulaymaniyya in the autumn of 1922, and declared himself king of Kurdistan. In 1930, he called on the British high commissioner to establish a Kurdish entity stretching from Zakho in the north to Khanaqin in the south.[83]

When the KDP was established in 1946, it included in its platform the following two objectives: "complete independence for Kurdistan" and "a struggle to establish a federal state in Iraq, which will be the Federal Democratic State of Kurdistan."[84] There was clearly a contradiction between the goal of complete independence and the goal of a *federal state*, which is by definition "a unity and partnership based on and regulated by an agreement."[85] In any case, the KDP itself quickly abandoned these two objectives and adopted the goal of autonomy.[86] Thus, although the slogan of independence continued to linger in the Kurdish world, it never became an operative objective.

The option of autonomy chosen by the Kurds was particularly problematic[87] because it was not well anchored in international law[88] and because it was generally perceived as a purely internal matter. The two types of autonomy, personal-cultural and territorial, are open to a number of interpretations: the minimalist interpretation, which is usually that of the party granting the autonomy, and the maximalist interpretation, which is that of the party seeking the right to autonomy. The fate of autonomy is ultimately determined by the balance of power between the granter and the recipient or, as a Kurdish leader puts it, "It [the autonomy] depends on our strength and that of our enemy's [*sic*]."[89]

One analyst defines autonomy as an artificial, purposeless, and dubious solution, suggesting that "autonomous relations in the twentieth century have mainly been a placebo intended to thwart liberation movements and repel separatist pressures. . . . Autonomy has been granted half-heartedly and has been accepted with ingratitude."[90] Criticism is also heard, mainly among Kurdish exiles, to the effect that the Kurdish national movement has abandoned the goal of independence and chosen autonomy. They see this as a cul-de-sac and the movement's main weak point. One critic says, "The demand for a truly autonomous Kurdish region for the Kurdish people in Iraq is like a thoroughbred horse seeking to hitch itself with a mule."[91]

The main questions that come to mind in this regard are: Why did the Kurds choose this way? When did they demand autonomy? And, how did the authorities respond to them?

The main reason for the Kurds' espousal of the autonomy option was their inherent weakness, which precluded them from aspiring to full independence. Autonomy seemed less threatening to the central government; thus, its prospects of being realized were more favorable. At the same time, autonomy could serve as a base and a springboard for more far-reaching objectives. Historical experience with semiautonomous principalities from the Middle Ages to the mid-nineteenth century was part and parcel of the Kurds' collective memory, and may have contributed to their opting for this route.

There was much unrest among the Kurds between 1918 and 1925, when the fate of the province of Mosul had yet to be decided. A variety of slogans was put forth in support of independence and autonomy. After Shaikh Mahmud Barzanji established the government of Kurdistan in the autumn of 1922, the British, who were in charge of regional administration, endeavored to appease the Kurds and draw their support away from him and the Turkish government. Due to the pressure exerted by Great Britain in December 1922, a far-reaching declaration on Kurdish autonomy was issued by the British and Iraqi authorities, despite the fact that it lacked legal grounding. According to the declaration, the governments of Great Britain and Iraq "recognize the rights of the Kurds living within the boundaries of Iraq to set up a Kurdish Government within these boundaries."[92] A special delegation of the League of Nations, which arrived in Mosul in early 1925 to ascertain the population's wishes and to make recommendations regarding the future of the region, reached the conclusion that the "Kurdish national sentiment" was strong and that the Kurds had a genuine desire to obtain full independence.[93] Nonetheless, the operative conclusion was the annexation of the province of Mosul to Iraq, with the provision of guarantees regarding the appointment of Kurds to positions in the administration and the legal and educational system of "their country" and the introduction of the Kurdish language as an official language. These promises, which were perceived by the Kurds as pledges of administrative and linguistic autonomy with international backing, were ignored after the annexation of Mosul. In addition they were not mentioned in the 1930 agreement between Britain and Iraq, which was supposed to pave the way for Iraq's admission to the League of Nations and hence to its independence. Even the term *Kurdistan* was not mentioned. The term *northern Iraq* was used instead.

Before its admission to the League of Nations in 1932, the Iraqi government issued a written declaration on the special status of minorities. It also enacted the Local Languages Law, which stipulated that "Iraq undertakes [*sic*] that in the *liwa*s [provinces] of Mosul, Arbil [Erbil], Kirkuk and Sulaymaniyya, the official language, side by side with Arabic, shall be Kurdish in the *qadha*s [district] in which the population is predominantly of Kurdish race."[94] The purpose of the law was to determine the boundaries of the area in which the Kurdish language would be spoken as the language of the administration, the courts, and the elementary schools.[95] Although the Barzani rebellions of 1931–1932 and 1943–1945 closely followed the declaration regarding the Local Languages Law, they did not result in any concessions to the Kurds. This remained the case until the elimination of the monarchy and the ascension of 'Abd-al-Karim Qasim to power in 1958.

Several days after Qasim's ascent to power, a Kurdish delegation presented him with a demand for administrative autonomy. Qasim rejected this demand, but granted far-reaching concessions to the Kurds during the first two years of his rule, including permission for the KDP to operate openly. In exchange, the party was forced to remove the autonomy paragraph from its platform in 1960.[96] In August 1961, when relations between Qasim and the Kurds deteriorated, the Kurds presented him with an ultimatum containing a demand for autonomy. Qasim responded by declaring war. Autonomy henceforth became the declared objective of the Kurdish rebellion.[97] The war, which broke out in September 1961, became known as the September Revolution (*thawrat aylul*) in the Kurdish discourse, in a way mirroring Qasim's July Revolution.[98]

After the first Baath regime came to power in February 1963, the Kurds presented it with a similar ultimatum. In April of the same year, the Kurdish ultimatum formulated, for the first time, a Kurdish plan that went so far as to speak, not of autonomy, but rather of federalism (*ittihad ikhtiyari*). The plan sought to include the provinces of Erbil, Sulaymaniyya, and Kirkuk in the Kurdish federative part as well as the districts and subdistricts populated by a Kurdish majority in Diyala and Mosul.[99] Interestingly, the demand to include Kirkuk has continued to bedevil the Iraqi state. The Baath rejected these demands immediately. It agreed only to a decentralization plan, which was actually a delaying tactic until the war that it had initiated in the summer of 1963 and that led to the Baath downfall in the autumn of the same year. When 'Abd-al-Salam 'Arif came to power and a cease-fire between 'Arif and Barzani was announced in February 1964, Barzani brought up the demand for autonomy.[100] However, 'Arif rejected these demands, and in February 1965 his interior minister declared that "Iraq does not intend to grant autonomy to the Kurds in the present or in the future."[101]

The Kurds intensified the pressure. The war, which continued intermittently until June 1966, induced the government of 'Abd-al-Rahman al-Bazzaz to agree to a cease-fire and to announce the twelve-point al-Bazzaz plan, which included the most extensive concessions to the Kurds up to then, although it still refrained from explicitly mentioning autonomy. Al-Bazzaz's plan was later ignored. The war resumed and continued for a year and a half after the ascension of the Baath on 2 July 1968.

The turning point came in March 1970. For the first time in Iraq's history, after a struggle that had lasted for more than fifty years, the government recognized the Kurds' right to autonomy.

Our discussion on Kurdish autonomy begins at this point.

Notes

1. Amir Hassanpour, *Nationalism and Language in Kurdistan 1918–1985* (San Francisco: Mellen Research University Press, 1992), p. 49.

2. Vladimir Minorsky, "Kurds," in *Encyclopedia of Islam*, 1st ed.

3. Quoted in Hassanpour, *Nationalism and Language*, p. 62.

4. A Kurdish memorandum, presented to the UN in November 1968, maintained that "the [Kurdish] nation has been ruled for the last 25 centuries by 25 Kings of the same family." Emir Kamuram Bedirkhan, Public Record Office, FCO17/872, 18 November 1968.

5. Maria O'Shea, "Tying Down the Territory: Conceptions and Misconceptions of Early Kurdish History," in *The Kurds: Nationalism and Politics*, eds. Faleh A. Jabar and Dawod Hosham (London: Saqi, 2006), p. 126.

6. Mordechai Zaken, *Jewish Subjects and Their Tribal Chieftains in Kurdistan* (Leiden: Brill, 2007), p. 1.

7. Kamal Fu'ad, "Introduction," in Muhammad Amin Zaki, *Ta'rikh al-Kurd wa Kurdistan*, vol. 1 (in Kurdish, 1931; in Arabic, Cairo: Matba'at al-Sa'ada, 1939), p. xii.

8. Abu Ja'far Muhammad bin Jarir al-Tabari, *Ta'rikh al-Umam wal-Muluk* (Beirut: Dar al-Qamus al-Hadith, 1968); Abu al-Hasan 'Ali bin al-Husayn bin 'Ali al-Mas'udi, *Muruj al-Dhahab*, vol. 3 (Paris: L'imprimerie Nationale, 1918), pp. 248–250. In al-Tabari, they are called Baqarda or Qarda. Muhammad Amin Zaki, *Ta'rikh al-Kurd wa Kurdistan*, vol. 1, p. 40.

9. Fu'ad, "Introduction," pp. xii, xiii.

10. Until 1970, Iraqi governments refused to use the term *Kurdistan*. Farid Asasard, *Al-Mas'ala al-Kurdiyya ba'd Qanun Idarat al-Dawla* (Cairo: Maktabat Madbuli, 2006), p. 26. Brendan O'Leary relates an anecdote whereby, when he was about to cross the border from Iraqi Kurdistan to Turkey in 2004, a Turkish soldier forced him to erase the

word "Kurdistan" from his computer and replace it with "northern Iraq." Brendan O'Leary, John McGarry, and Khalid Salih, eds., *The Future of Kurdistan in Iraq* (Philadelphia: University of Pennsylvania Press, 2005), pp. 3–4.

11. See, for example, the title of Jawad Mella's book *Al-Siyasa al-Isti'mariyya li-Hizb al-Ba'th al-Suri fi Gharb* [Western] *Kurdistan* (London: Kurdistan National Congress, 2004). A petition of 9 October 1930 from the Pizhdar to the League of Nations mentioned the term *Southern Kurdistan*. Public Record Office, CO 730/157/8, 9 October 1930.

12. *Al-Ittihad* (Baghdad, daily), 27 January 2005.

13. Mehrdad Izadi, *The Kurds: A Concise Handbook* (Washington, DC: Taylor & Francis, 1992), p. 99.

14. Osten Wahlbeck, *Kurdish Diasporas: A Comparative Study of Kurdish Refugee Communities* (London: Macmillan Press, 1999), p. 7.

15. Ibid., p. 115.

16. Hassanpour, *Nationalism and Language*, p. 53. On this epic, see Martin van Bruinessen, "Ehmedi Xanî's Mem û Zîn and Its Role in the Emergence of Kurdish National Awareness," in *Essays on the Origins of Kurdish Nationalism*, ed. Abbas Vali (Costa Mesa, CA: Mazda, 2003), pp. 40–57.

17. Joyce Blau, "Refinement and Oppression of Kurdish Language," in *The Kurds: Nationalism and Politics*, eds. Faleh A. Jabar and Dawod Hosham (London: Saqi, 2006), pp. 23, 108.

18. Mücahit Bilci, "Black Turks, White Turks: On the Three Requirements of Turkish Citizenship," *Insight Turkey* 11, no. 3 (2009): 30.

19. Ibid., p. 31.

20. Document no. 16, 21 August 1999, in Dilshad Nu'man Farhan, *Mu'anat al-Kurd al-Izidiyyin fi Zill al-Hukumat al-'Iraqiyya 1921–2003* (Duhok: Duhok University, 2008), p. 206.

21. Blau, "Refinement and Oppression," p. 109.

22. Wahlbeck, *Kurdish Diasporas*, p. 41.

23. For the full text of the study, see Mella, *Al-Siyasa al-Isti'mariyya*, pp. 94, 96.

24. Abbas Vali, "The Kurds and Their 'Others': Fragmented Identity and Fragmented Politics," in *The Kurds: Nationalism and Politics*, eds. Faleh A. Jabar and Dawod Hosham (London: Saqi, 2006), p. 49.

25. Jemal Nebez, *The Kurds* (London: Western Kurdistan Association, 2004), p. 7; Jawad Mella, *Kurdistan and the Kurds: A Divided Homeland and a Nation Without State* (London: Western Kurdistan Association, 2005), pp. 21–22. The term *Greater Kurdistan* was in use in the seventeenth century. Minorsky, "Kurds," p. 1146. This notion of Greater Kurdistan was extremely controversial: one Arab commentator referred to it as indicating the Kurds' "expansionist, racial, national approach." Salim Matar, *Al-Dhat al-Jariha* (Beirut: al-Mu'assasa al-'Arabiyya lil-Dirasat wal-Nashr, 1997), p. 480.

26. The short-lived Republic of Mahabad, established in Iran in 1946, was an exception that proved the rule.

27. Samir 'Ubayd, *Al-Quds al-'Arabi* (London, daily), 5 May 2006.

28. The raising of the Kurdish flag was considered as the beginning of such process. *Al-Musawwar* (Cairo, weekly), 8 September 2006; *Al-Hawadith* (London, weekly), 15 September 2006.

29. *Al-Mujtama'* (Kuwait, weekly), 20 August 2005.

30. 'Abd al-Fattah 'Ali Al-Botani, "Introduction," in Adib Mu'awwad, *Al-Qadiyya al-Kurdiyya* (Duhok: Duhok University, 2008), p. 10.

31. For such a debate, see Martin van Bruinessen, "Kurdish Paths to Nation," in *The Kurds: Nationalism and Politics*, eds. Faleh A. Jabar and Dawod Hosham (London: Saqi, 2006), pp. 24–29.

32. One example is that in 1991 Iraqi president Saddam Hussein issued a decree changing the nationality of non-Arabs to an Arab nationality: "In order to grant the Iraqi the right to choose his nationality (*qawmiyya*) and in accordance with the Arab Ba'th socialist party that an Arab is he who has lived in the Arab homeland, spoken its language and chosen Arabism as his nationality . . . the RCC decided that every Iraqi who has attained 18 years of age is entitled to change his nationality to Arab nationalism." The document is found in Farhan, *Mu'anat al-Kurd*, p. 203.

33. Hassanpour, *Nationalism and Language*, pp. 61–62; Wahlbeck, *Kurdish Diasporas*, p. 42.

34. Fred Halliday, "Can We Write a Modernist History of Kurdish Nationalism?" in *The Kurds: Nationalism and Politics*, eds. Faleh A. Jabar and Dawod Hosham (London: Saqi, 2006), p. 16.

35. Ibid., pp. 55–65.

36. Ibid., pp. 55–56.

37. Ibid., pp. 60–65. Among the Kurds of Iraq the term is written as *Kuradayti*. Document no. 10, in Mas'ud Barzani, *Al-Barzani wal-Haraka al-Kurdiyya al-Taharruriyya*, vol. 3: *Thawrat Aylul 1961–1975* (Erbil: 2002), p. 478.

38. Abbas Vali, "Genealogies of the Kurds: Constructions of Nation and National Identity in Kurdish Historical Writing," in *Essays on the Origins of Kurdish Nationalism*, ed. Abbas Vali (Costa Mesa, CA: Mazda, 2003), pp. 104–105.

39. Charles Benjamin, "The Kurdish Nonstate Nation," in *Nonstate Nations in International Politics*, ed. Judy S. Bertelsen (New York: Praeger, 1977), pp. 69–97.

40. Anthony D. Smith, *Nations and Nationalism in a Global Era* (Cambridge, UK: Polity Press, 1995), pp. 65–66.

41. Fredrick Barth, "Introduction," in *Ethnic Groups and Boundaries*, ed. Fredrick Barth (Long Grove, IL: Waveland Press, 1998), pp. 9–37.

42. Miroslav Hroch, *Social Preconditions of National Revival in Europe: A Comparative Analysis of the Social Composition of Patriotic Groups Among the Smaller European Nations* (New York: Columbia University Press, 2000), p. 74.

43. There were of course quite a few important essays such as the vanguard one by Minorsky, "Kurds"; and Serge Gantner, "Le mouvement national kurde," *Orient*, no. 32–33 (1964/1965): 29–120. In general, French scholars and journalists are among the vanguards in Western languages of the study of Kurdish nationalism: among them are Thomas Bois, Joyce Blau, and Basile Nikitine.

44. "The nonstate nation is defined as any entity that operates in a manner normally associated with a nation-state but is *not* a generally recognized nation-state. The defining characteristic of such a nation is its assertion or action implying sovereignty, while not being generally recognized as a sovereign entity." Judy S. Bertelsen, "Introduction," in *Nonstate Nations in International Politics*, ed. Judy S. Bertelsen (New York: Praeger, 1977), p. 2.

45. Stephen H. Longrigg, *Iraq, 1900 to 1950: A Political, Social, and Economic History* (London: Oxford University Press, 1953); Uriel Dann, *Iraq Under Qassem: A Political History, 1958–1963* (New York: Praeger, 1969); Hanna Batatu, *The Old Social Classes and the Revolutionary Movements of Iraq* (Princeton: Princeton University Press, 1978).

46. Majid Khadduri, *Independent Iraq, 1932–1958: A Study in Iraqi Politics* (London: Oxford University Press, 1960), pp. 60–61. The same is true for Bernard Lewis, *The Emergence of Modern Turkey* (London: Oxford University Press, 1965), pp. 260–261. Lewis devotes less than one page to the Kurdish problem in Turkey.

47. Khadduri, *Independent Iraq*, pp. 60–61. Interestingly, in a book that he published nine years later, he devotes a large part of the book to the Kurdish national movement.

Majid Khadduri, *Republican Iraq: A Study in Iraqi Politics Since the Revolution of 1958* (London: Oxford University Press, 1969).

48. Wadie Jwaideh, *The Kurdish National Movement: Its Origins and Developments* (Syracuse: Syracuse University Press, 2006).

49. Abdul Aziz Said, "Perspective of Abdul Said," in *Kurdish Identity: Human Rights and Political Status*, eds. Charles G. MacDonald and Carole A. O'Leary (Gainesville: University Press of Florida, 2007), p. 30.

50. Hassanpour, *Nationalism and Language*, pp. 171–175.

51. David Adamson, *The Kurdish War* (London: Allen & Unwin, 1964); Dana Adams Schmidt, *Journey Among Brave Men* (Boston: Little, Brown, 1964).

52. It is not my intention to give a comprehensive list of the books here. Readers will find them in the notes and the bibliography. Some of these are: Michael Gunter (*The Kurds of Iraq: Tragedy and Hope*); Kanan Makiya (*Cruelty and Silence: War, Tyranny, Uprising, and the Arab World*); Martin van Bruinessen (*Agha, Shaikh and State: The Social and Political Structures of Kurdistan*); Gareth Stansfield (*Iraqi Kurdistan: Political Development and Emergent Democracy*); Jonathan Randal (*After Such Knowledge, What Forgiveness? My Encounters with Kurdistan*); Susan Meiselas (*Kurdistan in the Shadow of History*); Denise Natali (*The Kurds and the State: Evolving National Identity in Iraq, Turkey, and Iran*); Quil Lawrence (*Invisible Nation: How the Kurds' Quest for Statehood Is Shaping Iraq and the Middle East*); David McDowall (*A Modern History of the Kurds*); Brendan O'Leary, John McGarry, and Khalid Salih, eds. (*The Future of Kurdistan in Iraq*); Joost R. Hilterman (*A Poisonous Affair*); David Romano (*The Kurdish Nationalist Movement: Opportunity, Mobilization and Identity*); Kerim Yildiz (*The Kurds in Iraq: The Past, Present and Future*).

53. Peter W. Galbraith, *The End of Iraq: How American Incompetence Created a War Without End* (New York: Simon & Schuster, 2006).

54. Eric Davis, *Memories of State: Politics, History, and Collective Identity in Modern Iraq* (Berkeley: University of California Press, 2005), pp. 11–112, 198–199.

55. Abbas Vali maintained that the absence of history writing did not mean that the past was not made use of in the production of meaning. Furthermore, the perception that they possess a common history has played a decisive role in the Kurds' struggle against the states. Abbas Vali, "Introduction: Nationalism and the Question of Origins," in *Essays on the Origins of Kurdish Nationalism*, ed. Abbas Vali (Costa Mesa, CA: Mazda, 2003), pp. 25, 38.

56. Zaki, *Ta'rikh al-Kurd*, vol. 1, 2 (in Arabic) (Cairo: Matba'at al-Sa'ada, 1939, 1945).

57. Zaki, *Ta'rikh al-Kurd*, vol. 1, p. *ya* (in Arabic). This criticism was later refuted by another Kurdish author, who explained that the Kurdish language had become a language of prose writing in only the second part of the nineteenth century. Fu'ad, "Introduction," p. xiii.

58. Blau, "Refinement and Oppression," pp. 103–104.

59. Zaki, vol. 1, p. 57.

60. Ibid., pp. 48–49. Years later, Jalal Talabani ridiculed the "imaginary stories" about the Arab origins of the Kurds: *Kurdistan wal-Haraka al-Qawmiyya al-Kurdiyya* (Beirut, 1971), p. 26; Mas'udi, *Muruj al Dhahab*, pp. 248–250.

61. Zaki, vol. 1, pp. 25–32.

62. Hassanpour, *Nationalism and Language*, pp. 191, 211–218. By 1970, there were hundreds of works in Kurdish. Fu'ad, "Introduction," p. xxi.

63. The books of two leading Kurdish politicians, Jalal Talabani, *Kurdistan wal-Haraka al-Qawmiyya al-Kurdiyya,* and Mas'ud Barzani, *Al-Barzani wal-Haraka al-*

Kurdiyya al-Taharruriyya, should also be mentioned. It is not my intent to provide a list of Kurdish historians and analysts, but only to mention that their number is becoming larger through time.

64. This view is held, quite exceptionally, by an Arab. See Mu'awwad, *Al-Qadiyya al-Kurdiyya,* p. 39.

65. Fu'ad, "Introduction," p. v.

66. In Gérard Chaliand, ed., *A People Without a Country: The Kurds and Kurdistan,* (London: Zed Press, 1980), p. 44.

67. Nebez, *The Kurds,* p. 74.

68. "Some Notes on the Kurdish Question," Public Record Office, FO195/2477, 3 December 1943.

69. Ibid.; Hassanpour, *Nationalism and Language,* p. 113.

70. This divergence is due to the absence of official statistics and to the disparate positions of various authors. For example, Mahmud al-Durra, an Iraqi officer who fought against the Kurds in the 1940s, gives their percentage in 1961 as 15.66 percent. Mahmud al-Durra, *al-Qadiyya al-Kurdiyya,* 2nd ed. (Beirut: Dar al-Tali'a, 1966), p. 15. By contrast, Ismet Sheriff Vanly, a member of the Kurdish national movement, says 28 percent for 1975. Ismet Sheriff Vanly, "Kurdistan in Iraq," in *A People Without a Country: The Kurds and Kurdistan,* ed. Gérard Chaliand (London: Zed Press, 1980), p. 157. Another Kurd states their percentage as 23.5 percent in 1990. Mehrdad R. Izady, *The Kurds: A Concise Handbook* (Washington, DC: Taylor & Francis, 1992), p. 117.

71. Nechirvan Barzani, the then KRG prime minister, speaks about fifty years of Barzani leadership. Not all Kurds of Iraq subscribe to this view. Opponents of the Kurdistan Democratic Party saw him as a traitor because of the 1975 debacle. Kurdish intellectuals, interviewed by the author, Sulaymaniyya, 2 May 2009. Hussein Tahiri accused him of causing division in the Kurdish ranks. Hussein Tahiri, *The Structure of Kurdish Society and the Struggle for a Kurdish State* (Costa Mesa, CA: Mazda, 2007), p. 129.

72. In an exchange between Mulla Mustafa Barzani and President 'Abd al-Salam 'Arif, the former stresses these very points. Barzani, *Al-Barzani wal-Haraka,* vol. 3, pp. 522–523.

73. For a discussion on this failure, see Khadduri, *Republican Iraq,* pp. 173–177.

74. For such fears, see *Al-Thawra* (Baghdad), 15 September 1991.

75. Cecil J. Edmonds, *Kurds, Turks and Arabs* (London: Oxford University Press, 1957), p. 398. Interestingly, in the referendum on Faysal in July 1921, the *liwa'* of Sulaymaniyya refused to participate and the *liwa'* of Kirkuk did so reluctantly, accounting (it was claimed) for the 4 percent negative vote. Significantly, neither Sulaymaniyya nor Kirkuk sent representatives to the accession ceremony held in Baghdad on 23 August 1921. Jwaideh, *The Kurdish National Movement,* p. 187.

76. Martin van Bruinessen, *Agha, Shaikh and State: The Social and Political Structures of Kurdistan* (London: Zed Books, 1992), p. 10.

77. Tahiri, *The Structure of Kurdish Society,* p. 17.

78. Jwaideh, *The Kurdish National Movement,* pp. 239–241.

79. Kurdish parties existed previously, but they were short-lived groups that lacked continuity and a centralized structure. The new party changed components in its name on three occasions. For simplicity's sake, I have used the name current in the period under discussion in this book.

80. Mulla Mustafa Barzani, for example, fantasized about obtaining one-third of Iraq's oil revenues, "a share proportionate to Kurdistan's population." Adamson, *The Kurdish War,* p. 147.

81. Martin Short and Anthony McDermott, "The Kurds," Minority Rights Group Paper no. 23 (London: Minority Rights Group, February 1975). The KDP claimed that Kurds were not usually admitted into Iraqi intelligence. "A Paper on the Kurdish Problem in Iraq," presented at the UN Seminar on the Rights of National, Ethnic, and Other Minorities, Ohrid, Yugoslavia, June–July 1974.

82. Sitting on the fence is not characteristic of the Kurdish national movement alone. Rather it is a phenomenon that has extended to national movements in Africa, for example. See Benyamin Neuberger, *National Self-Determination in Postcolonial Africa* (Boulder: Lynne Rienner, 1986), p. 63.

83. Farid Asasard, *Al-Mas'ala al-Kurdiyya ba'd Qanun Idarat al-Dawla* (Cairo: Maktabat Madbuli, 2006), p. 24. Six Kurdish members of the Iraqi parliament sent a memorandum in the same vein, adding a call to unite the Kurdish provinces into one unit. Ibid., p. 25.

84. David Andrews, ed., *The Lost Peoples of the Middle East* (Salisbury: Documentary Publications, 1982), p. 134.

85. Daniel Elazar, ed., *Federalism and Political Integration* (Ramat Gan, Israel: Turtledove, 1979), p. 3.

86. The KDP's sixth congress held in 1964 adopted this goal. Ismet Sheriff Vanly, *Le Kurdistan irakien entité nationale: Étude de la révolution de 1961* (Neuchâtel, Switzerland: Éditions de la Baconnière, 1970), p. 228.

87. The meaning of the word *autonomia* in Greek is independent leadership. This concept has undergone many transformations since it was first used in Greece in the second half of the fifth century B.C.E. Its current meaning is "the right of an institution or community to conduct its affairs according to its own laws." *The Hebrew Encyclopedia* (in Hebrew, Tel Aviv: The Encyclopedia Publication Company, 1958), p. 780. "Conditional or limited independence, based on law or custom, and subject to change by the authority which grants it." Walter John Raymond, *Dictionary of Politics* (Lawrenceville, VA: Brunswick, 1992), p. 30.

88. Robert A. Friedlander, "Autonomy and the Thirteen Colonies: Was the American Revolution Really Necessary?" in *Models of Autonomy*, ed. Yoram Dinstein (New Brunswick, NJ: Transaction Books, 1981), p. 136.

89. Adamson, *The Kurdish War*, p. 92.

90. Friedlander, "Autonomy," p. 136.

91. Ismet Sheriff Vanly, "Hawla al-Istratijiyya al-Siyasiyya wal-'Askariyya lil-Haraka al-Wataniyya al-Kurdiyya," *Dirasat Kurdiyya*, no. 1–2 (1985): 22–23.

92. Edmonds, *Kurds, Turks and Arabs*, p. 312.

93. Ibid.

94. Hassanpour, *Nationalism and Language*, p. 111.

95. Public Record Office, FO 371/15312, 11 June 1931.

96. *Al-Minhaj wal-Nizam al-Dakhili lil-hizb al-Dimuqrati al-Kurdistani* (Min Manshurat Pareti Dimuqrati Kurdistan, 1960).

97. In November 1962 a group of plotters approached Barzani, suggesting that he participate in a coup against Qasim. Barzani's reply was that the minimum that the Kurds would demand for such cooperation would be autonomy. Documents no. 9 and 10, in Barzani, *Al-Barzani wal-Haraka*, vol. 3, pp. 474–477.

98. Barzani, *Al-Barzani wal-Haraka*, from the book's subtitle, *Thaurat aylul.*

99. Barzani, *Al-Barzani wal-Haraka*, vol. 3, Appendix 12, pp. 483–488. Nechirvan Barzani mentioned that, between 1961 and 1975, (Mustafa) Barzani "led the Aylul revolution in Iraq." See Nechirvan Barzani, "Perspective of Nechirvan Barzani, Prime Minister, Kurdistan Regional Government," in *Kurdish Identity: Human Rights and Political*

Status, eds. Charles G. MacDonald and Carole A. O'Leary (Gainesville: University Press of Florida, 2007), p. 16.

100. Vanly, *Le Kurdistan irakien*, p. 228.

101. Emir Kamuram Bedirkhan, Memorandum to the UN, Public Record Office, FCO17/872, 18 November 1968. Serge Gantner, *The Kurdish National Movement* (in Hebrew) (Tel Aviv: 'Am Hasefer, 1968), p. 78.

Part 1

The Kurds and the Iraqi State, 1968–1980

Autonomy means "the reinforcement of Iraqi unity and the absolute rejection of partition."
                    —Saddam Hussein, *Al-Jumhuriyya,* 16 March 1971

Asked when he [Mulla Mustafa Barzani] had first become a nationalist, he answered that he had become one at the age of a few months old when he was imprisoned with his mother because of the Barzani rebellion (1905–1906). —David Adamson, *The Kurdish War*

2
The Long Road to Kurdish Autonomy

The Baathi Approach to Kurdish Nationalism: A Paradox

The advent to power of the Baath regime in July 1968 illustrates an interesting paradox as far as the Kurds were concerned. On the one hand, there was no room for another nation in the party's ideology of pan-Arab nationalism. According to Baathi ideologues and documents, the Kurds were part of the Arab nation because they lived on lands on which Arabs had lived for thousands of years.[1] On the other hand, this same regime went further than any other—either in Iraq or in any other country with a Kurdish population—in recognizing the existence of a Kurdish nation. Another paradox was that, although the agents for change led by Saddam Hussein and Mulla Mustafa Barzani were deeply suspicious of one another, they agreed to a marriage of convenience. To understand these paradoxes, it is necessary to analyze the problems facing the new Baath regime on its rise to power and to assess the balance of power between the Baath Party and the Kurds in the late 1960s.

To put it mildly, the Baath regime's ascent to power following the double coup of 17–30 July 1968[2] was received with a marked lack of enthusiasm in Iraq and abroad. This was partly due to the painful memories of the first, short-lived Baath regime of February–November 1963. Similarly, the Iraqi public was tired of the coups and countercoups that Iraq witnessed after independence and it lacked confidence in the ability of the various revolutionaries to improve the country's political and socioeconomic situation.

During the first two years of its rule, the Baath regime was perceived as weak, unstable, internally divided, violent, and extremist. The regime's weakness manifested itself in a struggle for power among the ruling elite and the absence of a political support base; in its isolation from the pan-Arab arena and lack of international support; and, finally, in its escalating conflict with Iran.

The struggle for power that characterized the first two years of the Baath

27

rule endangered the regime's very existence and precluded it from forming a comprehensive clear-cut policy. These struggles revolved around four major personalities: Ahmad Hasan al-Bakr, the president; Hardan 'Abd-al-Ghaffar al-Tikriti, the minister of defense and deputy prime minister; Salih Mahdi 'Ammash, the interior minister and deputy prime minister; and Saddam Hussein the assistant secretary general of the Baath Party Regional (*qutri*) Leadership. Although at first glance the struggle seemed of a clearly personal character, a more in-depth analysis shows that it also entailed important political questions. What would the regime's character and orientation be like? Would it be a military, or a quasi-military regime managed by people whose main base of support would be the army? Or, would it perhaps have a civilian character, with the Baath Party and its civilian faction at the apex? Each of the four players swept along on their coattails the elements that they sought to strengthen: Saddam promoted the party and its security apparatus, 'Abd-al-Ghaffar al-Tikriti advanced the army, 'Ammash promoted the army and the internal security forces, and al-Bakr apparently maneuvered between the army and the party.

The power struggle reached its climax at the end of 1969. In November and December of that year, constitutional and administrative changes transformed the regime into a quasi-presidential regime through the concentration of additional power in the president's hands. Saddam's standing was also considerably enhanced by his appointment as acting president and deputy chairman of the Revolutionary Command Council (RCC), the highest legislative and executive body in the state. Correspondingly, the standing of 'Ammash and 'Abd-al-Ghaffar al-Tikriti was weakened when both ceased to be deputy prime ministers. The concentration of power in the hands of the al-Bakr–Saddam duo and the corresponding weakening of the military did, as shown below, have an impact on the Kurdish question.

The initial consolidation of the Baathi regime led to confrontations with different sections of Iraqi society, including civilian and military sectors, religious and ethnic groups (Kurds, Shi'a, Christians, and Jews), political parties, and professional unions. The regime developed a system of uncovering spy networks and coup attempts, followed by systematic waves of purges—results were impressive from the regime's point of view. Hundreds of officers were dismissed, arrested, or executed. Well-known veteran politicians, including 'Abd-al-Rahman al-Bazzaz, the former prime minister, and Fu'ad al-Rikabi, the former Baath secretary general, were arrested or executed on charges of spying and conspiring against the regime. Political parties whose positions had been weak even before the ascension of the Baath—the leftist or pro-Syrian branch of the Baath Party, the National Democratic Party, and Nasserist factions—were dissolved. However, the weakening of its rivals did not automatically empower the regime because at that stage the Baath Party was still small and lacked public support. For its part, the army suffered severe upheavals due to constant purges and reshuffles.

From a public standpoint, the regime's popularity was low as it aroused the opposition of both the Kurds and the Shi'a. Baghdad's deteriorating relations with Iran and the hostility of the Shi'i religious establishment and Shi'i population—about one-half of the Iraqi population—toward the avowedly secular Baath precipitated a crisis in 1969, the most severe in the history of the Iraqi republic. The rioting included demonstrations in Shi'i centers and the use of arms to restore the peace.[3] Acts of open provocation on the part of the regime—such as the arrest of Shi'i clerics, the closure of Islamic institutions, and the granting of permission to sell alcoholic beverages in places holy to the Shi'a—also exacerbated the tension.

The regime's attempt to break out of its isolation by initiating a dialogue with the Iraqi Communist Party (ICP) Central Committee, with a view to establishing a national front, failed.[4] The ICP, the regime's strongest rival in Iraq, continued to regard the Baath Party with marked suspicion, not only because of the bloody rivalry between them during 'Abd al-Karim Qasim's rule and during the first Baath regime, but also because of the new regime's actions. Thus, alongside the calls for dialogue, the regime attempted to suppress the ICP while increasing its hold on the trade unions, the ICP's most important stronghold.

The Baath regime also suffered severe isolation abroad because of its own isolationist policies. The regime threw all of its weight behind stabilizing itself domestically while showing little interest in foreign policy. Paradoxically enough, the neighboring countries perceived the Iraqi regime as both weak and threatening, and as both isolationist and expansionist. Despite the Iraqi leaders' repeated declarations of a policy of goodwill toward the neighboring countries, relations were quite strained. Baghad's worst relations were with Syria, Saudi Arabia, Lebanon, Egypt, and—first and foremost—Iran. In fact, Baghdad accused the Arab states of not supporting it in its conflict with Iran.

The one outstanding factor that impacted the fate of the Kurds in Iraq and the regime's policy toward them was indubitably Iran. In this triangle of relations, a kind of axiomatic formula developed: bad relations between Iraq and Iran almost automatically led Iran to incite the neighboring Kurds to rebel against Baghdad.[5] On the other hand, the Kurdish rebellion not only weakened Baghdad's domestic position, but also affected its ability to contend with Iran. Relations between Iraq and Iran reached a low point because of the conflict over the Shatt al-Arab waterway and Iran's decision, in April 1969, to unilaterally suspend the 1937 agreement between Iraq and Iran. This agreement reaffirmed the 1847 agreement between the Ottoman and the Persian empires, which determined that the border between the two countries in the area of Shatt al-Arab was to pass on the eastern side of the river and not along the thalweg line,[6] except for the areas opposite the cities of 'Abadan and Khorramshahr. Control of the river was thus left in Iraqi hands.[7] The immediate pretext for the Iranian move reportedly was Iraqi provocation against Iranian ships. However, the main cause was Iran's general assessment that the Baghdad regime was too weak to obstruct such a move.

Baghdad's reaction included verbal protests, the deportation of Iranians and Shi'i clerics, pressure on the Shi'i population, and subversion of the Sunni Arab–populated, oil-rich region of Khuzestan in Iran, called Arabistan by Iraq. In April 1969, Iraqi interior minister 'Ammash went as far as to claim Arabistan for Iraq, on the grounds that it had been torn away from Iraq during the British Mandate.[8]

The Iran-Iraq conflict must be seen in a wider regional and global context; namely, the Iranian-Iraqi competition in the Gulf region, which was exacerbated by Britain's declaration in January 1968 of its intention to complete the evacuation of its forces from the region by late 1971. This prompted the major powers to intensify their efforts to fill the vacuum left by the British by deepening their influence in the Gulf states.

For their part, Iran and Iraq sought to advance their aspirations by securing the backing of the superpowers. However, while Iran, aiming to become the policing force of the Gulf with the blessings of the United States, grew stronger militarily and developed relations with both the Soviet Union and the United States, Iraq's international standing with the great powers was low. Baghdad had severed its diplomatic relations with the United States following the Six Day War of 1967, and relations with the Soviet Union remained lukewarm even though Baghdad had granted it the concessions on the Rumayla oil field.

From the outset, the Iraqi president had described the Soviet Union as occupying the premier position in Iraq's foreign relations. However, even if the Soviet Union viewed Iraq as a means for consolidating Soviet influence in the Gulf, it was not prepared at that stage to grant Iraq unconditional support. The Soviet Union was careful not to alienate Iran, with which it had developed friendly relations in recent years (although the Soviet policy was aimed at neutralizing Iran's influence in the Gulf and, consequently, that of the United States). Another reason was that the Soviet Union had serious reservations about the Baath regime's internal policy; particularly with regard to the Communists and the Kurds. The Soviet Union preached for the inclusion of the Communists in an Iraqi national front and for devising a peaceful solution to the Kurdish problem. The lack of progress on these two questions, together with Iraq's instability and isolation, compelled the Soviet Union to act with great caution.

The Kurdish Camp: The Good, the Bad, and the *Juhush*

On the eve of the Baath's advent to power, there was already de facto autonomy in certain parts of Iraqi Kurdistan. The *liberated areas*, as they were termed by the Kurds, covered about 35,000 square kilometers extending from Zakho in the northwest to Khanaqin in the southeast. The areas were not contiguous, given the central government's control over the cities and main roads. The Kurdish population in the autonomous region was estimated at approximately 1.0 million out of the 2.0 million to 2.5 million Kurds. The body that most symbolized Kurdish autonomy was the Peshmerga guerrilla army, which grew from 14,000 combatants in 1966 to 20,000 in 1970.[9]

The Revolutionary Council, which de facto is a Kurdish parliament, began functioning in 1964. In 1966, it included sixty-two members representing the guerrilla army; the Kurdistan Democratic Party, which was established in 1946; Kurdish tribes, which retained considerable power in Kurdish society; and independent figures. The Executive Committee, composed of seventeen members, drew its power from the Revolutionary Council and constituted a quasi-government. It was directed by the party, which held a majority in it. By contrast, the tribes had only one representative in the committee in 1966. The committee held a wide range of powers, including command of the guerrilla army, the administration, jurisprudence, tax collection, and supervision of the local police and prisons. The movement also had an intelligence organization, Parastin,[10] a Kurdish newspaper, *Kha-Bat*, and an underground radio station, Radio Iraqi Kurdistan.

The real power remained in the hands of one man until 1975: Mulla Mustafa Barzani, who bore two titles; namely, president of the Revolutionary Council and president of the KDP. Barzani (1904–1979) received his elementary schooling in Barzan and his religious schooling in Sulaymaniyya. He became involved in the Kurdish rebellion in 1931. When the rebellion was put down in 1934 he was exiled to southern Iraq, but later on was returned to Sulaymaniyya and put under house arrest until his escape in 1942. Between 1943 and 1945, he led another rebellion against Baghdad and then escaped together with *circa* 1,200 men to Iran, from where he led the fighting for the newly established Kurdish Republic of Mahabad. When Mahabad collapsed in early 1947, he escaped once again, this time to the Soviet Union, where he stayed until Qasim's revolution in July 1958. Following his return to Iraq in that year, he led what the Kurds call the September Revolution of 1961, which lasted intermittently until 1970 and earned him the title of national Kurdish leader.[11]

These Kurdish achievements should not be underestimated; neither, however, should their importance be overstated. The nascent political institutions were more on paper than on the ground. Autonomy, ostensibly obtained in a protracted war, was shaky as it failed to gain recognition from the central government. Hence, to prevent its liquidation by force, the Kurdish movement's main target was to achieve such political-constitutional recognition for their autonomy.

Kurdish accomplishments in the 1960s were due to the give and take between a charismatic leader and the party. Nevertheless, despite the fact that Barzani had distinguished himself as the leader of the Kurdish rebellion in the mid-1940s, in the absence of a strong organizational-political rear his rebellions had more of a tribal/local character than a national one. On the other hand, while the KDP gradually became a dominant political force in the Kurdish region, it did not succeed in breathing life into the movement during Barzani's exile in the Soviet Union. Herein lies one of the greatest paradoxes of this movement: just as the close cooperation between leader and party was vital for the formation of the movement in its initial stages and contributed greatly to its successes during the Qasim era, it was also a source of severe internal divisions.

The rift, which came out into the open in 1964, reflected internal tensions and conflicts of interests between Barzani—who operated primarily along the lines of a tribal leader with individualistic, authoritarian tendencies—and the party, which purported to represent a modern approach to politics, emphasizing the theoretical-ideological and organizational facets of the movement. The rift also reflected a struggle for power between a personality who had attained the status of national leader, Barzani, and a party leadership that sought to emphasize the concept of collective leadership.

Following the 1964 crisis, the Kurdish camp split into two. The dominant faction was headed by Barzani and the other by Ibrahim Ahmad and Jalal Talabani. Barzani's edge over the rival camp was clear. His faction controlled the Kurdish territory and established semi-independent institutions, while the guerrilla army remained almost entirely loyal to Barzani. In addition, an important segment of the party recognized the vital role that he was playing in the Kurdish national movement and continued to support him. The KDP itself split into two wings, each of which called itself *pareti* (the party, in Kurdish).

Barzani's wing lost the party's intellectuals, whose main representative was Ahmad, the party's general secretary before the split. It also lost the power to make independent decisions regarding Kurdish affairs. In addition, those who were promoted to senior positions in the party were selected not because of their intellectual abilities and ideological weight, but because of their loyalty to Barzani.[12]

By the time of the Baath coup, the leadership of Barzani's camp had already crystallized. The executive authority was in the hands of the KDP politburo, which came to include the following personages after the Seventh Congress of 1966: Habib Muhammad Karim, the party's secretary general and one of the leading Fayli Kurds, the majority of whom are Shi'a who live in the area surrounding Kirkuk and extending south to Khanaqin; Mahmud 'Uthman, Barzani's personal physician, one of his loyal assistants, and also his unofficial foreign minister; Salih al-Yusufi, the publisher of the daily *Al-Ta'akhi*, which started publication in 1966; and Nuri Shawis, who belonged to the dissident branch, but was subsequently reinstated in the KDP politburo. Two other personalities joined the politburo in 1969: 'Aziz Rashid 'Aqrawi, an officer in the Iraqi Army who deserted to join the Kurdish movement in 1962; and Muhammad Mahmud 'Abd al-Rahman, nicknamed Sami, director of the underground radio station Radio Iraqi Kurdistan and the closest person to Barzani aside from his sons.

From the late 1960s onward Barzani's sons (from two different wives), Idris and Mas'ud, played a significant role in political decisionmaking and created a triumvirate with their father. Idris obtained a command position in the guerrilla army in 1966, while Mas'ud took command of the Parastin. As far as is known, the nucleus of the Kurdish leadership maintained substantial internal cohesion until the collapse of the rebellion in 1975.

The dissident faction, headed by Ibrahim Ahmad and Jalal Talabani, was ephemeral. Ahmad, an intellectual who was involved in Kurdish activities as early as the 1940s, served as secretary general of the dissident faction until 1970. Talabani, his son-in-law, was initially close to Barzani and served in important positions, including as commander of the Peshmerga and in different diplomatic posts. After the split in 1964 the dissident faction found refuge in Iran, though it returned to Iraq two years later. Ironically, the faction that had opposed Barzani in 1964 for his "submission" to the 'Arif regime formed an almost open alliance against Barzani with the same regime merely two years later. However, despite Baghdad's assistance, the Talabani-Ahmad faction remained weak and isolated, and its anti-Barzani activities constituted more of a nuisance than a real threat.

An instructive description of the Kurdish camp was provided by a source that cannot be suspected of sympathy with the Kurds; namely, the internal publication of the Baath Party, *Al-Thawra al-'Arabiyya*. According to *Al-Thawra al-'Arabiyya*, there were three main forces in the Kurdish camp: the Barzani movement, the Talabani-Ahmad group, and the Salah al-Din Forces (quwwat Salah al-Din). It stated that the Barzani movement was the "central pillar of the Kurdish national (*qawmiyya*) movement," whose supporters were mainly peasants and workers. Its strength was based on "Peshmerga fighters, who were well trained, strong, and loyal to the movement"; on good military equipment and a fortified area from a natural and military standpoint; on the Kurdish fighters' intimate knowledge of field conditions; and on constant financial, military, and medical support from different sources. As to Barzani, *Al-Thawra al-'Arabiyya* noted that he was enjoying a unique leadership position.[13]

Al-Thawra al-'Arabiyya also pointed out that the Talabani group had adopted Marxist leanings. The group, the largest concentration of which was to be found in Sulaymaniyya, restricted its activities to the Baghdad area and several cities in the north. The group's fighters, who were equipped with small arms, "operate under the Iraqi Army's protection, and therefore camp in the vicinity of our camps." According to *Al-Thawra al-'Arabiyya*, the Talabani group, which was waging such a bitter war against Barzani's movement, was inferior to the latter in strength and influence.[14]

As to the Salah-al-Din forces (nicknamed *juhush*, or donkeys, by their opponents), *Al-Thawra al-'Arabiyya* disclosed that they were composed of "Kurdish tribes who supported the authorities" since the monarchy period. Those tribes "agreed to organize to fight the Kurdish movement, in exchange for monthly salaries paid to their tribal leaders. They were equipped with small arms supplied to them by the Iraqi Government." The party's organ characterized this group as a motley collection of armed men, which could not be defined as a political movement because it lacked both an organization and an ideology. The authorities therefore had not always been able to rely on its loyalty. As some of the Salah al-Din Forces revolted against the authorities, others secretly maintained friendly relations with the Barzani group while still others continued to fight against him due to historical, intertribal hostility. According to *Al-Thawra al-'Arabiyya*, one of the reasons for this inconsistency stemmed from their disappointment with the authorities, who had more than once abandoned them following reconciliation with the Barzanis.[15] Interestingly, Mulla Mustafa Barzani categorized the Kurds as "the good, the bad and the *juhush*."[16]

This instructive categorization gives us a glimpse into the Kurdish camp, especially the role of the tribes in the movement. From the very beginning, the tribes took a leadership position in the struggle against Baghdad and the British. Thus, for example, a petition by the Pizhdar to the League of Nations, filed on 9 October 1930, stated that "the Kurds have therefore decided to separate from the Arabs at all cost" in order to form a "Kurdish state within its natural boundaries, stretching from Zakho to the district beyond Kanaqin."[17] In fact, one cannot disconnect the tribes and tribalism from the Kurdish national movement. As Hamit Bozarslan explains,

> as a social organization, a tribe can have a tribal temporality, allowing it to manage its existence and its power relations with the outside world but at the same time, it can act as a national or trans-border regional actor. A tribal chief can find in his tribe the resources that allow him to become an actor in a national or supra-national sphere.

Bozarslan further emphasizes that "Kurdish nationalist movements . . . had and still have to take tribes into consideration either as allies or as enemies."[18]

Ripening Conditions for Dialogue

Two years before it came to power, the Baath Party established secret contacts with Barzani's camp, which were maintained until two months after the coup. However, at that stage, conditions were not yet ripe for a drastic change in Baghdad, which continued to toy with the idea of breaking up Barzani's camp until December 1969. The regime's three-pronged plan included: (1) a unilateral gesture to the Kurdish population to induce it to stop supporting Barzani; (2) support for the Talabani camp and its use against Barzani along the principle of divide and rule; and (3) the use of military force to break the rebels.

Shortly after its advent to power, the regime announced that it had decided to adopt the al-Bazzaz twelve-point plan as a basis for solving the Kurdish problem: establish a Kurdish Academy of Science and Arts and a university in Su-laymaniyya; grant general amnesty for those involved in "the incidents in the north";[19] establish a local police force manned by "residents of the northern area"; and proclaim 21 March—the Kurdish New Year, Nowruz—as an official holiday. In October 1969, the Baath announced a number of important cultural decisions, including Kurdish language instruction in high schools, universities, teachers colleges, the military, and the police academies; permission for Kur-dish authors and poets to establish their own union; and the use of historical Kurdish names to designate schools and offices in the Kurdish area.[20]

From the start, the regime sought to strengthen Talabani's group by ap-pointing Talabani supporter Taha Muhyi-al-Din Ma'ruf as minister without port-folio on 31 July 1968 and by licensing its daily *Al-Nur* (the light), which enthusiastically supported the regime. More importantly, Baghdad granted fi-nancial support and weapons to Talabani so that he would engage Barzani's forces. According to varying estimates, Talabani's forces numbered between 2,000 and 4,000 men; Baghdad paid each fourteen dinars per month.[21] This pol-icy had several advantages: Talabani's people knew the Kurdish terrain well and were trained in guerrilla warfare, something at which the regular army did not excel; internal fighting within the Kurdish camp could only harm its unity, which would benefit the regime; and internal fighting freed up regular army forces for other security missions. In October 1968, the Barzani forces clashed with the forces of Talabani near the Iranian border but, since the latter were no match for them, the Iraqi Army was forced to intervene to put an end to the fighting.

Clashes between the Iraqi Army and the Peshmerga took place intermit-tently from the fall of 1968 until December 1969. At one stage, the fighting was so intense that the army, committing two divisions to the battle, used heavy ar-maments (including tanks, heavy artillery, and aircraft) to bomb Kurdish vil-lages.[22] At the same time, a propaganda war continued between the camps: the regime accused Barzani of being unwilling to solve the problem peacefully and of collaborating with Iran and receiving weapons from Israel, which encour-aged the Kurds to "continue to cause problems."[23] Barzani and his spokesmen, for their part, accused the regime of genocide. In November 1968, they even re-quested the intervention of then UN Secretary-General U Thant, but did not re-ceive a response.

By the fall of 1969, it became clear that gestures of goodwill toward the Kurds did not undermine their support for Barzani. Neither did Talabani man-age to become a substitute for him in the Kurdish national movement, which continued to rally around Barzani and the KDP. Expenditures on the war, esti-mated at 0.25 million dinars per day,[24] severely damaged Iraq's economy.

The military solution again proved its limitations. Thus, "it was known that the government was increasingly concerned about the morale of the large forces tied down in the north, at [*sic*] the ever increasing expense of the war, and the apparent inability of the Army to force a decision."[25] The army was weakened by its power struggles with the civilian wing of the regime. In addition, the army, which numbered about 70,000 troops, was divided on several fronts: about 20,000 soldiers were stationed on the Kurdish front; 18,000 constituted the Iraqi expeditionary force on the eastern front (about 6,000 in Syria and 12,000 in Jordan); and the rest were on the border with Iran and in sensitive places on the domestic front.[26] Most importantly, the conflict with Iran, which broke out over the Shatt al-Arab waterway in April 1969, imposed severe limitations on the army's maneuverability and freedom of action in the Kurdistan region. On the one hand, the army had to divert resources and attention to the Shatt al-Arab area, where the Iranian Army had concentrated its forces. On the other hand, it also had to contend with the new-old phenomenon of deepening Iranian involvement in Kurdish affairs. Indeed, the conflict with Iran resulted in the tightening of the unholy alliance forged in the early 1960s between Iran and Barzani's camp. Despite the atmosphere of mutual suspicion, Iran and Barzani's camp had a common interest in destabilizing the Baath.

In the fall of 1969, collaboration, which had begun with arms shipments to the Barzani camp, evolved into direct Iranian aid to the Kurdish war effort, albeit on a particularly small scale.[27] This explains why the 1969 summer–fall offensive did not succeed, and the army failed to break into the heart of Kurdistan. In view of these developments, the regime had two options: come to an agreement either with Iran or with the Kurds. The regime preferred the first option, which was likely to kill two birds with one stone; namely, put an end to the conflict with Iran and block the source of support for the Kurdish national movement. An Iraqi delegation arrived in Tehran in the fall of 1969 to convince the shah to stop supporting Barzani, in exchange for far-reaching concessions on the part of Iraq.[28] Sensing that it had the upper hand, however, Iran rejected the offer. Thus, Baghdad's only choice was to reach an agreement with the Kurds. Such a course had the clear disadvantage of leaving Iran as a player seeking to exploit the Kurdish problem against Baghdad.

The Kurds thus came to the negotiating table from a position of strength.[29] Paradoxically, their main consideration was the Kurdish population's increasing exhaustion caused by a war that had continued intermittently since 1961. According to one estimate, close to 20,000 combatants and thousands of women, older people, and children were casualties of the nine-year war, and about 200 villages were obliterated by the Iraqi Air Force.[30] There is no doubt that Barzani, who was acutely aware of the population's difficulties, sought as he had many times in the past to enable the population to regain its strength. He expressed this in an anecdote about a prisoner bound to a tree who asked to be tied to another tree so that he would be able to take a few steps without constraints.

Barzani's camp was distrustful of the Kurdish alliance with the shah, however, fearing that the shah would abandon them whenever his interests so dictated. In an attempt to find new allies, Barzani sent letters to Turkey's president and prime minister in October 1968, in which he expressed his desire to strengthen ties with the Turkish people and government "who are a continuation of the Islam Ottoman Empire." Nothing came of it.[31]

The Kurds eventually realized that only the Iraqi regime was in a position to fulfill Kurdish demands. Barzani believed that this was an opportunity to gain autonomy for the Kurds, break the rival Talabani faction, and weaken the regime's military wing. Although the Kurds had from the outset suspected the Baath and its motives, countervailing considerations on their side were weighty enough to pave the way for negotiations.

Preparing the Baath Party's Conceptual Framework

Intensive preparatory work within the Baath Party preceded the accord on Kurdish autonomy. The Baath's aims were to adapt its ideology to the new political goals pertaining to the Kurdish question; to strengthen the civilian wing of the party, which supported a peaceful solution of the Kurdish problem at the expense of the rival military one; and to allay Kurdish fears of collaborating with a party that they perceived as nationalistic and chauvinistic.

The short-lived Baath government of 1963 left vestiges of deep animosity between the two camps. With its pan-Arab ideology, the Baath Party did not view favorably the Kurdish national movement, which in the Baathi view threatened both Iraqi unity and pan-Arab unification plans. For its part, the Kurdish national movement had deep misgivings about the Baathi ideology, which, if realized, was liable to lead to the absorption of the Kurds into a large Arab bloc. Mutual suspicion was further exacerbated against the backdrop of incidents in 1963. The autonomy plan, to which the Baath had committed itself before rising to power,[32] was replaced by a decentralization plan that did not even recognize the existence of the Kurdish national movement. Moreover, the war initiated in June 1963, at the height of negotiations, by the Baath against the Kurdish national movement was much more brutal than Qasim's war. Salih Mahdi 'Ammash, then defense minister, declared at the time: "I do not consider this a war. It is a national picnic by the Army assisted by civilians to put an end to these gangs."[33]

The first step toward clearing the atmosphere was outlined in the report of the Baath Party's Seventh Regional Congress at the end of 1968. The report indicated that "the national aspirations of the Kurds in Iraq were among the foremost questions facing the national movement." It further emphasized that the Baath Party "has always respected the Kurdish people's national and progressive aspirations, and regarded these as a legitimate right."[34] This revolutionary approach was accompanied by further moves, aimed at convincing party members of the need to settle the Kurdish problem peacefully and grant autonomy to the Kurds. Between April and October 1969, a comprehensive discussion was held on the Kurdish question in a series of articles in the Baath Party's internal organ *Al-Thawra al-'Arabiyya*. They were marked by a pragmatic approach, and refrained from the customary, harsh attacks against "Barzani's gang." The articles underlined that throughout Iraq's history, no Iraqi national movement had been spared wars, with northern Iraq as the theater of action. They even acknowledged that Barzani's movement was the strongest and most authentic movement in the Kurdish camp. Moreover, they reached the conclusion that "most of the political groups" in Iraq supported autonomy for the Kurds—at least in theory.[35] Previously, this point had been raised by Michel 'Aflaq, one of the founders of the Baath Party and the general secretary of the all-Arab (*qawmi*) leadership based in Iraq (to be distinguished from the competing all-Arab Baath leadership in Damascus). In the course of a speech that he delivered in June 1969, 'Aflaq declared that "the party does not oppose the Kurds' right to a certain kind of self-rule (*hukm dhati*)," adding in the same breath that "the Kurdish national movement is a legitimate part of the Arab revolution."[36]

The next step was to prepare Iraqi public opinion. On 17 December 1969, *Al-Thawra* published an article entitled "What Is the Way to Solve the Kurdish Problem?" The article reflects the dilemma the party faced, the upshot of the need to create a positive atmosphere with regard to the Kurdish question on the one hand, and a natural instinct to censure Barzani and his group on the other. This duality, characteristic of the article as a whole, was to become a major identifying mark of Baath-Kurdish relations. The article indicated that the Kurdish question, being a "national issue," dovetailed with the spirit of the period. However, presenting it as if it were in conflict with the national Arab cause was, according to the article, both mistaken and destructive. The article claimed that this was the basic mistake of the Barzani leadership—the very leadership that had also been responsible for the crisis of confidence with the Baath since 1963 and after the Baath's rise to power in 1968. It emphasized that the Baath Party understood the Kurdish question and was more capable than others to solve it, and called on "all Kurdish forces" to cooperate with the Baath. At the same time, it also alluded to military elements that sought to harm both the Kurds and the Baath, as was the case in 1963.[37]

The final stamp of approval for the reconciliation was given by the Baath Party's Tenth National Congress, which was held in early March 1970. The congress once more emphasized the need to solve the Kurdish problem peacefully, on the basis of autonomy within the framework of Iraqi unity while at the same time ensuring cooperation between the Arab and Kurdish peoples.[38]

The Labyrinth of Negotiations

Concurrently with the soul-searching of the Baath Party, the regime initiated direct negotiations with Barzani's movement in September 1969. The three main negotiation stages were set between September 1969 and March 1970. Because of the delicacy of the Kurdish problem, the discussions were held in almost complete secrecy, alternating between the capital of Baghdad and the headquarters of the KDP in Nawperdan (literally "between the two bridges") in the province of Erbil (Hawler) about 35 kilometers from the border with Iran.

Representatives of the Baath Regional Command and the military were involved in different stages of the negotiations on behalf of the regime, but there were substantial differences between them. While the military advocated a military solution, a growing bloc in the Regional Leadership was pushing for a peaceful one. The national leadership, which at the time had some influence over the regime, also supported a peaceful solution. The central Iraqi figure who initiated and pushed for an agreement with the Kurds was Saddam. He viewed a solution to the problem as a lever to oust his rivals in the army and thereby remove the army from politics, which would strengthen his position and that of the Baath Party. Saddam was directly involved in different stages of the negotiations and met Barzani a number of times. Other Regional Command members participated in the negotiations, as did Tariq 'Aziz, a veteran Baath member who later became Saddam's right-hand man. Participants from the military included Salih Mahdi 'Ammash, the interior minister; Hardan 'Abd al-Ghaffar al-Tikriti, the minister of defense; Hammad Shihab, chief of staff; and Sa'dun Ghaydan, commander of the Baghdad garrison. Among the National Command, the most prominent personality to participate in the negotiations was the general secretary, Michel 'Aflaq.

As to the Barzani camp, there apparently was a consensus regarding the line to be taken in the negotiations. Barzani played a decisive role in the negotiations, but did not leave his place of residence because of his deep mistrust of Baghdad's intentions. Rather, the different delegations came to him or his emissaries went to Baghdad. The Kurdish team, headed by Mahmud 'Uthman, who was known for his influence on the young generation of Kurds, included among others Barzani's two sons, Idris and Mas'ud.

'Aziz Sharif, who was appointed justice minister in December 1969, assumed the role of mediator. Sharif, a leftist and former Communist, apparently was encouraged by the Soviet Union to take on this mission. In fact, the Soviets played a not insignificant role in advancing the negotiations.[39] Already in September 1969, *Pravda* called on the Baath to "provide for the Kurdish people's national aspirations within the framework of the Iraqi state."[40]

Due to an inherent lack of trust between the parties, substantial problems regarding the nature of Kurdish demands, and a power struggle within the regime that made the decisionmaking process difficult, negotiations were protracted and tortuous. They seemingly followed two separate tracks: one inside the ruling group and the other pertaining directly to the dialogue between Baghdad and the Kurds. Between September 1969 and January 1970, the major problems were within the ruling group; only when these were surmounted, could negotiations in the second track move forward. In September Sharif, who had acted as mediator in the initial discussions, met with Barzani and with polit-buro members in the Kurdish region.[41] Reports maintained that it was Saddam who had established the first contacts with Barzani's representatives during a visit to northern Iraq in September 1969. Subsequently, secret meetings were held in Nawperdan, in the presidential palace in Baghdad, and even in Beirut where 'Aflaq resided. However, the negotiations came to naught at that stage as the Baath wing, which advocated a peaceful solution to the Kurdish problem, had to achieve the following objectives: (1) weakening the military who op-posed an agreement with the Kurds; (2) rallying the support of other military figures for the agreement; and (3) forming a kind of coalition with the National Command to grant ideological legitimacy to the agreement.

In October 1969, sixty senior pro-'Ammash officers were transferred from their positions, followed by the removal in November of 'Ammash and Tikriti from their posts as deputy prime ministers, and the appointment of Saddam as the deputy chairman of the RCC. In December, Saddam convened a meeting with 600 army officers to report on the talks with the Kurds, demanding that they accept the government's decision on the Kurdish issue.[42] However, the of-ficers continued to oppose any solution other than a military one. On 21 Jan-uary 1970, a conspiracy against the regime "with the help of Iran, the United States, and Zionism" was uncovered.[43] The conspirators were charged, among other things, with attempting to thwart an understanding with the Kurds. On the same day, thirty-three officers were executed. It is possible that parallel to this move, which severely damaged the support base of Tikriti and 'Ammash, a dialogue was held with other army officers to ensure their support of the agreement. The subsequent appointment on 3 April 1970 of Hammad Shihab to the post of defense minister, instead of Hardan al-Tikriti, and of Sa'dun Ghaydan to the post of interior minister, instead of 'Ammash, as well as other important reshuffles in the army may hint at some kind of prearranged pack-age deal.

Meanwhile, Saddam and 'Aflaq started closing ranks. The common de-nominators between the two were the fact that both were civilian members of the party, both were hostile to the army and sought to remove it from politics, and both were determined at that stage to solve the Kurdish problem peace-fully. In October 1969, 'Aflaq came to Baghdad to give his blessing to nego-tiations with the Kurds in the National Command meeting. He also gave his public seal of approval to the Kurdish national movement in the Iraqi press. Two months later, Dara Tawfiq met 'Aflaq in Beirut to obtain the National Command's approval of the agreement on the eve of the signing ceremony. Apparently, Barzani asked for 'Aflaq's approval to give the agreement greater validity.

Three days after the said conspiracy was uncovered on 21 January, Saddam revealed the existence of a dialogue between the Baath Party, the Iraqi government, and Barzani. On the same day, the RCC granted amnesty to those who had participated in the incidents in the north. According to the RCC, the motivation behind this move was to create suitable conditions for the implementation of the al-Bazzaz twelve-point plan of 29 June 1966. Radio Kurdistan broadcast a declaration on 3 February 1970 to the effect that the aspiration of the Arab and Kurdish peoples to achieve a peaceful solution had been satisfied, and that a new chapter had opened in the history of the Iraqi people. The announcement of the agreement was expected on 8 February, a symbolic date marking the anniversary of the Baath's first ascension to power in 1963. However, on 11 February, the Iraqi News Agency reported a postponement of the joint announcement until the parties had removed the obstacles standing in their way. On 15 February, contacts were suspended.

The main bone of contention was the Kurdish demand for territorial autonomy, which the Baath opposed at that stage and insisted on personal-cultural autonomy. An *Al-Thawra* article asserted that "Kurdish nationalism does not necessarily require the creation of a geographic area in which the Kurds can fulfill their national rights." Stating that the Baath opposed territorial autonomy, it explained that such a move would be perceived as the creation of a state within a state and would encourage separatist tendencies in the future. *Al-Thawra* then called on the Kurds to purge their ranks of "separatists and agents of imperialism and feudalism."[44]

Moreover, territorial autonomy carried with it the most difficult problem of the oil-rich province (*liwa'*) of Kirkuk, which the Kurds sought to include in the autonomous region, together with three other provinces: Sulaymaniyya, Erbil, and Duhok. The Kurds based their demand on the argument that they constituted a majority in that province.[45] In fact, as early as 1943, Mulla Mustafa Bazani demanded that the government create "an all-Kurdish province, embracing the *liwa's* of Kirkuk, Arbil, and Sulaymaniyya."[46] For its part, the regime would not concede such economic and strategic assets, which were liable to grant considerable power to the Kurds and prompt them to demand independence. The regime hence hastened to declare that the Kirkuk area had a mixed population, of which the Kurds constituted only a minority. As a preemptive measure, the Turkomans, who had a strong presence in the area, were granted various cultural rights on 24 January 1970. According to one source, however, the Turkomans, who had been brought in by the Ottomans to repel tribal raids, were thought to constitute less than 2 percent of the population.[47]

It is difficult to know the truth regarding this dispute, inasmuch as official statistics on the ethnic and communal composition of the area have not been published since 1947. As of early 2012, no census had yet been taken. According to the 1947 census, the number of Kurds in that year totaled 151,575 out of the 285,900 residents in the area.[48] In other words, the Kurds constituted a majority. However, since then, different administrative measures have been implemented, including population transfers (i.e., settling Arabs in the area) and dispersing the Kurds.[49] All in all, a vital question such as this could not be decided solely on the basis of strength of numbers, but rather on the ability of the more powerful side (in this case, the regime) to impose its will.

Another point of contention was the Kurds' demand to be included in the RCC, the decisionmaking body of the state, as opposed to the cabinet, which lacked any real authority. This demand was rejected on the grounds that Iraq was in a transitional stage and, for the time being, only Baathi members would be included in the RCC. Clearly, Baghdad's rulers were reluctant to share power. The Kurdish demand to establish a parliament within two years was likewise rejected.

Opinions also differed on the guerrilla army's future. While it was agreed in principle that part of the Peshmerga be transformed into a border guard, there was no consensus regarding the number of Kurds who would be included in it. While the Kurds demanded 10,000 fighters, the regime insisted on 5,000. This point illustrated the fundamental reservations that the two sides harbored toward each other and their need for safeguards in the event of a renewed armed conflict.

Despite these difficulties, discussions were renewed through the energetic mediation of 'Aziz Sharif. On 2 March 1970, the daily *Al-Jumhuriyya* attacked what it called "chauvinistic elements who were inciting a war and those who obtained temporary influence during the years of armed conflict between the citizens of the state" (an allusion to the army). The newspaper stated that the solution articulated by the party should serve as an example for all Arab countries suffering from a similar problem.[50]

It was Saddam who finalized the agreement. He stayed in Nawperdan for three days (8–10 March), not leaving it until all of the problems had been clarified and a highly detailed agreement had been formulated. Clearly, the parties had to retreat from their opening positions and make painful concessions. This applied primarily to the regime. Apparently, it was the regime's decision to recognize the principle of territorial autonomy that had brought the Kurds back to the negotiating table. For their part, though not conceding their demand for Kirkuk, the Kurds did agree to defer a decision until a census was taken in the area. The Kurds' demand to participate in the RCC was not met; instead, five Kurdish ministers and a Kurdish vice-president were to be appointed. The Kurds were also promised participation in an envisaged national alliance. With regard to the Peshmerga, a compromise was reached, according to which 6,000 men would serve in the projected border guard.

The way was now open for the 1970 March Declaration.

Notes

1. See, for example, *Nidal al-Ba'th fi Sabil al-Wahda al-Hurriyya wal-Ishtirakiyya* (Beirut: 1971), pp. 308–309; and Michel 'Aflaq, *Nuqtat al-Bidaya* (Beirut: Al-Mu'assasa al-'Arabiyya lil-Dirasat wal-Nashr, 1974), pp. 107–108.

2. See Phebe Marr, *The Modern History of Iraq* (Boulder, CO: Westview Press, 1985), pp. 204–214; Ofra Bengio, "Iraq," in *Middle East Record (MER) 1968*, ed. Daniel Dishon (Jerusalem: Israel Universities Press, 1977), pp. 516–521; Marion Farouk-Sluglett and Peter Sluglett, *Iraq Since 1958: From Revolution to Dictatorship*, 3rd ed. (London: I. B. Tauris, 2001), pp. 107–116; and Charles Tripp, *A History of Iraq* (Cambridge: Cambridge University Press, 2002), pp. 193–199.

3. Regarding the crisis with the Shi'a, see Avraham Hayim, "The Shi'a in Iraq," *Hamizrah Hehadash* 19, no. 4 (1969): 323–354 (in Hebrew); Tripp, *A History of Iraq*, pp. 202–204; and Graham E. Fuller and Rend Rahim Francke, *The Arab Shi'a: The Forgotten Muslims* (New York: Palgrave, 2001), pp. 100–101.

4. The Iraqi Communist Party (hereafter ICP) was divided into two main groups. The dominant group, called the ICP Central Committee, is the one mainly referred to in this book. The second group, the ICP Central Leadership, was greatly weakened with the surrender of its general secretary 'Aziz al-Hajj to the police in the spring of 1969. Regarding the breakdown of the talks between the Baath and the ICP Central Committee, see Edith Penrose and E. F. Penrose, *Iraq: International Relations and National Development* (London: Ernest Benn, 1978), p. 360.

5. It was one of the open secrets in the Middle East that "the Iranian government have [*sic*] in the last decade given the Kurds . . . considerable support in money, equipment, training and rear communications." Public Record Office, FCO17/872, 2 October 1968.

6. A *thalweg line* is a line connecting the lowest points along a river or valley.

7. *Iran–Iraq Boundary*, International Boundary Study no. 164, the Geographer Office of the Geographer Bureau of Intelligence and Research, 13 July 1978.

8. Beirut Regional News Service, 22 April 1969, cited in *Daily Report*, 23 April 1969.

9. Abbas Kelidar, "Iraq: The Search for Stability," *Conflict Studies*, no. 59 (1975): 11; Ismet Sheriff Vanly, *Le Kurdistan irakien, entité nationale: Étude de la révolution de 1961* (Neuchâtel, Switzerland: Éditions de la Baconnière, 1970), pp. 246–249; Public Record Office, FCO17/1237, 2 April 1970. On the Peshmerga, see Michael G. Lortz, "Willing to Face Death: A History of Kurdish Military Forces—The Peshmerga—From the Ottoman Empire to Present-day Iraq" (master's thesis, Florida State University, 2005).

10. The Israeli Mossad was said to have helped set up the Parastin (meaning protection in Kurdish) back in 1966. The Parastin was commanded by Mas'ud Barzani, who had trained intensively in Kurdistan and Israel. Jonathan C. Randal, *After Such Knowledge, What Forgiveness? My Encounters with Kurdistan* (Boulder, CO: Westview Press, 1999), pp. 190–191.

11. For a background see Michael M. Gunter, *The Kurds of Iraq: Tragedy and Hope* (New York: St. Martin's Press, 1992), pp. 7–14.

12. Chris Kutschera, *Le mouvement national kurde* (Paris: Flammarion, 1970), pp. 251–252.

13. *Al-Thawra al-'Arabiyya* (Baghdad), no. 7–12 (1969), pp. 287–292.

14. Ibid.

15. Ibid.

16. Personal communication with Barzani associate.

17. Public Record Office, CO 730/157/8, 9 October 1930.

18. Hamit Bozarslan, "Tribal Asabiyya and Kurdish Politics: A Socio-historical Perspective," in *The Kurds: Nationalism and Politics*, eds. Faleh A. Jabar and Dawod Hosham (London: Saqi, 2006), p. 133.

19. *The north* is an alternate term for the Iraqi Kurdistan area. The authorities sought to avoid the term *Kurdistan*, which might have separatist connotations.

20. Radio Baghdad, 9 October 1969, cited in BBC, 11 October 1969.

21. Kutschera, *Le mouvement*, p. 265.

22. *Al-Hayat*, 12 March 1970. According to another source, four divisions were involved in the fighting. See Kutschera, *Le mouvement*, p. 268.

23. Hardan 'Abd-al-Ghaffar al-Tikriti in an interview by *Kayhan International*, 9 December 1968. It should be noted that this rare disclosure was published in a non-Iraqi journal.

24. *Al-Ahram* (Cairo, daily), 13 March 1970.

25. Public Record Office, FCO17/1237, 2 April 1970.

26. *International Herald Tribune* (Paris and Zurich , daily), 13 March 1970; Varda Ben-Zvi, *Middle East Record 1969–1970* (Tel Aviv: Tel Aviv University, 1977), pp. 562–563; *Al-Ahram*, 13 March 1970.

27. Kutschera, *Le mouvement*, p. 272.

28. Ibid. The author did not detail what the defined proposals were.

29. The following was their assessment of the situation: "In 1970 the Baathist regime were [sic] weak and knew . . . that [it] would not remain in power if it continued the fight." Public Record Office, FCO8/2307, 22 July 1974.

30. *Ha'aretz* (Tel Aviv, daily), 15 March 1970.

31. Public Record Office, FCO17/872, 14 October 1968.

32. Uriel Dann, *Iraq Under Qassem: A Political History, 1958–1963* (New York: Praeger, 1969), p. 344.

33. Derek Kinnane, *The Kurds and Kurdistan* (London: Oxford University Press, 1964), p. 76.

34. Radio Baghdad, 6 February 1969, cited in BBC, 8 February 1969.

35. A series of articles appeared in *Al-Thawra al-'Arabiyya*, pp. 203–600. It seems that the author of the articles was 'Abdullah Sallum al-Samarra'i who served as minister of culture and information during 1968–1969. Ferhad Ibrahim, *Die Kurdische Nationalbewegung im Iraq* (Berlin: Klaus Schwarz Verlag, 1983), p. 576.

36. 'Aflaq's remarks were quoted in *Al-Thawra*, 11–12 March 1973.

37. *Al-Thawra*, quoted by Iraqi News Agency, 17 December 1969, cited in *Daily Report*, 19 December 1969.

38. Radio Baghdad, 13 April 1970, cited in *Daily Report*, 14 April 1970.

39. *Al-Musawwar* (Cairo, weekly), 20 March 1970; *Pesh Merga*, August–December, (Helsinki) 1976. Subsequently, the ICP also claimed that it had played an important role in negotiating the agreement between the Kurds and the regime. *World Marxist Review* (Toronto, monthly), June 1974.

40. *Pravda*, 21 September 1969, as quoted by *Mizan Supplement* (London), September–October 1969.

41. Sa'ad Jawad, *Iraq and the Kurdish Question, 1958–1970* (London: Ithaca Press, 1981), p. 255.

42. Kutschera, *Le mouvement*, p. 274.

43. *Al-Hawadith* (Beirut, weekly), 30 January 1970.

44. *Al-Thawra*, quoted by *Le Monde* (Paris, daily), 19 February 1970.

45. In later years, the Kurds argued that Kirkuk was sacred to them.

46. Wadie Jwaideh, *The Kurdish National Movement: Its Origins and Developments* (Syracuse: Syracuse University Press, 2006), p. 232.

47. Cecil J. Edmonds, *Kurds, Turks and Arabs* (London: Oxford University Press, 1957), pp. 430–438. According to other sources, the Turkomans numbered about 80,000 and constituted about one-fifteenth of the Kurds in the early 1960s. In 1970, their percentage in the population was estimated at between 1.5 percent and 2.5 percent. Bernard Vernier, *L'Iraq d'aujourd'hui* (Paris: Librarie Armand Colin, 1963), p. 60; *Area Handbook for Iraq* (Washington, DC: American University, 1971), p. 62. In the mid-1970s,

their number was evaluated at 330,000. Munir H. Nasser, "Iraq: Ethnic Minorities and Their Impact on Politics," *Journal of South Asian and Middle Eastern Studies* 8, no. 3 (1985): 24. The city of Kirkuk, which lies in the center of the province, is a mixed city of Arabs, Kurds, and Turkomans. For two eye-opening analyses on Kirkuk, see Henry D. Astarjian, *The Struggle for Kirkuk* (Westport, CT: Praeger Security International, 2007); and Gareth Stansfield, *Crisis in Kirkuk: The Ethnopolitics of Conflict and Compromise* (Philadelphia: University of Pennsylvania Press, 2009).

48. Edmonds, *Kurds, Turks and Arabs*, pp. 430–438.

49. The Baath regime was the first to initiate a policy of Arabization in the Kurdish area in 1963. Forty thousand Kurds were displaced from the Kirkuk area alone. Kutschera, *Le mouvement*, p. 237.

50. *Al-Jumhuriyya*, 2 March 1970.

3

Paved with Good Intentions

The March Declaration (*bayan adhar*) of 1970, which was intended to solve the Kurdish problem peacefully, was an official document containing the most far-reaching concessions ever made by any Iraqi regime to the Kurds; namely, recognition of their right to autonomy (*hukm dhati*). However, not everyone in Baghdad was reconciled to solving the problem in this way. Even its architects, who had expressed boundless enthusiasm for the March Declaration at the time, did so by force of circumstances and were fully cognizant that their fate in particular, and the fate of the Baath in general, depended on a solution being found to the Kurdish problem.

On 11 March 1970, President Ahmad Hasan al-Bakr read the "Declaration (*bayan*) of the RCC" about the Kurdish question, including an introduction and fifteen articles, on Radio Baghdad. The wording of the document pointed to the many difficulties entailed in its formulation. Its sophistication was evidenced by the use of the word *declaration*, which the regime no doubt had selected because it created the impression of a unilateral gesture on its part. The term *agreement*, on the other hand, would have acknowledged that the two parties involved in the negotiation were of equal standing. Unlike al-Bakr, the Kurds used the term *agreement* in their announcement.[1]

The introduction to the agreement highlighted two issues:

1. Solving the internal Iraqi problems, chief among which was the Kurdish problem, and creating Iraqi national unity (*wahda wataniyya*) would enable the state to "divert all its resources to the fateful battle of the nation" (*al-ma'raka al-qawmiyya*); that is, the battle for Palestine.[2] This emphasis was intended to preempt possible criticism by the military and to anchor the agreement in the Baathist ideological commitment to the Palestinian cause.[3]

2. Emphasizing the fact that the all-Arab national leadership had laid the conceptual-theoretical foundation for a solution to the problem at its Seventh

Regional Congress in late 1968, thus granting it greater credibility in the eyes of the Kurds.

It was no coincidence that the main point of the declaration was inserted at the end of the document. Article 14, which spoke of the unification of provinces with a Kurdish majority into a single administrative unit, incidentally mentioned that the Kurdish residents in this unit "shall enjoy autonomy" (*hukm dhati*). This revolutionary phrasing was nonetheless qualified by three reservations:

1. The autonomy was to be in the framework of the Iraqi republic, which meant rejection of separatism.
2. Exploitation of natural resources was to be within the purview of the republic, which meant oil resources would remain in central government control.
3. Autonomy was not to enter into effect immediately, but after four years. Although this qualification was not included in the text, there was a verbal understanding relating to it.

Article 10 was an important article, stating that "the Iraqi people (*al-Sha'b*) is composed of two primary nations (*qawmiyyatan*), the Arab and the Kurdish." However, it had already appeared in 'Abd-al-Karim Qasim's interim constitution. In one way or another, many articles repeated items included in the al-Bazzaz twelve-point plan of 1966. The Kurdish language would become the official language, alongside Arabic, in areas where Kurds constituted a majority. Kurdish officials or speakers would be appointed to the administration apparatus of areas with a Kurdish majority. Amnesty would be granted to people involved in the incidents in the north. Arabs and Kurds would be resettled in their former places of residence. Indemnities would be paid to injured parties or their relatives. The Kurdish radio station and heavy armaments would be handed over to the authorities "in the final stages of the agreement."[4] And the Kurds would have proportional representation in the proposed legislative authority.

Other articles included the establishment of independent organizations for Kurdish women, youth, and students; the appointment of a Kurd to the post of vice-president; and agrarian reforms to be carried out "immediately" in the Kurdish area. Such agrarian reforms probably intended to weaken the Kurdish leadership that drew its power from old, tribal agrarian-based frameworks.

As to the several secret clauses included in the agreement, the government alluded to them by stating that a number of articles, "having [only] secondary importance," were not included in the declaration.[5]

According to these clauses,

1. the Kurds were to keep a force of ca. 6,000 as national border guards (*haras watani lil-hudud*), to be financed by Baghdad;

2. Iraqi Army forces were to withdraw from their "normal positions" in the Kurdish north;
3. the Salah al-Din Forces (quwwat Salah al-Din) and the faction of Ibrahim Ahmad and Jalal al-Talabani were to be disbanded;
4. the KDP would be allowed to operate freely in the Kurdish region and to publish its own newspaper;
5. a nationwide census would take place within a year, and thus define the region of Kurdish majority.[6]

The content and spirit of the agreement pointed to an unprecedented gain for the Kurdish national movement. This was the first time in the twentieth century that an Iraqi regime recognized the Kurds' right to territorial autonomy. Or, as a Kurdish author put it, "It recognized openly the existence of people possessing land and having the right to establish its own national (qawmiyya) government on that land."[7] This move was all the more important given that it had been made by a pan-Arab, radical party. It also had no counterpart in other countries in which the Kurds had settled. Official approval was also given to the standing of Mulla Mustafa Barzani, who is noted as having given his approval to the declaration. The regime's unofficial commitment to disbanding the groups opposing Barzani left him as the uncontested leader of the Kurdish camp.

Nonetheless, this agreement had serious limitations and obstacles from the Kurdish standpoint. The most serious was a four-year deferment of the implementation of autonomy, which according to Barzani had been imposed on the Kurds by the government. The fact that it was a "declaration," and not an agreement anchored in international law, left autonomy to the mercy of the central government. Moreover, the fact that several of the more complicated problems—such as the issues of Kirkuk, Kurdish representation in the central government, and the revival of parliament—were left pending also constituted seeds for future tribulations.

From Baghdad's point of view, the agreement seemed like out-and-out submission to the Kurds. Out of the fifteen articles of the agreement, fourteen contained concessions to the Kurds while only one mentioned the Kurds' surrender of arms in the final stages of the implementation of the agreement. None even hinted that the Kurds ought to cease hostilities against the government. One can only surmise that the regime sought to avoid mentioning this point so as not to acknowledge that a rebellion was indeed taking place, that the government was not strong enough to suppress it, and that it was compelled to secure quiet in the north at the price of heavy concessions and not as a gesture of goodwill on its part.

In fact, the regime's gains were to manifest themselves in the longer term. In the meantime it sought to consolidate its power, strengthen the economy, increase oil output, and channel military resources to deter Iran. The Iraqi weekly *Alif-Ba'* emphasized that a solution to the Kurdish problem would enable Iraq "to play a national role, not only on the front line on the eastern front, but also in confronting Iranian aspirations in the Arab Gulf."[8]

Euphoria Meets Reality

The days following the agreement were marked by euphoria, and 12 March 1970 was celebrated as peace day (*yawm al-salam*), an interesting terminology reminiscent of peace agreements between states. Hundreds of thousands of Arabs and Kurds demonstrated in the streets of Baghdad in support of the agreement. President al-Bakr appeared before the demonstrators, accompanied by Mahmud 'Uthman and Barzani's two sons, Idris and Mas'ud. It was the first public exposure in Baghdad for the Kurds in nine years.[9] Al-Bakr and 'Uthman delivered enthusiastic speeches and, when 'Uthman stated on behalf of Barzani that the Kurds would stand by the Arabs in the wars against Israel, the crowd cheered. Demonstrations of support were also held in the Kurdish north with the participation of the Peshmerga. The three days following the agreement were established as official holidays, and Radio Baghdad broadcast patriotic songs and cables of support in both Arabic and Kurdish.

Barzani, whose suspicions of Baghdad had not been allayed, did not take part in the festivities. However, he did send a cable signed with the title "leader of the Kurdish movement (*haraka*) and head of the KDP," which was read on Baghdad television by 'Uthman. Emphasizing that he and his party had taken part in formulating the declaration, Barzani indicated that only the weakness of previous regimes had precluded a "peaceful solution" of the problem. Barzani declared that the Kurdish people supported the "just struggle being waged by the Arab nation against its enemies" and was committed to implementing the articles of the declaration in spirit and in letter.[10] On the whole, Barzani considered the agreement as a great achievement for the Kurds because it acknowledged the principle of autonomy and was drafted between two parties after protracted and difficult negotiations.

Jalal Talabani too sent a congratulatory cable but, in a book that he published shortly afterward, he attacked the agreement, stating that the regime had gone down the wrong road when it chose to negotiate with "opportunistic elements" instead of relying on "true, progressive and revolutionary Kurdish forces."[11]

The most enthusiastic support for the agreement came from its architect Saddam Hussein who stated that "the solution will not be another temporary cease-fire as it was in the past. Rather, it is a full, fundamental, political, and constitutional solution which will guarantee brotherhood between the Arabs and Kurds forever."[12] Saddam, who signed the agreement with Barzani sometime before its publication, returned to the Kurdish region on 21 March to celebrate the event. He was the only leading personality to make such a gesture and was welcomed by Barzani himself. He even participated in the Kurdish New

Year festival, Nowruz, where 300,000 people were gathered to receive him. He was reportedly taken by car for a distance of two miles, amid waves of enthusiasm cheered by an enthusiastic crowd.[13]

In an interview with *Al-Ahram*, Saddam disclosed that "we had to wage a struggle within the party and the army to lay the foundation for the new concept," emphasizing that the leadership would implement "the articles of the agreement" as swiftly as possible lest "hostile circles" act against it.[14] In fact, people in the Baath Party itself were opposed to the agreement.[15] Saddam expected the agreement to have far-reaching implications in the region, particularly in Iran, because "the Iranians are bound to find themselves in serious trouble . . . as Iraq found itself in a constant state of self-defense due to the Iranian plots and attempts to exploit the Kurdish problem."[16] Saddam believed that the Iranians might attempt to obstruct the agreement so as to prevent its impact on the Iranian Kurds. On another occasion, he expressed his belief that Iraq's soldiers would be able to "teach this shah a lesson, and soon."[17]

The shah reacted angrily, fearing that the strengthening of Iraq was liable to disrupt his plan to expand his hegemony in the Gulf. From the Iranian point of view, there was now a potential danger of the Kurds in Iran raising demands similar to those of their brethren in Iraq. Above all, the loss of the Kurdish bargaining card could have serious repercussions for the shah. Turkey likewise was far from pleased with the agreement and now demanded that full minority rights be granted to the Turkoman residents of Iraq who numbered 700,000 according to Turkish estimates. It further warned against the kindling of the "Barzani flame," which might endanger "the territorial integrity of both Turkey and Iraq."[18]

Meanwhile, Baghdad initiated moves to implement the agreement. These included the establishment of a peace committee (*lajnat al-salam*) to supervise the implementation of the agreement; the introduction of Kurdish as a language of instruction in middle and high schools in the Kurdish area;[19] the granting of permission to establish a Kurdish cultural association and a Kurdish science academy and to teach the Kurdish language in high schools throughout Iraq; and the appointment of five Kurds from Barzani's camp as ministers in the Baghdad government.

Salih Mahdi 'Ammash and Hardan 'Abd-al-Ghaffar al-Tikriti were expelled from their key positions as interior minister and defense minister, respectively, and were appointed as vice-presidents. This measure indicated Saddam's victory over his rivals in the military wing, but it also a priori weakened the status of a future Kurdish vice-president, should one be appointed.[20] Similarly, the powers of the Kurdish ministers were limited, given that they did not hold key positions in a cabinet that itself was a rubber stamp for the Baath Party and the RCC.

Although the agreement stipulated that the Kurds hand over their radio station in the final stages, as a goodwill gesture Radio Kurdistan ceased broadcasting on 23 March 1970. Even more important was the elimination of the administrative structure that the movement had established in 1964. In May the authorities permitted the publication of the official daily of the KDP, *Al-Ta'akhi* (i.e., solidarity), which was published in both Arabic and Kurdish. The agreement gave a boost to Kurdish cultural activities. Poets and writers published their writings in twenty-nine new periodicals, and Kurdish intellectuals from various parts of Iraq became "Kurdicized" and began writing in Kurdish.[21]

In the meantime, there were reports on the withdrawal of Iraqi forces, of the Salah al-Din auxiliary forces, and of the Peshmerga to locales designated by the authorities. The RCC approved the Peshmerga Law in July 1970, discharging 14,000 men from this force and transposing 6,000 others as border guards to whom all terms of the Iraqi police applied.[22]

The agreement had an immediate effect on the internal balance of power within the Kurdish camp as well as on the triangular relations between the Kurds, the Communists, and the Baath Party. The KDP's new status was evidenced by the very fact that it could convene its Eighth Congress in Nawperdan in July 1970.[23] The congress was unique in that it was held publicly, with the participation of representatives of the KDP; Kurdish delegations from Lebanon, Europe, and the United States; the Baath Party; and even the Palestine Liberation Organization (PLO).

Barzani was reelected as president and Habib Muhammad Karim as general secretary. New members of the politburo included Mahmud 'Uthman, Muhammad Mahmud 'Abd al-Rahman, 'Ali 'Abdullah, Nuri Shawis, Salih-al-Yusufi, and 'Aziz 'Aqrawi. For the first time, the central committee, whose membership grew from seventeen to twenty-two, included Barzani's two sons, Idris and Mas'ud, and a women's representative, Zakiyya Isma'il Haqqi.[24] Mas'ud Barzani was ranked second, behind the general secretary, since he had obtained more votes than 'Uthman who was considered the leader of the leftist branch.

The decisions of the congress comprised twenty-three articles, the most salient of which were the KDP's struggle to achieve autonomy for the Kurds in Iraq, to place the national Kurdish movement's achievements on a par with those of the Arab nationalist movement in Iraq, to act for the establishment of an elected democratic regime, to support the Kurdish struggle in other parts of Kurdistan, and to insist on the distribution of oil revenues in proportion to the percentage of Kurds in the population.

The KDP congress also served as a stage for the secret and public disputes among its different participants, the most important of which was the establishment of a national front (*jabha wataniyya*), which was itself only the tip of the iceberg of the question of the division of power in Iraq. Since its advent to power, the Baath Party had repeatedly declared its intention to establish a national front that would include the opposition. Initially, the regime's effort had been directed at the ICP Central Committee with the aim of driving a wedge between the latter and the KDP. Indeed, at a certain stage in the discussions, Saddam stipulated that the inclusion of the ICP in the envisaged national front be linked with the cessation of Communist support for Barzani in the Kurdish war against the regime.[25] Now, because of the regime's agreement with the Kurds, relations between Baghdad and the ICP began to deteriorate while the Baath Party exploited its alliance with the KDP to weaken the Communists. KDP-ICP relations also deteriorated inasmuch as the KDP threatened the ICP's status among the Kurdish population, which formed an important base of support for the Communist movement.

Another immediate effect of the agreement was the breakdown of Talabani's group. In April, the RCC prohibited the publication of his daily *Al-Nur*; Taha Muhyi-al-Din Ma'ruf, considered one of Talabani's people, was dismissed from the government; and, most importantly, 4,000 of his supporters surrendered their weapons to the authorities. Paradoxically, Talabani, Barzani's harshest rival, once again joined the KDP, despite the opposition of other members such as 'Umar Mustafa and Hilmi Sharif. As for Barzani, now the party's indisputable leader, he sought to bring Talabani's group to the fold so as to eliminate the schism in the Kurdish camp.[26] Barzani initiated a reconciliation meeting with Talabani, which was held in August 1970 at the Rawanduz road junction. The internal discussions within Talabani's group continued until February 1971, when it was finally decided that this faction would disband and join the KDP.

Opening Pandora's Box

No sooner was the March Declaration issued than the Pandora's box of oil-rich Kirkuk opened. As of this writing (early 2012), the Kirkuk problem has remained the main bone of contention between the Kurds and Baghdad. With regard to Kirkuk, a number of problems have emerged that are mainly on matters concerning ethnic and religious minorities. Reflecting the multiethnic nature of the state, the struggle is no longer between the Baathi regime and the Kurds alone but has come to include other minorities, adding further complications to the issue at hand.

Hardly four months passed since the March agreement in 1970 when ominous signs began to surface. Relations between the Kurds and the regime developed as if on two levels. Verbally, the two parties gave the impression that they aspired to implement the agreement. On the ground, however, relations deteriorated to the point of completely eclipsing the original goals. This duality reflected the ongoing power struggle within the regime, one manifestation of which was the debate regarding the Kurdish question. While the civilian faction headed by Saddam continued to support (for a limited period) a peaceful solution, the military headed by 'Ammash sought to thwart the agreement. President al-Bakr remained on the fence.

In fact, the picture was even more complex, revealing Baghdad's underhanded dealings with the Kurds. Although Saddam appeared to be a most enthusiastic supporter of the agreement, in time it became clear that he did not intend to implement the agreement's more problematic articles, which he had signed merely to gain time to eliminate his rivals and gain a foothold in the army.

The problems that arose in the aftermath of the agreement were of two types. One concerned sporadic incidents such as the attempt to assassinate Barzani's son Idris and, later, Mulla Mustafa Barzani himself. The second was related to disputes over fundamental questions such as the demarcation of the borders of the autonomous region and the issue of the national front.

On 17 July 1970, the second anniversary of the Baathi coup, an interim constitution was issued. Article 5(b) stipulated: "The Iraqi people is composed of two main nations (*qawmiyyatan*), the Arab nation and the Kurdish nation. This constitution recognizes the national rights (*huquq qawmiyya*) of the Kurdish people and the legitimate rights of *all minorities* in the framework of Iraqi unity (*wahda*)" (italics added). Article 7(b) further specified that "the Kurdish language shall be, alongside Arabic, the official language in the Kurdish area." However, in Kurdish eyes these important points were marred by the Preamble to Article 5, which stated that Iraq was "part of the Arab nation."[27] The Kurds sought wording to the effect that the Arabs in Iraq were part of the Arab nation. Identity issues thus bedeviled the parties from the very beginning.[28]

The one issue on which the agreement could stand or fall was the demarcation of the autonomous region and problems related to it; namely, the call for a census, the problem of Kirkuk, and the status of other minorities in the Kurdish region. On 18 June 1970, the planning minister Jawad Hashim announced the regime's intent to conduct a census on 26 October of that year. However, five days before the designated date, the RCC decided to postpone the census until March 1971. In fact, the census was never to take place.

Seen in retrospect, the census, which was intended to settle the dispute regarding Kirkuk and allow for the announcement of the March agreement, was a hard-pressed tactical solution that could not be implemented. Baghdad, which from the outset had been opposed to the inclusion of the Kirkuk area in the autonomous region, regarded such a census as a capitulation to the Kurds. It feared that a census would clearly demonstrate that the Kurds were the majority in the area, thus compelling Baghdad to respond to their demands. For their part, the Kurds too had their qualms with regard to a population count. Although they were absolutely certain that a Kurdish majority existed in Kirkuk, they feared that the regime would take measures to influence the census, either by forging its results or relocating the population in order to change the demographic situation in Kirkuk.

The Kurdish misgivings were illustrated in Barzani's statement to *Jeune Afrique* on the eve of the scheduled time of the census in October 1970: "I view

such a census as superfluous. It is a fact that this area is Kurdish."[29] Furthermore, he indirectly accused the authorities of attempting to influence the results of the census, "Inside the government, there are probably persons of bad
faith, who wish to seize the opportunity to act. . . . We will not accept a wrong
verdict." With this statement, Barzani played into the hands of the authorities,
which hastened to postpone the census.

Between October 1970 and March 1971, several attempts were made to
find a compromise formula. The Kurds proposed that a new census be conducted on the basis of the 1957 census so as to exclude Arabs or other non-
Kurds who had meanwhile settled in the controversial areas.[30] However, at this
stage the regime apparently felt that it was strong enough to not conduct a census at all. It subsequently argued that the agreement to defer the census had
been reached by mutual consensus.[31]

Refusing to accept the fait accompli, Barzani sent a memorandum to President al-Bakr in which he protested the fact that the authorities had done everything to avoid conducting the census and had taken measures to create "an Arab
population concentration in the city of Kirkuk and its environs to obtain a non-
Kurdish majority in this district—the richest in oil—in the next census."[32] President al-Bakr's response was no less vehement: "The Iraq Army . . . shall not
hesitate to intervene [against the Kurds] to bring about respect for the law."[33]

Meanwhile, the concept of autonomy also underwent changes forced
through by Saddam. In an interview on the occasion of the first anniversary of
the March agreement Saddam referred to claims that Kirkuk was a Kurdish
area, stating that "autonomy was given to the people, not to the land."[34] This signified that he had retreated to a concept of personal autonomy, which at the
time had been rejected by the Kurds.

In anticipation of the census and the demarcation of an autonomous region,
each party hastened to create a fait accompli on the ground and improve its own
position. The race did not stop, even when it became clear that the census would
not take place. In the face of Kurdish claims that the Kirkuk area was Kurdish
from a historical, geographic, and demographic standpoint, the Turkomans
maintained that they had inhabited the area before the Kurds and had outnum-
bered them until the mid-twentieth century.[35] In fact, Hanna Batatu suggested,
the Turkomans were originally the predominant element in the town of Kirkuk,
which had been "Turkish through and through" and represented one-half the
population in 1959 while the Kurds constituted only one-third.[36] For its part,
the regime attempted to bring the Turkomans to the fold and encourage them to
oppose the local Kurdish administration in the area. It should be pointed out
that an atmosphere of enmity had long prevailed between the Kurds and the
Turkomans. It stemmed, among other things, from the fact that the Sublime
Porte, namely the Ottoman sultan, settled Turkomans in the Mosul and Kirkuk
area in the nineteenth century to put down Kurdish rebellious activities there.
The Kurds, who regarded the Turkomans as uninvited guests, exploited every

opportunity to take revenge on them. In a later incident in Kirkuk in June 1959, the Kurds—together with members of the Communist Party—were involved in the massacre of Turkomans.[37]

The regime sought to exploit this enmity to gain the Turkomans' support. Recall that, at the height of discussions regarding the March agreement, the regime granted cultural rights to the Turkomans (in January 1970). In June of the same year, when preparations for the census intensified, the regime and the Kurds stepped up their pressure on the Turkomans. The Kurds apparently attempted to present certain Turkoman tribes as Kurdish. The Turkoman leader even accused the Kurds of threatening to massacre his people if they did not support the Kurds. In any case, in the struggle for the minds and hearts of the Turkomans, the regime had the advantage of being able to grant them privileges and protection. The Turkomans themselves were reluctant to collaborate with the Kurds and did not wish to be included in the Kurdish autonomy. Turkey, which did not look favorably on Kurdish autonomy in Iraq, acted behind the scenes to thwart the possibility of Turkoman support for the Kurds.[38]

The controversy surrounding the Fayli Kurds, which surfaced in the spring of 1971, was also linked to the question of the demarcation of an autonomous region.[39] The Faylis originated in Luristan, Iran. Although religiously they are Shi'a, there are differing opinions regarding their nationality. The Kurds claimed that the Faylis were Kurds whereas others argued that the Faylis themselves did not identify themselves as such.[40] The Faylis began to migrate to Iraq in the nineteenth and early twentieth centuries, and the Kurds estimated their number at 100,000 in 1971, compared to the authorities' estimation of 15,000. The Kurds repeatedly demanded that the authorities grant the Faylis Iraqi citizenship, arguing that the parties had agreed to this.[41] They even argued that the authorities discriminated in favor of non-Iraqi Arabs by giving them various key positions while obstructing the promotion of the Faylis.

The regime's daily, *Al-Jumhuriyya*, denied the existence of an agreement on the Faylis. Regarding discrimination in favor of the Arabs, it emphasized that the constitution explicitly stipulated that Iraq was part of the Arab nation, and that it was not stated anywhere that the Kurdish people (*qawm*) in Iraq were part of a larger nation, extending from Iran to the Soviet Union, for that would mean "clear separatism" (*infisal sarih*). *Al-Jumhuriyya* concluded that Kurdish autonomy was an integral part of "Arab unity."[42] Meanwhile, the regime took practical steps to prevent the "naturalization" of the Faylis. In the winter of 1971–1972, about 60,000 Shi'a, including 40,000 Faylis, were expelled from Iraq on the pretext that they were not Iraqis.[43] Furthermore, between 1972 and 1979 the Baath made sure that no Fayli could occupy a high-ranking position. Thus, it rejected the Kurdish nominee for the post of vice-president, Habib Muhammad Karim, because it "seemed to think that its acceptance of a Fayli Kurd as Iraq's vice-president would be tantamount to officially recognizing all members of the Fayli community as Iraqi citizens."[44]

The difficulties facing the Yezidis, another Kurdish-speaking people that lived in Iraq since ancient times, were no less complex as they suffered from severe persecution and Arabization, especially under the Baath.[45] Their neighbors called them "Satan's worshipers," but their religion is actually a mixture of elements from different religions and beliefs with roots going back to a pre-monotheistic era.[46] They were persecuted mainly by Muslims and much less by Christians. The Yezidis, who lived in small isolated groups for the most part in the Sinjar Mountains west of Mosul and in Shaykhan in the province of Erbil, were more isolated than other ethnic or religious groups. The dispute between the Kurdish movement and the Iraqi regime concerned Yezidi nationality. According to the regime, the Yezidis were Umayyad Arabs (members of the Arab dynasty that ruled in Damascus from 661 to 750 C.E.)[47]—hence the regime's attempts to Arabize them. The Kurdish camp, however, adhered to its claim that the Yezidis were Kurds.[48] A well-known researcher, Basile Nikitine, has no doubt about the Kurdishness of the Yezidis; in this he follows the views of another researcher, according to whom all the Kurds were Yezidis before they adopted Islam.[49] Interestingly, an Arab scholar asserted as early as 1945 that the Yezidis were nationalist Kurds, even more so than their Muslim Kurdish brethren.[50] However, his was a lone voice. Both this dispute and the Arabization project initiated by the regime obfuscated their real numbers.[51] One estimation put the number of Yezidis at 75,000 in 1957.[52] In any case the Yezidis, known for their rebelliousness against each and every regime, ultimately also defied the Baath, thus bringing into focus the conflict between the regime and the Kurdish camp.

Not limiting itself to verbal announcements, Baghdad meanwhile escalated its move to Arabize Kirkuk and other strategically important areas by establishing Arab "colonies" in the heart of the Kurdish region. In fact, a new document revealed that the policy of Arabization had started as early as 1929, using this very term (*ta'rib*) because the Arabs in that oil-rich region accounted for only 20 percent of the population. The Baath policy was unique in that it had a twofold aim: settling Arabs and evacuating the Kurds.[53] Responding to the charge of Arabization, Saddam went as far as to justify it by saying: "Nothing prevents members of the larger [Arab] nation from moving to live on the land populated by members of the smaller nation which enjoys self-rule." To think otherwise, he said, indicated "a chauvinistic mentality . . . whose goal is separatism."[54] Later, the Baath Party denounced the "false charges," according to which it was Arabizing mixed areas while accusing the KDP of the "Kurdization" of the same areas.

Burning the Bridges of Trust

While the autonomy border dispute continued, a series of events took place that further undermined the already shaky trust between the Kurds and the regime.

On the night of 6 December 1970, Barzani's son Idris, who had come to Baghdad to congratulate the leadership on the occasion of the three-day celebration marking the end of the Ramadan fast ('Id al-Fitr), escaped an assassination attempt against him. The car used for the assassination attempt had been the authorities' gift to Barzani.

Barzani strongly denounced the assassination attempt and demanded that the authorities bring the guilty parties to justice, five of whom he claimed were Kurds belonging to the Talabani faction. He emphasized that many people wished to sabotage peace, including several leading figures in the government and especially in the army.[55] Barzani further stated that despite the doubts that this incident aroused in him, he would continue to adhere to the agreement. *Al-Thawra* also strongly denounced the assassination attempt and promised to bring the culprits to justice. On 3 February 1971, it announced that the suspects had been located and would be put on trial "soon."[56] Nothing came of it.

After the assassination attempt, the government took quick action to appease the Kurds. This included a monthly indemnity of 10 dinars for each family that had lost a son in the battles of 1961–1970, a monthly grant of 10 dinars for each Peshmerga member who had been discharged and had no permanent income, and the allocation of 4 million dinars for construction in the north. However, the regime's gestures apparently failed to appease the Kurds: in fact, in December 1970 there were reports of a renewed flow of Bulgarian and Czechoslovakian weapons to the Kurdish camp.[57]

On the political level, despite the façade of an alliance between the Baath and the KDP, the latter's activities caused much annoyance in the regime. Although the KDP operated openly, pursuant to the agreement, it was perceived as threatening the entire political fabric in Iraq because it insistently called for the democratization of the political system, the reestablishment of parliament, and the formation of a national front.[58] The Baath and the KDP also competed for new party members, particularly in the Kurdish north.

Equally irritating to the Baath was the fact that the KDP newspaper *Al-Ta'akhi* expressed independent and oppositionist views, which not only boosted the newspaper's circulation but also led to repeated attempts by the government to clip its wings. In mid-May 1971, a sharp debate was sparked between *Al-Ta'akhi* and the regime's newspaper *Al-Jumhuriyya*. The latter attacked *Al-Ta'akhi* journalists for having devoted themselves "to the spread of liberal and bourgeois ideas" and for advocating "a free economy and a parliamentary system."[59] *Al-Jumhuriyya* attempted to draw a distinction between *Al-Ta'akhi* and the KDP, suggesting that *Al-Ta'akhi* did not represent the KDP's views, which was denied categorically by the newspaper. In any case, Saddam sent a cable to the two newspapers shortly afterward, asking them to stop feuding. In fact, the controversy reflected a deepening rift between the Kurds and the regime.

Concurrently, the RCC established a High Committee for Affairs of the North (al-lajna al-'ulya li-shu'un al-shamal), which was headed by Saddam and became the "RCC of the Kurdish problem."[60] In other words, the powers of the RCC were granted to the committee in order to expedite the implementation of the March agreement. Saddam's tendency to appease the Kurds at that stage was demonstrated by gestures such as the decision to confiscate all the weapons from the Kurdish Baathi auxiliary Salah al-Din Forces by 1 June 1971. Saddam also held a meeting with Idris Barzani with the intention of solving outstanding problems. On 22 June, he visited the fifth branch of the KDP in Baghdad and the Kurdish Women's Association, where he called for the strengthening of the alliance between the two parties and warned against reactionary and rightist forces seeking to damage it.

As against this, the Iraqi ground and air forces attempted to occupy the area in the vicinity of the city of Barzan by bombing several Kurdish villages in early July 1971. The Kurdish ministers were recalled to the north in protest. Barzani accused the authorities of fraud and the KDP Central Committee decided to send a delegation to Baghdad, presenting the authorities with a choice between upholding the agreement or all-out war. For his part, al-Bakr sent envoys to Barzani, explaining that the operation had been initiated by several officers without his knowledge. Whether true or not, around the time of the attack, a plot (real or imagined) to topple the regime was uncovered. Dozens of senior officers were subsequently arrested, including the air force commander.

Capping these moves was the attempt to assassinate Barzani on 29 September 1971, which undoubtedly did much to unsettle the Kurdish camp and destroy the trust between Baghdad and Barzani. Believing that Barzani's death would put an end to the Kurdish rebellion, different governments in Baghdad had attempted to kill Barzani from 1935 onward and even falsely announced his death.[61] This time, the attempt was made by nine clerics, who claimed that they had been sent by the authorities in Baghdad to promote the dialogue with the Kurds and were to meet with Barzani and 'Uthman. Two clerics, who had bombs strapped to their bodies, exploded immediately at the outset of the meeting, but Barzani and 'Uthman managed to escape before fighting broke out between the other clerics and Barzani's bodyguards. The fight ended with the death of eight clerics and two drivers whose cars were found to contain additional explosives. The official Kurdish announcement claimed that all the clerics had been killed. But one actually survived and it was he who disclosed the details of the plot to Barzani.[62]

As soon as the assassination attempt became known, the Baath Party regional command sent a cable to Barzani in which it expressed its deep regret about the incident and accused "malicious elements" and "agents of imperialism" of attempting "to sabotage the March Declaration." In a series of articles, the authorities washed their hands of any connection to the incident.[63] Once again they established an investigative committee, but its conclusions were never published.

Who was behind the assassination attempt? The regime's version, which was put forward after the uncovering in July 1973 of the general security director Nazim Kzar's "conspiracy" (see below), was that Kzar was behind it. A second version maintained that the military was responsible and that it had even planned a large attack against the Kurds in the event that the attempt succeeded. Yet a third version claimed that Saddam had instigated it because the agreement no longer served his purposes. Saddam now sought to divert the army's energy to targeting the Kurds while he remained free to continue eliminating his rivals.

Years later, it became known that not only had Saddam been behind the assassination attempt, but that he had also involved Barzani's eldest son 'Ubaydullah, who had found refuge in Baghdad around the same time, in the assassination attempt.[64] The background to this strange episode was the growing animosity between Barzani and his son because of a family conflict that began in the early 1960s. At that time 'Ubaydullah murdered his wife, the daughter of Barzani's uncle, Shaikh Ahmad, following a love affair with an Assyrian girl. He thus aroused the anger of his father who sought to kill him. However, 'Ubaydullah managed to flee with the rebellion's treasury, finding refuge first in Russia and then in Iran. From there, he was extradited and sent to his father who kept him under house arrest until he fled to Baghdad. Saddam established a relationship with 'Ubaydullah, obtaining his cooperation by promising 'Ubaydullah the succession after his father's murder.[65]

A short time before the incident, Saddam met with Barzani and promised to send clerics to him to complete bilateral discussions. Barzani's suspicions were not aroused because one of the members of the delegation was a well-known cleric from the Barzani tribe. After the fact, it emerged that Saddam had kept the plot secret from these clerics as well; in fact, the tape recorders with which he equipped the clerics were actually time bombs and were intended to kill them along with Barzani. Saddam even prepared a plan for the military seizure of the area after the assassination was carried out.[66]

It therefore seems that the assassination attempt was part of an integrated operation intended to liquidate Barzani, who was perceived as the core of the national Kurdish movement, and to confer prestige on the army, which would in turn lead to the strengthening of Saddam's position in the army.

Notes

1. Voice of Iraqi Kurdistan, 11 March 1970, cited in BBC, 13 March 1970. In this study, the term *agreement* was used, except in cases of direct quotations in which the term *declaration* was used. It should be indicated that the Soviet Union used the term *declaration* (*New York Times* [New York, daily], 24 March 1970) whereas the ICP used the term *agreement* (*World Marxist Review* [Toronto, monthly], June 1974). For the text, see Radio Baghdad, 11 March 1970, cited in BBC, 13 March 1970 and *Al-Thawra* (Baghdad, daily), 12 March 1970.

2. It is necessary to highlight the different meanings of *qawmiyya* and *wataniyya* as expressed here. *Qawmiyya* refers both to pan-Arab nationalism and to an ethnic group (e.g., the Kurds). *Wataniyya* indicates unity and patriotism.

3. The most vociferous attack came from pan-Arab nationalists, especially from Baathi Syria. Farid Asasard, *Al-Mas'ala al-Kurdiyya ba'd Qanun Idarat al-Dawla* (Cairo: Maktabat Madbuli, 2006), pp. 31–33.

4. It should be noted that the text itself uses the term *agreement* here, which could have been a slip of the pen. Alternatively, it could have been done on purpose to make it binding for the Kurds who had to fulfill their part in it.

5. *Al-Sayyad* (Beirut, weekly), 26 March 1970.

6. Public Record Office, FCO17/1237, 2 April 1970.

7. Asasard, *Al-Mas'ala al-Kurdiyya*, p. 31.

8. Quoted by Midle East News Agency, March 1970.

9. Public Record Office, FCO17/1237, 6 April 1970.

10. *Al-Thawra*, 12 March 1970.

11. Jalal Talabani, *Kurdistan wal-Haraka al-Qawmiyya al-Kurdiyya* (Beirut: Dar al-Tali'a, 1971), p. 384.

12. *Al-Thawra*, 12 March 1970.

13. *The Guardian* (London, daily), 11 May 1974.

14. *Al-Ahram* (Cairo, daily), 12 March 1970.

15. The British ambassador to Iraq described Saddam Hussein as the architect of the agreement "against considerable opposition in the party." Public Record Office, FCO17/1238, 19 November 1970.

16. *Al-Ahram*, 12 March 1970.

17. *Al-Jumhuriyya*, 13 May 1970.

18. Ankara, *Ulus*, 16 July 1970, cited in *Daily Report*, 21 July 1970. It seems that Turkey's estimate of the number of Turkomans was excessive.

19. Until then, Kurdish was taught only in elementary schools. Asasard, *Al-Mas'ala al-Kurdiyya*, p. 41.

20. In the final analysis, no Kurd was appointed as vice-president.

21. Joyce Blau, "Refinement and Oppression of Kurdish Language," in *The Kurds: Nationalism and Politics*, eds. Faleh A. Jabar and Dawod Hosham (London: Saqi, 2006), pp. 109–110.

22. According to a confidential report, there was "a virtual frontier post between arm-controlled [*sic*] Iraq and Pish Merga-controlled Kurdistan." J. H. Simons, British Embassy Baghdad, Public Record Office, FCO17/1237, 13 June 1970.

23. The Seventh Congress was held in November 1966 amid the confusion preceding the collapse of the al-Bazzaz twelve-point plan.

24. Haqqi, a Fayli Kurd, was later elected head of the Women's Union of Kurdistan. Saad B. Eskander, "Fayli Kurds of Baghdad and the Ba'ath Regime," in *The Kurds: Nationalism and Politics*, eds. Faleh A. Jabar and Dawod Hosham (London: Saqi, 2006), pp. 180–202.

25. *Al-Sayyad*, 9 October 1969. After 1963, ICP members found refuge in the Kurdish area. They were even permitted to establish combat units, which operated in the framework of the Peshmerga forces but nonetheless achieved a certain degree of autonomy. They fought alongside the Kurds until the agreement was signed. Ismet Sheriff Vanly, "Kurdistan in Iraq," in *A People Without a Country: The Kurds and Kurdistan*, ed. Gérard Chaliand (London: Zed Press, 1980), p. 172.

26. Interestingly, with regard to Talabani, Barzani's sons "were much more intransigent than he. Mulla Mustapha himself had mellowed with the years." Public Record Office, FCO17/408, 5 October 1968.

27. *Al-Jumhuriyya*, 17 July 1970.

28. The Kurds also criticized Article 43, which stipulated that the armed forces would be subordinate to the RCC, a body that excluded Kurds.

29. *Jeune Afrique* (Paris, weekly), 22 September 1970, cited in *Daily Report*, 28 December 1970. Years later, a Kurdish author depicted Kirkuk as: "Kirkuk is in the Kurds' conscience as is al-Quds in that of the Palestinians." Asasard, *Al-Mas'ala al-Kurdiyya*, p. 34.

30. *Jeune Afrique*, 15 December 1970. The Kurds claimed that the 1957 census showed that the Kurds numbered 173,085 out of the total population in the province, which was 258,900. *Al-Jadid* (Beirut, weekly), 27 October 1972.

31. *Settlement of the Kurdish Problem* (*Al-Thawra*, Thawra Publications, n.d., n.p.), pp. 38–39.

32. *Le Monde*, 25 May 1971.

33. Ibid.

34. *Al-Kifah* (Beirut, daily), 16 March 1971.

35. Arshad al-Hirmizi, *The Turkmen Reality in Iraq* (Istanbul: Kerkük Vakfı, 2005), dedicated the entire book to this issue.

36. Hanna Batatu , *The Old Social Classes and the Revolutionary Movements of Iraq* (Princeton: Princeton University Press, 1978), p. 913.

37. Uriel Dann, *Iraq Under Qassem: A Political History, 1958–1963* (New York: Praeger, 1969), pp. 223–225; Avshalom H. Rubin, "Abd al-Karim Qasim and the Kurds of Iraq: Centralization, Resistance and Revolt, 1958–1963," *Middle Eastern Studies* 43, no. 3 (2007): 365; al-Hirmizi, *The Turkmen Reality*, pp. 102–103.

38. For Turkish policies, see Wahram Petrosian, *Siyasat Turkiyya tujah Kurdistan al-'Iraq wa-Amerika 1991–2003* (Duhok: University of Duhok, 2008).

39. For a detailed discussion of the Faylis, see Saad B. Eskander, "Fayli Kurds of Baghdad and the Ba'ath Regime," in *The Kurds: Nationalism and Politics*, eds. Faleh A. Jabar and Dawod Hosham (London: Saqi, 2006), pp. 180–202.

40. Harvey Henry Smith and Richard F. Nyrop, *Area Handbook for Iraq* (Washington, DC: American University Press, 1971), p. 63; Basile Nikitine, *Les Kurdes: Étude sociologique et historique* (Paris: Éditions d'Aujourd'hui, 1965), p. 157.

41. During its negotiations with the KDP in 1970, the Baath Party insisted that the Fayli issue not be discussed because it claimed that the Fayli had no connection with the broader Kurdish issue. Eskander, "Fayli Kurds," p. 195.

42. *Al-Jumhuriyya* (Baghdad, daily), 13, 17, and 20 May 1971.

43. See also Eskander, "Fayli Kurds," p. 195.

44. Ibid., p. 199.

45. For a detailed discussion, see Dilshad Nu'man Farhan, *Mu'anat al-Kurd al-Izidiyyin fi Zill al-Hukumat al-'Iraqiyya 1921–2003* (Duhok: Duhok University, 2008).

46. See Nelida Fuccaro, *The Other Kurds: Yazidis in Colonial Iraq* (London: I. B. Tauris, 1999).

47. Ismet Sheriff Vanly, *Le Kurdistan irakien entité nationale: Étude de la révolution de 1961* (Neuchâtel, Switzerland: Éditions de la Baconnière, 1970), p. 198. It is likely that the regime grabbed at the name Yezid, which sounds similar to Yazid, a caliph of the Umayyad dynasty, thus arguing in favor of the Arab origins of the Yezidis. The Ottoman Empire considered the Kurds as Yezidis. Farhan, *Mu'anat al-Kurd*, p. 7.

48. In the 1990s, a "Yezidi cultural movement" was formed with the aim of forging a new collective identity separate from the old Kurdish and Arab national movements that had been trying to win them over to their side. Idan Barir, "This Is Our Story: The Yezidi Cultural Movement and the Processes of a Collective Identity Constructing

Among the Yezidis in Kurdistan and the Diaspora" (master's thesis, Tel Aviv University, 2009).

49. Nikitine, *Les Kurdes: Étude sociologique et historique*, p. 225.

50. Adib Mu'awwad, *Al-Akrad fi Lubnan wa-Suriyya* (1945; reprint, Duhok: University of Duhok, 2008), pp. 62–73.

51. In the censuses of 1977, 1987, and 1997, the Baath registered them against their will as Arabs. Farhan, *Mu'anat al-Kurd*, p. 8.

52. Farhan, *Mu'anat al-Kurd*, p. 29

53. Asasard, *Al-Mas'ala al-Kurdiyya*, pp. 61, 80–81.

54. *Al-Jumhuriyya*, 16 March 1971.

55. *Newsweek* (New York, weekly), 7 December 1970.

56. *Al-Thawra*, 3 February 1971.

57. *Al-Hayat* (London, daily), 30 December 1970.

58. The release, in late 1970, of former prime minister 'Abd-al-Rahman al-Bazzaz is attributed in no small way due to pressures exerted by the Kurds.

59. *Al-Jumhuriyya*, 13, 17, and 20 May 1971. I do not have at my disposal the issue of *Al-Ta'akhi* from which *Al-Jumhuriyya* quotes. I know of the dispute only from *Al-Jumhuriyya*.

60. Radio Baghdad, 12 May 1971, cited in *Daily Report*, 13 May 1971.

61. 'Abd al-Fattah 'Ali al-Botani, *Dirasat wa-Mabahith fi Ta'rikh al-Kurd wal-'Iraq al-Mu'asir* (Erbil: Hajji Hashim, 2007), p. 370.

62. A Mossad agent reported that, at the very time of the attempt, the head of the Mossad Zvi Zamir was in Kurdistan for talks with Barzani. Eliezer (Geizi) Tsafrir, *Ana Kurdi* (in Hebrew) (Or Yehuda: Hed Artzi, 1999), pp. 145–149.

63. *Al-Thawra*, 4, 10, and 11 October 1971.

64. *Al-Nahar Arab Report*, 11 October 1981.

65. Anonymous, interviewed by the author, 13 March 1982.

66. *Ruz al-Yousuf* (Cairo, weekly), 11 October 1971; *Al-Nahar Arab Report*, 11 October 1971.

4

Unholy Alliances

By the end of 1971, relations between the Baathi regime and the Kurds had become increasingly subordinate to the broad and complex problems swamping the region such as the competition between Iraq and Iran for hegemony in the Gulf, the struggle of the superpowers for influence in the Middle East in general and the Gulf in particular, Iraqi political initiatives on the inter-Arab level, and Iraq's involvement in the 1973 October War.

Thus, while for one and a half years relations had mainly been a function of domestic developments, they henceforth became determined more and more by Iraqi foreign relations. Meanwhile, a widening gap opened up between Baghdad's policymaking and that of the Kurds: Baghdad excelled in its ability to make initiatives, dictate moves on the tactical and strategic level, set the rhythm of events, and act with sophistication, cunning, and flexibility, but Kurdish policies lagged far behind. And while Baghdad formed alliances in the open, the Kurds were forced to build alliances in the dark. This made the Kurds a pawn in the hands of powers with greater political experience.

The Iran-Iraq-Soviet Triangle

On 30 November 1971, the traditionally tense relations between Iraq and Iran turned into an open crisis following Iran's seizure of three islands located in the Strait of Hormuz at the entrance to the Gulf—Abu Musa, the Greater Tunb, and the Lesser Tunb.[1] Although the islands had no real strategic importance in themselves, this step symbolized Iran's superiority in the Gulf and was a slap in the face to Iraq, which viewed itself as Iran's main rival in this area, after Great Britain had announced its withdrawal from the Gulf in January 1968.[2] What particularly worried Iraq was the US Nixon Doctrine, according to which Iran could play the role of "policeman" in the Gulf. This explains the regular supply of US arms to Iran in 1969;[3] the quiet consent of Britain, the evacuating power, to Iran's seizure of the islands; and, no less important, the weakness and apathy of the Arab countries in the Gulf and elsewhere, thus precluding any anti-Iranian measures.

Failing in its attempt to mobilize the Arab world to curb Iran, Iraq severed its diplomatic relations with Iran on 1 December 1971, the only Arab country to take such a drastic step.[4] At the same time, it also severed its relations with Great Britain. Iran reciprocated by severing its diplomatic relations with Baghdad while sending an open threat to Iraq on the subject of the Kurdish issue. In an interview with a French newspaper, the Iranian foreign minister stated, "To date, we have not offered them [the Kurdish rebels] military aid, but we could be led to do so if an open conflict started."[5]

Faced with this turn of events, Iraq deemed a rapprochement with the Soviet Union to be the best means for curbing Iran. The rapprochement, which began in the summer of 1969, culminated in the signing of a friendship treaty on 9 April 1972. This farsighted strategic move was to address Iraq's major problems and promote its political, economic, and strategic interests. Iraq sought a strong ally to help it promote its aspirations in the Gulf and counterbalance the support Iran had rallied from the United States and Britain.[6] On the inter-Arab level, the Iraqi-Soviet friendship agreement sought to eliminate Iraq's isolation, which was reflected among other things in the failure of the March 1972 Iraqi initiative to unite Iraq, Egypt, and Syria. Even more important was the backing that Iraq hoped to secure from the Soviet Union in its struggle against foreign oil companies, which in fact ended with the nationalization of Iraqi oil in June 1972. The technical assistance and arms deals that Saddam Hussein signed with the Soviet Union during his visit to Moscow in February of that year were intended to strengthen the regime domestically and to consolidate it politically, economically, and militarily. The regime expected these moves to have a cumulative effect: by drastically weakening the Kurds vis-à-vis the central government, they would remove the Kurdish question from the political scene.

The Kurdish reaction to the Iraqi-Soviet agreement was a mixture of fear, anger, and frustration. In an interview with *Le Figaro* on the day after the agreement was signed, Mulla Mustafa Barzani attacked Saddam harshly: "It is the police which is administrating this country according to the directives of Saddam Husayn, who is nothing but a lunatic thirsting for power. He liquidated Tikriti and 'Ammash; he wanted to liquidate me; he will liquidate Bakr." As to the friendship treaty, he said, it was directed primarily against the Kurds:

> This rapprochement was effected at our expense. The arms which the Russians are about to supply in great quantities to Baghdad will not be used against the Iranians, with whom the Russians most surprisingly have particularly good relations, and not even against the Israelis, whom Baghdad would never attack, its declarations notwithstanding. They will use these arms against us.[7]

Looking back on these developments, a Kurdish intellectual saw in the friendship agreement "an important Ba'th victory" in Baghdad's "diplomatic chess game"; the agreement "left the Kurdish national movement with its back against the wall" and compelled it to seek other "unnatural" alliances.[8] In this case, too, the Kurds were all but paralyzed. Barzani had indeed asked the Soviets to bring the Kurds into the secret pact between the Soviet Union and Iraq before it was signed. But the Soviets ignored his request and the Kurds heard about the agreement for the first time on Radio Baghdad. After signing the Iraqi-Soviet pact, Soviet premier Aleksey Kosygin promised the Kurdish ministers in Baghdad that he would raise the Kurdish question with the Baathi leaders, but nothing came of it.

The friendship treaty between Iraq and the Soviet Union had an immediate impact on relations between Baghdad and the Kurds as well as on the Baath-KDP-ICP triangle. As far as the Soviets were concerned, the March agreement between the Baath and the Kurds solved an internal contradiction between its declared ideology of supporting oppressed peoples and national liberation movements on the one hand, and its political and economic interest in a rapprochement with the Iraqi regime. Thus, after the March agreement, the Soviet Union's interest in the Kurdish issue lessened. At the same time, the Soviets pressured Baghdad to promote the ICP's standing. Here too, the Soviets sought to resolve the contradiction between its backing of the "national" regime of the Baath and its support for the ICP, which was being persecuted by the same regime. Indeed, in the past when the Soviet Union's vested interests dictated that it tighten its relations with any regime, even at the expense of the Communist parties, it did not hesitate to do so.[9] It was nevertheless patently clear that the Soviets preferred a middle way between the two interests; the solution this time was to move Baghdad to include the ICP in a national front.

With these developments, Baghdad began to change its policy gradually from an alliance with the KDP to one with the ICP—an inevitable tactical change since it realized that, if it wished to obtain the cooperation of the Soviet Union, it must conciliate the ICP. Thus, despite the deep animosity between the Baath and the ICP, the latter appeared to be a much less dangerous rival than the KDP so that a coalition with it would require fewer concessions than a coalition with the KDP. The Baath also sought to obtain the ICP's support for the nationalization of oil, as it was known that the ICP enthusiastically supported such a move. Finally, well versed in divide-and-rule tactics, the regime saw in a rapprochement with the ICP a means to foment discord in the ranks of the opposition.

The first manifestation of the Baath's changing policy was the publication of the National Action Charter in November 1971, which was to prepare the ground for the integration of the Communists into the national front, in accordance with the Soviet Union's request. While the KDP rejected the charter, the ICP approved it wholeheartedly in early 1972, describing it as a "turning point" and a "new state of affairs" in the Iraqi political arena.[10] The regime gave the ICP permission to openly celebrate the anniversary of its inauguration, thus manifesting its improved status. On 14 May, for the first time in Iraq's history, two senior members of the ICP joined the government: Makram Talabani (a Kurd) was appointed irrigation minister and 'Amir 'Abdullah became minister without portfolio. The decision regarding the appointments was apparently made during Kosygin's visit to Baghdad, when he requested the inclusion of the Communists in the government as a precondition for the Iraqi-Soviet pact. Following the cabinet changes, Baghdad went out of its way to describe the ICP as a "patriotic [party] . . . aware of its national obligations," and prepared to help "defend the revolution and its achievements." Baghdad described its own move as an unprecedented step in the history of Iraq in general and of the Communist Party in particular, and also as a "fatal surprise blow" against all enemies of the revolution, "especially Iranian forces of reaction and Zionism."[11]

Concurrently with the tightening of the alliance with the ICP, the Baath let the ties with the KDP die a slow death. The joint committees and meetings virtually ceased convening; the second anniversary of the March agreement was celebrated with little fanfare and without the participation of senior Baathi figures. Representatives of the KDP were not invited to the festivities of the Baath's anniversary, to which the ICP had been invited, nor were they summoned to discussions on the formation of a national front. Worst of all, the Baath stopped paying subsidies to the Peshmerga, thus putting Barzani's camp in a difficult financial position.[12]

When asked about the role of the partners in the national front, Saddam responded that the Communists accepted the Baath leadership whereas the Kurds were making excessive demands, emphasizing that "whoever does not agree [to the Baath's conditions], let him go."[13]

Iran Plays the Kurdish Card

The friendship agreement between Iraq and the Soviet Union rang a warning bell in Iran. Although the Soviet Union had maintained contacts with the shah before the signing of the Iraqi-Soviet friendship agreement to allay his fears regarding the agreement's objectives, the shah viewed it as being directed primarily against Iran. Tehran feared that the agreement would set against it a strong, radical neighbor with pan-Arab tendencies that would pose a direct threat to Iran, disrupting Iranian plans for hegemony in the Gulf. It saw no less of a danger in the deepening of Soviet penetration into Iraq, which it viewed as a pincer movement to encircle Iran in the north and the west. No less worrying were Iran's fears of the spread of Marxist ideology in the Gulf. These fears were evidenced by the strong criticism leveled by Iran against the introduction of two Communist members in the Baghdad government.

The very fact that it initiated a border incident, the most serious one since April 1969, only two days after the agreement was signed, revealed the extent to which Iran felt threatened. The mutual propaganda attacks and saber rattling reached new peaks. An editorial by the newspaper *Ayandegan* declared, "The Iraqi regime is not eligible to fight, but if *Saddam Husayn* insists and speaks of war with Iran, it will not be a problem to punish him and his clique" (emphasis added).[14]

Despite the deepening hostility, Iran was by no means interested in direct military confrontation with Iraq. Its strategy was to undermine the Iraqi regime from within by using the Kurdish card against it. However, this strategy posed several problems. The increasing animosity between the Baath and the Kurdish movement notwithstanding, the latter did not altogether slam the door on a dialogue with the Iraqi regime. It was therefore necessary for the Iranians to present convincing arguments in favor of the chances for success of a renewed Kurdish rebellion in Iraq. In addition, Barzani feared the Iranian ruler and distrusted him no less than he did the rulers of Baghdad. He was aware of the mercenary role that the Kurds had been assigned by the shah, describing it as: "The shah wants the Kurds with their heads over the water, with him holding their forelocks."[15]

The shah also was wary of Barzani and suspected his intentions. The mutual animosity had historical roots since Barzani was one of the four generals who had waged war against the shah when the Republic of Mahabad was established in Iran in 1946. The shah also had an obsession with the "Red Kurds," who had haunted him ever since Barzani and his followers returned to Iraq from exile in the Soviet Union where they had stayed from 1947 to 1958. The March agreement between the Kurds and the Iraqi regime added a new layer of antagonism between the two parties. One day before signing the agreement, the shah summoned Barzani who categorically denied that he intended to sign an agreement with the regime. Above all, Iran had to walk a fine line between inciting the Kurds of Iraq and preventing any spillover effects on the Kurds of Iran. Iran's fears regarding its own internal Kurdish problem, which was indeed still latent at that stage, made it difficult from a psychological-tactical standpoint for Iran to provide direct aid to the Iraqi Kurds. On the other hand, Iran's fear that Baghdad would reciprocate in kind—by inciting the Arabs in Khuzistan as it had done in the past—moved it to maintain a low profile on its own role in inciting the Kurds of Iraq while seeking US involvement in the matter.

The "Hidden Hands" of the United States

On his way back from a summit conference with Soviet president Leonid Brezhnev, US president Richard M. Nixon met with the shah in Tehran on 30 May 1972. At that meeting, which was also attended by Henry Kissinger, then head of the US National Security Council, different strategic questions were discussed, including that of inciting the Kurds in Iraq to rebel. Nixon gave his approval to an increase in arms shipments to Iran as well as a green light to the shah's plan regarding the Kurds, including an agreement in principle to provide the Kurds with some US assistance. The United States thus deviated somewhat from its former, consistent line of maintaining its distance from the national Kurdish movement and denying it support.[16] The main motive behind this traditional US policy was the need to accommodate its two allies, Iran and Turkey, which were sensitive to any strengthening of the Kurdish movement in a neighboring country because of their own internal Kurdish problem.[17] Neither did the United States have a strategic interest in the Kurdish question or believe in the validity of that struggle. Furthermore, the US State Department was of the opinion that "a high degree of autonomy or independence for the Iraqi Kurds would be disruptive of area stability and inimical to our interests in the long run."[18]

Motivated by their belief in US power and a somewhat naïve, mystical notion that US support would dramatically change things in their favor, the Kurds, and especially Barzani, persisted in their attempts to obtain US support. Already in 1962, Barzani had made a strong plea for US support for his movement, but the answer had been that the United States did not interfere in Iraq's internal affairs and would not support Kurdish activities in any way. Following the fall of 'Abd-al-Karim Qasim, Mulla Mustafa Barzani once again appealed to the United States. In a letter to President John F. Kennedy in August 1963, he requested the president's support for Kurdish autonomy. He received no reply. A similar fate met another appeal in September 1967. In August 1968 Barzani sent an envoy to Washington, DC, apparently to revive a long-standing request for arms, money, and diplomatic support from the US government. The expected answer, as on previous occasions, would be a lemon.[19] The other side of the coin was the inherent Kurdish suspicion of the Soviet Union, which was fed by Barzani's personal hostility toward Communism. This mistrust stemmed from the refusal of the Soviet Union to provide tangible support to the Kurdish rebellion, even during nadirs in its relations with Baghdad (e.g., the first Baath regime in 1963). This unease, which was reinforced by the tightening of Iraqi-Soviet relations, provided a common ground for US covert support to the Kurds.

Secret contacts took place between Barzani and the Central Intelligence Agency (CIA) in March 1972, for instance, when the CIA received a message from the Kurdish leader, suggesting that he come personally to the United States to discuss Iraqi-Soviet relations.[20] On 3 April, Barzani's emissary met with a US official in Washington. The emissary appealed for direct, or indirect, US assistance for the establishment of an Iraqi Arab Kurdish "liberation movement" in Iraqi Kurdistan "with the aim of overthrowing the Ba'athi regime in Baghdad." The appeal was rejected.[21] Another source reported that Idris Barzani and Mahmud 'Uthman led a Kurdish delegation to Washington to meet with Richard Helms, then head of the CIA.[22]

Meanwhile, another partner, wary of Baathi radicalism and Baghdad's declaration against it, had entered the picture; namely, Jordan, which started cooperating with Iran and the United States to contain Baghdad. Even before the signing of the Iraqi-Soviet friendship agreement, a Jordanian delegation was sent to Iran and Kurdistan to discuss the situation in Iraq and to plan a coup.[23]

A number of considerations lay behind the US policymakers' approach to the Kurds. On the global level, there was an intense, albeit controlled, competition between the two superpowers in this strategic region. And the United States attempted to curb the spread of the Soviet Union by weakening its ally, Iraq, by way of the Kurds. On the regional level, the United States sought to assist Iran, which was feeling "threatened by its neighbor" Iraq.[24] Iran asked the United States to serve as the shah's guarantor vis-à-vis the Kurds, who feared that the shah would abandon them when his interests so dictated. Another US consideration was the need to limit the threat posed by a radical Iraq to the conservative Gulf states and to the oil routes in the region. Finally, there was a need to divert Baghdad's attention away from the Arab-Israeli conflict. Herald Saunders, of the National Security Staff, summarized the US approach toward the Kurds. His principal arguments were that: (1) permitting or encouraging the Kurds to remain a source of instability in Iraq would thwart the Soviet effort to promote a national unity government as a sounder base for the Soviet position; (2) the Iranians, Jordanians, and Israelis had intermittently supported the Kurds as a means of tying down Iraqi forces at home and the security of those countries was in the US interest; and (3) additionally, there was now the prospect of active Iraqi meddling in the Gulf, which domestic instability would help weaken.[25]

Considerations opposing this policy were no less weighty. At the time, its policy of rapprochement with the Soviet Union was coming to fruition so the United States had to proceed with maximum caution to avoid undermining it. Similarly, although Iran was actually urging it to help the Kurds of Iraq, the United States still had fears of the Kurdish rebellion spreading to Turkey and Iran itself.[26] In addition, although the United States wished to see a weak Iraq, it was not interested in a total disruption of the existing order. Neither was it interested in strengthening separatist movements. It should be remembered that precisely at that time more vigorous contacts were being held between the United States and Iraq, apparently to preclude Baghdad's absolute dependence on the Soviet Union. In the summer of 1972 after a high-level Iraqi delegation headed by 'Izzat al-Duri, then minister of agrarian reform, made a secret visit to Washington, the United States decided to increase the number of its representatives in Baghdad despite the fact that US-Iraqi relations remained officially suspended.[27]

There were also domestic considerations that did not favor US involvement, however. The State Department consistently opposed "such initiatives" in the region.[28] As one official put it, "Even if we were to decide to help them,

I would assume we would want our hand to be hidden."[29] It can also be assumed that, following the US entanglement in Vietnam, public opinion would oppose any involvement overseas.

The US initiators of the plan to aid the Kurds devised solutions that could be described as having one's cake and eating it.[30] It should be pointed out that relations between Kissinger, who pushed for the plan in the United States, and the State Department, headed by Secretary William Rogers, were extremely tense. Kissinger attempted to circumvent the State Department by outlining a policy that was not always consistent with the department's approach.

From the Kurdish point of view, the main shortcoming of the US plan was the total secrecy with which it had been designed and executed. The rationale for this secrecy was that the shah wished it to be so, that Kissinger did not want to antagonize the Soviets too greatly, and that opposition by the State Department had to be circumvented. In this context, it should be indicated that Rogers was not privy to the plan. He apparently did not know of its existence until the summer of 1973. This meant that the US aid plan was not an official, institutionalized, and binding plan that had undergone the customary decisionmaking process in the United States. Rather, it was a "partisan" initiative of a US security arm. Although it had received the president's blessing, the plan bore a secret, "underground" character, and could be shrugged off and disavowed at any time.

Despite the fact that the aid program was designed not to be binding on the United States, its initiators on the US side nonetheless intentionally created the impression among the Kurds that it was somewhat of a guarantor who would protect them against the eventuality of Iran's sudden defection. Barzani would subsequently say, "Although they never gave us a defined, written commitment, we always thought, based on our discussions with them, that they would not abandon us at a difficult time."[31] To allay the Kurds' suspicions regarding this absolute secrecy, the United States developed a cover story to the effect that it was intended to spare Barzani the embarrassment of being a US client. Accordingly, the United States precluded contacts between the Kurds and senior US officials. Such contacts as existed were maintained mainly in Europe between CIA personnel and Barzani's people.[32]

Another drawback of the plan from the Kurdish point of view was the strategy of "no victory," which the United States had mapped out for the Kurdish struggle and which was kept in strict secrecy from them: "The President, Dr. Kissinger, and the foreign head of state (the shah) hope that our client (the Kurds) will not have the upper hand."[33] In other words, the initiators of the plan wanted the Kurds to be strong enough to sap the strength of the Iraqi government, but not enough to obtain autonomous rule. This point further highlights the fact that the Kurdish cause per se had no place in the totality of considerations and developments pertaining to the plan. The desire of its initiators to prevent US involvement or entanglement compelled them to seek indirect channels to implement it, one of which was Israel.

Israel and the Kurds: My Enemy's Enemy

Relations between Israel and the Kurds began developing shortly after the out-break of the Kurdish rebellion in the autumn of 1961, apparently at Israel's ini-tiative.[34] Israel acted according to the principle of "my enemy's enemy is my friend." It sought to exploit the Kurdish rebellion in order to weaken the Bagh-dad government, which maintained a radical position on the Arab-Israeli con-flict, and also sought to disrupt the dispatch of Iraqi forces against Israel. The latter's interest in the Kurdish struggle was anchored in the "doctrine of the pe-riphery," then current in Israel, which maintained among others that it should seek an alliance with non-Arab states as well as with minorities in the Middle East so as to face the large Arab bloc.[35] Based on this policy, Israel moved closer to Iran and the Kurds. However, Iran and Israel had a diametrically opposed at-titude toward the Kurds: while Iran feared the absolute strengthening of the Kurds, Israel hoped for it and supported it.

Unlike Iran and the United States, whose approach was purely oppor-tunistic, Israel's interest in the Kurds was also emotional and humanitarian. The more deeply that Israelis became involved in the field, the stronger the bond became. Occasionally, it even interfered with what were practical political con-siderations. Criticism of the fact that Israelis operating in Kurdistan became emotionally involved is contained in a report on the activity of the Mossad (In-stitute for Intelligence and Special Operations) in Kurdistan:

> The Mossad was responsible for contacts with the Kurds. The personal con-nections between Mossad representatives, who witnessed Kurdish suffer-ing and bereavement, and the Kurds had a profound effect. The Israelis became emotionally bound to their Kurdish friends, and identified with their problems. For example, the Kurds wanted heavy equipment, tanks, and ar-tillery, and the Israeli representatives in the field supported their request. In the second stage, the Kurds initiated moves Israel had advised against. When they began to founder, the third, almost inevitable, stage was set in motion: the Kurds blamed the party which had helped them, namely Israel, for their failures.[36]

Israeli public opinion apparently was sympathetic from the outset, prompt-ing the Israeli government to help the Kurds.[37] This possibly stemmed from an unconscious comparison of the Kurdish problem with Zionism and Israel's struggle for independence. Kurdish activist Ismet Sheriff Vanly maintained that the Jews of Kurdistan—who he asserted had lived fully integrated lives, free of discrimination, among the Kurds—helped create sympathetic public opinion on the Kurdish question when they immigrated to Israel. In fact, the picture was much more complex than the one presented by Vanly.[38] Nevertheless, it should be noted that over time Israel's involvement in Kurdistan bore further fruit, which was both unexpected and unrelated to Israel's initial motives. It included facilitating the emigration of some 5,000 of Iraq's remaining Jews, who had not been permitted to leave Iraq legally following the massive immigration in the early 1950s.[39] Another by-product was the provision of important intelligence information for Israel.[40] In fact, even Israelis who were hoping for peace talks with the Iraqi government thought that the best means to achieve this was via the Kurds.

For their part the Kurds had their own motives for attempting to approach Israel, the most important of which were the geographical and political isolation that they faced and the fact that they were craving for help, whatever the source. As a graphic explanation to a KDP member who questioned the Kurdish policy, Barzani asked whether a blind man who had to cross a busy street would not accept help from everybody.[41] Another possible explanation was that the Kurds sought to get inspiration from the Zionist enterprise and emulate it in Kurdistan. In fact, in 1966 then Iraqi defense minister 'Abd-al-'Aziz al-'Uqayli warned of the danger of a "new Israel" being established in northern Iraq.[42] In addition, the Kurds thought that Israel might be the best venue for them to realize an old dream; namely, that of US support. More importantly, they regarded Israel as being more credible and less fickle than Iran because it did not have an ambivalent attitude toward the Kurdish people and because a political settlement between Israel and Iraq was not on the horizon whereas the threat of a political settlement hovered constantly over the Iraq-Iran-Kurdish triangle of relations.

That said, ties with Israel were nevertheless particularly equivocal for the Kurds because such ties were liable to present them as traitors to their country and religion and to arouse domestic and Arab public opinion against them.[43] Indeed, the Israeli presence in Kurdistan weighed heavily on the Kurds who understood that crossing such lines would make it virtually impossible for them to be reconciled with the central government. Consequently, they maintained a conspiracy of silence on the subject. At the time, only a few Kurds were privy to the secret relations with Israel, and those Israelis who happened to be in the area or who were active in Kurdistan were dressed up in traditional Kurdish dress. Nonetheless, the internal Kurdish debates with regard to Kurdish-Israeli relations led its opponents to uncover the ties. The main opponent of the relationship was Jalal Talabani. His motives were both political, that is, cooperation with the Baghdad authorities and rivalry with Barzani, the person who had cultivated the Kurdish relationship with Israel and ideological, that is, affiliation with the leftist camp. In fact, Talabani's newspaper *Al-Nur* had already leaked Israel's support of the Kurds in early 1969.[44]

Baghdad itself was aware of the secret relations between Israel and the Kurds, but quite surprisingly it also preferred to maintain a conspiracy of silence, at least for a while, and to refrain from using that knowledge as a propaganda tool against the Kurdish movement.[45] The Baghdad government was extremely embarrassed by the Israeli presence (which, at times, consisted of fewer than five people). This, and the fact that it was not even able to get its own house in order, could have put Baghdad's pretensions of heading a war against

Israel in a ridiculous light. It is also possible that intelligence and tactical considerations motivated Iraq to not disclose the Kurds' connections with Israel in real time.

Iran, which served as the exclusive channel for Israeli aid to the Kurds, also kept silent on the issue because it did not wish to arouse unfavorable domestic public opinion or bring forth pressure from Arab countries. No less important was its wish to refrain from mounting tension with the Iraqi government, with which it hoped to eventually reach an agreement. Finally, Iran itself felt uneasy about Israel's involvement and the complex problems it aroused. Although Iran did respond positively to Israel's request to allow it to provide aid to the Kurds through Iranian territory, a measure that could also have served Iran's own interests, it never dropped its suspicions of Israeli intentions.[46] Iran was afraid of losing control as well as of Israeli aid developing beyond the limits set by the shah: "I want the fire of the rebellion to flicker, but I do not want a flame."[47]

Therefore, Iran insisted that an Iranian liaison officer always be present during the various operations involving Israeli aid to the Kurds. This liaison officer was to report to Savak (the Iranian secret police) headquarters. Israel was well aware of the fact that its conduit to the Kurds was Iran and that there was no logic in doing things behind the Iranians' back. Israel occasionally also served as advocate for the Iraqi Kurds vis-à-vis the shah. At times, Iran refused to permit the transfer of arms to the Kurds and only intensive diplomatic moves on the part of Israeli liaison officers softened its position.

Different versions exist about how and where relations between Israel and the Kurds initially developed. What is clear beyond all doubt is that Barzani decided in favor of the relationship and threw all of his weight behind it whereas other figures in the Kurdish leadership accepted this policy as a fait accompli. One explanation for Barzani's stance was the strong relationship that he had formed with the Jewish Kurdish community, especially with a Jewish friend, David Khawaja Khinno.[48] Barzani covertly visited Israel twice, in 1968 and 1973. Second-echelon Kurdish figures also visited Israel, including Barzani's sons, Mas'ud and Idris, and 'Aziz 'Aqrawi.[49] Aware of the problematic nature of the relationship, Barzani customarily maintained a separation between the Kurdish team that was in contact with Baghdad and the one that maintained contacts with Israel. The objective was to prevent internal contradictions or information leaks.

The first official Israeli acknowledgment that Israel provided aid to the Kurds dates to 29 September 1980 (a few days after the outbreak of the Iran-Iraq War). Then prime minister Menachem Begin disclosed that Israel had extended aid to the Kurds "during their uprising against the Iraqis in 1965–1975" and that the United States was aware of the fact. Begin added that Israel had sent instructors and arms, but not military units.[50]

Initially, Israeli aid was limited to humanitarian aid such as the construction of a field hospital in 1966. It expanded gradually to eventually include the supply of small arms and ammunition. Later, it encompassed more sophisticated arms such as antitank and antiaircraft equipment. The supply of arms was usually airborne via Iranian airspace. The aid included military training for Kurdish combatants, conducted in Kurdistan itself (thus requiring the routine maintenance of an Israeli team on-site), in Iran, and in Israel (apparently to a more limited degree). However, due to logistical problems and the lack of infrastructure in the Kurdish region itself, the bulk of the training was carried out in Iranian camps.[51]

One reliable source claimed that all training of the Kurds was provided by Israel. Refa'el Eytan, who visited Kurdistan in 1969, before he became Israel's chief of staff, stated that almost all of the Israeli trainers were paratroopers. Israelis also served as advisers. In fact, Eytan's visit served this very purpose. But it should be stressed that Israelis were never involved directly in battles and never assumed any command role whatsoever.[52] Sometimes Israeli aid was vital, so much so that according to one source the rebellion of 1966 would have collapsed without it.[53] Israelis also helped in a number of activities such as propaganda campaigns in Europe, courses for Kurdish medics, or writing schoolbooks in Kurdish. However, anyone who expected all this to be translated into direct Kurdish support of Israel in its wars against the Arab states was proven wrong. In the Six Day War, the Kurds did nothing to tie up Iraqi armed forces on the Iraqi domestic front.[54] Nonetheless, Israel did not suspend its aid and apparently maintained it to some extent even after the March agreement of 1970. Israel apparently recognized the fact that the speed by which it had concluded the Six Day War had not given the Kurds the opportunity to engage Iraqi troops. Perhaps Israel also appreciated the constraints that prevented the Kurds from taking measures that would be seen as a stab in the back of Iraq and might result in the burning of all possible bridges between the Kurds and Iraq. Above all, it seemed that Israel had accepted Barzani's explanations and excuses, which he provided on various occasions, to the effect that there was no need for the Kurds to fight against the Iraqi Army since this army was already preoccupied by a strong Kurdish national movement.

The Kurds, who also placed exaggerated hopes on Israel's ability to help them, were compelled to lower their expectations, given that Israel was operating under constraints, for example, the serious limitations that Iran placed on it. However, in the summer of 1972, when the Iranian-US-Israeli plan to stir up the Kurds was concocted in secret, none of the concerned parties—least of all the Kurds—knew with any certainty where all this would ultimately lead.

Activating the CIA Aid Plan

In June 1972, a détente agreement was signed between the United States and the Soviet Union, in which the parties declared their willingness to concede claims of any special influence in the world and give up any "attempts to exploit tensions to obtain unilateral advantages."[55] But even before the ink had dried on this agreement, Iran and the United States were already examining ways to exploit the tension between the Kurds and the Iraqi regime for their own ends. Several weeks after President Nixon's visit to Iran on 30–31 May and his agreement in principle to use the Kurds to destabilize the Baath, Barzani was summoned to a reconciliation meeting with the shah. It should be recalled that the shah was greatly angered by the March agreement. Immediately after it was signed, he recalled his representative from Kurdistan and sought to remove the Israeli "representatives," but the latter convinced him of the need for them to remain in Iraq.

The content of the discussions at these meetings is not known. Neither is it known what the shah asked of the Kurds. In any case, it is clear that Barzani remained unconvinced and did not conceal his reservations about the shah's plans. Meanwhile, Nixon informed the shah of his final decision regarding aid to the Kurds in mid-July 1972 through a special envoy, John Connally. This decision did not go through the usual channels for approval and few CIA personnel were involved in it.[56] At this stage, after Barzani had rejected the shah's appeal, a Kurdish delegation—which included Barzani's sons, Mas'ud and Idris, and Muhammad Mahmud 'Abd-al-Rahman—traveled to the United States to hold talks with CIA representatives. In the final analysis, the delegation decided to accept the US aid plan.

Barzani's sons lacked diplomatic experience and were not aware that ties with the CIA, which were not binding on the governmental echelon, would present such a stumbling block. In his talks with Barzani, 'Abd-al-Rahman emphasized the problematic nature of such a connection. Barzani, who was enthusiastic about establishing ties with the United States, argued they represented real gains, however. Furthermore, he apparently also believed that they would provide an adequate US guarantee against the shah's betrayal. It is also possible that Barzani preferred secret relations with the United States because it permitted him to keep an open channel to the regime. It should be noted that secrecy was maintained within the Kurdish camp. Initially, only Barzani, his two sons, and several members of the politburo were privy to the plan. Thus, decisionmaking on fateful issues in the Kurdish movement was the province of a mere handful of people, sometimes only Barzani himself. With time, however, all members of the politburo were apprised of the plan. Only one member, Salih al-Yusufi, was opposed to it.[57]

The CIA aid plan took effect in August 1972 and was adhered to until March 1975. At an estimated cost of about $16 million, it included financial aid, the provision of Russian- and Chinese-made arms and ammunition, and a high-powered radio station that brought Radio Iraqi Kurdistan to the entire Middle East.[58] The US aid was insignificant compared to Iranian support and, in any case, the Kurds ascribed more political than military importance to it. Given that the United States sought to avoid direct involvement in the aid program, the bulk of the program was implemented through Israel, which was presumably privy to the secret program from the beginning.[59] Moreover, with time Israel found itself lobbying for the Kurds in Washington and urging an increase in aid. No detailed information was as yet available on the total volume of aid from the three countries—Iran, Israel, and the United States. However, it clearly exceeded the Kurds' absorptive capacity, partly due to the absence of a suitable administrative and military infrastructure.

To sum up, these overt and covert alliances raised the moral question of betrayal. As a nation unto itself, the Kurds claimed that they were entitled to take actions that would safeguard their national identity and sovereignty. As part of the Iraqi state, they were presented as traitors. This issue was to remain the main core of the debate between Arabs and Kurds for years to come.

Notes

1. As to the island of Abu Musa, the shah and the ruler of al-Shariqah had an agreement regarding the establishment of an Iranian outpost on the island. The other two islands were seized by force, which breached a prior understanding with Great Britain that such seizure would not be effected until after Britain had completed its obligations to its allies on 1 December 1971. See J. B. Kelly, *Arabia, the Gulf, and the West* (London: Weidenfeld & Nicolson, 1980), p. 95.

2. The shah suggested that control over these islands would ensure the passage of oil tankers in the Gulf. However, the Iranians actually had better strategic points from which to ensure this. The real reason for the seizure was their expectation of finding oil on the sea bottom in the area of the islands. Ibid., pp. 88–89.

3. Regarding the supply of US weapons to Iran, see Shmu'el Segev, *The Iranian Triangle* (in Hebrew) (Tel Aviv: Sifriyat Ma'ariv, 1981), p. 44; and Daniel Pipes, "A Border Adrift: Origins of the Conflict," in *The Iran-Iraq War*, eds. Shirin Tahir-Kheli and Shaheen Ayubi (New York: Praeger 1973), p. 19.

4. Iraq sought to equalize the struggle for the "Arab Gulf" with that of the struggle over Palestine. *Ruz Al-Yusuf* (Cairo, weekly), 1 May 1972.

5. *Le Combat*, 8 December 1971, cited in *Arab Report and Record*, 1–15 December 1971.

6. Although the Soviet Union viewed the alliance as a tool to deepen its penetration of the Gulf, unlike Iraq it did not regard it as a move against Iran. The Soviet Union sought to maintain good relations with Iran and did not wish to antagonize it. See Robert O. Friedman, *Soviet Policy Towards the Middle East Since 1970* (New York: Praeger, 1978), pp. 76–81; and Kelly, *Arabia*, pp. 281–282.

7. *Le Figaro*, cited in *Ma'ariv* (Tel Aviv, daily), 21 April 1972.

8. Ismet Sheriff Vanly, "Kurdistan in Iraq," in *A People Without a Country: The Kurds and Kurdistan*, ed. Gérard Chaliand (London: Zed Press, 1980), p. 183.

9. Uriel Dann, "The Communist Movement in Iraq Since 1963," in *The U.S.S.R and the Middle East*, eds. Michael Confino and Shimon Shamir (Jerusalem: Israel Universities Press, 1973), p. 385; Friedman, *Soviet Policy*, p. 23.

10. The positive responses of the ICP leaders were highlighted in the Iraqi media

such as *Al-Jumhuriyya* (Baghdad, daily), 24 February 1972; Iraqi News Agency, 2 April 1972, cited in *Daily Report*, 4 April 1972.

11. *Al-Jumhuriyya*, 19 May 1972.

12. Memorandum for Director of Central Intelligence declassified PA/HO Department of State, "Barzani-US-USSR," 12 June 1972.

13. *Al-Nahar* (Beirut, daily), 13–14 April 1972.

14. *Ayandegan*, 16 April 1972, cited in *Daily Report*, 17 April 1972.

15. Anonymous, interviewed by the author, 13 March 1982. Barzani expressed more than once to US representatives his distrust of the shah's intentions who, he claimed, viewed the Kurds as a mere playing card. *Village Voice* (New York), 16 February 1976.

16. In 1947, the United States rejected Barzani's request for political asylum in the United States. It also rejected an appeal in 1962 to assist the Kurdish rebellion. Dana Adams Schmidt, *Journey Among Brave Men* (Boston: Little, Brown, 1964), p. 203. For an important documentary source book, see Lokman I. Meho, *The Kurdish Question in U.S. Foreign Policy: A Documentary Sourcebook* (Westport, CT: Praeger, 2004). For a general discussion of US policy toward the Kurds, see Michael Gunter, "United States Foreign Policy Toward the Kurds," *Orient* 40, no. 3 (1999): 427–437; Mariana Charountaki, *The Kurds and US Foreign Policy: International Relations in the Middle East Since 1945* (London: Routledge, 2011); and Peter J. Lambert, "The United States and the Kurds: Case Studies on the United States Engagement" (master's thesis, Naval Postgraduate School, 1997).

17. According to new documents from the State Department, the United States opposed Iranian support to the Kurds because it sought to maintain good relations with Baghdad as well. Meho, *The Kurdish Question*, pp. 463–465.

18. Ibid., p. 465.

19. Public Record Office, FCO17/408, 13 August 1968; Meho, *The Kurdish Question*, pp. 442–443, 451, 470.

20. CIA, declassified PA/HO Department of State, "Barzani-US-USSR," 9 March 1972.

21. Memorandum of conversation, declassified PA/HO Department of State, "Barzani-US-USSR," 3 April 1972. A later source claimed that Barzani had been summoned to the United States, but that Kissinger refused to meet with him. Fadil Barrak, *Mustafa al-Barzani: Al-Ustura wal-Haqiqa* (Baghdad: Dar al-Shu'un al-Thaqafiyya al-'Amma, 1989), p. 255.

22. Eliezer (Geizi) Tsafrir, *Ana Kurdi* (in Hebrew) (Or Yehuda: Hed Artzi 1999), p. 158.

23. Ibid., p. 154. A secret report revealed that Jordan also was supporting the Kurds. Memorandum to Henry Kissinger, National Security Council, declassified PA/HO Department of State, "Barzani-US-USSR," 7 June 1972.

24. The secret US aid for the Kurds was perceived mainly "as a favor for our ally" Iran. *Village Voice*, 16 February 1976.

25. Memorandum to Henry Kissinger, National Security Council, declassified PA/HO Department of State, "Barzani-US-USSR," 7 June 1972.

26. Memorandum to Henry Kissinger, National Security Council, declassified PA/HO Department of State, Barzani-US-USSR, 7 June 1972.

27. *Al-Hawadith*, 8 September 1972.

28. Memorandum for Director of Central Intelligence, declassified PA/HO Department of State, "Barzani-US-USSR," 12 June 1972.

29. Memorandum to Henry Kissinger, National Security Council, declassified PA/HO Department of State, "Barzani-US-USSR," 7 June 1972.

30. The CIA used the code words "ethnic group," and "our ally" to refer to aid to the

Kurds and Iran respectively. *Investigation of Publication of Select Committee on Intelligence Report* (Washington, DC: US Government Printing Office, 94th Cong., 2d. sess.1976). *Village Voice*, 16 February 1976.

31. *Jerusalem Post*, 23 March 1975.

32. In November 1971, such contacts were held in Beirut. CIA, declassified PA/HO Department of State, "Barzani-US-USSR," 9 March 1972.

33. Many details of the US aid plan were leaked to the *Village Voice* in February 1976 as part of a comprehensive report by the Special Senate Committee, which was established in 1975 to examine the methods of operation of the US intelligence community. Following the publication in the *Village Voice*, a commission was established to check the leak itself; the reports were granted great credibility since the people investigated did not deny their content. The entire episode was published in *Investigation of Publication of Select Committee on Intelligence Report* (Washington, DC: US Government Printing Office, 94th Cong., 2d. sess., 1976).

34. Israeli officials, interviewed by the author, 13 March 1982 and 28 July 1985. In 1962 the KDP claimed that Israel had offered support in Europe and that the Kurds had rejected it because they feared Arab reaction. Meho, *The Kurdish Question*, p. 443. According to another version, the first contacts with the leaders of the Kurdish national movement were established by Re'uven Shiloah in the early 1930s, when he worked as a reporter for the *Palestine Bulletin* newspaper. See Tom Segev, *1949, The First Israelis* (in Hebrew) (Jerusalem: Domino, 1984), p. 34.

35. For this doctrine, see Ofra Bengio, *The Turkish-Israeli Relationship: Changing Ties of Middle Eastern Outsiders* (New York: Palgrave Macmillan, 2004), pp. 33–71.

36. Ze'ev Schiff, *Ha'aretz* (Tel Aviv, daily), 7 June 1985. I also interviewed someone who had been in the field for a long time and made a contrary claim to the effect that he and others like him, aware of Barzani's limitations, had actually restrained policymakers in Israel. Anonymous Israeli official, interviewed by the author, 9 September 1985. Generally speaking, acccording to the rules of the division of labor between the army and the Mossad, the latter is responsible for contacts with states that do not maintain diplomatic relations with Israel, especially when the matter involves an enemy country.

37. Sa'ad Jawad, *Iraq and the Kurdish Question, 1958–1970* (London: Ithaca Press, 1981), p. 301.

38. See Mordechai Zaken, *Jewish Subjects and Their Tribal Chieftains in Kurdistan* (Leiden: Brill, 2007).

39. Mas'ud Barzani supervised the action. Barrak, *Mustafa al-Barzani*, pp. 273–275; Tsafrir, *Ana Kurdi*, pp. 148–152.

40. Shlomo Nakdimon, *Broken Hope: The Israeli-Kurdish Relations, 1963–1975* (in Hebrew) (Tel Aviv: Yedi'ot Ahronot, 1996), pp. 100–112, 314–324; Barrak, *Mustafa al-Barzani*, p. 232.f

41. Quoted in Barrak, *Mustafa al-Barzani*, p. 234.

42. Mahmud al-Durra, *Al-Qadiyya Al-Kurdiyya*, 2nd ed. (Beirut: Dar al-Tali'a, 1996), p. 388.

43. Indeed, years later, Barrak dedicated a whole book to Barzani's "treasonous" affairs. Barrak, *Mustafa al-Barzani*.

44. Public Record Office, FCO17/872, 5 April 1969.

45. In one case, Baghdad accused the Kurds of conveying intelligence information to Israel through Iran and of acquiring Israeli goods. *Settlement of the Kurdish Problem* (*Al-Thawra*, Thawra Publications, n.d., n.p.), p. 56.

46. Israel initiated the contact with Iran regarding the Kurdish matter and not vice versa. It should furthermore be noted that, without Iran's knowledge, Israel initiated contacts with the Kurds before initiating them with Iran. Israel also found it somewhat dif-

ficult to inform Iran about this connection. Anonymous Israeli officials interviewed by the author, 13 March 1982; 28 July 1985; 22 September 1985.

47. Anonymous Israeli official interviewed by the author, 22 September 1985.

48. See Zaken, *Jewish Subjects*, pp. 67–79, 113–120.

49. For a detailed account of this, see Shlomo Nakdimon, *Broken Hope*, passim.

50. Radio Israel, 29 September 1980, cited in BBC, 1 October 1980.

51. Jean Larteguy, *The Walls of Israel* (New York: M. Evans, 1969), p. 92. Larteguy's book was immediately translated into Arabic by the Iraqi Defense Ministry. Barrak, *Mustafa al-Barzani*, p. 206. The first course taught to Kurdish officers by Israeli instructors was held in August 1965. See Segev, *The Iranian Triangle*, p. 215.

52. Barrak claimed that they did participate in battles. Barrak, *Mustafa al-Barzani*, p. 227.

53. Anonymous Israeli official interviewed by the author, 9 February 1982; Refa'el Eytan, *Raful, The Story of a Soldier*, with Dov Goldstein (in Hebrew) (Tel Aviv: Sifriyat Ma'ariv, 1985), p. 117.

54. According to a US intelligence source, "Just before the war started an Israeli agent reportedly visited Mulla Mustafa to arrange, if possible, some Kurdish action to tie down the Iraqi army. He did not succeed." Meho, *The Kurdish Question*, p. 471.

55. Stanley Hoffman, *Primacy or World Order* (New York: McGraw-Hill, 1978), p. 64.

56. Plans of this type required the approval of a special committee known as the Committee of 40. However, the committee received information on the plan only after the US envoy had informed the shah about it. Its approval was only a rubber stamp. *Village Voice*, 16 February 1976.

57. Another leading member, Hashim 'Aqrawi, told Barrak that he opposed these links, which prompted Barzani to marginalize him. Barrak, *Mustafa al-Barzani*, p. 222.

58. It was established in Mawat, Iran. Ibid., p. 238.

59. According to one assessment, Iran suggested Israel as an additional guarantor for the Kurds. Ferhad Ibrahim, *Die Kurdische Nationalbewegung im Iraq* (Berlin: Klaus Schwarz Verlag, 1983), pp. 711–712.

5

Deteriorating Relationships

The open and secret realignments in the region began to change the balance of power between the Baath and the Kurds in Baghdad's favor. The war of words that ensued between the two camps in the wake of these developments was telling. It was indeed quite unique that, in an authoritarian and closed state like Iraq, significant facts were uncovered simply because the dirty laundry was aired in public. The discourse underwent deep changes as the narrative of the two parties increasingly reflected a clash between two national movements represented by the Baath and the KDP. Henceforth, the Baath's main line of propaganda was to make a clear distinction between the Kurdish people on the one hand, and the KDP and Mulla Mustafa Barzani on the other—with the aim of excluding the latter from politics, precisely because they were perceived as being the moving spirit behind the Kurdish national movement. Clearly on the defensive, Barzani and the KDP, for their part, sought to prove that they and the national movement were inseparable.

The Nationalization of the Kirkuk Oil Fields

On 1 June 1972 Baghdad nationalized the Kirkuk oil fields, thus dealing a severe blow to the Kurds. Well prepared by the Iraqi authorities and with the backing of the Soviet Union, this move pulled the rug from under Kurdish demands that the Kirkuk area be included in the autonomous zone. The transfer of Kirkuk's fifty-five oil wells from the Iraq Oil Company to the Iraqi state put an end to Kurdish claims to the oil of the region. Various economic, strategic, and political motives were behind the nationalization move, the most important of which was to create a fait accompli with regard to the Kirkuk question. This was evidenced by the fact that nationalization began in Kirkuk and only later came to include Mosul and Basra.

Another blow to the Kurds was the austerity program adopted in the wake of the nationalization of the petroleum industry that was a direct upshot of the drop in oil revenues and the difficulty of marketing oil from Kirkuk. The more than 50 percent cutoff of the allocations for development programs hit the Kurds in particular since they held a lion's share in them. No less serious was the fact that the Kurdish movement had lost a major means of putting pressure, not only on the regime, but also on foreign companies. The KDP responded with re-strained anger. On the one hand, it could not publicly censure an act that sym-bolized Iraqi patriotism. But on the other hand, it could not support it because oil nationalization harmed vested Kurdish interests. The party's silence con-trasted sharply with the enthusiastic support of the ICP and its active mobiliza-tion in favor of Iraq's nationalization policy.

A few days later nationalization riots broke out in Sinjar, which is popu-lated by Yezidi Kurds, and eventually spread from there to Kirkuk and Su-laymaniyya. The flare-up was spontaneous, embracing disparate groups of people that were apparently not acting on behalf of the KDP, but enjoyed its support after the fact. What caused the outbreak was the fact that Yezidi tribes, which used to get protection money from the oil company, had lost these priv-ileges because of the nationalization policy. Moreover, on the very day that nationalization was implemented, the government began to disarm the Yezidis in accordance with the March agreement. Concurrently, the regime began set-tling Arab tribes in this area, a move that resulted in violent confrontations be-tween the Kurdish tribes and the Arabs. This led to the Iraqi Army's intervention—including the shelling of Kurdish areas by the air force—and Barzani's dispatch of reinforcements to defend the Kurdish tribes. Apparently only one division of the Iraqi Army was involved in these incidents. For the first time since the March agreement, martial law was declared in order to re-store quiet.[1]

Amid these developments, *Al-Thawra* called on the authorities to act res-olutely against "groups and pockets which are not acting on behalf of the supreme national interest, but are acting as if only their narrow interests were of import in the life of the homeland, while the homeland is waging the most difficult struggle in its history." Alluding to the connection between the na-tionalization of oil and the hostile position of the "agent government of Iran" and the riots, the newspaper called for placing the national interest above every narrow consideration.[2]

In retrospect *Al-Thawra*'s response was apparently the opening salvo of a strident, protracted debate with the Kurdish movement and its newspaper, *Al-Ta'akhi*, in which *Al-Thawra* served as the spearhead of the Iraqi media in flog-ging the Kurds. This reflected a profound political development, which entailed a gradual change in the positions of Saddam Hussein who shifted from enthu-siastically supporting the agreement to acting against it, and from presenting the KDP as the Baath's partner to an attempt to neutralize it completely in the political arena. Asked about the Kurds' claim that Baghdad was not adhering to the agreement, he stated that the nationalization of oil was more important than any other issue: "We reject the selfish approach when solving problems. What is important today is the homeland as a whole."[3]

Saddam changed his strategy because he had exhausted the advantages that the agreement held for him. In fact, he sought to sweep the party and public opinion and did so through *Al-Thawra*, whose editor-in-chief Tariq 'Aziz eventually became Saddam's right-hand man. In contrast, from the outset President Ahmad Hasan al-Bakr was not enthusiastic about the agreement, but attempted to preserve it nonetheless.

The Second Assassination Attempt on Barzani

On 15 July 1972, a second attempt to murder Barzani was uncovered. The KDP spokesman, who announced the attempt only five days later, reported that a man who posed as a reporter of the Iraqi News Agency had carried out the assassination attempt. In his confession the man revealed that he had been sent on his mission by "officials of the highest level in the General Security Directorate" (*mudiriyyat al-amn al-'amma*), which is subordinate to the Iraq Ministry of Interior.[4]

The Baath reacted by banning the issues of *Al-Ta'akhi* in which the report had been published. In addition the Ministry of Interior attacked the KDP for reporting the incident conspicuously and unilaterally, for accusing governmental agencies without having legal proof of its charges, for not informing the Ministry of Interior in advance, and for deviating from the rules of quiet dialogue that had been common practice between the Kurds and the regime since the March agreement. Meanwhile, the KDP revealed that the person involved in the assassination attempt against Barzani, a Kurd of Syrian origin, acknowledged that he had been hired for the mission by the interior minister Sa'dun Ghaydan. According to *Al-Hayat*, the general security director Nazim Kzar was also personally involved in the episode.[5] Pointing an accusing finger at the authorities, Mahmud 'Uthman stated that "the government should not think that we believe that all [murder] attempts which it devises against us are the acts of the oil companies and imperialism, as it claims."[6] In any case, nothing came of the investigation.

Al-Thawra used the episode to settle accounts with the KDP, accusing it, in two editorials, of acting independently in the Kurdistan region and in disregard of the central government. *Al-Thawra* accused the KDP of collecting taxes from the inhabitants, keeping its own prisons, arresting and putting Kurds and Arabs in detention on charges of "cooperation with the authorities," and of extraditing Iranian Kurds who infiltrated KDP areas that were under the "influence" of the Iranian government.[7]

Al-Thawra argued that the regime had fulfilled its promise regarding the Peshmerga by establishing the border guard, which numbered about 6,000 troops. However, it stated that this guard, which was supposed to be part of the Iraqi Army, "behaves as if it were a regular force subordinate to the KDP. It is outside state control, save for the state's distribution of salaries and supply of arms and equipment [to its members]." The newspaper added that the guard engaged in operations against the army, police, and civilians, and that it guarded "Iran's borders" instead of Iraq's. It claimed that the border guard had surrendered an Iraqi position, Zayn al-Qaws in the Khanaqin area, to Iran.[8]

The Baathi newspaper further accused the KDP of equipping 120,000 Kurds with forged identification cards of Peshmerga personnel so as to enable them to evade conscription, and of flooding markets in areas "under KDP influence" with Iranian and Israeli goods to the detriment of the Iraqi national economy. *Al-Thawra* stressed that "the extraordinary conditions in the area" made it nearly impossible for the Baathi authorities to apprehend Iranian smugglers. Therefore, though one might have expected the KDP and the "apparatuses" (i.e., the Peshmerga) at its disposal to demonstrate patriotism and eliminate this severe problem, they did not do so. Another claim was that the KDP showed disloyalty to the regime when it granted refuge to persons accused of conspiring against the Baath and established a training base for them. However, the most serious accusation was that Iran had supplied the KDP with heavy weapons, training bases, and a radio station.[9]

The Iraqi government in all probability received such reports from Kurdish informants. In fact, the number of Kurds cooperating with the government was identical to the supporters of the KDP and Barzani.[10] In any case, the charges unintentionally highlighted Baghdad's sense of weakness vis-à-vis the KDP, which was depicted as an omnipotent ruler in the autonomous zone.

Following the publication of the above articles in *Al-Thawra*, the Baghdad government sent 'Aziz Sharif on a mediation mission, which resulted in *Al-Thawra* and *Al-Ta'akhi* declaring their willingness to put a stop to the debate between them. Nevertheless, the KDP found other ways to pursue its claims. In a public statement by a KDP member in Hamburg in mid-August, the KDP claimed that the government had introduced into the area an entire army division (the 2nd Division), which launched an attack against the Kurds with the support of tanks, artillery, paratroops, and the air force. The offensive, which went on for several weeks, resulted in the flight of thousands of Kurds and the destruction of the houses of Kurds known for their support of the KDP. The KDP also claimed that the regime had escalated its policy of Arabizing Kurdistan by acquiring land from Kurdish and Arab feudalists in preparation for expelling Kurds and settling Arabs in their place. The KDP asserted that thirteen Kurdish villages in the district of Kirkuk alone had been subjected to this policy.

The failure of the second assassination attempt against Barzani, and the realization that the KDP had, precisely through the March agreement, become too strong an organization moved Saddam to develop a new strategy as of the summer of 1972. His strategy involved two goals: (1) to drive a wedge between the KDP and the Kurdish people; and (2) to sever the linkage between the KDP and the March agreement. In other words it was an attempt to reach out to the Kurdish people, over the heads of the KDP, by conveying the message—through economic, social, and cultural favors—that the regime would indeed continue to adhere to the March agreement for the sake of the Kurdish people, but no longer in partnership with the KDP.

Nonetheless, the difficult economic situation caused by the nationalization of Kirkuk's oil resources required that the regime refrain from an open confrontation with the KDP at this stage. Accordingly, it continued to maintain outwardly normal relations with the KDP while attempting to undermine its influence. The KDP also continued to play a double game for similar reasons. While maintaining open channels to Baghdad, it also acted to undermine the central government. The KDP gave refuge to the anti-Soviet faction of the Maoist Communist Party (ICP Central Leadership), enabling this faction to relocate its activity from the Basra area in the south to northern Iraq, and also signed a secret agreement with different opposition groups with a view toward toppling the central regime.

The deterioration of relations between the Kurds and the regime in the summer of 1972 sounded warning bells in Moscow. The Soviet Union was motivated by its desire to see a strong Iraq, particularly after the expulsion of Soviet advisers from Egypt, which occurred around the same time and turned Iraq into its main stronghold in the Middle East. Deterioration of relations between Baghdad and the Kurds was liable to endanger the Baath; limit the Soviet Union's political, military, and economic gains; and deny it its last remaining influence in the Kurdish camp. Neither did the Soviets like the tightening of relations between the KDP and the Maoist faction of the ICP, which was liable to hurt the pro-Soviet faction of the ICP. On the other hand, the Soviet Union did not want the Baath regime to become too strong, enabling it to monopolize power and remove the ICP and the KDP from positions of influence. Hence, it sought to maintain a certain balance between the KDP and the regime while also keeping open channels of influence on the Kurdish side.

After the second attempt to assassinate Barzani, the Soviet Union endeavored to break the chill in its relations with the Kurds caused by the Baghdad-Soviet friendship agreement. The Soviets sent an official invitation to Barzani to visit Moscow, apparently with the aim of arranging a meeting with President al-Bakr, who was scheduled to arrive in Moscow on 14 September 1972. Barzani turned down the invitation, arguing that the circumstances did not permit him to leave Kurdistan. Actually, Barzani was angry because Soviet premier Aleksey Kosygin had not visited him when he was in Baghdad in April. He obviously did not have much faith in the Soviets and their readiness to act on behalf of the Kurds. The Kurds' secret ties with the United States no doubt added to the hardening of Barzani's position.

While al-Bakr was in Moscow, the Soviet Union pressured him to engage in a dialogue with the KDP. In fact, shortly after al-Bakr's return to Baghdad, the parties began a new dialogue. Iran, which feared losing an important bargaining card should Baghdad and the Kurds reach an understanding, appealed to Baghdad through the foreign minister of a third country, offering Baghdad a barter deal according to which Iran would guarantee quiet in the Kurdish north in exchange for Iraq's public abrogation of the 1937 border agreement.[11] Baghdad did not respond to the appeal.

Narratives in Closed Circles

On 23 September 1972, the Baath Party's Regional Leadership sent a memorandum to the KDP aimed at mending fences with the party.[12] Although the document included serious charges against Barzani's Kurdish movement, it still referred to it by the positive title of "freedom movement" (*haraka taharruriyya*)—not to be confused with a national liberation movement (*harakat tahrir*). It also presented the KDP as the legitimate representative of the Kurdish people.

The document, which was full of contradictions, emphasized that the Baath had issued the March Declaration from a position of strength, based on a fundamental, strategic outlook with no connection whatsoever to the bellicose situation that prevailed at the time between the Baath and the KDP. This outlook was based on the principle of a peaceful solution to the Kurdish question and the granting of national (*qawmiyya*) rights to which the Kurds were entitled. At the same time, the document added, the Baath Party maintained a dialogue with the KDP because it understood that disregarding an important component in the Kurdish movement was liable to thwart its peace efforts. The document further maintained that the Baath had gone far beyond the demands of the Kurds during negotiations and that it was the Baath that had offered to grant autonomy.[13] Nevertheless, it claimed, the KDP sought to present the March Declaration as a "victory" and a "decision forced" by the KDP on the Baath rather than a national (*wataniyya*), democratic understanding.[14]

The memorandum stated that the March Declaration contained two main components; namely, "guaranteeing the national, legitimate rights of the Kurds" and "the strengthening of Iraqi unity, i.e. the unity of the people, the homeland, and the constitutional regime." Regarding the first component (i.e., the Baath's part in the declaration), the memorandum listed thirty-three acts by the Baath, including the allocation of 50,000 dinars as the first payment to 5,000 discharged members of the Peshmerga, and between 30,000 and 50,000 dinars as a monthly payment to Barzani's headquarters. Stating that six articles had yet

to be fully implemented, the memorandum put the blame for their nonimple-
mentation on the KDP itself.[15]

As to the strengthening of national unity, to which the KDP was committed in the agreement, the memorandum asserted that not only did the KDP not
fulfill its obligations but it also went as far as to maintain links with Iran, which
seriously damaged national unity and Iraqi sovereignty. The memorandum specified fifteen areas of Kurdish-Iranian cooperation, including the flow of heavy
and light Iranian weapons to the Kurds, the supply of a radio station, the training of Kurdish members of the Peshmerga in Iranian training camps, the transfer of military intelligence information to Iran, the smuggling of goods and
people, and the exchange of visits between members of the KDP leadership and
Iranian officials.

The KDP was further blamed for preventing the central government from
maintaining its control over the Kurdish area, including by preventing the army
from carrying out exercises or deploying forces in certain areas in the north,
putting obstacles in the way of officials of the central government, and failing
to hand over guard posts adjacent to the Iranian border. The memorandum
pointed to hundreds of criminal acts, including murder, carried out by KDP
members against Kurds suspected of collaboration with the authorities.

The memorandum stated that the KDP had acted with duplicity toward the
Baath. Although the KDP was a partner in government, it behaved like an opposition party; for instance, by instilling a sense of separatism among the Kurds.
Acknowledging that the Baath Party had made several mistakes—because of a
lack of understanding among some of its leadership of the importance of the
March Declaration and because of negative attitudes on the part of the KDP itself—the memorandum asserted that, unlike the KDP, the Baath had worked
hard to correct its mistakes.

The memorandum finally put forward thirty-one conditions for the
restoration of relations with the KDP, including severance of KDP links with
Iran, commitment not to disrupt the army when it carried out its missions, and
subordination of the border guard to the Iraqi Army. The memorandum concluded with a call for "serious, objective" dialogue to find solutions to these
problems.[16]

Nonetheless, relations deteriorated quickly, with the Baath endeavoring to
delegitimize the KDP. All of this took place against the background of power
struggles within the regime and with Saddam, who was now seeking to lead
matters to a military confrontation, while al-Bakr attempted to calm tempers.
One explanation for Saddam's about-face was his desire to ride the wave of
anti-Kurdish sentiment in the army to strengthen his position there.

In mid-October 1972 the crisis broke out into the open. The Baath leaked
the memorandum described above to the foreign press whereas the KDP made
public its conditions for the continuation of a dialogue, one of which was the
resignation of Ghaydan and Kzar, who were both suspected of involvement in

the conspiracy to murder Barzani. In exchange, the KDP offered to hand over some of its heavy weaponry and to cease political activity against the regime. The KDP also issued two ultimatums; namely, that a population census be conducted immediately and that the Arabization of the Kurdish area cease without delay.

The response of the Baathi authorities came on 19 October 1972 in the form of the merging of the Ministry of Agriculture (headed by a Kurd) with the Agrarian Reform Ministry, and the appointment of the non-Kurd 'Izzat al-Duri to head the unified ministry. *Al-Ta'akhi* strongly criticized this move because it was not made in consultation with the KDP, it deprived the Kurds of an important ministry, and it violated the March agreement that assigned five ministries to the Kurds. Justifying the merger as an economizing measure, *Al-Thawra* indirectly attacked the Kurdish ministers for behaving in a "tribal fashion," stating that "the appointment of a Kurd to a governmental post does not mean that he and the ministry which he heads must only be interested in the affairs of the Kurdish area."[17]

The mutual accusations leveled by *Al-Ta'akhi* and *Al-Thawra* with regard to the ministers was actually part of a vociferous debate that *Al-Thawra* initiated on 17 October 1972. The debate, which went on for a month, was conducted in fourteen *Al-Thawra* editorials on the Kurdish question, under the heading "For the Sake of Preserving Peace and Strengthening National Unity," and in *Al-Ta'akhi*'s response to these editorials.[18] The decision to bring the debate into the open apparently stemmed from Saddam's desire to present the KDP in a negative light, mobilize Arab and Kurdish public opinion against it, and gradually delegitimize it as a partner in the March agreement.

Al-Thawra, which was under Saddam's tight control, directed its editorials against *Al-Ta'akhi*, which had become a thorn in the side of the Baath owing to the unprecedented critique and opposition that it voiced. The freedom to criticize that it had appropriated to itself led to unceasing attacks against the regime and its policies in all areas of life in Iraq. In its unceasing struggle to democratize government practices, *Al-Ta'akhi* thus became a channel for the wider public's complaints, not just those of the Kurds. On the whole, *Al-Ta'akhi*'s public pronouncements and the trenchant debate between the two newspapers were quite out of the ordinary in this type of regime where the media were state controlled. Hence, the special interest in this debate.

Al-Thawra's editorials contained unbridled attacks against the KDP, *Al-Ta'akhi*, and the KDP's internal publication *Al-Kadir* (the Cadre), quotes from which were presented as proof of the KDP's separatist tendencies. The editorials blamed the KDP of anti-Iraqi acts, the most significant of which was helping smuggle Jews out of the country. Unlike the memorandum that described Barzani's Kurdish movement as a liberation movement, the editorials referred to it as an "armed" (*musallaha*) movement controlled by reactionary and unpatriotic circles. The editorials further challenged the KDP's claims to exclusive leadership of the Kurdish national movement, its part in the March Declaration, and its demand for the incorporation of only KDP members in the government to the exclusion of other Kurds. *Al-Thawra* stated, "Inasmuch as the Ba'th Party directs and is responsible for all affairs of the homeland, it cannot grant the KDP absolute ideological, political, and organizational power over Kurdish citizens."[19]

The editorials also sought to negate a future role for the KDP:

> In essence, the March Declaration is not a pact between the Arab Socialist Ba'th Party and the revolutionary authorities on the one hand, and the KDP leadership and the armed Kurdish movement on the other. If the KDP leadership . . . fulfills them [i.e., previously mentioned conditions], its role will remain bound to the declaration. Otherwise, it will face isolation within the Kurdish national movement and in national life in Iraq.[20]

The Kurdish leadership responded by submitting a secret memorandum to the Baath Party on 28 October 1972, which they apparently leaked to the Lebanese press before delivering it to Baghdad. They also published a series of responses in *Al-Ta'akhi*, entitled "For the Sake of Peace, National Unity, and the Implementation of the March *Agreement*" (emphasis added). It is interesting to note that, in the case of the Kurds too, the secret memorandum appeared more moderate than the editorials in *Al-Ta'akhi*. While the KDP responded with a stormy counterattack in the memorandum, it nonetheless left the door open for reconciliation. For example, it spoke of the need to establish strategic relations between the two parties. A key point, which infuriated the Baath, was the KDP's demand for equal power sharing.[21]

On the whole, the memorandum was a defense against accusations leveled at the KDP in the Baath memorandum and in *Al-Thawra*. The most salient point was the KDP's attempt to defend its status as an exclusive partner in the March agreement. The party emphasized that this was an agreement and not a declaration, that the peaceful solution which they had obtained in March was not achieved without "an heroic war on the part of our Kurdish people to defend its national (*qawmi*) existence," and that the KDP—and no other group—was the central power in the Kurdish camp with which a dialogue should be maintained. The memorandum advised the Baath to stop attempting to revise the KDP's status in the Kurdish national movement since that approach, which had already been tried by the Baath and its predecessors, led only to "disaster, tragedy, and great suffering."

The KDP pointed out that relations with the Baath began to deteriorate in the summer of 1971. The memorandum mentioned nearly two dozen areas in which the regime attempted to harm the Kurdish nation in general and the KDP in particular, the most salient of which were the Arabization of Kurdistan; the drive to weaken the KDP leadership by two attempts on Barzani's life; the organization of Kurdish armed groups against the KDP and its supporters; and the shelling of the Kurdish villages of Sinjar, Barzan, and Shaykhan with aircraft and artillery.

Admitting that a significant number of articles of the March agreement had been implemented—mainly clauses regarding education, culture, and construction—the memorandum nevertheless emphasized that substantial problems remained. It expressed reservations about the Baath Party's activities among the Kurds because "the party's slogans and history are entirely bound up with Arab national (*qawmiyya*) aspirations" so that it would never strike roots among Kurdish ranks. Another argument was that the Baath was carrying out political activity in the Kurdish area only for procuring "mercenaries" to act against the KDP.[22]

The KDP rejected claims that it maintained contacts with foreign elements (Iran was not mentioned explicitly) but it indicated that, if contacts existed on any level, the blame lay with the Baath and the deterioration of its relations with the KDP after 29 September 1971, that is, the failed attempt on the life of Barzani. Like the Baath, the KDP also presented conditions for restoring the damaged relations. These included the cessation of the policy of Arabization and Baathization and of "activities among the Kurdish people, carried out behind the back of its leadership"; the integration of the Kurds into the executive and legislative body, the army, and the university; and the designation of a date and framework for an autonomy based on the "establishment of a national entity (*iqamat kiyan qawmi*) in the framework of national unity."[23]

Al-Ta'akhi's editorials were more trenchant than the memorandum.[24] First of all, *Al-Ta'akhi* acknowledged Kurdish ties with Iran, mainly in the medical and humanitarian fields. Nonetheless, it stated that Iran also served as a transit country for arms and food procured by the KDP abroad (but not from Iran itself). *Al-Ta'akhi* placed the blame for these connections at the doorstep of various Iraqi regimes, including the Baath, which had pushed the Kurds into political isolation and compelled them to seek relations with whichever partner. Accusing the regime of hypocrisy *Al-Ta'akhi* stated that, while the Baath Party was purporting to support the Kurds of Iran, it was also maintaining contacts with no less than four foreign countries to put an end to its conflict with Iran, without submitting any preconditions to Iran regarding its Kurds. Aside from this, *Al-Ta'akhi* protested, if the Kurdish cause was so dear to the Baath, why did it not defend the Kurds in Turkey? *Al-Ta'akhi* emphasized that the Kurdish movement in Iraq stood for the entire Kurdish nation and that Barzani's influence went well beyond Iraq's borders, even though the KDP slogans were restricted to Iraqi Kurdistan.[25]

With regard to the smuggling of Jews through Kurdistan, *Al-Ta'akhi* stated that the KDP had no hand in the matter; that the Jews were fleeing from all parts of Iraq; and, moreover, that they were leaving for Europe through official channels.[26] The newspaper concluded that these accusations were intended to tarnish the Kurds' image in the eyes of the Arabs.

Al-Ta'akhi acknowledged the existence of a KDP intelligence apparatus, the Parastin, similar to that of the Baath, which operated independently from the governmental apparatus. It stressed that the conspiracies against the KDP had compelled it to establish its own intelligence apparatus. Blaming the Baath for replacing ideological principles with "political tactics," *Al-Ta'akhi* attacked the "reactionary" circles and "chauvinistic" ideas that were gradually taking control of the Baath and causing it to retreat from principles it had developed before the March agreement regarding the rights of the Kurdish nation. *Al-Ta'akhi* stressed that the KDP had never sought separation from Iraq, and preferred a "voluntary union" or federalism (*ittihad ikhtiyari*). Nonetheless, it did not renounce "the Kurdish people's right to self-determination."[27]

While saber rattling between the newspapers went on in full force, armed forces began to concentrate in the areas of 'Aqra, Sinjar, and Shaykhan in the province of Mosul as well as in the Sulaymaniyya province under the pretext of military exercises. The Kurds also reinforced their forces as 500 Kurds deserted the Iraqi Army and joined Barzani's forces. The latter continued to receive arms from Iran and maintained contacts with Iraqi opposition figures in Iran.[28]

President al-Bakr threw his full weight behind the attempt to prevent further deterioration of relations while the wing headed by Saddam was in fact behind the *Al-Thawra* attacks and sought to marginalize the KDP. On 'Id al-Fitr, the three-day feast of the end of the Ramadan fast that began on 6 November 1972, President al-Bakr visited the branch of the KDP in Baghdad, a move that was considered unusual for him. He met with KDP leaders to discuss the tense relations. As a goodwill gesture, he contributed a full year's rent to the KDP headquarters in Baghdad as well as allocating funds for building a new wing at the headquarters. Interestingly, *Al-Thawra* did not report this move at the time, although *Al-Ta'akhi* did. *Al-Thawra* eventually responded too. Dismissing the implication that the visit symbolized a schism in the Iraqi leadership, *Al-Thawra* stated that al-Bakr's visit was normal in view of the holiday.[29]

Meanwhile, reassured by promises of US support in case of military encounters between the Kurds and the Baath, the Parastin initiated a series of attacks against Baath government institutions and offices in Kurdistan, thus frustrating any plans of reconciliation between the KDP and the Baath.[30]

Stratagems for Isolating the KDP

In the following months, the regime undertook a number of measures to undermine the KDP and weaken its status as a partner of the Baath and a leading force in the Kurdish camp. *Al-Thawra* initiated a new round of attacks against the KDP. Entitled "Free Opinions," *Al-Thawra*'s articles became once again a rostrum for vilifying the KDP, albeit in a more sophisticated manner.

The articles took issue with the terminology used by the KDP, which in their opinion reflected the party's true intentions. The author perceived veiled separatist goals in the use of the term "Southern Kurdistan."[31] He stated that the distance between this term and "the state of Kurdistan" (*dawlat Kurdistan*) was not big. In his opinion, the term "Kurdish revolution" also harbored military intentions nowhere near the spirit of the March understanding. According to *Al-Thawra*, the KDP's use of the terms "Arabization" and "*tab'ith*" to describe the regime's policy indicated that it was seeking absolute exclusivity for itself in the northern region by prohibiting the regime and the party from acting with the same freedom of action as that enjoyed by the KDP in other parts of Iraq. Moreover, the articles maintained, Kurdish figures who were friends or members of the Baath automatically became "mercenaries" (*ma'jurin*) in the KDP's lexicon. The author rejected the term "March agreement," to which the KDP adhered because as far as he understood an agreement is signed between two equal parties. However, in this case, such equality did not exist inasmuch as the Baath was simultaneously a party and the ruling authority (*sulta*), whereas the KDP was only a party. The author opined that as the ruling party, the Baath was superior to the KDP, hence its responsibility for preserving the spirit of the March Declaration. Furthermore, the author accused the KDP of leading tribal struggles "as if it were a super tribe" as well as of exploiting other minorities—such as the Turkomans and Assyrians—for tactical purposes.[32]

Concurrently, attempts were made to drive a wedge between the KDP and the ICP, among other things by inviting the ICP to participate in December 1972 in tripartite discussions between the Baath, the KDP, and the ICP on the implementation of the March agreement. This measure, which was adopted after three months of futile discussions between the Baath and the KDP, was actually intended to break the KDP's monopoly on the handling of the Kurdish question.

Another measure, no less serious from the viewpoint of the KDP, was the establishment in December 1972 of the Kurdistan Revolutionary Party (KRP; al-hizb al-thawri al-kurdistani). That party's manifesto, which was signed by "a group of cadres from the KRP," presented itself as the continuation of a party headed by Jalal Talabani and Ibrahim Ahmad (the manifesto did not mention them by name) and disbanded in early 1971 after which it eventually became part of the KDP. However, several days later, in a public statement signed by Talabani, Ahmad, and others, they washed their hands of the KRP and called on the Kurdish people to unite around Barzani. It later transpired that the group that called itself the Kurdistan Revolutionary Party was headed by 'Abd-al-Sattar Tahir Sharif, a reserve member of the KDP's central committee in 1970. Crossing the lines to the regime's side enabled him to advance quickly in the party and regime hierarchy. In November 1973 he became general secretary of the KRP, and in April 1974 he entered the government as minister of labor and construction. In a statement by the KRP, the party called on the Kurdish people to wash its hands of Barzani's leadership, the KDP, "rightists," and of "perfidious" groups, and to commit itself to "Arab-Kurdish unity."[33]

Concurrently, the regime made efforts to solve several problems in the Kurdish area, with a view to neutralizing the KDP's support base. These measures included granting an exemption from military service to Yezidis in exchange for monetary compensation (November 1972), facilitating the naturalization of Fayli Kurds born in Iraq (February 1973), and granting pardons to Assyrians who had been involved in the 1933 incidents and renaturalizing them as Iraqis (January 1973).[34] This last measure should be understood against the backdrop of competition between the Baath and the KDP for the support of other minorities, especially the Assyrians. The latter had identified with the Kurdish population and had joined its guerrilla fighters when the Levies mercenary corps to which they belonged was disbanded after World War II.[35] In fact, in one of its articles, *Al-Ta'akhi* stressed the Assyrians' support for the Kurdish national movement, indicating that the Assyrians had fought on the movement's side since the Kurdish revolution in 1961, which created a strong feeling of solidarity between Christians and Kurds.[36]

Meanwhile, the government announced an increase in financial resource allocation for the development of the north, with special emphasis on education including instruction in the Kurdish language. Emphasis was also placed on building highways and houses to offset the damage caused by the war between the Kurds and the Iraqi Army since Qasim's time. At the same time, however, the regime also acted to impede the progress of various Kurdish associations linked to the KDP or whose activity strengthened Kurdish national identity. This primarily involved the students union, the teachers union, and the Kurdish writers union. The regime demanded that the latter be linked organizationally to the General Iraqi Writers Union. However, it granted Kurdish writers no influence in a body strictly controlled by Arabs. On another level, the Baath initiated discussions with Iran in December 1972 and in April 1973 with a view toward settling the conflict between them. These initiatives produced no results, however.

To sum up, within two years of the March agreement, the Kurds and Baghdad had gone back to square one—not yet a fully fledged military confrontation, but nevertheless a war between two narratives that could not coexist.

Notes

1. *Al-Hayat* (London, daily), 3 July 1972; *Al-Nahar*, 12 July 1972.
2. *Al-Thawra* (Baghdad, daily), 9 July 1972.
3. *Akhir Sa'a* (Cairo, weekly), 16 August 1972.
4. Iraqi News Agency, 20 July 1972, cited in *Daily Report*, 21 July 1972.
5. *Al-Hayat*, 13 August 1972; Deutsche Presse Agentur, 15 August 1972, cited in *Daily Report*, 16 August 1972.

6. *Al-Hayat*, 8 September 1972. The first Baath regime of 1963 offered a reward for the killing of Barzani.

7. *Al-Thawra*, 25, 26 July 1972.

8. Ibid. In fact, Iraq regained this position several days before the Iran-Iraq War began on 22 September 1980.

9. *Al-Thawra*, 25, 26 July 1972.

10. Anonymous Israeli official interviewed by the author, 13 March 1982.

11. *Village Voice* (New York), 16 February 1976. The 1937 border agreement confirmed the 1847 Treaty of Erzerum, which set the boundary at the eastern bank of the Shatt al-Arab so that the entire waterway remained under Iraqi control.

12. The memorandum was published in *Al-Thawra*, 16 November 1972.

13. After the collapse of the rebellion, Saddam claimed that Barzani had signed the March Declaration for tactical reasons because Barzani did not believe in autonomy, but in the rule of the gun. Saddam Husayn, "Khandaq Wahid Am Khandaqan," in *Al-Thawra wal-Nazra al-Jadida* (Baghdad: Dar al-Hurriyya lil-Tiba'a, 1981), pp. 242–243.

14. *Al-Thawra*, 16 November 1972.

15. Ibid.

16. Ibid.

17. *Al-Thawra*, 22 October 1972.

18. I had at my disposal only two of *Al-Ta'akhi*'s responses.

19. *Al-Thawra*, 19 October 1972.

20. *Al-Thawra*, 14 November 1972; the rest of the articles appeared on 17, 18, 19, 29, 30, and 31 October 1972, and on 1, 2, 5, 6, 14, 15, and 16 November 1972.

21. The KDP's memorandum was quoted in *Al-Thawra*, 16 November 1972. It is likely that it had been rewritten because *Al-Hawadith* published a much more sharply worded version of the memorandum on 10 November 1972.

22. *Al-Thawra*, 16 November 1972.

23. Ibid.

24. The two *Al-Ta'akhi* articles at my disposal were dated 15 and 21 November 1972.

25. *Al-Ta'akhi* (Baghdad, daily), 15, 21 November 1972.

26. Starting in May 1971, the Iraqi government adopted a quiet policy, permitting the Jews to leave Iraq, albeit under constant, tight control. This policy began to change in the fall of 1972, when the persecution of Jews resumed. *Jerusalem Post*, 8 January 1973. An émigré from Iraq confirmed to me that, in 1971, the Iraqi government permitted older Jews to leave for Europe on Iraqi passports.

27. *Al-Ta'akhi*, 15, 21 November 1972.

28. Middle East News Agency, 6 November 1972, cited in *Daily Report*, 7 November 1972; Deutsche Presse Agentur, 9 November 1972, cited in *Daily Report*, 10 November 1972; *Al-Hayat*, 5, 9 November 1972.

29. For Bakr's visit, see, Middle East News Agency, 8 November 1972, cited in *Daily Report*, 8 November 1972.

30. Ferhad Ibrahim, *Die Kurdische Nationalbewegung im Iraq* (Berlin: Klaus Schwarz Verlag, 1983), p. 607.

31. As was mentioned above, in the pan-Kurdish terminology *Southern Kurdistan* means Kurdistan in Iraq.

32. *Al-Thawra*, 7, 8, 10, 11, 14, 22, 31 December 1972; 3, 15, 19, 22, and 26 January 1973.

33. *Al-Hayat*, 11 December 1972.

34. Ironically, it was the Iraqi Army that massacred hundreds of Assyrian villagers in August 1933.

35. Dana Adams Schmidt, *Journey Among Brave Men* (Boston: Little, Brown, 1964), p. 72.

36. *Al-Ta'akhi*, 9 January 1973. A famous Peshmerga commander was an Assyrian woman, Margaret George Malik, killed in 1966. David McDowall, *A Modern History of the Kurds* (London: I. B. Tauris, 2004), p. 381.

6

Marginalizing the Kurds

Three years after the March agreement had been finalized, the Baathi regime seemed more self-confident and wielded more power than ever. The fact that it had succeeded in solving most of the problems related to the nationalization of oil within a few months resulted in an unprecedented strengthening of Saddam Hussein's position. In the face of the opposition of experts and a lack of enthusiasm on the part of other members of the leadership, Saddam subsequently defined himself as the architect of nationalization.[1] The KDP, on the other hand, started losing its bargaining power. The irony was that the March agreement, which paved the way for nationalization,[2] had now become its main victim. Although the regime did not renounce the March agreement publicly, it chose to empty its contents and all but ignore the KDP. Saddam even went so far as to indirectly define the KDP as a party with separatist tendencies, which should be exposed publicly and countered with full force.[3] Moreover, in his first interview with a US newspaper, Saddam contended that under no circumstances would the Baath concede any of its authority to the Kurds and that no Kurd would be included in the Revolutionary Command Council.[4]

Well aware of the regime's consolidation and growing attempts to marginalize it, the KDP launched a propaganda campaign in which it attempted to counterattack the Baath by emphasizing points that, in a way, echoed the Baath's arguments:

1. The centrality of Mulla Mustafa Barzani and the KDP in the Kurdish national movement in general and the March agreement in particular: "The attempts to suppress the shining role (of the party), belittle our party's importance within the national (*wataniyya*) Kurdish movement, weaken its role in political life, damage its unity, and divide its ranks—these attempts will lead to perdition."[5]
2. The Kurdish movement's perception of "Arab-Kurdish brotherhood" —

not through the prism of its relations with the government, but as people-to-people relations.[6]

3. Emphasis on the centrality of democracy in KDP thinking and on the Gordian knot between democracy and Kurdish national rights.

As part of its struggle to mobilize favorable public opinion the KDP continued, through its newspaper *Al-Ta'akhi*, to criticize different aspects of the regime's social, economic, and bureaucratic policies as well as its policy regarding Kurdistan. The Baath did not ban the publication of these articles but for the most part would not respond to them, given the opinion that "barking dogs never bite, and the storm will pass." This disregard symbolized the political chasm that had opened between the Baath and the KDP—a chasm that the KDP tried to bridge by submitting its own program for autonomy while inducing the Baath to respond to it.

The KDP submitted its program on 9 March 1973. It included the following principles: The Iraqi republic is one and indivisible. It is composed of two primary nations, the Arab and the Kurdish, and several national minorities. The Kurdish people's participation in government shall be relative to its proportion in the population, including in key or sensitive positions in the army, government, and central legislative institutions such as the RCC and the future parliament. A Kurdish vice-president shall be selected by the legislative assembly. The region (*iqlim*) of Kurdistan shall have a legislative assembly to be elected by the population in free, direct elections. The executive council of the region shall be approved by the legislative assembly, which will also elect its head. Its members shall have the rank of minister and be appointed officially by the president of the republic. The executive council shall be composed of thirteen ministries, including education, culture, local administration (e.g., local police and local security), finance, planning, agriculture, industry, and commerce. The Kurdish region's share of the state budget shall be proportional to the Kurds' share in the population. The constitution, foreign policy, armed forces and internal security, oil production, general budget, and legislation of general laws shall be under the purview of the central government. Any law or legislation (promulgated by the central government) pertaining to autonomy must be approved by the local legislative assembly.[7] At the time these demands seemed far-fetched, yet little did the Kurds know that thirty years later their achievements would be even greater.

The plan, submitted at the request of the Baath Party itself, was as shown below far removed from the Baath's concept of autonomy. As soon as the Baath received the proposal, they filed it away and imposed a complete blackout on the matter. Eight months later, when it became clear that nothing had been done regarding the plan, the KDP publicized it.

After keeping silent for many months, Barzani finally granted a provocative interview to a US reporter. Barzani stated that the nationalization of oil in the Kirkuk area, which was located within the boundaries of the Kurdish region, was to the disadvantage of the Kurds. Dropping a not-so-subtle hint to the United States he stressed that, with sufficient support, he would have seized the oil fields in Kirkuk to be operated by a US company: "We act in a way which is consistent with the United States' policy in the area, if the United States will protect us from the wolves." Highlighting Kurdish fears of a renewed military confrontation, Barzani called on the United States to provide assistance to the Kurds—be it humanitarian, political, or military, open or hidden, direct or indirect, through Iran, or even through Israel.[8] Four days later, limited clashes between the army and Peshmerga were reported in the areas of Halabja, Qal'a Diza, and Handrin. Similarly, clashes broke out between supporters of the KDP and those of the ICP only days after the rapprochement discussions between the first secretary-general of the ICP and Barzani.

As the tension in the north grew, a coup attempt was staged on 30 June 1973, shortly before President Ahmad Hasan al-Bakr's return from a visit to Bulgaria and Poland. The failed attempt was led by Nazim Kzar, general security director (*al-amn al-'amm*), and ended with the killing of Kzar himself and of the defense minister Shihab. The interior minister, Sa'dun Ghaydan, was injured. At the time, most observers maintained that Saddam had also been targeted during the coup. However, after the fall of the Baath in 2003, Hamid al-Juburi, one of Saddam's close associates, revealed that it had actually been Saddam who masterminded the coup and that the KGB had forewarned al-Bakr of the imminent putsch.[9] In any case, the close proximity between the clashes in the north and the coup attempt convey the impression that the plotters chose this particular timing to heat up the atmosphere in the north so as to divert the attention of the army, al-Bakr's main prop, from what was happening in the capital.[10]

Barzani's camp watched the events in Baghdad with unconcealed satisfaction. The shock visited on the central government was perceived as quite likely to curb the regime's consolidation and to strengthen its dependence on non-Baathi elements, especially the Kurds. The elimination of Kzar unintentionally fulfilled a central demand of the Kurds who had sought his removal because of his uncompromising attitude toward the Kurdish question and because of the involvement of his security services in the two assassination attempts on Barzani. Also, what appeared to be the weakening of Saddam was perceived as a positive development by the Kurds, given that his views on the Kurdish question had become extreme and to the Kurds' detriment. However, their hopes of reaping the fruits from this crisis were quickly dashed.

The worst blow was the establishment of a national front excluding the KDP. Ever since the Baath Party's ascension to power, political circles had been discussing the establishment of a front and there was an unwritten agreement that the KDP and the ICP would not join the front separately. The ICP, however, decided to go it alone because of the numerous inducements offered by the

Baath. For the first time, the ICP would obtain official recognition from an Iraqi regime; its representatives in the national front would be equal to the number of Kurds (if and when they decided to join the front); and it would be allowed to publish its own daily, *Tariq al-Sha'b*. No less important, the ICP now perceived an opportunity to oust the KDP from its senior position vis-à-vis the Baath as well as from its position in the Kurdish north where the ICP drew a major segment of its members. It is possible that the ICP joined the front at the urging of the Soviet Union.

Before long, it transpired that the main beneficiary of this move was the Baath regime. The ICP, by contrast, did not even gain the position of junior partner. It was not brought into the RCC and was prohibited from engaging in any activity in sensitive places, for example the army and the police, a prohibition carrying the death penalty. The front itself was devoid of power. The regime's gains were patently clear as it expanded its base of support without paying a real political price. This measure symbolized the healing of the rift between the nationalist and the Communist camps, a rift that hung like a cloud over Iraqi society for many years and reached its peak during the 'Abd-al-Karim Qasim and the first Baathi eras (1958–1963). Most importantly, the Baath's policy of divide and rule had succeeded in driving a wedge between the KDP and the ICP, which had until then been united on one issue: a shared hostility toward the Baath.[11]

The Baath and the ICP invited the KDP to join the national front, but the latter rejected the invitation outright. The KDP described the front as a bilateral agreement between the Baath and the ICP that had been negotiated hastily with the intent to pressure the Kurds into accepting the accord, and accused the Baath and the ICP of informing the KDP of the agreement only four days before it was made public. A joint response by the Baath and the ICP came a month later in the form of a declaration by the Supreme Committee of the National Front, which attacked what it termed the KDP's negative position on the front and the barriers it had put up to thwart its activities.[12]

The day after the establishment of the front, the KDP leaked the autonomy proposal (which it had submitted to the Baath several months earlier without receiving a response) to the Beiruti newspaper, *Al-Hayat*. With this move, it sought to remind the other two partners that the KDP was still the main power in the Kurdish region and could not be excluded from any discussions regarding the autonomy plan. It quickly became clear, however, that not only did the Baath not wish to discuss the plan presented to it by the KDP, but it also did not wish to involve the KDP in discussions concerning the Baath's own plan. Thus, in the first meeting of the Supreme Committee of the National Front, which was held on 28 August 1973 with the participation of representatives of the Baath and the ICP (albeit not the KDP), the foundation lines of the autonomy plan were discussed.

In response to the stance of the ICP *Al-Ta'akhi* published the Communist Party's draft autonomy plan, which had been published in July 1970 in the ICP publication, *Al-Fikr al-Jadid*, and was close in spirit and content to the KDP proposal. Neither the ICP nor the Baath responded. Actually, Saddam had already passed judgment on the KDP. In his last public discussion about autonomy, he said:

> We must not blur the borders between our Kurdish people and the KDP to the extent of creating an overlap [between the two]. It is also impossible for the Ba'th to be in conflict with our Kurdish people, since the Ba'th regards itself as—and indeed is—the leader of the Iraqi people, not the leader of the Arabs among the Iraqi people.[13]

This was to be the main Baathi argument for many years to come.

The establishment of the national front further contributed to the deterioration of relations between the Kurds and the central government. On 19 August 1973, the army launched an offensive against the Kurds in the Sinjar area. The KDP claimed that "aircraft, tanks, heavy artillery, and mercenaries" participated in the offensive while the Baath explained that the attack was a response to "extensive sabotage operations" carried out by "armed elements" belonging to the Kurdish movement of the KDP. The following day the regime took another, far-reaching measure by executing, for the first time since the March agreement, four KDP members convicted of spying for Iran. The KDP attempts to intervene with the Baath to prevent the executions and to bring about the cessation of the attack in Sinjar failed. In protest, the KDP called for a general strike on 25 August 1973. The strike, which lasted twelve hours and included all the Kurdish districts, was a unicum in the political panorama of the Baath regime.[14]

While *Al-Ta'akhi* presented the strike as an important victory for the KDP, *Al-Thawra* ridiculed it: "We can close every store in Iraq within one hour if we use rifles to organize the strike." Emphasizing that the Baath and other parties also had considerable influence there, *Al-Thawra* contended that the parties did not find their proper expression because "the language of the rifles now prevails."[15] Hammering home the Kurdish national factor, *Al-Ta'akhi* insisted that the Kurdish question was the problem of an entire people and that the struggle for autonomy was the concern of every Kurdish patriot. As to the strike, its success was authentic, and not produced "by the force of rifles." *Al-Ta'akhi* asked, "If the language of rifles prevails in Kurdistan, which language rules in the center and the south—the cooing of doves?" Blaming the Baath for attempting "to reduce" the power of the KDP, the newspaper stressed that "the national Kurdish movement headed by Barzani is fully entitled to claim the representation of the Kurdish people throughout Iraq." Therefore, the "attempts to act fraudulently, take back with the left hand what the right hand proffers, and to place barriers and different stumbling blocks in the way of this movement . . . will commend no one."[16]

While the saber rattling continued at full force in the area, the October War of 1973 broke out, for a while diverting attention to another theater that was nonetheless not completely separate from the Kurdish question.

The Kurdish Question and the October War

The October War, which began on 6 October 1973, posed a challenge to both the Iraqi regime and to the Kurds. A regime like the Baath—one with a pan-Arab ideology and a declared commitment to the Palestinian cause, which was in constant competition with the Syrian Baath for the "authentic" representation of a pan-Arab ideology—could not stand by idly while a war was raging between Israel and an Arab coalition led by Egypt and Syria. According to an Iraqi commentary, Iraq could only "be the vanguard in the battle and take full part in it, based on a pan-Arab (*qawmiyya*) outlook, which regards the quest of liberation—of Sinai, the Golan, and Palestine—as its mission and duty, just as it is the duty and obligation of Egypt, and Syria, of the Palestinians, and all Arabs."[17] Hence, Baghdad decided to take part in the war only hours after it broke out.

However, another Iraqi commentary indicated that no other Arab country confronting Israel operated under the same constraints as Iraq. Therefore, no other Arab country was required to make the same sacrifices as Iraq since participation in the October War meant the withdrawal of Iraqi forces stationed along the long border with Iran on the one hand and exposure of the domestic front to "serious internal security" problems on the other hand.[18] An Iraqi book, published in 1975 and dealing with Iraq's role in the October War, discusses Baghdad's strategic difficulties on the outbreak of the war. It points out that

> tension along the Iranian-Iraqi border, distrust of Barzani's intentions, and the possibility that Barzani would cause renewed fighting in the north had [in the past] forced the Iraqi leadership to station more than 70 percent of its infantry and about 20 to 30 percent of its armored forces on the eastern border . . . and on the southern border of the collaborationist Kurdish enclave.[19]

The Kurds, for their part, faced a dilemma of their own. On the one hand, the war provided them with a golden opportunity to attack the Iraqi Army, which was then busy on another front, and to attempt to realize the dream of a real autonomy or even Kurdish independence—an idea that the KDP leadership had begun to cultivate secretly during the same period. On the other hand, choosing such a route could be viewed as a betrayal of Islam and the homeland, and arouse public opinion in the Arab and Muslim world against the Kurdish leadership. Mahmud 'Uthman subsequently indicated that certain people in the regime sought to prove that the Kurds were willing to stab the Arab nation in the back and that, if the Kurds were to initiate fighting at the time, some people in the regime would eagerly prey on such a move.[20]

As soon as the war began, Barzani proclaimed Kurdish solidarity with the Arab states in their war against Israel. He directed his people to refrain from any confrontation with the Iraqi Army. He also sent a message to al-Bakr, stating the KDP's willingness to reenter into a dialogue with the authorities. Al-Bakr rejected the appeal and chose to focus on another side of the triangle; that is, on reaching an understanding with Iran. The advantages were self-evident since such an understanding was likely to neutralize two enemies simultaneously given the unlikelihood of the Kurds declaring war against the Iraqi Army without Iranian support.

The day after the outbreak of the war Iraq informed Iran of its willingness to renew diplomatic relations, which had broken off following Iran's seizure of the three islands mentioned in Chapter 4—Abu-Musa, the Greater Tunb, and the Lesser Tunb—and immediately begin negotiations to solve the outstanding disputes between them and thus safeguard "the interests, rights, and sovereignty" of the two states. Iraq explained that its motive was the need "to free up Iraq's military potential" for the pan-Arab battle, emphasizing that its decision was not "tactical" and it would adhere to it in all circumstances.[21] It is not clear whether Iraq managed to negotiate a deal with Iran by dint of Baghdad's promise to concede Iraqi sovereignty over the Shatt al-Arab waterway. In any case, Iran had other considerations that favored reaching an understanding with Iraq, including its desire to obtain support for an increase in oil prices and to buttress Islamic solidarity.

Iran's immediate response paved the way for the dispatch of an Iraqi expeditionary force of 16,000–18,000 troops and about 100 tanks to the Syrian front on 10 October 1973. Three days earlier, the Iraqi Air Force had already begun providing support on both the Egyptian and Syrian fronts.[22]

Iraq's participation was substantial, comprising three-quarters of its air force, two-thirds of its armored corps, and one-fifth of its infantry corps. The extent to which the understanding with Iran satisfied the Iraqi government with regard to the Kurdish front is evidenced by the fact that it felt sufficiently confident to dispatch its strongest units to Syria, units that were stationed on the Kurdish front at the time. These included the Special Forces Brigade and the 5th Mountain Brigade under the command of 'Abd-al-Jawad Dhanun who would become the chief of staff of the Iraqi Army in 1983. The army chose to send these units precisely because of their high level of military capabilities, sophisticated equipment, and the experience they had gained "during the pacification operations against the Barzanis."[23]

The Iraqi-Iranian agreement dealt a severe blow to the Kurds because it robbed them of both a political bargaining card and a military option. Indeed, during the war, Israel probed the Kurds as to the possibility of opening a front in Kurdistan to distract the Iraqi armed forces or at least prevent them from further reinforcing the Syrian front. This possibility proved impractical, however. It became clear to the Kurds that, without the Iranian rear, an offensive on their part would not achieve much.

Moreover, Kurdish consultations with the United States regarding such a move met with strong resistance. Secretary of State Henry Kissinger's cable of 16 October 1973 to the US liaison clarified unequivocally that "we do not think that it would be wise to carry out the offensive military measure which the other government [read: Israel] suggested to you. For your information, we have consulted with our ally [read: Iran] through the ambassador, and both made the same recommendation."[24] Nonetheless, some Israeli officials viewed Kissinger's opposition as an excuse seized by Barzani to evade the Israeli request.

Opinions are divided regarding the United States' motives with respect to this development.[25] Kissinger's questionable explanation was that Iranian, US, and even Israeli intelligence thought that the Kurds would be defeated should such an offensive be mounted. In retrospect, some viewed this development as a cynical move that prevented the Kurds from making significant gains at the expense of the Iraqi Army, which was then occupied on another front. Be it as it may, in the light of these internal and external constraints, the Kurds rejected Israel's appeal to mount an offensive against the Iraqi Army. Although Israel understood these constraints, it was nevertheless bitterly disappointed by the Kurdish position. Israel did, however, continue to support the Kurds after the war, apparently based on the argument advanced by Barzani that the presence of strong Kurds tied up Iraqi military divisions.

As to the Kurds, it could be said with the wisdom of hindsight that the October War was a lesson they failed to learn. The illusory pact they made with the United States came to nothing at the very first test, but they failed to draw the appropriate conclusions. One way or another, the Kurds eventually became convinced that it was the October War that had postponed a confrontation between them and the Iraqi Army for six months.

Baghdad's resumption of relations with Iran strengthened the Baath's confidence to the point that it was able to continue maneuvering the KDP into a corner even during the war. One day after the dispatch of the Iraqi expeditionary force to the Syrian front, the Baath extended invitations to 200 "independent" Kurdish figures via *Al-Thawra* asking them to participate in discussions on the Kurdish autonomy. The list did not include a single representative of the KDP. This was no doubt an intentional provocation through which the Baath sought to clarify to the KDP that the latter would not be able to use the war as a means of pressuring the regime and that the KDP was not to be a partner in any discussions on autonomy. The KDP responded by immediately publishing its own autonomy program in *Al-Ta'akhi*.[26] It also asked the Baath to cancel the said meeting with the 200 Kurdish figures, but to no avail.

In one of these meetings, Saddam candidly declared that the KDP had indeed submitted its own program, "but we did not discuss this plan. The truth is that we regard this plan as being far from the concept of autonomy. One thing is certain, namely that we must discuss the programs in the spirit of one single people."[27]

The KDP-ICP Conflict: A Diversionist Exercise?

Late in October 1973, the focus shifted for a short time from the KDP-Baath conflict to the lesser conflict between the KDP and the ICP. This latter conflict, one of the most bitter in the history of KDP-ICP relations, brought to the surface problems that had remained latent for many years and reflected the complexity of the relations between the two parties.

The roots of the conflict lie in the historically ambivalent KDP-ICP relationship, which can be viewed as a partnership-competition dichotomy. Except for certain periods (e.g., a short spell under Qasim's rule), the two were partners in a joint struggle against the central government.[28] This partnership was evidenced on the one hand by the KDP granting refuge to ICP members and their incorporation in the Kurdish armed struggle against the central government, and on the other hand by the Kurdish question being rated as the primary pillar of ICP ideology. At the same time, the KDP and ICP competed fiercely on two levels. One level concerned competition for the central government's largesse as well as each party's fear of the other reaching an agreement with Baghdad, thus abandoning the partnership and isolating the other. The second level concerned competition for the minds of the Kurds. While the strength of the KDP was based entirely on the Kurds, that of the ICP was based on the Kurds to a significant degree but also included Arabs and other non-Arab minorities.[29] The homogeneity of the KDP versus the heterogeneity of the ICP constituted a constant source of mutual suspicion.

Under the Baath, new problems surfaced when the Baath first allied with the KDP and then with the ICP. The KDP, which had signed the March agreement with the Baath, became an object of suspicion and jealousy to ICP members. At a later stage, the ICP established the national front with the Baath and in turn became the object of suspicion and jealousy, this time to the KDP. To this muddle should be added the hidden Baath activity that aimed to inflame the conflict between the KDP and the ICP.

The deterioration of KDP-ICP relations, which began with the establishment of the national front, took a turn for the worse during the October War when a sharp debate broke out between the KDP newspaper, *Al-Ta'akhi*, and that of the ICP, *Tariq al-Sha'b*. The dispute was unprecedented in the history of modern Iraq because both newspapers were now operating legally and concurrently, having worked underground for a long time. They now took advantage of the freedom that they had been granted to settle old and new accounts.

While the Baath kept silent on the KDP's position with regard to the October War, *Tariq al-Sha'b* published an ICP appeal to the KDP on 21 October 1973, urging it "to adopt a position of greater solidarity with the Arab people, which is waging a just liberation war." *Al-Ta'akhi* responded angrily in an editorial headlined "He Who Lives in a Glass House, Should Not Throw Stones." *Al-Ta'akhi* attacked the self-righteousness of the ICP and its attempts to cast doubt on KDP positions on the war when the ICP approach was itself a target of strong criticism.[30] Making a mockery of the ICP, *Al-Ta'akhi* stated that "the ICP's central committee is not authorized to render formal legal opinions [i.e., fatwa, usually in the sense of opinions on religious questions rendered by clerics] and to provide evaluations on the positions of others regarding the Palestinian question."[31] The distance between such comments and the outbreak of armed hostilities was quite negligible.

On 15 November 1973, the ICP Central Committee issued a statement accusing the KDP of waging "a war of annihilation" (*harb ibada*) against ICP members and organizations in the Kurdish area. It claimed that the KDP's hostile actions against the ICP had commenced two years earlier, when the Baghdad authorities stopped persecuting the Communists, and reached a peak with the establishment of the national front. These acts included the extortion of disavowal (*bara'a*) documents from ICP members, incitement against the ICP in mosques, the kidnapping of hundreds of members and sympathizers of the ICP and their imprisonment without trial, and the persecution of writers who issued statements in favor of the national front.[32] Indeed, a non-ICP source stated that it was the Parastin, the Kurdish secret services, that mounted a series of attacks against Communist Party members and thus increased the tension between the two parties.[33]

Al-Ta'akhi's rendering of the events was that the recent outbreak was due to acts of provocation by ICP members, the most recent being the transfer of "thousands of weapons" and much ammunition from "certain governmental circles" to ICP members behind the back of the KDP.[34] According to *Al-Ta'akhi*, this was done in order to establish, with the help of the authorities, fortified camps next to the headquarters of the KDP, which the Communists were not allowed to set up anywhere else.[35] *Al-Ta'akhi* pointed to the ICP's tactical position on the Kurdish question, which changed to suit the convenience and needs of the ICP, as the root of the conflict: "[The Communist Party] demonstrates maximum commitment to the rights of our Kurdish people when the relations of the communists with the government—any government—are bad. However, this commitment weakens significantly when relations between the communists and the government thaw."[36]

The newspaper stated that the KDP had remained faithful to the ICP even after the March agreement, proof of which was the refuge it granted to ICP members hunted down by the regime after the agreement was signed and the fact that the Second ICP Congress was held in the heart of Kurdistan, "specifically in the area where Barzani and the politburo of his party reside." In *Al-Ta'akhi*'s view, the turning point came when the ICP began to collaborate with the Baath, which led it to "wash its hands of the Kurdish question, disavow its previous positions, and mount a campaign of criticism and false accusations against our party." *Al-Ta'akhi* criticized ICP attempts to undermine the influence of the KDP in the Kurdish area, emphasizing that "for 12 years, the true authority in most parts of Kurdistan has been the authority of the Kurdish revolution." As to the differences of opinion between the KDP and the ICP with respect to relations with the Soviet Union, the newspaper stated that the KDP did not oppose the friendship pact with the Soviet Union, but was disappointed because the Soviet Union had ignored it. At the same time, the newspaper attacked the ICP for following the Soviets in every respect, including supporting the Baath.[37]

Although it did not deny that it had received weapons, *Tariq al-Sha'b* rejected the claim that this had kindled the dispute. According to the ICP, the true cause of the dispute was of a political nature and originated in the grudge that the KDP bore toward the ICP for participating in a united front with the Baath. The ICP stressed that there had always been currents in the KDP that sought to eliminate the Communist organizations in Kurdistan, adding that "it is unwise to color the Kurdish national movement red." The ICP pointed out that it had been established in Kurdistan before the establishment of the KDP, that it had championed the struggle on behalf of the Kurds years before the establishment of the KDP, and had always been committed to this struggle.[38]

Throughout this entire period, the regime maintained almost complete silence. The one time when *Al-Thawra* referred to the conflict, it directed its critical barbs at the KDP, warning it against attempting to harm the national front. The regime also expressed its support for the ICP by arresting 300 KDP members on charges of attacks against Communists.[39] Clearly, the Baath was only too happy that its job was being done by others. Neither should it be ruled out that it was Baghdad that had actually provoked the conflict between the ICP and the KDP. Indirect support of this premise can perhaps be found in the distribution of arms to ICP members during the October War and in the regime's attempts to divert the Kurdish leadership's attention to side issues.

The conflict abated briefly in mid-November 1973, among others due to the intervention of the Soviet Union, which viewed the tension with concern and sent two envoys on a secret visit to Barzani when the crisis was at its peak. The envoys brought Barzani a note from Leonid Brezhnev, reprimanding Barzani for his position on the Baath and for "the liquidation operations carried out by the KDP against the ICP in the north."[40] At the same time, Salih al-Yusufi and Dara Tawfiq went to Moscow for consultations. In Iraq, 'Aziz Sharif again played the role of mediator.

On 18 November 1973, *Al-Ta'akhi* and *Tariq al-Sha'b* responded to Sharif's call for a resolution of the dispute between them. In the following two days, meetings were held between representatives of the two parties, among others Barzani and Sharif. The parties concluded with a joint statement, calling for an immediate cessation of all acts of hostility, for periodic meetings between the sides, and for strengthening the alliance between them.[41] A subsequent disclosure by the KDP revealed that the agreement included a singular commitment by the ICP to disband Communists who had been armed and employed against the KDP in the latest flare-up.

On 12 February 1974, the KDP announced a unilateral cessation of hostilities as "the interests of the Kurdish and the Iraqi people are not served by diverting attention from primary problems in order to treat secondary problems, chief among which is the KDP dispute with the ICP."[42] Careful reassessment of the conflict by both parties no doubt stemmed from the realization that the KDP-ICP partnership was stronger than any partnership of either one of them with the Baath. The short-term gains of the ICP, resulting from a rapprochement with the Baath, did not allay the party's suspicion toward the latter. The ICP also understood that a final break with the KDP would considerably weaken its hold in the north, damage a particularly important source for the recruitment of new members, and cause the loss of a refuge that it might need in the future. In addition, the ICP realized that its role in the coalition had remained marginal. For its part, despite being the stronger party, the KDP did not wish to face a joint front comprising the Baath and the ICP.

Tariq al-Sha'b aptly summarized the common danger facing the ICP and KDP when the conflict between the two was at its height: "Our party has no intention of going the way of disputes, hatred, and conflicts with it [the KDP], and it is not in its interest to do so, based on a growing awareness that this would entail great damage and demand a heavy price, not just of us . . . but also of them."[43]

Notes

1. Fuad Matar, *Saddam Hussein, the Man and the Cause, and the Future* (Beirut: Third World Center, 1981), p. 233.

2. In an interview on the occasion of Nationalization Day, Saddam disclosed that nationalization was a strategic program and its planning had begun in July 1970. *Al-Thawra* (Baghdad, daily), 1 June 1973. Although Saddam did not point to a connection between nationalization and the March agreement, such a connection seems obvious.

3. *Al-Thawra*, 19 March 1973. Saddam did not explicitly mention the KDP. However, from the context, it is clear that he was referring to it. By contrast, 'Abd-al-Khaliq al-Samarra'i, who had attempted to mediate with the Kurds several months earlier, gave an interview to *Al-Ta'akhi*, in which he spoke of the alliance between the Baath, the KDP, and the ICP. *Al-Ta'akhi* (Baghdad, daily), 11 March 1973.

4. *New York Times*, quoted in *Ha'aretz* (Tel Aviv, daily), 19 April 1973.

5. *Al-Ta'akhi*, 18 March 1973.

6. *Al-Ta'akhi*, 11 March 1973.

7. *Al-Ta'akhi*, 16 October 1973.

8. *International Herald Tribune*, 22 June 1973.

9. Interview of Hamid al-Juburi, Aljazeera, 2, 5 June 2008.

10. Considering that a visit to Barzani by a US reporter was rare, and assuming that the reporter did get a green light from the authorities, one is left with the impression that even the interview in the *International Herald Tribune*, 22 June 1973, was part of a diversionary tactic by the planners of the coup.

11. On the ICP during this period, see 'Abd al-Fattah 'Ali al-Botani, *Dirasat wa Mabahith fi Ta'rikh al-Kurd wal-'Iraq al-Mu'asir* (Erbil: Hajji Hashim, 2007), pp. 257–271.

12. The committee was officially headed by President Ahmad Hasan al-Bakr.

13. *Al-Thawra*, 25 September 1973.

14. *Al-Ta'akhi*, 26 August 1973.

15. *Al-Thawra*, 28 August 1973.

16. *Al-Ta'akhi*, 11 September 1973.

17. *Al-Thawra*, 11 October 1973.

18. *Al-Thawra*, 12 October 1973.

19. *Dawr al-Jaysh al-'Iraqi fi Harb Tishrin 1973* (Beirut: al-Mu'assasa al-'Arabiyya lil-Dirasat wal-Nashr, 1975), p. 50. The book, which was written under the auspices of the Iraqi authorities, refers to the March agreement as "a cease-fire agreement" or "a temporary agreement" (pp. 139, 147).

20. *Le Monde Diplomatique* (Paris, monthly), 14 April 1974.

21. *Al-Thawra*, 8, 12 October 1973.

22. On the Iraqi Army's role in the war, see *The Iraqi Army in the Yom Kippur War* (in Hebrew) (Tel Aviv: Ma'arakhot, 1986).

23. *Dawr al-Jaysh*, pp. 1, 140, 147.

24. *Village Voice* (New York), 16 February 1976.

25. Henry Kissinger, *White House Years* (Boston: Little, Brown, 1979), p. 1265.

26. As stated, the plan was leaked earlier to *Al-Hayat*.

27. *Al-Thawra*, 19 October 1973.

28. In October 1962, the KDP suggested that they act jointly with the ICP to unseat 'Abd-al-Karim Qasim, but the ICP refused. Al-Botani, *Dirasat wa Mabahith*, p. 268.

29. During the peak period of ICP power (1949–1955), all of the general secretaries of the ICP and 31 percent of its central committee members were Kurds. Hanna Batatu, *The Old Social Classes and the Revolutionary Movements of Iraq* (Princeton: Princeton University Press, 1978), p. 699.

30. The ICP adopted the Soviet Union's line regarding the establishment of the State of Israel and, subsequently, of a political solution of the Arab-Israeli conflict. Batatu, *The Old Social Classes*, pp. 599–601; Uriel Dann, "The Communist Movement in Iraq Since 1963," in *The U.S.S.R. and the Middle East*, eds. Michael Confino and Shimon Shamir (Jerusalem: Israel Universities Press, 1973), p. 386.

31. *Al-Ta'akhi*, 23 October 1973.

32. *Tariq al-Sha'b* (Baghdad, daily), 15 November 1973.

33. Ferhad Ibrahim, *Die Kurdische Nationalbewegung im Iraq* (Berlin: Klaus Schwarz Verlag, 1983), p. 606.

34. The Baath Party was said to have armed the ICP and encouraged it to establish control over mixed townships mainly in the Sulaymaniyya area. Public Record Office, FCO8/2307, 13 February 1974.

35. *Al-Ta'akhi*, 14 January 1974. *Al-Hayat* claimed that the Communists had begun to seek refuge in the vicinity of army camps in order to secure help in the event of a confrontation with the KDP. *Al-Hayat* (Beirut, daily), 17 February 1974.

36. *Al-Ta'akhi*, 12 November 1973.

37. *Al-Ta'akhi*, 13, 17 November 1973. A few years earlier, an ICP member admitted that his party had accepted Soviet dictates without questioning. Al-Botani, *Dirasat wa Mabahith*, p. 270.

38. *Tariq al-Sha'b*, 15, 17 November 1973.

39. *Al-Hayat,* 12 December 1973.

40. *Al-Anwar* (Beirut, daily), 21 November 1973; Public Record Office, FCO8/2307, 13 February 1974.

41. Public Record Office, FCO8/2092, 5 December 1973.

42. *Al-Ta'akhi*, 12 February 1974.

43. *Tariq al-Sha'b*, 15 November 1973.

7

An Imposed Autonomy

By the time the KDP had overcome its conflict with the ICP, the regime managed to adopt a number of measures toward the final neutralization of the KDP. On 12 December 1973, the Baath submitted its preliminary autonomy plan to the KDP. Immediately afterwards, the Iraqi media published a cable of support on behalf of a so-called rival KDP. The KDP leadership protested, claiming that it had sent no such cable. The Baath acknowledged that there had been a mistake. Prior to this, three central figures in the KDP leadership moved to Baghdad "with the planning and encouragement of several circles hostile to the Kurdish national movement leadership." These were 'Aziz Rashid 'Aqrawi, a member of the politburo; Hashim 'Aqrawi, a member of the KDP Central Committee; and Isma'il Mulla 'Aziz, another member of the Central Committee and the person in charge of the KDP's fifth branch in Baghdad. The KDP claimed that "the group of three . . . have [sic] become guests and protégés of several government agencies."[1]

Meanwhile, the Eighth Regional Congress of the Baath Party, which was held in January 1974, formulated its final position toward the KDP. Saddam Hussein played a central role in the congress, both in the debates and in the formulation of the report. Regarding the Kurdish question the report stated that, when the Baath leadership decided to cooperate with the KDP in the framework of the March Declaration, "it did not disregard the misguided policies pursued by certain segments of the KDP that have suspicious connections with separatist and reactionary circles, as well as separatist tendencies." At the same time, the Baath was aware of the different currents within the KDP and perceived that it had a responsibility "to help create suitable conditions, allowing for the Kurdish movement's commitment to Iraqi national (wataniyya) unity."[2]

Although the report acknowledged certain mistakes made by the Baath and by state apparatuses, it attacked the positions of the KDP, which it said had from the outset viewed the March Declaration as a means to obtain "tactical gains" and to put forth additional demands. Moreover, it added that "the separatist, suspect agents and the reactionary elements" within the KDP leadership were on the ascent after the agreement and started collaborating with "reactionary" and "imperialist" states to put a stop to the revolution. However, the report emphasized that the Kurdish question should not be addressed on the basis of the behavior and attitude of such factions "since this is a national question." The report stressed that the strategy adopted by the Baath to solve the problem peacefully had proven its effectiveness so that the task of "provocative elements" urging mutiny and destruction had become much more difficult.[3]

While the report left no doubt as to the Baath's intentions regarding the KDP, the regime continued for some time to behave as if the KDP was still party to the negotiations. On 16 January 1974, discussions were held in Baghdad on the autonomy plan of the national front, this time with the participation of the KDP. The Kurdish delegation was headed by Habib Muhammad Karim and the Baath delegation by Saddam. Although the meetings were presented as discussions between the national front and the KDP, the truth of the matter was that the KDP was asked to accept the plan without raising objections: "If the previous stage left room for debate and friction . . . the current stage is completely different."[4] The Lebanese newspaper *Al-Nahar* even reported that the plan would go into effect on 11 March 1974—with or without the approval of the KDP.[5]

On 29 January 1974 the "group of three," which meanwhile had been expelled from the KDP,[6] sent a scathing memorandum to Mulla Mustafa Barzani, which made headlines in the Iraqi weekly *Al-Rasid*. The memorandum, which according to the weekly highlighted "a deep rift within the KDP," contained twenty-two accusations, the most important of which included: activities contrary to democratic procedures and the principle of collective leadership within the KDP; the linking of the Kurdish people's fate with that of Barzani; collaboration with parties hostile to Iraq and the Kurds; attempts to establish a barrier between the Kurdish people and the Iraqi national movement; and, finally, the purging of true, committed party members and the advancement of opportunistic elements within the party. The message conveyed to Barzani was that "we have decided to liberate ourselves from your personal rule and influence."[7] *Al-Ta'akhi* responded to the "inflated" message in *Al-Rasid* with the claim that the KDP regarded the memorandum as part of a comprehensive plan aimed at weakening the Kurdish leadership and providing a pretext for stopping serious discussions, thus avoiding the finding of a definitive formula for autonomy.[8]

Toward the end of February 1974, the RCC issued two decrees. One prohibited the activity of parties that did not belong to the national front; namely, the KDP. The other disbanded the Supreme Committee for the Affairs of the North, which had until then included KDP members, and reconstituted it to include Saddam as its head and Baath Party members only.

Preparing the Ground for an Imposed Autonomy

While discussions with the KDP gave out, Saddam devoted all of his energy to strengthening his own position and that of the regime. One result of the Eighth Congress, whose decisions were to a large extent Saddam's, was the recognition of the latter as Iraq's de facto leader despite the fact that Ahmad Hasan al-Bakr continued to be the official head of state. A symbolic expression of this occurred on the anniversary of the ascension to power of the Baath on 8 February 1963 when Saddam was the only party member to be decorated with the al-Rafidayn Medal, First Class, as a token of appreciation for his action on behalf of the party and the revolution. On the same day, a committee headed by Saddam that had been established two weeks earlier announced a series of popular measures, including a significant increase in the earnings of all salaried workers—first and foremost in the army and the security services—a reduction of taxes, and the provision of free education at all levels.

Saddam increasingly emphasized his own position in the army. A symbolic manifestation of this was the medal that he received from the Iraqi Air Force in February 1974 in appreciation of "his outstanding services" for the force. The urge to increase his influence in the military stemmed not only from Saddam's need to create a counterweight to President al-Bakr and overcome the "military inferiority complex" that had hounded him because he had not served in the army, but also from his assessment that the army would soon be needed to enforce the autonomy plan.

As the targeted date for autonomy to take effect approached, the front with Iran heated up. Starting in early 1974, when negotiations over the Shatt al-Arab waterway reached an impasse, a series of border incidents occurred between Iraq and Iran, the most serious one on 10 February, with each country blaming the other for initiating hostilities.[9] Iran's attempts to disrupt Baghdad's move were prompted by Iran's perception of a twofold danger in the implementation of autonomy for the Kurds in Iraq: the loss of the Kurdish card, which was Iran's most important bargaining chip against Iraq, and the creation of an autonomy model, which the Kurds in Iran might wish to imitate. Some observers believed that, although it was Iraq that brought up the border incidents for discussion in the United Nations, the incidents in fact served Iraqi interests in that they allowed Baghdad to move divisions to the Kurdish region under the cover of responding to an Iranian threat.

At the same time, the 8th Division was established, with its headquarters in Erbil and Taha al-Shakarji as its commander. Al-Shakarji became familiar with the area in 1963 when he "gained distinction" for his brutal acts against the Kurds.[10] In Kirkuk, North Koreans were said to be helping train a mixed army and paramilitary group controlled by Baghdad.[11] Two weeks before the publication of the Autonomy Law, the Iraqi Army was put on high alert.

On 25 February 1974, Saddam paid a secret three-day visit to Moscow, apparently to seek the Soviet Union's blessing for the autonomy plan. The inclusion of Iraqi chief of staff 'Abd-al-Jabbar Shanshal in the delegation reinforced the assumption that Saddam also sought to obtain additional arms from the Soviets against the backdrop of Iraq's arms race with Iran and the possibility of a renewed war against the Kurds. On 3 March, Saddam convened a meeting of the national front to discuss the results of the visit and the implementation of autonomy on the planned date. The front approved the final wording of the autonomy draft and referred it to the RCC to enforce it as a law.

Meanwhile, Barzani made a last attempt to engage in a dialogue with the Baath. On 8 March, his son Idris arrived in Baghdad at the head of a Kurdish delegation to meet with Saddam. Since the Kirkuk issue was the main bone of contention, the parties discussed no less than eight alternative solutions to the problem. During the talks, Idris vowed that the Kurds would burn all "their bridges" with Iran should an agreement be reached with the Baath.[12] However, instead of drawing closer to the Kurdish proposals, the Baath extraordinary congress of 9 March decided to pass the Autonomy Law at the designated time. It also put forth two proposals in the form of an ultimatum to solve the Kirkuk question. One entailed a joint administration of the province, which would come under the auspices of the central government. The other entailed the division of the province so that two of its districts would be annexed to the autonomous region and the rest would be placed under the central government's control. The Kurds were allowed fifteen days to accept one of the two proposals.

Idris, who regarded the government's action as an ultimatum, stopped the discussions and went back to Kurdistan. However, on 10 March 1974, Dara Tawfiq arrived in Baghdad with an alternate proposal for a joint administration under the auspices of the autonomous government. Barzani declared that he would fully agree to the regime's autonomy program should his proposal be accepted. However, the Baath rejected this as well as two other proposals, signaling the failure of all attempts to hold a dialogue.[13]

The Baath Autonomy Model

On the fourth anniversary of the March Declaration, the regime issued the Autonomy Law, proclaiming its commitment to implement the declaration. At the same time, it published an amendment to the interim constitution, which included an article stating that "the area (*mintaqa*) containing a Kurdish majority shall enjoy autonomy."[14]

A closer examination of the law would show that it disregarded some of the important demands that had been made by the KDP: the demarcation of the autonomy boundaries and the inclusion of Kirkuk within them; the appointment of Kurds to all state apparatuses, including the army, in proportion to their percentage in the population; and the allocation of resources to the Kurds in proportion to their percentage in the population. The law indicated that the security apparatuses and nationality (*jinsiyya*) police shall be subordinate to the Ministry of Interior, which shall appoint and dismiss officials in this sector.

The Autonomy Law did allow the establishment of a legislative body for the Kurds,[15] but the ensuing paradox was that the Kurds would have an elected legislative assembly (*al-majlis al-tashri'i*) while no such body existed in the center.[16] The law also permitted the establishment of an executive council. But in contrast to the Kurdish proposal, the head of the council was not to be elected by the legislative assembly, but was to be appointed by the president of the state who was also authorized to dismiss the head and to disband the executive council.

The main step by which the regime attempted to insure itself against deviations on the part of Kurdish legislative or executive bodies was to authorize a supervisory body composed of the Court of Appeals in Baghdad to repeal any decision made by these two or any other bodies in the autonomous region. The fact that the president was given the authority to disband the legislative assembly provided another safety valve. Erbil, rather than Sulaymaniyya, was established as the administrative center of the autonomous zone because of its greater accessibility and because it could be controlled more easily than Sulaymaniyya, which had been a stronghold of Kurdish nationalism for many generations.

Immediately after publication of the law, Radio Baghdad broadcast statements made earlier by Saddam in a meeting of the national front. Saddam explained that the Baath had, up to the last minute, attempted to reach an agreement with the KDP on the Autonomy Law—attempts which the KDP had thwarted. He mentioned three reasons for the regime's determination to promulgate the Autonomy Law at this time, the KDP's requests for a postponement notwithstanding. First, the Baath Party sought to strengthen its bonds of trust with the Kurdish people in light of the disappointments inherited from previous regimes and recent attempts to cast doubt on the regime's intentions to grant autonomy to the Kurds. Second, it sought to prove that "the Kurds are sons of our people, and we are more devoted in our concern for their future than those who call themselves members of the Kurdish nation (*qawmiyya*)." Finally, according to a subsequent issue of *Al-Thawra*, Saddam hinted that the KDP had sought to thwart the implementation of the March Declaration and the Autonomy Law since "they wanted [to establish] a new state in Iraq."[17]

As to the dispute over the borders of the autonomy and the KDP demand that Kirkuk be included within these borders, Saddam maintained that the Baath did not view autonomy as a rift between Iraqis and Kurds, but as a "full merger alongside the demarcation of an area in which national rights will be upheld." He emphasized that it was impossible to track down "the shadow" of every Kurd and grant autonomy to any piece of land where a Kurd happened to live. Saddam stressed that, if this had been feasible from a "legal" and "psychological" standpoint, such autonomy would have been designated as "autonomy for

Iraq" and not for the Kurds since it would have pertained to all Iraqis. He dismissed the argument that the Kurds had "a historic right" to the Kirkuk area because it had been Kurdish in the past and emphasized that, by the same logic, the Arabs would now have to claim Spain for themselves.[18]

Saddam disclosed that the KDP had been willing to accept the Autonomy Law until the very last moment on the condition that the Baath would concede Kirkuk. However, the regime rejected this, stating that it was non-negotiable. Saddam also rejected Kurdish demands for state budget allocations proportional to their percentage in the population, arguing that such a formulation might be applicable in a federal union, but not in the framework of autonomy. Regarding elections for the Kurdish legislative assembly, he candidly and undiplomatically rejected the possibility of holding such elections in the near future.[19]

Finally, Saddam presented the KDP with an ultimatum to join the front and to accept the Autonomy Law within fifteen days, underlining that "during this time period, we will not seek an alternative to you . . . [but] subsequently, we will not agree to an alliance with you. . . . After this date, other representatives of the KDP will possibly represent the party in the national front."[20]

In retrospect, it can be said that the Baath did advocate autonomy, but only as a means to assimilate the Kurds and strengthen their linkage to the nation-state. This contrasted sharply with the Kurdish movement's aspirations to establish a separate identity for Kurdistan and to weaken its links with the center. Thus, the clash of identities and interests did not weaken over time, but actually intensified. The Baath's ambivalent outlook may explain the paradox of a regime with a pan-Arab, nationalistic outlook—such as that of the Baath—recognizing another nation's right to autonomy within its borders. From a practical standpoint, the regime sought to use the autonomy framework as a springboard for achieving the following objectives: (1) to win the support of the Kurdish people and stifle its urge for rebellion; (2) to neutralize Kurdish guerrilla resistance and bring about the army's control over the area without waging war; and (3) to drive a wedge between the Kurdish leadership and the Kurdish population with the final goal of getting rid of that leadership.

Closing the Circle

On the morrow of the publication of the Autonomy Law, the Iraqi media reported with great fanfare a cable from the KDP expressing enthusiastic support for the law. It was signed by three of its leaders: ʻAziz Rashid ʻAqrawi, Hashim ʻAqrawi, and Ismaʻil Mulla ʻAziz. This was a broad hint that the group of three was destined to function as an "alternative" KDP. Another shadowy supporter of the law was the Kurdistan Revolutionary Party (KRP), headed by ʻAbd-al-Sattar Tahir Sharif. On the same day, hundreds of pamphlets produced by the KRP and calling on the Kurds to support the law were distributed in Baghdad and in other cities. The Iraqi media reported on the support of two other Kurdish personalities: Shaikh 'Uthman Barzani, the son of Barzani's older brother Ahmad, and Barzani's own son 'Ubaydullah. In his cable, 'Ubaydullah stated that "our Kurdish people . . . are now being asked to realize their legitimate right to autonomy in cooperation with our noble and good Iraqi people and all the patriotic forces to whom Iraq's unity and the happiness of its people are important."[21]

While expressing support for the law, the ICP sought to leave an opening for the KDP to join the national front and help implement autonomy. *Pravda*, the newspaper of the Soviet Communist Party, also praised the Autonomy Law and warned against the emergence of "rightist forces" that were attempting to arouse separatist tendencies.

For its part, the KDP kept silent. The 12 March 1974 issue of its newspaper, *Al-Ta'akhi*, disregarded the Autonomy Law altogether and announced its decision to stop publication. Two days later, Radio Kurdistan renewed its broadcast after a four-year hiatus. In its first broadcast, it urged the Kurdish people to take up arms "to save Kurdish land from *Iraqi hands*" (emphasis added).[22] Even prior to the government's announcement, there were rumors that all able-bodied men had moved out of the towns and that, in some cases, "entire villages were evacuated to the hills."[23] Shortly afterward, Barzani initiated skirmishes with the Iraqi Army along the Turkish border. Following his initial successes, Kurds from various government sectors flocked to the movement's camp. These included Kurdish officers and soldiers from the Iraqi Army, policemen, engineers, physicians, students, clergy, and others. Some sources put the total number of those who joined the movement at 100,000, including 60 physicians, 4,500 teachers, 5,000 policemen, 160 engineers, 100 officers, and many students.[24]

In the meantime, an Iranian newspaper article was published in indirect support of the Kurds. It stated that "while the Iraqi Army has prepared itself for many years of war, enthusiasm for and faith in gaining actual autonomy has also strengthened manifold among the Kurds" over the past few years.[25] Meanwhile, a right-wing Likud member of Israel's parliament (Knesset), Yedidya Be'eri, appealed to Israeli foreign minister Abba Eban, demanding that the government officially declare its support of the Kurds.[26] His demand was not acted on, however. Neither were Barzani's attempts to bring the United States publicly to the Kurds' side any more successful. Nonetheless, Barzani's contacts with the United States regarding the supply of arms and other assistance continued behind the scenes.

On 23 March 1974 Soviet defense minister Andrey Grechko visited Iraq. The timing of the visit, close to the end of the ultimatum, was no coincidence since it was aimed to pressurize the Kurds into accepting the Autonomy Law. A later report maintained that Grechko sought to mediate between the Baath and the Kurds but that, on advice of Iran and the United States, Barzani had rejected the mediation efforts.[27] Nevertheless, it stands to reason that, if this had indeed been the case, such advice would merely have reinforced an earlier decision by Barzani that had matured against the background of developments over a number of years. On the other hand, based on the circumstances and timing of Grechko's visit, it did not seem that Grechko still harbored hopes of reconciling the two sides, but rather of giving his seal of approval to the Baath initiative. During his visit to Moscow on 25 February 1974, Saddam had apparently reached an understanding with the Soviet Union regarding its support of the regime, but both the Soviets and the Iraqis postponed the official declaration until the end of the ultimatum period so as to put the blame on the Kurds for thwarting a solution. At the end of Grechko's visit, a joint declaration was issued on the strengthening cooperation between Iraq and the Soviet Union in the military as well as in other fields. The declaration also contained an indirect message to both the Kurds and Iran to the effect that the Soviet Union would stand by Iraq in any future war.

On 26 March 1974, the final date for the Kurds to respond to the ultimatum, the Baath issued the Law on the Legislative Assembly of the Kurdistan Area. According to Article 10, the members of the first legislative assembly may be appointed (*ikhtiyar*) without a formal election procedure (*'an ghayr tariq al-intikhab*).[28] This represented a significant erosion of the Autonomy Law, which had stipulated that members of the assembly were to be elected, not appointed.

Soon afterward, the regime initiated sweeping personnel changes aimed at weakening Barzani's camp. On 4 April 1974, three Kurdish district governors loyal to Barzani were replaced by regime loyalists. On 7 April, the five pro-Barzani Kurdish ministers were replaced by pro-Baath Kurds. The Ministry for the Affairs of the North was also disbanded. Among the new ministers was Barzani's son 'Ubaydullah, minister without portfolio. Explaining 'Ubaydullah's appointment, Saddam stated that "our loyalty in our new politics is not family or tribal loyalty. These patterns have passed from the world. We believe and do know that there are other people in the Barzani family who are responding positively and without deceit to our policy. . . . In the future, you will see from whence come the people who support our policy."[29]

On 21 April, Taha Muhyi-al-Din Ma'ruf was appointed vice-president. Radio Kurdistan strongly attacked the new "star" as an opportunist who represented only himself, who was willing to collaborate "with a band of dictators in their criminal actions and to kill and slaughter his own people in return for a contemptible post that does not represent any real power in the regime, although it may appear to be an important position."[30]

The KDP's response to the Autonomy Law came only after the armed struggle had already begun. The response, which was intended to justify rejection of the law, was no longer directed at the authorities, but was intended to gain the support of the Kurdish camp and international players—especially

Western countries. In an interview with the *New York Times*, Barzani stated that "Kurdistan has become an important factor in the military and political equation of the Middle East. It is the duty of Western governments to advise us of the role it should play." However, he also emphasized that the Kurds had yet to obtain the "serious, comprehensive, and firm" support of the West.[31]

The rejection of autonomy was based on three arguments: past experience with the Baath; the way in which autonomy was established; and, most importantly, the substance of autonomy. The KDP pointed to the tactical approach of the Baath after the conclusion of the agreement. The overall objective of this approach—manifested, among other things, by two assassination attempts against Barzani—was to undermine the KDP's authority; to maneuver it into an isolated position in the Kurdish camp; and, finally, to exclude it from a settlement of the Kurdish problem. As to the way in which the Autonomy Law had been approved, the KDP stressed that it entailed a unilateral action by the Baath, which underscored the Baath's "arrogant" and "chauvinistic" character, and was intended to confront the KDP and the entire Kurdish camp with a fait accompli. As evidence, the KDP cited the fact that the Baath had disregarded the KDP's autonomy plan and refused altogether to discuss any changes in its own plans. Describing the Autonomy Law as "emasculated, fraudulent, distorted, and false," the KDP argued that the Baath had emptied autonomy of all content and had changed it into a mere decentralization program.[32]

The KDP pointed out the many weak points in the law, the most important of which were the following: the central government was to control the legislative and executive bodies of autonomy; there was no mention of a fair representation in central institutions, including sensitive posts in the government and the army; and the Kurds would have no say in the formulation of domestic and foreign policy, which was to be within the exclusive purview of the Baath. Most importantly, the Baath had not moved closer to the Kurds regarding Kirkuk, "although all historical, geographic, population and economic facts show beyond any doubt that Kirkuk province is a Kurdish area."[33] Above all, the absence of democratic institutions in the center was perceived by the Kurds as a main flaw because it precluded a real guarantee for the implementation of genuine Kurdish autonomy.

These arguments notwithstanding, it seemed that the main motive behind the rejection of the Autonomy Law by the Kurds was their deep distrust of the regime. In the KDP's view, accepting such autonomy would be tantamount to signing a writ of submission that would lead not only to its own demise, but to that of the entire Kurdish national movement. However, this stance was not the outcome of a feeling of weakness as the KDP, headed by Barzani, continued to be the undisputed ruler of the Kurdish north. In addition, the Kurdish movement remained relatively unified despite the regime's ongoing attempts to divide it and sow dissension within its ranks, given that Jalal Talabani's camp continued to back Barzani's decisions, at least at this stage. In the spring of

1974, the leftist elements in the Kurdish camp—who initially had ardently supported the agreement with the Baath and were among the most vociferous opponents of relations with Iran—also reached the conclusion that the Baath did not desire an understanding with the KDP. Besides, Kurdish supporters of the Baath were not part of the Kurdish elite and did not enjoy much influence with the population. The support of Barzani's son 'Ubaydullah had more propagandist than political value. Another important factor that strengthened the Kurds' resolve was their belief that the United States would support them, at least behind the scenes. Against this background, one can understand the following statement by one of Barzani's followers regarding the Kurds' ability to thwart an Iraqi offensive: "Barzani is not stupid. He would not say no to the Iraqis if he thought that he could not repel an Iraqi offensive."[34] These assertions notwithstanding, Barzani's decision would become the cause of a fierce debate in the Kurdish camp, especially against the backdrop of future developments.

For its part, in deciding to impose autonomy unilaterally, the regime was motivated by a feeling of unprecedented strength and the conviction that it would finally be possible to crush the Kurdish rebellion headed by Barzani. The regime's feeling of power was somewhat justified. Its alliance with the Soviet Union, which took on added weight with the visit of the Soviet defense minister, intensified the regime's feeling that it had received the backing of a major power. Correspondingly, the army was greatly strengthened by a flow of modern arms. The economy also became stronger, having received an important boost from the increase in world oil prices and the flow of money to the state treasury. Another victory was the regime's success in driving a wedge between the KDP and the ICP, and the fact that the ICP had for the very first time aligned itself with the Baath—its historical and ideological rival. Above all, the regime was confident that the Kurds' willingness to fight had weakened significantly, due to the relative well-being and quiet that prevailed in the north following the 1970 agreement. Saddam's feeling of confidence prompted his declaration that "the maximum that we could consider was that Barzani should raise the white flag . . . we will never sit at the same table with these agents and negotiate with them because Mulla [Mustafa] Barzani has benefited extensively from such tactics in the past."[35]

The road to war was paved.

Notes

1. *Al-Ta'akhi* (Baghdad, daily), 11 February 1974.
2. *Revolutionary Iraq 1968–1973*, Report of the Eighth Regional Congress of the Arab Ba'th Socialist Party, Iraq, January 1974 (October 1974), pp. 102–108.
3. Ibid.
4. *Al-Thawra* (Baghdad, daily), 17 January 1974.
5. *Al-Nahar* (Beirut, daily) 8 February 1974.

6. According to another source, they were expelled before they left for Baghdad because they had disagreed with Barzani's policies. David McDowall, *A Modern History of the Kurds* (London: I. B. Tauris, 2004), p. 337.

7. *Al-Rasid*, as quoted by Syrian Arab News Agency, 10 February 1974, cited in *Daily Report*, 13 February 1974.

8. *Al-Ta'akhi*, 11 February 1974.

9. Public Record Office, FCO8/2307, 13 February 1974.

10. *Al-Nahar*, 18 March 1974. Shakarji was to be dismissed during the war in 1974 because of the high number of casualties among Iraqi soldiers. Ismet Sheriff Vanly, "Kurdistan in Iraq," in *A People Without a Country: The Kurds and Kurdistan*, ed. Gérard Chaliand (London: Zed Press, 1980), p. 179.

11. Public Record Office, FCO8/2307, 13 February 1974.

12. Chris Kutschera, *Le mouvement national kurde* (Paris: Flammarion, 1970), pp. 295–296.

13. Ibid., pp. 295–298.

14. The Autonomy Law was published in *Al-Thawra*, 12 March 1974. The Arabic term, which the KDP uses to refer to the autonomous area, is *iqlim*, a defined geographical region of land, as opposed to the term *mintaqa*, a region in the general sense and not one with clear demarcations and defined geographical features.

15. The wording of the law is "the elected (*muntakhab*) legislative body in the area."

16. The parliament, which was disbanded at the time of 'Abd-al-Karim Qasim's ascension in 1958, was revived in 1980 and included Baathi members only.

17. *Al-Thawra*, 15, 28 March 1974.

18. Ibid.

19. Ibid.

20. Ibid.

21. *Al-Thawra*, 13 March 1974; Iraqi News Agency, 12 March 1974, cited in BBC, 14 March 1974.

22. *Al-Hayat*, 15 March 1974.

23. Public Record Office, FCO8/2307, 10 March 1974.

24. *New York Times* (New York, daily), 1 April 1974; Vanly, "Kurdistan in Iraq," p. 180.

25. Radio Tehran, 16 March 1974, cited in BBC, 18 March 1974.

26. *Ma'ariv* (Tel Aviv, daily), 18 March 1974.

27. *New York Times*, 12 February 1976.

28. *Al-Thawra*, 27 March 1974.

29. *Al-Sayyad* (Beirut, weekly), 18–25 April 1974.

30. Voice of Iraqi Kurdistan, 22 April 1974, cited in BBC, 25 April 1974. Ma'ruf was believed to be a supporter of Talabani's faction.

31. *New York Times*, 1 April 1974.

32. Voice of Iraqi Kurdistan, 5 April 1974, cited in *Daily Report*, 9 April 1974.

33. Ibid.

34. Israel Defense Forces Radio, 29 March 1974, cited in *Daily Report*, 1 April 1974.

35. Iraqi News Agency, 25 April 1974, cited in BBC, 27 April 1974.

8

A Time for War

The eminent scholar of the history of war, Michael Howard, argues that "from the very beginning the principle of nationalism was almost indissolubly linked, both in theory and practice, with the idea of war." He further adds that "as nations came to define themselves and trace their origins, the history of their conflicts with one another became a central part of this process of definition, and the concept of 'nation' became inseparably associated with the war it fought." Thus, war has "epitomized national solidarity and self-sacrifice."[1] The case of the Kurds of Iraq is no different from that of other nations. What came to be termed as the fifth Kurdish war, which began in March 1974 and lasted an entire year, proved beyond doubt that the Kurdish movement had transcended tribal loyalties and was developing clearer national traits. However, the eventual Kurdish defeat caused a severe setback so that it would take another twenty years and another four wars, one of which was a civil war, for a more cohesive national movement to crystallize.

The Kurdistan Theater

The war of 1974–1975 was fiercer and bloodier than any of its predecessors. It was unique in that, unlike in the past, the Kurdish movement now employed conventional combat methods, with all that this implied for a movement trained only in guerrilla warfare. In addition, the Iraqi regime also had for the first time gained the open backing of a superpower, the Soviet Union. And perhaps most importantly, Iran became involved directly in a war that ended not due to the political engagement between the Iraqi government and the Kurds, as had been the case in the past, but between the Iraqi government and the Shah of Iran.

The development of a war revolving around the Iran-Iraq-Kurdish triangle strongly suggests that we should examine the war objectives of all three players. As it despaired of reaching an understanding with the Baath, the Kurdish movement now aimed to topple the regime and achieve through military superiority substantial autonomy, which would also include the province of Kirkuk within its boundaries. This region constituted a central objective in the Kurds' strategy because control over the oil resources it contained would grant them economic autonomy, enhance worldwide interest in the Kurdish problem, and strengthen their bargaining power vis-à-vis the central government. Even if the Kurds had a more far-reaching objective, that is, that of achieving independence, they would be wary of expressing it publicly—mainly out of fear of arousing animosity from their patron, Iran.[2]

As to Iran, its first objective was to topple the Baath regime, which constituted an ideological and political threat to the Iranian regime. Iran was nonetheless willing to be satisfied with a less far-reaching objective; namely, weakening the Baath to the point where it would moderate its radicalism and agree to concede its sovereignty over the disputed area in the Shatt al-Arab waterway. The Kurds would serve as a means to obtaining this goal—without, however, deriving any benefit from its achievement.

The Baath Party, for its part, sought to eliminate Mulla Mustafa Barzani's movement once and for all and to cut the KDP's Gordian knot with Iran while granting the Kurdish population a form of autonomy that would not pose a threat to the state's unity, but would be sufficiently enticing to distance the Kurdish masses from Barzani and ensure their loyalty to the Baath.

In surveying the developments pertaining to the war, we come across a major difficulty, the censorship that Baghdad imposed in real time on the war's very existence. Subsequently, Baghdad explained this policy by saying that "the battle was particularly sensitive and delicate because of its being an internal problem."[3] The absence of an on-the-spot official version of the war naturally makes it difficult to obtain a sufficiently balanced picture of it. We thus have to rely extensively on Kurdish, Arab, and non-Iraqi sources, which, unlike the Iraqi media, devoted great attention to the subject.

This was an all-out war conducted on several levels: military, socioeconomic, psychological-propagandist, and political. While the Kurds held the military initiative at the outset, Baghdad had the initiative on all other levels because it understood that superiority could be obtained only by a flexible combination of all four levels.

Regarding leadership in the Kurdish camp, Barzani was a vital force and unifying personality since "for most Kurds, Barzani came immediately after God."[4] The picture was less clear regarding the Iraqi regime's camp. One would have assumed that President Ahmad Hasan al-Bakr, who was supreme commander of the armed forces and who enjoyed extensive support in army circles, would be the one to lead the battle. However, eight years later, after al-Bakr's death, the Baath's political report of the Ninth Regional Congress claimed that Saddam Hussein "had planned the strategy of the battle against the rebellion and defined the battle tactics on the military, political, economic, psychological, and social levels."[5] It is reasonable to assume that this was a rewriting of history. But even if we accept the Baath report at face value, it is highly doubtful whether Saddam was as charismatic and as unifying a figure as Barzani, or that he could have mobilized extensive popular support to the extent that Barzani could, since the government did not issue any statements about the war for a long time.

The Kurds initiated the war on 12 March 1974, one day after the ultimatum came into force and as a protest against it. During the first stage of the war, which lasted until mid-April, the Peshmerga fighters succeeded in gaining control of a border strip 725 kilometers long—that is, the entire length of the border with Turkey and about 400 kilometers of the border with Iran—and an area of about 25,000 square kilometers.[6] They besieged garrisons at seven different locations, including at Zakho and Sulaymaniyya, and defeated or cut off the supply sources of some 12,000 troops positioned at strategic locations. The crowning achievement was the capture of the city of Rawanduz, which was especially important because of its location on the so-called Hamilton Road. This road, named after the British engineer who built it, extended from Erbil to the Iranian border, passing through the high mountain ridges of Mounts Handrin (2,825 meters) and Zawzaq (2,757 meters). It had become an exclusive lifeline, connecting the Kurds with Iran. The capture of Rawanduz boosted morale given that, until then, the Kurdish movement had had no control of any cities in Kurdistan, in all of which Iraqi Army garrisons were operating. In addition, the headquarters of the movement was located in three positions along Hamilton Road—at Nawperdan, Galala, and Hajj 'Umran—since the Kurds customarily switched headquarters out of fear of shelling.

A Kurdish memorandum explained the movement's initial success, pinpointing to the fact that "the whole Kurdish people stood firm behind its leadership," their prime motive being Kurdish patriotism. It mentioned that 100,000 people had left the towns for the liberated areas, including "many thousands of soldiers, non-commissioned officers, and officers."[7] Similarly, many Peshmerga fighters were operating in the framework of the border guard and thus faced no great difficulty in clearing army forces from these areas. Despite their thorough preparations, the Baathi authorities seemed surprised by the operational speed of the Kurds, as evidenced by the fact that they began to mobilize their reserves only in early April. The timing of the offensive, before the spring thaw in the mountains, and the inability of armed forces to move freely at that time of the year were also of great help to the Kurds. On the other hand, Baghdad sought to give the impression of having exhausted its political options and of having renounced large-scale military operations at the very moment when a response to the proposed ultimatum was expected. Indeed, immediately afterward, on 15 April, the Iraqi Army's spring offensive began. Its main goal was to liberate besieged garrisons and to break through the strongholds that had been seized by the Peshmerga. In mid-May, after weeks of bitter fighting, the army succeeded in regaining control of Zakho. This was of strategic importance, owing to both its location on the route connecting Iraq with Turkey and its status as a particularly important commercial route. The army apparently also succeeded in liberating the garrison forces at Shaqlawa and at Salah-al-Din near Erbil. However, it failed to regain control of 'Aqra, Rawanduz, and Qal'a Diza, despite the intense battles fought there.

Clashes on a smaller scale continued throughout June and July 1974, the initiative remaining primarily in the hands of the Peshmerga who used guerrilla methods to enter Kurdish cities under the cover of darkness, including Sulaymaniyya, Erbil, and Dohuk, where they carried out sabotage operations against governmental facilities, police stations, and military posts. There also were, albeit not overly successful, attempts to hit oil installations in Kirkuk.

The Iraqi Army's summer offensive began in August, reportedly with the assistance of Soviet instructors.[8] The objective of the offensive—which was a two-pronged offensive against Qal'a Diza and Rawanduz—was to besiege the main outposts of the guerrilla army, the headquarters of the rebellion, and the road connecting Kurdistan with Iran. Qal'a Diza fell on 19 August. The Kurds thus lost an important outpost from which they had been able to threaten Erbil, Sulaymaniyya, and Kirkuk. On 22 August, Rawanduz also surrendered. Nonetheless, the army did not succeed in gaining control of Hamilton Road, its main objective since 1961, because the Kurds controlled the two mountain ridges overlooking it; namely, the Zawzaq and the Handrin. Intense battles, which claimed many casualties on the Iraqi side, continued throughout September. In early October, the army managed to gain control of a segment of the Zawzaq ridge. The Kurdish movement itself acknowledged that the Iraqi Army's impressive gains had put the movement in a difficult situation. The Iranian assessment was that the Kurdish situation was critical and that, as the shah observed, they "seemed to have lost their previous fighting spirit."[9]

Nonetheless, the Iraqi goal of gaining control over the entire Kurdish area before the onset of winter was thwarted because of the military assistance Iran provided—for the first time quite directly and openly—to the Kurds. It included arms and ammunition, guided antitank missiles to stop large armored attacks, and ground-to-air missiles. Direct Iranian support also included army units in Galala, Ranya, and Qal'a Diza. According to various estimates, there were between 400 and 1,000 Iranian troops and officers in Iraq, some of them disguised as Peshmerga. In addition, Iranian forces on the border also provided support with their heavy artillery, which could reach Erbil. Iraq had no suitable response to this threat. Fearing the collapse of the Kurds before its objectives were achieved, Iran continued to support them in the following months by supplying food and training and dispatching guerrilla groups from Iran. This made it possible for the Kurds to stop the Iraqi Army's advance and at times even to push it back.[10] Though close to victory, the Iraqi Army was thus compelled to prepare for another round of war, a round that would have to be deferred because of the coming winter when the army could lose the advantage of armored and air force due to the rain and snow. As for the Kurds, their position was not good either. In contrast to the large area they had commanded at the start of the war, in early 1975 they were limited to a narrow, 80-kilometer-long border strip on the Iranian border. While sporadic engagements continued throughout January and February 1975, it became increasingly clear to Baghdad that it would not achieve military superiority as long as Iran continued to help the Kurds.

In conjunction with its military activities, the Iraqi regime developed a three-pronged strategy toward the Kurdish civilian population, aimed at breaking the Kurdish national movement's popular support base while increasing support for the regime. To erode support for the movement, the regime imposed an economic blockade, adopted terror tactics against the population, and pursued a policy of Arabization. At the beginning of the war, Saddam had already declared, "We are determined to impose a severe (*qasi*) economic blockade on the [Kurdish] area not under our control. . . . This is part of [our] military activity."[11] The embargo caused much harm, especially in the Badinan area, which extended along the Turkish border from Zakho to Barzan and had a population of about 500,000 people. It had devastating consequences, given Kurdistan's economic dependence on the center, the virtually hermetic sealing off of the border on the Turkish side, and the growing strain of keeping a supply route open into the area. Consequently, a near-famine situation had arisen in the area by the end of 1974. Food staples were in short supply and prices skyrocketed; at times, there was a three- to tenfold increase in prices. The black market, which the Kurdish leadership could not control, experienced a boon. The economic paralysis was also apparent in the villagers' inability to market their produce; mainly, tobacco and fruit. Baghdad worsened the situation by burning cultivated fields and rendering agricultural machinery inoperable. In fact, Baghdad's aim was "to starve out the occupants."[12]

Another Baghdad strategy was the indiscriminate aerial bombing of civilian populations. According to Kurdish claims, the Iraqi Air Force carried out about 1,328 sorties between April and June 1974 alone, destroying 300 Kurdish villages. In April the Iraqi Air Force attacked the city of Qal'a Diza, which had become a refuge for students and university faculty who had fled from Sulaymaniyya, killing 135 people.[13]

The air force dropped napalm bombs and phosphorous chemicals, newly acquired from the Soviets, the use of which was a clear breach of the Geneva Convention to which both Iraq and the Soviet Union were signatories. To further demoralize the Kurdish population, the Iraqi Army parachuted toy explosives to children, causing death and severe injury.[14]

Kurdish sources claimed that Soviet pilots flew some of these aircraft. Indeed, a secret document revealed that the Soviets had supplied "arms for use in the campaign," "advisors" and technicians, and "probably also a small number of pilots."[15] Furthermore, the Kurds also maintained that "the Russians have made Kurdistan a testing ground for the efficacy of their new weapons."[16] Baghdad never acknowledged such attacks against the civilian population. Therefore, no official source has ever allowed verification of the numbers of sorties reported by the Kurds. But even if the Kurdish data are exaggerated, aerial bombardments were apparently used as a tool to break the morale of the civilian population. It should be remembered that bombing of the Kurdish population in the 1920s had been a main tactic of the British Royal Air Force.[17] In an attempt to limit the number of civilian casualties, Barzani imposed a daytime curfew at the beginning of the war. Journalists in the area reported that students were forced to study in dark, poorly lit rooms. However, in the final analysis, the Kurdish leadership was powerless in the face of these attacks, especially given the clear asymmetry between the two camps: while the Iraqi population in the center was not subjected to the war at all, the Kurdish population bore its main brunt. At the same time, Arabization or de-Kurdization operations continued in three principal areas: Sinjar, Kirkuk, and Khanaqin.[18]

All of this created a major refugee problem. In the first stage, refugees fled from cities and villages into the heart of Kurdistan where they found refuge in caves. However, when the economic and military pressure became still more onerous, refugees began to flee to Iran. In April 1974, Barzani appealed to the shah to accept Kurdish refugees in his country. By September the stream of refugees totaled 100,000, and by December 135,000. A further 100,000 attempted to cross the Turkish border, which was closed to them.[19] Thus, the number of displaced people reached 500,000 by the end of the year. In addition to causing a humanitarian problem, the mass flight also constituted an economic, ethical, and organizational burden for the Kurdish leadership. Instead of focusing on military-organizational problems, it was forced to contend with the need to find housing and food for refugees whose escape route passed through the area under KDP control. The refugee problem also became a burden for Iran, which opened twelve refugee camps and allocated $100 million to them.[20] Nonetheless, Iran cleverly used the refugees as a propaganda tool with the world and as a bargaining card with the Kurdish leadership and Baghdad.

Another channel through which the authorities attempted to influence the Kurdish population was by waging a propaganda war, spearheaded by Barzani's son 'Ubaydullah and nephew Shaikh 'Uthman. Also recruited were Kurdish ministers, members of the progovernment Kurdish parties, and members of the national front. The propaganda campaign was aimed at destroying Barzani's image. In interviews with the Iraqi and foreign press, Barzani's opponents disclosed his connections with Iran, Israel, and the United States. They denounced him as a traitor to the homeland, as the leader of a tribal gang, as senile and adventurous, as a reactionary feudalist who did not care for the Kurdish people's welfare, and as a man who did not represent the Kurdish people's national aspirations. 'Ubaydullah went as far as to declare that "we don't regard this as a war of liberation. It's a mopping up operation."[21] On more than one occasion,

Baghdad proclaimed Barzani's end to be near. In September, it leaked a report on his flight to Iran; in December, it reported his death.[22]

At the same time, the regime sought to develop a locus of support for the Baath by establishing institutions of autonomy. But their attempts to establish such institutions quickly met with numerous difficulties. The main difficulty stemmed from the volatile military situation and from a weakening of state control over the Kurdish cities during the initial months of fighting, which limited the regime's freedom of action in the area. Another difficulty, mentioned by Saddam himself, was a "volatile political situation which had not yet settled" and which precluded the publication of the names of members of the autonomous institutions immediately after the introduction of the Autonomy Law.[23] The KDP claimed that the regime found it difficult to staff the institutions of autonomy with Kurds. This claim could perhaps be confirmed by the fact that the Baath announced a list of members of the (appointed) legislative assembly as late as 30 July 1974. Moreover, the list was only partial, given that it included a mere sixty of the eighty members stipulated by the law. The Iraqi Revolutionary Command Council's announcement clarified that the names of the remaining twenty members of the assembly would be published in another RCC resolution "when political conditions permit Kurdish citizens to join the assembly, who, in the current circumstances, cannot fulfill their national duty."[24] However, in the second round of appointments on 24 September, the regime also came up short, failing to fill the last eight seats in the assembly. It seems that the Kurds refrained from joining the assembly out of a sense of true Kurdish solidarity inasmuch as it was clear to everyone that a legislative assembly, whose members are appointed, is "an assembly in name [only]" and has nothing to do with true autonomous institutions. Potential collaborators with the regime also feared that Barzani would seek revenge against them if he were to become stronger. Saddam echoed these fears when he stated that "the Kurdish citizens have always feared that the day would come when those who fight on the side of the revolution [i.e., the Baath] would again be under Barzani's scepter." But he vowed, "this day will never come."[25]

On 5 October when the military situation was somewhat more favorable to the regime, seventy-two members of the legislative assembly, some of whom were said to be Arabs, attended the opening session[26] headed by Babakr Pishdari. At the same time a fourteen-member executive council, headed by Hashim 'Aqrawi, was appointed. However, this measure was of a purely symbolic and propagandist nature. According to foreign correspondents, 4,000 Iraqi troops provided security for the participants of which more than 100 were journalists. In fact, few Kurds participated in the ceremony. Security measures included helicopter air cover.[27] Al-Bakr and Saddam were absent from the ceremony, which bore a makeshift, spur-of-the-moment character, as it took place in a school because the council had no premises of its own. The oath, taken in the Arabic language, included the words "to preserve the safety of the Iraqi republic and its territorial integrity." The ceremony did not generate much popular en-thusiasm.[28] All the council members moved to Baghdad the following day; they did not reconvene in 1974 or in 1975. A member of the legislative assembly, Ra'uf Mustafa Ghaffur, was arrested in February 1975 and executed in May 1975 for unknown reasons.[29]

The Kurdish camp, for its part, attempted to attract international support. Foreign reporters constituted a vitally important channel for bringing the Kur-dish cause to world attention.[30] In general, the Kurds received extensive and sympathetic reports worldwide, with the exception of Lebanese newspapers such as *Al-Sayyad*, *Al-Shay'*, and *Al-Hawadith* whose reporting was hostile. Kurdish appeals were also channeled through international organizations. In early June, the movement appealed to the Secretary-General of the United Na-tions to intervene in what it termed the genocide that was being carried out in Kurdistan. The appeal went unanswered, however.[31] Even the Red Cross was not permitted to help injured Kurds because the Iraqi government insisted that the Kurdish question was a domestic issue in which intervention by interna-tional organizations was not warranted. The Kurds reacted by establishing the Kurdistan Red Crescent in the United Kingdom—a move that elicited protests from Baghdad on the ground that the term *red crescent* was restricted to inde-pendent Muslim countries and that Iraqi Kurdistan, which was headed by "a handful of unknown adventurers," did not need such assistance.[32]

When the Arab summit conference convened in Rabat between 19 and 26 October 1974, Barzani sent the conferees a cable asking that they appoint a commission to investigate events in Kurdistan and help "end the war between brothers" and "save the Iraqi people."[33] This appeal went unanswered, too. The Kurdish camp also tried its hand at propaganda, of which Radio Kurdistan was an important tool, occasionally even making direct appeals to the Iraqi Army. In one such appeal, the radio station called on army officers to rebel against the Baath regime, which it claimed had provoked internecine warfare, had dis-criminated in favor of Baathist officers by removing them from the areas of fighting, and had prohibited official burial services for other Iraqi officers who were killed in battle.[34] But the main target audience of the broadcasts was the Kurdish population itself, which was called on to enlist in the war effort. How-ever, it seems that these broadcasts sometimes missed their mark. In the opin-ion of the Kurdish national activist, Ismet Sheriff Vanly, the daily reports of Radio Kurdistan on the shelling of the civilian population caused confusion among the Kurds and hastened their flight.[35]

A Balance of Weakness

Despite the large military forces involved in the fighting, this war again re-vealed both sides' basic weakness and inability to bring about a decision by force of arms. The mobilization for the war in the Kurdish camp was unprecedented. Many Kurds abandoned their jobs, even in governmental institutions, and joined the Peshmerga. According to some estimates, at one point the Pershmerga forces reached a peak of more than 50,000 regular combatants.[36] However, more than one-half were new forces, who were just then joining the rebellion and lacked military experience and training. Military equipment, which increased quantitatively, continued to consist mainly of light arms. The supply of arms depended primarily on one source, Iran. Facing this guerrilla army was a well-trained and well-equipped regular army, which according to various estimates included between 80,000 and 85,000 troops, in addition to—as should be emphasized—20,000 mostly Kurdish mercenaries, approximately 600 tanks, and 200 aircraft. These numbers are especially impressive when compared to the Iraqi Army's order of battle in 1974–1975. According to the Institute for Strategic Studies in London, the order of battle in those years included 100,000 soldiers, 218 aircraft, and 1,390 tanks.[37] No less important were the military supplies provided by the Soviet Union, the quantity of which increased throughout the fighting in 1974 and in early 1975. An agreement on the sale of French arms to Iraq, signed in January 1975, further intensified the Soviet Union's wooing of Iraqi arms buyers.

In view of this awesome military machine, the Kurdish movement was apparently compelled to take measures that were to create problems in the long term. The first entailed a transition to conventional combat on Iran's advice. This move greatly hampered Kurdish combatants who were not trained in conventional warfare. The second was Barzani's request during a meeting with the shah at the end of October 1974 for direct help from the Iranian Army to prevent the collapse of the movement. The shah was, by his own confession, facing a dilemma. He had to support the Kurds. If he did not, either the Baath regime in Iraq would become unacceptably strong or the Kurds would all go Communist—or both.[38] This request, and the ensuing Iranian military involvement, had ramifications on three levels: it further increased the Kurds' dependence on Iran; it brought Iran and Iraq to the brink of a military confrontation; and it denied Iraq a military victory. The Kurdish dependence on Iran was not only military and economic, but political as well. One manifestation of the Kurdish movement's lack of political freedom was the fact that, although it challenged the regime's autonomy program and the autonomous institutions established in October, it did not establish its own autonomous institutions, being satisfied with the appointment earlier, in April 1974, of a "government" composed of nine Kurdish ministers. It can be assumed that Iran's sensitivities played an important part in the movement's deliberations inasmuch as the Kurdish movement established autonomous institutions of its own; for example, as it had done in 1962 when its dependence on an outside power was not yet so great.

The economic blockade imposed by the regime on the liberated parts of Kurdistan increased the Kurdish economic dependence on Iran and revealed a serious infrastructural problem in the Kurdish area. Given considerations of control and management, successive Iraqi governments had been careful not to connect the different villages in Kurdistan with one another via an internal road network. Rather, they connected the villages with only the main cities in their districts, which were in turn connected to the capital. Kurdistan's dependence on the center, which stemmed from this, made it extremely difficult for Kurdish combatants to reach many of the more remote villages because the main cities of the district were not under their control. Consequently, the Badinan area was cut off in the winter of 1974–1975 and it was difficult for the leadership to satisfy the population's basic needs. This traffic network also created serious logistical problems for the movement. For example, Kurdish guerrilla fighters who wished to move from the district of Sulaymaniyya to the northern Baliq region were forced to go via the cities of districts in Iranian territory and, from there, back into Iraqi Kurdistan. The Kurdish leadership also proved incapable of solving serious problems that developed in the rear, namely among the noncombatants. True, identification with the Kurdish national cause was greater than at any time in the past and morale was high. However, high spirits could not sustain the population in the face of a well-oiled war machine. Indeed, the refugee problem was the movement's Achilles' heel. The number of casualties was also relatively high, estimated at approximately 2,000 killed and a much higher number of injured civilians and combatants.[39]

Another weak point, but with much deeper roots, was the gap between the movement's leadership and the largely rural combatants on the one hand, and the intellectuals and urban dwellers who were then joining the ranks of the movement en masse on the other. The leadership failed to bring the latter into the fold. Most of them did not participate in the war itself, nor did they assume command and leadership roles.[40] Thus, the leadership missed the opportunity to meld all layers of Kurdish society into the national crucible. The mutual suspicion that prevailed between the two camps constituted a nearly insurmountable barrier to a true partnership. However, organizational problems also played a part. In hindsight, it seems that the Kurdish leadership continued to act more or less along tribal patterns and did not have the competence to conduct an all-out war. Neither was it capable of organizing and training new volunteers while conducting a war and simultaneously tending to the rear. The KDP's worst shortcoming was its failure to prepare alternative political and military plans. Instead, it was pulled along by events.

From the outset, the Baghdad government had been optimistic about achieving a quick victory through military means. It estimated that it would liquidate Barzani's movement within two months.[41] There were indeed grounds for optimism. The economic situation was strong thanks to the large revenues, which were given a boost by the dizzying increase in oil prices following the October War of 1973. The domestic political situation also seemed stable due to the regime's consolidation, the Communists' almost unreserved support of the

Baath (the KDP accused the ICP of participating in the war against the Kurds), and the mobilization of a significant segment of Kurds to help in the war against the Barzanis. I have already mentioned the powerful forces that were at the regime's disposal, including the backing of the Soviet Union and Turkey's cooperation against the Kurdish movement (see Chapter 4).

Despite all the factors that initially favored the regime, Baghdad was forced to change its estimations time and again: in the spring, it predicted victory for the coming summer; in the summer, for the coming fall; in the fall, for the coming winter. The blitzkrieg became a protracted war of attrition that damaged the regime's prestige and credibility.

Paradoxically, following the military successes in October 1974, there were clear signs of the regime's difficulties in contending with the war. In a meeting between Saddam and the commanders of divisions involved in the war, the latter "pointed out that they could not achieve their military aims in the north" and expressed their desire for a political solution.[42] This was evidenced by the fact that the Iraqi Army had to entrench itself in its positions, expedite arms procurements, and conduct a comprehensive call-up of reserves for the third time in November. These successes were costly. Total state expenditures during the year of war were estimated at about $4 billion.[43] However, even if the regime could contend with the economic problem relatively easily, it was much harder for it to contend with the problem of casualties, which had always been a sensitive subject. At the end of the war, the Iraqi chief of staff 'Abd-al-Jabbar Shanshal reported that 1,640 soldiers had been killed and 7,903 injured.[44] Later on, Saddam admitted to much higher numbers: 16,000 killed or wounded in the army and 60,000 killed or wounded among army personnel and civilians combined.[45] The great disparity between these figures reflects Baghdad's extreme sensitivity. Only after a lengthy period of time could the regime provide numbers that seemed closer to the truth.

Unresolved conflicts posed serious dangers to the Baath, the most imminent of which was the possibility of the army's intervention to topple the regime—as had happened to the first Baath regime in 1963. In fact, the fighting in Kurdistan was reported to be going badly for the Iraqi Army, which was on the brink of revolt.[46] Baghdad's pressing need for arms increased its dependence on the Soviet Union. Soviet backing, which was considered an important political and military asset for Baghdad at the outset of the war, thus became a burden as Iraq sought to find alternative ways to end the war. Finally, it should be remembered that Iraq's military successes in the autumn of 1974 drew Iran into the war, a development that was liable to involve the two countries in a direct, massive confrontation.[47]

Signs of the regime's internal difficulties became apparent in the fall of 1974. In early October, the RCC issued two laws. One stipulated the death penalty for economic violations "that endanger the national economy."[48] According to Kurdish claims, it was used against persons who attempted to smuggle food and other vital products into the blockaded Kurdish area. Another law stipulated the death penalty for all spies, and not just for those who spied for Israel or an enemy country, as had been the case in the past. On 13 October when this law was issued, Baghdad announced the uncovering of a spy network that worked for Iranian intelligence, with the goal to "spread and deepen sectarianism (*ta'ifiyya*) among the people and spread rumors to damage the people's morale."[49] The disclosure of this network (whether true or fabricated) and the language of the announcement indicated that agitation was widespread among the Shi'a, as can be deduced from the use of the expression *sectarianism*, which in Iraqi terminology refers to the Shi'a. Another problem implied by the language of the announcement was the population's declining morale, apparently due to the growing number of war casualties. In November it became known that death sentences had been handed down against five Shi'i clerics and scholars, and prison terms imposed against others on the charge of belonging to "an illegal Islamic party" called al-Da'wa (the Call).[50] It is not clear whether a connection actually existed between the spy network mentioned above and al-Da'wa because the Baghdad government had never mentioned the latter in public. In any case, the appeals of Shi'i leaders in Iraq, including Ayatullah Abu al-Qasim al-Musawi al-Kho'i, as well as those of Shi'i clerics and politicians in Lebanon and of Amnesty International, to commute the death sentences were of no avail and the five were executed on 5 December. According to a subsequent statement by Amnesty International, the background of the executions and imprisonments was the criticism leveled by the Shi'i population against the war[51] since, as is well known, most of the rank-and-file soldiers were Shi'a. Therefore, they constituted a higher proportion of the casualties.

The military high command also paid a heavy price. In the summer and fall of 1974, several senior commanders were discharged, including the commander of the 8th Division, General Taha al-Shakarji; the commander of the Republican Guard, Dawud al-Janabi; and the commander of the air force, Husayn Hiyyawi. Baghdad acknowledged only the transfer of the air force commander "to another military position," but denied that the transfer was a direct outcome of the unrest in the army. The *Daily Mail* claimed that the discharges had stemmed from the uncovering of a military conspiracy and ended in the execution of twenty-one senior officers.[52] The causes of the military unrest were manifold, including doubts about the aims of the Kurdish campaign, civilian interference in military affairs, and the numerous casualties.[53]

Shake-ups were also visible at government level. On 11 November 1974, personnel changes were carried out in twelve ministries: four ministers were dismissed and eight others were transferred. The transfers pertained to three ministries: the Ministry of Oil, the Ministry of Finance, and the Ministry of Agriculture and Agrarian Reform. The changes pointed to growing economic difficulties. In addition, they also placed persons close to Saddam in top-ranking positions; for example, 'Izzat al-Duri, minister of the interior; Taha Yasin

Ramadan, minister of industry and planning; and Tariq 'Aziz, minister of information. These people, who accompanied Saddam after his ascension to the presidency in 1979, would constitute the nucleus of his supporters until the fall of his regime in 2003. Their appointment indicated the strengthening of Saddam's position at the expense of the faction of al-Bakr.[54] Another indication for the political weakening of al-Bakr (who at the same time was personally affected by the death of his wife on 7 November) was the dismissal of Sa'dun Ghaydan, al-Bakr's confidant, from the position of interior minister. Ghaydan's ouster conceivably also reflected difficulties encountered by his ministry in recruiting soldiers. Another significant change was the appointment of Sa'dun Hammadi, a Shi'i and veteran party member with close relations with Iran, to the position of foreign minister. Some viewed this appointment as paving the way for a political option.

Tortuous Negotiations with Iran

Baghdad's understanding that the war would not end as quickly as initially seemed likely and that it entailed the danger of a direct military confrontation with Iran, which Baghdad most certainly did not want, led Iraq to seek alternative ways to solve the imbroglio that was threatening to unbalance the country. Aware that the way to eliminate the Kurdish movement passed through Iran, Baghdad initiated two complementary moves. The first concerned Iraq's political orientation and its image in Iranian eyes. The rulers in Baghdad, and especially Saddam, understood that Iran's fears of a friendship pact between Iraq and the Soviet Union were the main impetus to Iran's renewed involvement in the Kurdish question. It is for this very reason that Iraq sought to appease Iran by lowering its radical profile and softening its pro-Soviet orientation.[55] *Al-Nahar* defined this development as a desire "to be inside and outside the socialist camp at the same time."[56] However, it was precisely the war that made this development complicated. As the war became more protracted, Baghdad's dependence on military assistance from the Soviet Union increased so that it became more difficult to weaken political ties with it.

Nonetheless, Baghdad succeeded in opening up new economic and political options: forging economic links with the United States; renewing diplomatic relations with Great Britain in April 1974; cultivating political, economic, and military relations with France; lowering its profile with respect to the strategic pact between Iraq and the Soviet Union; leaking reports regarding Baghdad's differences of opinion with the Soviet Union; and, finally, opting for a rapprochement with pro-Western Arab countries, including Saudi Arabia, Jordan, and Egypt. The latter actually provided a bridge to a direct dialogue with Iran. It was clear that the indirect process of lowering the profile of Iraq's relations with the Soviet Union would not satisfy Iran; hence, the need to open a direct channel for dialogue. Given their close relations with the shah, Jordan and Egypt played an important role in the establishment of such channels of communication. The process began with preparatory discussions between representatives of Iran and Iraq held in Istanbul, in August 1974. The topic under discussion was an Iranian demand for delineating the border in the Shatt al-Arab waterway according to the thalweg line. Indeed, Iraq's consistent refusal to recognize the thalweg principle as a basis for negotiations was the main stumbling block to success.[57] For its part, Iraq demanded the cessation of Iranian aid to the Kurds. Previously, border incidents had become more numerous. It could reasonably be assumed, although not with complete certainty, that this was Iranian muscle flexing, intended to put pressure on Iraq during negotiations. Although border incidents intensified throughout the discussions in Istanbul, they failed to prompt Iraq to make concessions regarding the Shatt al-Arab. Referring to the link between the Iranian attacks and the discussions in Istanbul, Baghdad stated that the goals of the attacks were: (1) "to put pressure on Iraq during the negotiations, for the purpose of extortion"; and (2) "to provide assistance to the defeated clique of its agent, Mulla Mustafa Barzani." As to Iran's attempt to assist Barzani, Baghdad said that "it [Baghdad] has decided conclusively and unequivocally to eliminate completely and resolutely the perfidious clique" and that it was prepared to pay any price.[58] The negotiations were suspended on 28 August. The next day, Iraq complained to the United Nations about a large-scale concentration of Iranian forces, comprising five divisions, along its border. Meanwhile, an envoy from Egyptian president Anwar al-Sadat traveled to Baghdad and Tehran to mediate.

The second stage of the dialogue was set at the Arab summit conference in Rabat in October 1974, when Saddam headed the Iraqi delegation. The conference recommended that President Sadat, King Hassan II of Morocco, and King Hussein of Jordan launch a mediation mission. In November, Baghdad asked King Hussein to act as mediator between Iraq and Iran because of his good relations with the shah and his prior experience as arbiter, albeit in a failed conciliation effort, in 1969. In December, Sadat and Algerian president Houari Boumédienne engaged in intensive mediation activity, but failed in their endeavor because of Iraq's refusal to concede its sovereignty on the Shatt al-Arab. The shah, for his part, continued to demand this as an absolute condition while simultaneously conveying a positive message to Iraq to the effect that Iran did not encourage the Kurds to achieve independence in Iraq, given that the Kurds demanded only "some degree of autonomy within Iraq."[59] Indeed, the shah's main purpose was "to continue to keep the Kurds afloat" without being involved in a direct war with Iraq.[60]

The third stage in the mediation effort between Iraq and Iran began on 6 January 1975, when the shah visited Jordan (for the first time in ten years) and then Egypt from 8 to 12 January. An important part of the discussions in Jordan and Egypt concerned the conflict with Iraq. The talks resulted in a number of meetings in Istanbul between Iraqi foreign minister Sa'dun Hammadi and Iranian foreign minister 'Abbas 'Ali Khalatbari between 14 and 18 January—without, however, producing any results. In the meantime tension along the border escalated and, with it, Iranian aid to the Kurds. Escalation along the border continued into the first half of February. On 11 February, Saddam declared Iraq's "adherence to its sovereignty and its readiness to defend its territory and territorial waters in the Shatt-al-'Arab."[61] However, a few days later, a somewhat different tone crept into his remarks. Speaking to the Egyptian newspaper *Al-Ahram*, Saddam stated that "never has the political and military situation in the northern area been so good." He emphasized that Barzani had withdrawn under the pressure exerted by the army and that the Kurdish masses were abandoning him, so that "he remained [only] with his Israeli military advisers, while receiving protection and aid from abroad." In this context, he mentioned the aid provided by Arab elements, meaning Syria. Saddam, it should be noted, refrained from mentioning Iran's massive aid to the Kurds. In fact in his comments on the conflict with Iran, he spoke in a conciliatory tone, emphasizing the desire "to establish good-neighborly relations with it." Saddam clarified, in very practical tones, that the troubled relations were a result of a "*unilateral* violation of the 1937 treaty regarding navigation in the Shatt-al-'Arab" (emphasis added), but he did not insist, at least not this time, on Iraq's sovereignty over the Shatt al-Arab.[62]

The last stage of the negotiations occurred from 4 to 6 March 1975 in Algiers during a conference of the Organization of Petroleum Exporting Countries (OPEC). The shah and Saddam met twice during the conference, through the mediation—and in the presence of—Algerian president Boumédienne. In the final session of the conference, Boumédienne announced that an agreement had been signed between the shah and Saddam. In a surprising gesture of conciliation, the two met at the center of the meeting hall, shook hands, and embraced to the sound of wildly cheering attendees.

A Kurdish Defeat by Proxy: The Algiers Agreement

The core issue of the Algiers Agreement was the cessation of Iranian aid to the Kurdish national movement in Iraq, in exchange for Iraq's concession of its sovereignty over the Shatt al-Arab, which meant the delineation of the border according to the thalweg line.[63]

At different times, Baghdad had presented various versions of the circumstances that produced the agreement. Here, I will concentrate on two. The first version, which was presented when the agreement was signed, claimed that the agreement was anchored in the RCC resolution of 7 October 1973 regarding the settlement of the border problem between Iran and Iraq (which resulted in the Iraqi-Iranian reconciliation on the eve of the October War) and resolutions of the Eighth Baath Party Congress of January 1974. According to this version Iran, not Iraq, had opposed the terms of the agreement that subsequently took shape at Algiers.[64] The second version, which Saddam made public on the eve of the Iraq-Iran War in September 1980, stated that Iraq was compelled to take this "courageous, [and] serious" measure because of a nearly complete lack of ammunition, given that the Iraqi Air Force had only three heavy bombs with which to carry on the war against the Kurds. He also claimed that the Soviet Union was not upholding its military commitments to Iraq.[65]

Both this later version and the claim that the Soviet Union had failed to supply arms were factually incorrect. In fact, an especially large new arms deal had been signed with the Soviet Union in January 1975. The assertion about a lack of ammunition seemed like an ex post facto pretext intended entirely to deflect criticism from the army to the Soviet Union. And the first version, though accepted by some researchers, is not borne out when examined under close scrutiny. Neither the RCC decision of October 1973 nor the resolutions of the Eighth Congress of 1974 spoke of an Iraqi concession to Iran regarding the Shatt al-Arab. On the contrary, the political report of the Eighth Congress, while expressing a desire to solve the problems with Iran peacefully, emphasized "its determination to defend Iraq's legitimate rights."[66] In addition, the claim that the shah had opposed the terms of the agreement until the last moment ignored the fact that he had secretly offered Iraq a cessation of Iranian aid to the Kurds as early as the summer of 1972, in exchange for Iraqi concessions regarding the Shatt al-Arab. Iraq rejected his offer, however. It should also be remembered that the shah never departed from his demands regarding the Shatt al-Arab nor was there any Iraqi personality who demonstrated a readiness to make any concessions at all.

There were several, particularly important, internal motives for presenting the first version. First, it was intended to provide a pretext for and justify a protracted war that might have been prevented had Iraq accepted Iran's conditions from the outset. Putting the blame on Iran also served the goal of preserving the honor of the army, which had not been strong enough to defend Iraq's interests in the Shatt al-Arab and defeat the Kurds. This version also disclosed an attempt by Saddam to give ideological "depth" to a measure that was apparently highly controversial, and thereby receive the approval of senior political and party institutions. It is not known whether Saddam held prior consultations with the political or military echelon before going to Algiers, but there is no doubt that he went without a decision reached by the higher political echelons. It was four days after the Algiers Agreement was signed that the RCC and the regional and national leadership of the Baath Party approved it. The fact that it was not signed by President al-Bakr, who was the shah's counterpart, but instead by Saddam, indicates two things that are not necessarily contradictory: first, that Saddam's was a partisan move that implied the proclamation of his status as the actual supreme leader of Iraq;[67] and, second, that al-Bakr, at the very least, had reservations regarding this move. This is indicated by the long speech that al-Bakr delivered on 7 April 1975, the Baath's anniversary. For the most part, his speech was devoted to the Kurdish issue and to relations with Iran. Although he praised the agreement, he completely disregarded the Iraqi concession regarding the Shatt al-Arab. He also disregarded any connection between this concession and the successful elimination of the Kurdish rebellion: according to his version, the rebellion had been crushed thanks to the army's strength and courage—and nothing else.

The reason for this disregard of the Algiers Agreement—or apologetic, evasive wriggling around it—lies in the fact that it entailed an especially painful Iraqi concession. By means of this agreement, Iraq voluntarily gave up on an agreement anchored in an international law from 1937, which had given Iraq control over the Shatt al-Arab. This was a prime, vital, strategic interest because the Shatt al-Arab was Iraq's only outlet to the sea and, until that date, its most important outlet for the export of its oil. In addition, the demarcation of the land borders based on the Constantinople Protocol of 1913 (Article 1 of the Algiers Agreement) was, both in theory and in practice, an Iraqi concession of the district of Khuzestan/Arabistan in Iran, which Iraq had claimed because of its Arab population.

The key question, therefore, is what motivated Iraq to take such far-reaching action. A number of cumulative reasons can be distinguished; for example, Iraq's desire to end its isolation in the Arab world, to consolidate its political and economic position, to break away from its dependence on the Soviet Union, and to advance its position in OPEC. However, the most important reason was, of course, Saddam's determination to put an end to the Kurdish rebellion. Since a solution by peaceful means had failed and the military solution had proved quite inadequate, a third way remained open to Iraq: to arrive at a political solution through Iran, which could be particularly costly, but would open up the possibility of solving the Kurdish problem as well as the chronic problems with Iran. It should be indicated parenthetically that this agreement was very much an anomaly in the history of the Kurds' relations with their host countries. In the Ottoman and Persian empires, and throughout the twentieth century, the Kurds exploited rivalries between the two empires or states to advance their own interests; or, alternatively, these states exploited the Kurds for their wars against the neighboring state. Now, for the first time, rival states were joining hands against the Kurds in order to put an end to the rivalry between them.

Saddam apparently viewed Iraq's loss of control over the Shatt al-Arab as a tactical rather than a strategic concession, especially because he hoped to be compensated for this concession by Iraq's assumption of control or leasing of the two Kuwaiti islands, Warba and Bubiyan, which would ensure it free access to the sea.[68] Iraq initiated actions toward this goal, in parallel with the dialogue with Iran. On 1 December 1974, Iraqi forces infiltrated Kuwait and established military positions in the area of Samita.[69] A Kuwaiti official charged Iraq with attempting to take control of the two islands. At the OPEC conference in Algiers, Saddam held discussions with the emir of Kuwait regarding the islands—discussions that led to nowhere.

As for the shah, he was motivated to reach an agreement for the following reasons: his unwillingness to be entangled in a war with Iraq, and fears of a strong Kurdish autonomy neighboring Iran; his desire to curb the Soviet Union's influence; and Iran's aspiration to be the leading power in the Gulf. Iran's concession of its support of the Kurds, which had obviously become increasingly onerous, did not seem to be too high of a price for an agreement that would give it such impressive gains.

The Kurds Between the Hammer and the Anvil

While Baghdad acted feverishly to bring the conflict with Iran to an end, the Kurds remained passive. One should not, however, assume that they were unaware of Baghdad's activities since the latter made a point to publicize the dates and objectives of its meetings with Iran. It makes more sense to assume that the Kurds were hopeful that Iraq and Iran would not be able to reach an agreement. In addition, the Kurdish leadership was almost entirely focused on war efforts and on providing assistance to the civilian population. It devoted fewer, if any, efforts to establishing diplomatic and political contacts, in which it obviously lacked experience. Perhaps the sad truth, from their standpoint, was that the Kurds had no external political action channels besides Iran. True, there was a US guarantee never to abandon them, but this dubious guarantee caused severe damage to the movement because it lulled the Kurds into a false sense of security. The leadership's attempt to clutch at the US promise indicated naïveté, not to say total detachment from reality. This was indicated by the cable that Barzani sent to the United States on 16 January 1975, which included an appeal for it to declare Kurdistan "the 51st State of the United States."[70] This did, in any case, reflect the concerns raised in the Kurdish camp following the renewal of discussions between Iraq and Iran that January. On 22 January Barzani sent a message to Henry Kissinger, then US secretary of state, to which the latter finally replied a month later by claiming that the Kurds' messages had "received the most serious attention at the highest levels of the United States government." Kissinger, however, also added that he could not invite Barzani to Washington because relations had to be kept secret and because of concern for Barzani's personal safety.[71] The Kurds' concern regarding the future was also evident in the dispatch of Kurdish envoys to Egyptian president Sadat in February with the hope that they would uncover relevant information. There are some reports that Barzani himself arrived in Tehran on 26 February to get some clarifications, but that the shah did not meet with him. Barzani was nevertheless informed that an agreement that would "benefit" the Kurds was to be signed between Iraq and Iran. Even if the version that the Kurds had prior information of the impending Algiers Agreement is accepted, news of an Iraqi-Iranian agreement no doubt must have caught them completely unprepared and would have been a severe blow. Even the Kurdish intelligence service, the Parastin, was taken unaware. The dizzying pace of events preceding the Algiers Agreement left them utterly powerless.

Within hours of signing the agreement with Iraq, Iran ceased all aid to the Kurds. Iran closed the border with Iraq, evacuated Iranian soldiers and heavy arms from Iraqi territory, and returned all arms and food depots that were intended for the Kurds to Iranian territory. Simultaneously, the Iraqi Army began a major offensive against the Kurds in the Sulaymaniyya area. The attack found the Kurdish combatants with a limited quantity of ammunition and almost no heavy arms. In particular, they had no defense against Iraqi aircraft, which could carry out low-altitude sorties nearly undisturbed. For about a week, intense battles raged in which both sides suffered heavy losses. At the same time, despite the Kurdish camp's inferiority, it managed to prevent the Iraqi Army from advancing toward the Iranian border. While the fighting continued, Barzani's headquarters sent a secret appeal to the CIA representative on 10 March 1975, stating, "Our people's fate is in unprecedented danger. Complete destruction hovers over our heads. There is no explanation for all of this. We appeal to you and to the United States administration to intervene pursuant to your promises."[72] Kissinger reportedly received a letter from Barzani on the same day stating:

> Our hearts bleed as we see that the direct byproduct of their agreement [the agreement between Iraq and Iran] is the unprecedented ruin of our defenseless people, inasmuch as [your ally Iran] has closed the border and completely ended all assistance for us, while [its enemy Iraq] has begun the greatest offensive ever waged, which is continuing at this very time. . . . We feel, your Excellency, that the United States has a moral and political responsibility toward our people.[73]

Barzani requested that the United States intervene with Iraq to stop the military offensive and to begin negotiations with the Kurdish movement. He also requested that the United States intervene with Iran to permit the Kurds to continue their minor guerrilla war until the Kurdish problem was resolved in the framework of comprehensive negotiations.[74]

According to later statements, Kissinger did not respond to these urgent appeals, because he himself was secretly involved in the rapprochement between Iran and Iraq. In this way, Kissinger hoped to obtain Iraq's goodwill and hence its quiet consent to the military disengagement measures between Egypt and Israel in which he was involved at the time.[75] As disclosures regarding this episode began to appear in the United States in late 1975 and early 1976, and following the public storm caused by the United States' cynical policy that resulted in the elimination of the Kurdish movement, Kissinger was quoted as saying in defense of this strategy that "secret activity should not be confused with missionary activity."[76]

In his memoirs, Kissinger justified the abandonment of the Kurds by saying that saving them would have entailed the intervention of two Iranian divisions and $300 million in US aid, which neither Iran nor the United States wanted to give.[77] Kissinger did not explain why he initially had made promises that he did not intend to keep. Another version of the events maintained that Iran had not consulted with the United States regarding the Algiers Agreement.

The multiplicity of versions makes it difficult to fathom the truth. However, it is clear that the administration of President Gerald R. Ford did not view itself bound to the secret promises of Ford's predecessor, Richard M. Nixon. Neither did it see any need to disrupt the growing rapprochement between Iran and Iraq or perceive the Kurds as a strategic asset warranting US intervention on its behalf.[78] The United States totally reneged on its pledge: it discontinued all financial aid, refrained from all intervention with the Baghdad government to obtain better terms for the Kurdish movement, and refused to provide humanitarian aid such as admitting refugees into the United States. The US departure also obstructed the continuation of Israeli aid, which, in any case, was conditional on Iran's full consent.

On 13 March 1975, Iraq announced its willingness to stop the Iraqi Army's advance into the area of Kurdistan for two weeks. Radio Baghdad explained that this was a gesture to the shah who, during discussions in Algiers, had requested "a grace period" for the Kurdish combatants. At the time, the shah presumably offered the Kurds two options: either move to Iran "in a permanent and final manner" or submit to the Iraqi authorities. Radio Baghdad emphasized that this decision did not mean a cease-fire with a "collaborator enclave (*jayb 'amil*)" or the intention to hold a dialogue with it. It added that, at the end of the grace period, "our armed forces will resume their advance to liquidate the last positions of the agent pocket and impose full sovereignty on the homeland's borders, as well as spreading law and order and stability."[79] Iran's intervention in favor of a cease-fire was intended to salvage the remnants of the shah's credibility among the Kurds; to appear to the world as having prevented genocide; and, most importantly, to ensure the establishment of precise procedures in the time interval preceding the implementation of the agreement, so as not to provide Iraq with an excuse to pull back from it.

For its part the Kurdish leadership, which did not view itself bound by the cease-fire, decided to continue fighting despite the cessation of Iranian aid. On 16 March 1975 a staff meeting was held at Galala between Barzani, members of the Kurdish politburo, and military commanders, with the aim of planning an attack on the Rawanduz front. However, in another meeting held two days later, Barzani announced his personal decision to stop the fighting and to move to Iran. Though he left the option open for others to continue fighting, the leadership decided to follow in Barzani's footsteps. At the same time, the KDP made a desperate attempt to pursue political channels. On 19 March, the politburo sent a cable to President al-Bakr and Saddam, offering to open an "immediate dialogue" so as "to find a firm and reasonable solution between us, in a way that cannot be exploited by others." President al-Bakr and Saddam's reply was unequivocal: no negotiations. The regime was resolved "to purge the soil of Iraq of its traitors."[80] On 20 March, Barzani cabled the commanders, telling them to stop fighting and move to Iran. On 21 March, Radio Kurdistan discontinued its broadcasts.

Among the questions that preoccupied the Kurdish movement and resulted in sharp criticism being leveled at its leadership were the following: Why did Barzani change his mind so abruptly? What caused him to stop the fighting and, thus, bring about the collapse of the movement? Did events vindicate this decision? According to different sources, the immediate cause for Barzani's decision was a message he received from Iran—apparently after the foreign ministers of Iraq and Iran had reached a final agreement on 17 March 1975 on the implementation of the Algiers Agreement—in which Iran threatened to cooperate with the Iraqi Army against the Kurds if the Kurds did not stop the fighting.[81] It is impossible to verify this version but, even if there was no such direct threat, the shah retained the effective option of pressuring Barzani by controlling the fate of Kurdish refugees in Iran whom he held hostage. Beyond that were several cumulative factors that tipped the balance in favor of eventually stopping the fighting. The movement had come under heavy psychological pressure: it felt cut off from its central lifeline; its three traditional enemies—Iraq, Iran, and Turkey, which had closed its border to Kurdish refugees to improve relations with Baghdad[82]—were collaborating against it; the United States was not responding to any of its appeals for aid, even humanitarian aid; Israel's hands were tied because of Iran's policies; and the Baghdad government had slammed the door on negotiations. Another central factor that favored the cessation of fighting was the Kurdish population itself. Although a segment of the movement supported the continuation of the struggle, Barzani once more decided against it in order to prevent further human suffering. Another factor, which also played a significant role in Barzani's decision, was the fact that he felt frustrated and was old and sick. This certainly had an influence on the movement, whose very existence and resolve depended on him. By virtue of the exclusive position that Barzani held in the movement, his decision did not arouse opposition among other members of the leadership. This was to become the main target of criticism leveled against the leadership after the rebellion collapsed.[83]

Criticism was also directed against the close relations that the movement had developed with the shah who, critics maintained, was willing to fight Iraq "to the last Kurd." Barzani, for his part, justified these relations by saying that Iran under the shah was the only party willing to help the Kurds.[84]

The harshest criticism concerned Barzani's secret ties with the United

States. After the rebellion collapsed, both the Kurds and foreign observers concluded that the course of events would have been different had the Kurds not been enticed to forge ties with the United States. In a letter to President Ford in 1977, Barzani claimed that "I could have prevented the calamity which befell my people had I not fully believed in the promise of America. This could have been done merely by supporting the Ba'th policy and joining forces with them, thereby taking a position contrary to American interests and principles and causing trouble for Iraq's neighbors."[85] Without attempting to justify the US policy, it could be said that it was naïve to cast the entire blame on vague, secret promises of the United States. In truth, the crux of the issue was a genuine clash between two national movements. External elements did not create this clash, although they inflamed and exploited it for their own purposes. Even Barzani's contention that, were it not for the US promise, the Kurdish leadership would have reached an understanding with the Baath was utterly refutable. The entire course of events pointed to a deepening of the mutual distrust between the Kurdish leadership and the Baath after the March agreement. Moreover, the Baath had pushed the Kurdish leadership into a corner and had left it with no alternative but to initiate the rebellion. It therefore seems that even if the Kurds had wanted to reach an understanding (which is doubtful), the Baath Party, which was in a position of strength, would not have been willing to do so. This was borne out by the fact that the Baath manipulated the situation to push the Kurds to the brink of war. The fact is that the Kurdish rebellion was not a response to outside directives or demands from Iran, the United States, or Israel.

From a historical perspective, Barzani's and his movement's abandonment of the rebellion repeated a pattern of action seen in previous periods: when any Kurdish movement was close to making gains, it frequently stopped fighting—in response to internal or external pressures—in the hope of renewing the rebellion at a time of more favorable conditions. Examples of this were the 1880 rebellion of Shaikh 'Ubaydullah against the Persian Empire with the support of the Ottoman Empire; the 1925 rebellion of Shaikh Sa'id against Turkey; the Republic of Mahabad (headed by Qazi Muhammad), which was supported by the Soviet Union and collapsed in 1947; and, finally, the insurrections mounted by Barzani who ended the fighting several times when he sensed the ground burning under his feet in the expectation of resuming the battle at a later stage. His flights to Turkey, Iran, and the Soviet Union were part of this pattern. Another important characteristic of these rebellions was the unique role played by leaders both in the outbreak and the collapse of the rebellion.

The Collapse of the Rebellion

"We are alone without friends. The Americans gave us no help or refuge. I think that we are in for gloomy days."[86] These remarks were made by Barzani immediately after his decision to stop fighting. Indeed, within several days, the movement collapsed and the fruits of a struggle that had been ongoing since 1961 were lost in one fell swoop and, with it, the dream of genuine autonomy. A mood of despair, mourning, anger, frustration, and confusion prevailed all over the Kurdish region when the decision to stop fighting became known. The decision was kept secret until the last moment, but the hardship caused to the population by the fighting was now intensified by the sudden realization that the entire struggle had been for naught and that the chances of renewing it were slim. It was especially difficult for the people to digest the report that Barzani, the legendary hero, had decided to stop fighting. As a result, even hardened people collapsed in tears or committed suicide, others burned down their homes before leaving for Iran, and still others killed the commanders who had brought the bad tidings that the fighting was to be stopped.[87] The Kurds now had three alternatives, each one more problematic than the other: to continue fighting without any support, to seek refuge in Iran, or to surrender to the Baghdad government. The rebellion's leadership, headed by Barzani, opted to go to Iran. Barzani refused to submit to Baghdad because he was quite sure that he would be put to death by the Baath. On 30 March 1975 he moved to Iran, together with the Kurdish political leadership. By 1 April, many other fighters had managed to reach the border. They disarmed, handed their weapons over to the Iranian authorities, and joined the Kurdish refugees who by that time had reached an estimated 250,000.[88] According to the agreement between Iraq and Iran, the Kurdish refugees were to be granted a pardon and could return to Iraq. However, Saddam stated that he would not permit the return of four people: Barzani, his two sons, and one of Barzani's nephews. Of the Kurds who remained in Iraq, 2,000 fled to the mountains to continue the guerrilla fighting, but the majority surrendered to the Baghdad authorities after handing over each of their weapons in exchange for $350.[89]

The darkest hour for the Kurds was the finest hour for the Iraqi Army. The Algiers Agreement handed over Kurdistan on a silver platter. The army thus achieved in fifteen days what it had failed to do in fifteen years of fighting. After a period of grace, the Iraqi armored forces pressed forward, without air support and without meeting any resistance, since the Peshmerga military strongholds had all been dismantled. Radio Baghdad reported that the residents "welcomed the armed forces, applauding and cheering" when the Iraqi Army entered Barzani's headquarters at Galala on 2 April 1975.[90] Within a few days, it took over all northern areas, including the mountain passes between northern Iraq and Iran. One military commander who had participated in the campaign said, "There is no need for aircraft, there is no opposition. Not one shot was fired, and not one drop of blood has been shed. The mission of taking control of the border (area) was completely successful."[91] The Baghdad authorities exploited the rapid, easy seizure of Kurdistan to balance their concession of the Shatt al-Arab and to raise the army's morale, which the Algiers Agreement had undermined. Saddam kept a low profile, apparently in order not to completely burn his bridges with the Kurdish population. Al-Bakr, who was less sophisticated and sensitive, gave an enthusiastic speech on 7 April, in which he described the seizure of Iraqi Kurdistan as "a major historical event" and "a magnificent Iraqi patriotic (*watani*) and pan-Arab (*qawmi*) holiday . . . because the reactionary, treacherous rebellion in (certain) northern parts of the homeland had been eliminated forever." Describing the battle as "difficult and onerous" and the enemy as a difficult enemy "who was equipped by imperialism [*sic*] with large quantities of the most modern weapons," al-Bakr praised the heroism and ability of the "new" Iraqi Army, which according to him was the most important component in the victory.[92]

Barzani however had a different view of how this victory had been achieved: "Our soldiers left the battlefield undefeated. Despite its enormous material superiority, the Iraqi army could not score one single victory. In one year of war it has advanced only a few kilometers, and suffered heavy losses. No, the decision against us was in the political arena."[93]

The Kurdish poet Sami Shoresh summed up the Kurds' trauma and hope in these verses in his poem "The Uprising":

Tell the mountains, the plains, and the valleys
The sun, and the shadows,
The rifles, and the daggers,
The survivors of the deep trenches,
The day shall come when a storm of anger shall break forth
In front of the gate of the governor's house in Sulaymaniyya.

The clouds of red revolution shall move,
The angry waves of the Peshmerga shall roar.

Notes

1. Michael Howard, "War and Nations," in *Nationalism*, eds. John Hutchinson and Anthony Smith (Oxford: Oxford University Press, 1994), pp. 254–255.
2. Except for rare statements by Barzani and his confidants, for example, Barzani's interview in *Newsweek* (New York, weekly), 22 July 1974.
3. *Al-Thawra* (Baghdad, daily), 27 January 1983. At the end of the war, different versions appeared; the facts presented in these versions are suspected of having been altered.
4. *Le Monde* (Paris, daily), 10 July 1974.
5. *Al-Thawra*, 27 January 1983.
6. The hard core of the Peshmerga force amounted to 45,000 troops—with 60,000 reservists. Anthony McDermott, "The 1975 Crisis," Minority Rights Group Report no. 23 (London: Minority Rights Group, 1977), p. 16. For border lines, see also *New York Times* (New York, daily), 1 April 1974.

7. Public Record Office, FCO8/2307, 22 July 1974.

8. McDermott, "The 1975 Crisis," p. 19. In addition, there were Indian instructors. Chris Kutschera, *Le mouvement national kurde* (Paris: Flammarion, 1970), pp. 304, 316.

9. Public Record Office, FCO8/2307, 11 September 1974.

10. Public Record Office, FCO8/2308, 14 October 1974; Public Record Office, FCO8/2309, 31 December 1974; "The War in Kurdistan," *Strategic Survey* 75, no. 1 (1974): 84.

11. *Al-Thawra*, 28 April 1974.

12. Public Record Office, FCO8/2308, 26 November 1974.

13. "The War in Kurdistan," p. 83; *New York Times*, 10 March 1975; "The Days of Qala Diza and Halabja," available at www.kdp.pp.se/old/chemical.html.

14. Public Record Office, FCO8/2308, 28 October 1974; Public Record Office, FCO8/2309, 13 December 1974.

15. Public Record Office, FCO8/2309, 27 November 1974.

16. Public Record Office, FCO8/2309, 13 December 1974.

17. Geoff Simons, *Iraq: From Sumer to Saddam* (London: St. Martin's Press, 1994), pp. 179–181.

18. George Black, "Introduction," in *Genocide in Iraq: The Anfal Campaign Against the Kurds* (Washington, DC: Human Rights Watch; Middle East Watch Report, 1993).

19. Public Record Office, FCO8/2308, 19 September 1974; Public Record Office, FCO8/2309, undated.

20. McDermott, "The 1975 Crisis," p. 17.

21. Quoted in ibid., p. 16.

22. Public Record Office, FCO8/2309, 5 December 1974.

23. *Al-Thawra*, 28 April 1974.

24. *The Baghdad Observer* (Baghdad, daily) , 31 July 1974.

25. *Al-Thawra*, 28 April 1974.

26. Public Record Office, FCO8/2308, 10 October 1974.

27. Public Record Office, FCO8/2308, 21 October 1974.

28. Public Record Office, FCO8/2308, 10 October 1974.

29. *Amnesty International Report, 1975–1976* (London: Amnesty International, 1976), pp. 183–187; *Free Kurdistan* (London, irregular), no. 7, January 1976.

30. Baghdad attempted to prevent journalists from visiting the Kurdish area. Public Record Office, FCO8/2308, 16 October 1974.

31. For the world's indifference to the Kurdish fate, see Denise Natali, *The Kurdish Quasi-State* (Syracuse: Syracuse University Press, 2010), pp. 21–28.

32. Public Record Office, FCO8/2308, 26 October 1974. A Kurdish activist told me that, in order to smuggle a French journalist into Kurdistan, they had to walk one entire month from Syria via Turkey to Kurdistan to meet Barzani. Interviewed by the author, 15 June 2010.

33. *Al-Hayat* (London, daily), 1 November 1974.

34. Voice of Iraqi Kurdistan, 16 May 1974, cited in *Daily Report*, 17 May 1974.

35. Ismet Sheriff Vanly, "Kurdistan in Iraq," in *A People Without a Country: The Kurds and Kurdistan*, ed. Gérard Chaliand (London: Zed Press, 1980), p. 179.

36. Public Record Office, FO973/32, March 1979.

37. Total manpower including regular, reserve, and irregular was estimated at *circa* 200,000. Public Record Office, FCO8/2308, 26 November 1974; McDermott, "The 1975 Crisis," p. 16

38. Public Record Office, FCO8/2308, 24 October 1974.

39. Ofra Bengio, *The Kurdish Revolution in Iraq* (in Hebrew) (Tel Aviv: Hakkibutz Hameuhad, 1989), p. 153.

40. Kutschera, *Le mouvement*, p. 316.

41. *Al-Sayyad* (Beirut, weekly), 30 May 1974.

42. Public Record Office, FCO8/2308, 29 October 1974. Senior officers also repeated their preference for a political solution in November. Public Record Office, FCO8/2308, 26 November 1974.

43. Kutschera, *Le mouvement*, p. 324.

44. Arab Report and Record, 1–15 May 1975.

45. *Al-Thawra*, 18 September 1980.

46. Public Record Office, FCO8/2308, 20 November 1974.

47. One thousand Iranian troops were engaged in the war. McDermott, "The 1975 Crisis," p. 16.

48. *Al-Jumhuriyya* (Baghdad, daily), 4 October 1974.

49. *Al-Thawra*, 13 October 1974.

50. *Al-Hayat*, 21 November 1974. The al-Da'wa Party reached the peak of its activity in 1979–1980 after the Islamic Revolution in Iran.

51. *Amnesty International Report, 1975–1976*, pp. 183–187.

52. *Daily Mail*, quoted by *Ma'ariv* (Tel Aviv, daily), 30 September 1974.

53. Public Record Office, FCO8/2309, 27 November 1974.

54. Public Record Office, FCO8/2308, 19 November 1974.

55. See this thesis in Hayim Shemesh, *Soviet-Iraqi Relations, 1968–1988: In the Shadow of the Iraq-Iran Conflict* (Boulder: Lynne Rienner, 1992), p. 123.

56. *Al-Nahar* (Beirut, daily), 11 April 1974.

57. Public Record Office, FCO8/2309, 10 December 1974.

58. Radio Baghdad, 30 August 1974, cited in *Daily Report*, 3 September 1974.

59. Arab Report and Record, 16–31 December 1974.

60. Public Record Office, FCO8/2309, 18 December 1974.

61. Radio Baghdad, 11 February 1975, cited in *Daily Report*, 12 February 1975.

62. *Al-Ahram*, 21 February 1975, cited in *Daily Report*, 26 February 1975.

63. For the text of the first agreement, see *Al-Thawra*, 7 March 1975. For the text of the full agreement signed in June, see *Orient* 16, no. 3 (1975).

64. Edmund Ghareeb, *The Kurdish Question in Iraq* (Syracuse: Syracuse University Press, 1981), p. 172; Iraqi News Agency, 10 March 1975, cited in *Daily Report*, 11 March 1975.

65. Radio Baghdad, 17 September 1980, cited in BBC, 19 September 1980.

66. *Revolutionary Iraq 1968–1973*, Report of the Eighth Regional Congress of the Arab Ba'th Socialist Party, Iraq, January 1974 (October 1974), p. 217.

67. Some defined the agreement as "completely a personal deal." *The Guardian* (London, daily), 22 March 1975.

68. An Iranian official mentioned that Iraq's possible victory over the Kurds would turn Baghdad's attention "to their number two target, namely Kuwait." Public Record Office, FCO8/2307, 11 September 1974.

69. Reuters, 1 December 1974, cited in *Daily Report*, 2 December 1974.

70. *Village Voice* (New York), 16 February 1976.

71. Mas'ud Barzani, *Al-Barzani wal-Haraka al-Kurdiyya al-Taharruriyya*, vol. 3, p. 699.

72. *Village Voice*, 16 February 1976.

73. Ibid.

74. Ibid.

75. For Kissinger's changing policy toward Iraq, see Kenneth W. Stein, "Henry Kissinger to Iraq in 1975: 'We can reduce Israel's size.'" *Middle East Quarterly* (Fall 2006): 71–78.

76. *New York Times*, 12 February 1976.

77. Henry Kissinger, *White House Years* (Boston: Little, Brown, 1979), p. 1265.

78. Brent Scowcroft, Kissinger's deputy, was later quoted as saying: "We ended our support. It was just small potatoes." Quil Lawrence, *Invisible Nation: How the Kurds' Quest for Statehood Is Shaping Iraq and the Middle East* (New York: Walker; distributed by Macmillan, 2008), p. 28.

79. Iraqi News Agency, 13 March 1975, cited in *Daily Report*, 14 March 1975.

80. Iraqi News Agency, 19 March 1975, cited in *Daily Report*, 20 March 1975.

81. Kutschera, *Le mouvement*, p. 329.

82. Public Record Office, FCO8/2309, 19 December 1974.

83. Thirty-five years later, PUK supporters regarded Barzani's move as an act of treason. Being members of Peshmerga, they were convinced that the Kurds should have continued fighting in spite of all the difficulties. Kurdish intellectuals interviewed by the author, Sulaymaniyya, 4 May 2009.

84. Author interview with an anonymous official who was close to Barzani, 22 September 1985.

85. Ferhad Ibrahim, *Die Kurdische Nationalbewegung im Iraq* (Berlin: Klaus Schwarz Verlag, 1983), p. 610.

86. *Jerusalem Post* (Jerusalem, daily), 23 March 1975.

87. For a description of these dramatic days, see Kutschera, *Le mouvement*, pp. 326–333.

88. McDermott, "The 1975 Crisis," p. 17. Phebe Marr, *The Modern History of Iraq* (Boulder, CO: Westview Press, 1985), p. 234. Marr estimated the number of refugees at between 100,000 and 200,000.

89. Ofra Bengio, *The Kurdish Revolution in Iraq*, p. 189.

90. Iraqi News Agency, 2 April 1975, cited in *Daily Report*, 3 April 1975.

91. *Daily Star* (Beirut, daily), 4 April 1975.

92. *Al-Thawra*, 7 April 1975.

93. *Die Welt*, 1 April 1975, cited in *Daily Report*, 2 April 1975.

9

Interregnum

The Algiers Agreement and the suppression of the Kurdish rebellion ushered in a new era in the history of Iraq: for the first time in many years, the Baath Party became the sole, unshakable ruler in all of Iraq. Saddam Hussein continued to strengthen his position in the ruling elite.[1] The easy victory that Saddam had achieved for the army in Kurdistan paved the way for his meteoric rise in the military hierarchy. Thus, on Army Day in January 1976, President Ahmad Hasan al-Bakr awarded Saddam the rank of general, applied retroactively to July 1973. In July 1979, after meticulous preparations, Saddam became president—in actuality, the omnipotent ruler of Iraq.[2]

The Baath—The Best of All Times

Seen in retrospect, the period between 1975 and 1980 was the best of all times for the Baath regime. Politically speaking, not only had the Kurdish threat been removed, albeit for a brief period of time only, but the Baath's marriage of convenience with the Communist Party was no longer necessary. In fact the latter lost, in one fell swoop, its role as the balancing power between the regime and the Kurds—becoming, in the eyes of the Baath, a nuisance that had to be eliminated gradually and without unduly antagonizing the Soviet Union. This process, which began with the signing of the Algiers Agreement, led to an open rift in 1979 when the ICP went underground again.

On the socioeconomic level, the end of the war in Kurdistan released resources for other purposes. The country experienced an economic boom as never before. The growing revenues from a nationalized oil industry were invested in ambitious development programs in both the civilian and the military sectors. One of these programs was the strategic oil pipeline completed in 1977, which extended from the Gulf through Kurdistan to Turkey. The pipeline increased oil output and liberated Iraq from its dependence on the oil pipeline passing through Syria. The construction of the pipeline, completed without significant disruptions on the part of the Kurds, enhanced the strategic importance of the Kurdish areas to the export of Iraqi oil. A considerable portion of the revenues were allocated to different welfare and reconstruction programs intended to benefit the people and find favor in their eyes, thus contributing directly to the strengthening of Saddam's position. Paradoxically, ending the war in Kurdistan did not bring about a reduction in military expenditures. On the contrary a large part of the budget was allocated to the accelerated buildup of the army, which included the diversification of arms sources, an increase in the size of the army, and the commencement of construction of a nuclear reactor in 1975.[3]

An important motive for the military buildup was Iraq's complex relationship with Iran. In theory, the agreement ratified in June 1975 opened up an era of détente between the two countries and "ended a 40-year conflict," according to Radio Tehran.[4] However, beneath the appearance of close friendship and cooperation, hostile and suspicious attitudes continued to percolate. These were fed by Iraq's loss of sovereignty over the Shatt al-Arab waterway, Iran's large military buildup, basic differences between the two regimes' political orientations, and the continued rivalry between them for supremacy in the Gulf.

Since its hands were no longer tied by the Kurdistan war of 1974–1975 and the conflict with Iran, Iraq could begin to fortify its regional position and attempt to achieve the leadership status that it coveted in the Gulf and in the Arab world in general. One means to do so was by formulating a less radical foreign policy, as manifested in a growing rapprochement with pro-Western Arab countries such as Jordan, Saudi Arabia, and Egypt. On the other hand, relations with a radical Syria, which had been tenuous for a long time, deteriorated even further after the signing of the Algiers Agreement. Syria indirectly denounced the agreement because, as Damascus contended, it had conceded Arab sovereignty over the Shatt al-Arab and Arabistan (Iranian Khuzestan). Practically speaking, the agreement posed a threat to Syria because it facilitated Iraq's military buildup. In the summer of 1976, Iraq even concentrated forces on its border with Syria in response to Syria's involvement in Lebanon. The oil pipeline to Turkey was also a thorn in Syria's side. All of these factors, together with old and new rivalries with Baghdad, prompted Damascus to become the Kurds' new patron. Kuwait also had good reason to fear the implications of the Algiers Agreement and Baghdad's incessant pressure to gain a foothold on the islands of Warba and Bubiyan. However, Kuwait was successful in repelling these pressures, arguing that Iraq no longer had a reason to seek access to the Kuwaiti islands since an agreement had been reached that allowed Iraq free navigation in the Shatt al-Arab.

Another outcome of the agreement and the elimination of the rebellion was a somewhat more balanced Iraqi East-West policy. Relations with France gathered momentum in all areas. As for the United States, although diplomatic relations would remain nonexistent for another decade, relations on the economic level grew rapidly. Correspondingly, though Iraq remained bound by its friendship pact with the Soviet Union—its main arms supplier—it sought to become less dependent on the Soviets. In pursuing this policy, Iraq was acting on the basis of an understanding, reached at Algiers, regarding the need to reduce the presence of the major powers in the Gulf. This implied a reduction of Soviet influence in Iraq. With the elimination of the Kurdish rebellion, Iraq could afford to break away from its dependence on the Soviet Union that had increased because of the uprising. Another consideration was the large-scale development that Iraq was planning, and for which it needed Western technology and know-how. Iraq's ambition to achieve a leadership role among the nonaligned countries—and, consequently, its need to present an image of nonalignment with either one of the two blocs—also played an important role in Iraqi policies.[5] Finally, Saddam's own ambivalent attitude toward the Soviet Union, combining cooperation with growing feelings of antipathy and distrust, must be considered.

Within five years of signing the Algiers Agreement, Iraq had positioned itself as a regional power in a prominent leadership role. This development was facilitated by Iraq's relative domestic stability and quiet; by its economic and military strength, acquired thanks to oil revenues; and by the political vacuum in the Arab leadership following the Camp David agreement between Egypt and Israel, which was signed on 17 September 1978 and exploited by Iraq at the summit conference in Baghdad that same fall. Another vacuum developed simultaneously in the Gulf after the fall of the shah and the establishment of the Islamic Republic in Iran in early 1979.

Reeducating the Kurds

In his famous treatise, *The Prince,* Niccolò Machiavelli gives the following advice on the best way to administer a conquered territory: "There is no surer way of keeping possession than by devastation. Whoever becomes the master of a city accustomed to freedom, and does not destroy it may expect to be destroyed himself."[6] The Baath attempted to do just this. An internal Baath Party memorandum, circulated in April 1975, stated the following: "Our strategic goal is for the so-called Kurdish problem not to resurface in this or in subsequent generations."[7] On the way toward achieving this, Baghdad targeted several interim goals: to destroy Kurdish national identity and assimilate the Kurds into Arab society; to break up the traditional Kurdish leadership; to sever the Kurdish ties with the outside world and, thus, prevent Kurdish reorganization; to expel the Kurds from strategic areas; and, finally, to attempt to establish a new base of support for the regime. The vacuum left by the leadership of the Kurdish movement and the shock to the Kurdish population after the collapse of the rebellion helped Baghdad implement its plan. Although the momentum of the plan subsided after a year, some of its components persisted for quite a while.

The government's long-range goal was to strike at Mulla Mustafa Barzani, his sons, and the Barzani clan because of their central role in the Kurdish movement. Barzani's exile to Iran apparently solved a difficult problem for the regime. In actuality, the vendetta against the Barzanis was to go on for many years. Even when he was outside of Iraq in exile, Barzani continued to raise Baghdad's concerns, both because of his continuing influence over the Kurds and because of his vitality and survival skills. When Barzani was in Iran in 1975, Baghdad made three, albeit unsuccessful, attempts to assassinate him.[8] Baghdad's apprehension notwithstanding, for both the man and the leader, this was indeed the end because Barzani no longer had the strength for another round of war. After a forced stay of several months in Iran, he was granted political asylum in the United States where he died of cancer in March 1979. His followers buried him in Iran, not in Barzan his hometown, out of fear of the authorities' reprisals. It seems that even in death, Barzani frightened his opponents. According to the KDP, Iraqi agents made an attempt to steal his body in 1981. Barzani's tragic end concluded an era in the history of the Kurdish struggle in Iraq, which one observer describes as the end of the strongest "Kurdish state" since the rule of Bedir Khan.[9] Barzani's exit from the stage severely damaged a Kurdish movement that had lost its charismatic, unifying figure. In the opinion of one scholar, the main factor that contributed to the great awakening of the Kurdish national movement in the 1960s and 1970s was not the nationalist propaganda disseminated by intellectuals in the KDP, but Barzani's military successes that constituted a source of Kurdish pride and a focus of identification.[10]

The next in line in Baghdad's hit list were Barzani's sons: in January 1979, an attempt was made to assassinate Mas'ud while he was in Vienna. In November 1980, 'Ubaydullah, a longtime collaborator of Saddam's, was killed when he became involved in an argument with Saddam during a government meeting. In the fall of 1983 Barzani's two other sons, Sabir and Luqman, were assassinated because they were suspected of aiding Iran.[11] Fifteen Barzanis were killed along with them. At the same time about 8,000 male members of the Barzani clan, young and old, and their supporters were rounded up and taken to Baghdad. They disappeared and their remains were found twenty years later.[12] When Idris died of a heart attack in February 1987, Baghdad Radio did not conceal its joy: "To hell with him, as this is his final home."[13]

One more problem confronting Baghdad was that of the Kurdish refugees in Iran. Contending that the refugees constituted a social, economic, and political time bomb for Iran, it exerted ongoing pressure to return them to Iraq. Left with no other choice, Iraq time and again responded by announcing a general amnesty for the refugees in order to induce them to return. They went back in waves, the largest in October 1975 when 50,000 resettled in Iraq. Nonetheless, many Kurds, especially among the leadership, feared for their lives and refused to do so. In order to "persuade" them, Iran exerted pressure of its own such as random arrests, the imposition of a curfew, the dispersion of Kurds in different locations in Iran,[14] and the refusal to give them the status of citizen or refugee. As a result most Kurds, with the exception of about 30,000 individuals, had returned to Iraq by 1976. Iraq's policy goal, however, was to turn them into refugees in their own country. Among those who returned or surrendered themselves to the authorities were veteran members of the leadership such as Salih al-Yusufi, Dara Tawfiq, Habib Muhammad Karim, and ʻUmar Mustafa, all of whom received minor government posts far from the Kurdish region. The Peshmerga and other Kurds whose lot was less fortunate were detained or arrested. According to a report by Amnesty International, nearly 200 were executed within a year of the signing of the Algiers Agreement.[15] However, Kurdish émigrés in Europe claimed that the number was much higher than that.

In line with Machiavelli's advice on the importance of scattering and dispersing conquered populations,[16] Baghdad exiled large numbers of Kurds to the Shiʻi area in southern Iraq, including the provinces of Dhi Qar, al-Qadisiyya, al-Muthanna, and al-Ramadi, with the objective of assimilating them into a new Arab-Shiʻi environment. This policy posed a special threat to the Kurds because it uprooted them from their natural environment and created difficult climatic and social conditions. Iraqi officials claimed that 30,000 to 50,000 Kurds were included in the plan whereas Kurdish sources spoke of 200,000 to 300,000. A later source placed the number of displaced persons at 600,000.[17] They belonged in one of three categories: refugees who had returned from Iran, including Peshmerga personnel; Kurds from areas bordering on Iran, Turkey, and Syria; and Kurds from autonomous areas in dispute (e.g., Kirkuk or Khanaqin) and other strategic areas.

According to the then information minister Tariq ʻAziz, the Kurds were moved in small groups of 5 to 100 families to Arab villages "so that they could learn to understand their Iraqi, Arab brothers" and so that they could travel freely throughout Iraq once their reeducation was complete. Regarding KDP and Peshmerga activists, ʻAziz stated that they spent time in special camps where they heard lectures from Baath members on "national unity and Kurdish autonomy."[18]

According to the Kurds, these were instead nothing but concentration camps in which KDP activists received intensive Baathist indoctrination. ʻAziz stressed that several leaders of the movement had received governmental positions, although "we could have executed them."[19] Three of them—Dara Tawfiq, Salih al-Yusufi, and Habib Muhammad Karim—were indeed killed in 1980–1981. In July 1976, Saddam referred to the displacement policy, acknowledging that the Baghdad authorities had transferred the residents of several villages on the border and in strategic areas "to other parts of the republic." Saddam also acknowledged that the Kurds who had recently returned from Iran had been transferred to central and southern Iraq.[20] At the same time, he

declared that the Iraqi government had decided to stop these measures completely because, according to him, national unity, security, and stability now
prevailed in the region.[21] It is possible that the motive for ending this policy
was quite the opposite; that is, renewed agitation among the Kurds and apparent friction between the Kurds and the Shi'a in the new Kurdish areas of residence. According to Iraqi sources only 6,000 Kurds remained in the south in
late 1976, most of them Barzanis.[22] They were permitted to return to Kurdistan only in 1979.

Another important stage in Baghdad's plan was to purge infiltrators from
the borders of Iran. The border agreement, signed with Iran in June 1975, dealt
at length with the problem. It stipulated hard-and-fast methods for controlling
infiltrations. In June 1976, an agreement was signed regarding border control
with Turkey as well (followed by three more accords with Turkey in 1978, 1979,
and 1984). One measure entailed the establishment of a 10- to 20-kilometer-
wide security belt along the northern border by means of evacuating the entire
Kurdish population from their villages and transferring them to the heartland of
the Kurdish territory or even to southern Iraq. The objective was to prevent infiltration by and cooperation between Kurds on both sides of the border. Iraqi
border guard units, composed of non-Kurds, manned the evacuated areas. No
less serious from the Kurdish point of view was the way the province of Kirkuk,
which the Kurds had sought to include in the autonomous region, was dealt
with. In order to block Kurdish claims on Kirkuk once and for all, the regime
initiated a massive population transfer that included the expulsion of Kurds and
the resettling of Arab residents in their stead. There are claims that even Egyptians were brought in to settle in these areas.[23] In February 1976, administrative
measures were taken to dismember the province: areas populated by a Kurdish
majority were torn away from Kirkuk and added to provinces such as Sulaymaniyya whereas the city of Kirkuk itself and the province of Huwayja (both
rich in oil) were merged into one small district. Moreover the ancient name of
the province was now changed to Ta'mim (nationalization), thus indicating the
nationalization of both the region and its oil as well as its expropriation from the
Kurds and hence stressing its new Arab character.

The change of Kirkuk's name was part of an intensive, protracted process
of obliterating the Kurdish national identity and Arabizing Kurdistan. The
name of Khanaqin, another oil-rich area, was changed to 'Uruba (Arabism).
Hajj 'Umran, the movement's headquarters, became al-Nasr (victory). Other
villages received new names; for example, al-Karama (honor), al-Hurriyya
(freedom), Haifa, Yafa, and al-Quds (Jerusalem). The use of the term *Kurdistan* was prohibited. It was replaced by the neutral term *the northern region*
(*mintaqat-al-shimal*) or *the autonomous area* (*mintaqat al-hukm al-dhati*).
The terms *Kurds* and *Kurdistan* were also removed from textbooks and from
the names of professional associations. When a Baathi women's activist was
asked to explain the deletion of the term *Kurdish* from the name of the Kur-

dish women's association, she responded, "We will never use this poisonous word again."[24] Other measures included: prohibiting the teaching of the Kurdish language in schools in areas not included in the autonomy area; putting an end to the activity of the Kurdish women's association, the teachers association, and the Kurdish cultural association; disbanding the Kurdish Academy of Science and Arts and putting obstacles in the way of progress at the University of Sulaymaniyya, which had been a stronghold of Kurdish nationalist activism. The government transferred Kurdish teachers to other universities, reduced the faculty, increased the percentage of Arabs at the University of Sulaymaniyya, and eventually moved the university to Erbil in 1981 in the hope of exercising a tighter control over its activities. Three pro-Iraqi Kurdish newspapers were closed down. In February 1976 *Al-Ta'akhi*, which had long been a tool in the service of the Baath, was closed and its editor 'Aziz Rashid 'Aqrawi arrested. Thus, even Kurdish supporters of the regime were not saved from Baghdad's vindictiveness. A newspaper that reflected this new spirit, *Al-'Iraq*, was published in its stead. Attempts to Arabize Kurdistan also included the removal of Kurdish officials from the autonomous area and their replacement by Arabs; the provision of a 500 dinar inducement for Arab men to marry Kurdish women;[25] and a far-reaching, long-range plan in 1975 that involved the granting of Iraqi citizenship, alongside various concessions and incentives, to Arabs from other Arab countries so as to reduce the percentage of Kurds in the population.[26]

At the same time the government announced extensive development plans worth millions of dollars, including the construction of "model villages," the paving of strategic roads, the implementation of agrarian reform, and the construction of factories and vacation sites in the north. While these plans were also intended to appease the Kurdish population and present a positive showcase to the world, they were mainly intended to break old social patterns from which the traditional Kurdish leadership had drawn its power and to strengthen the central government's hold on the north. About 250,000 Kurds living near the border and in other Kurdish areas were transferred to the model villages, which were built in areas offering easy access to the authorities.[27] These residents were uprooted from their traditional sources of influence and leadership, and were now under the controlling eye of the army. Moreover, inasmuch as the Kurds were experiencing social and economic difficulties, it was easy for the regime to recruit them to the army in exchange for remuneration. Under the cover of agrarian reform, the Baghdad authorities transferred ownership of land from Kurdish to Arab hands, primarily south of the autonomy area.[28] They also expropriated the assets of large Kurdish landowners.[29] Thus, the latter lost their main source of power. In addition, industrial development was announced with the goal of increasing urbanization, cultivating new social bonds, and breaking traditional tribal loyalties. However, the Kurdistan region "remained tied to an unproductive agricultural sector."[30] The new strategic roads that spread throughout the north were intended to prevent guerrilla fighters from regaining their hold over the land, to bring remote settlements under the regime's control, and to permit the rapid deployment of the Iraqi Army. As it turned out, modernization proved to be a two-edged sword. While it did allow Baathi penetration into the Kurdish heartland, it also strengthened Kurdish national identity.

The implementation of autonomy was a key method by which the regime sought to find a way into the heart of the Kurdish population and to undermine the foundation of the Kurdish movement. Although Baghdad did not disavow autonomy, even when it had the power to do so, it changed it to autonomy in name only, devoid of the authority of self-rule. Saddam, who continued to preach autonomy, expressed the special character that the regime wished to confer on it: "Our decision to develop autonomy *in order to strengthen Iraqi unity* is final" (emphasis added).[31] The extent to which this kind of autonomy sought to serve Iraqi unity and the Baath is evidenced by the fact that, during the second term of the Kurdish legislative assembly, beginning in October 1977 the members of the legislative assembly were appointed by the RCC. Moreover the chairman of the new executive council, Ahmad 'Abd-al-Qadir al-Naqshbandi, who was derisively nicknamed "Mr. Autonomy" by the Kurds, was the chairman of the Baath Party in the north. Neither the legislative assembly nor the executive council had any real power. Even the position of vice-president of the republic, held by Taha Muhyi-al-Din Ma'ruf, remained ceremonial as did the positions of the four Kurdish ministers. These officials, who acted as go-betweens, were highly unlikely to express the Kurdish population's desire for autonomy and were in fact used as pawns to promote the Baath policy.

Another policy trend, reinforced by the suppression of the rebellion and running counter to the substance of Kurdish autonomy, reflected the party's attempts to disseminate the Baathist doctrine among the Kurds by espousing a clear, pan-Arab ideology. The Baath Party established branches in all provinces of the north, including in the model villages. It openly preached the recruitment of Kurds into the Baath Party and even provided incentives to those who joined the party; for instance, by granting positions in governmental ministries to Kurdish party members and blocking the advancement of Kurds who refrained from becoming members. On a tour of the provinces of the north in March 1979, Saddam called on Kurdish citizens to join the Baath Party because, he said, no contradiction existed between being Kurdish and being a member of the Baath Party nor between being Kurdish and being "a part of the Arab nation." The regime's attempts to create an overlap between Kurdism and Arabism reached the point where Saddam declared that Salah-al-Din al-Ayyubi, a Kurdish Muslim hero born in Tikrit, was Arab.[32] It should be noted, however, that not all Kurds took pride in Salah al-Din al-Ayyubi, precisely because he did not champion the Kurdish cause.

A Renewed Struggle for Autonomy

The Kurdish war of 1974–1975 delivered a severe blow to the Kurdish national movement. But it was not the deathblow sought by the regime and feared by the movement itself. Barzani mirrored and reinforced such fear when he declared in May 1975, while in Iran, that "the war for autonomy has come to an end and will never be resumed."[33] However, on other occasions, Barzani did express the hope that the struggle would be resumed by his successors. Indeed, the quiet enforced by the regime in Kurdistan was disrupted about a year after the end of the fighting. The Kurdish movement began to reorganize from an initial position of inferiority vis-à-vis the Baath. Through its military, police, and administrative arms, the government ruled Kurdistan high-handedly. In fact, a not insignificant part of the Peshmerga and the KDP had made their peace with the Baath. Two Kurdish parties, the pro-Baath (dissident) KDP and the KRP, became Baath agents in all but name. The Kurdish population was deeply frustrated by the Kurdish national struggle and the leadership's incompetence. The leadership was, above all, fragmented. There was no central movement to lead the struggle, but various distinct groups that were all engaged in bitter infighting. Nonetheless, two basic factors that constituted the sine qua non for the movement's survival persisted: a Kurdish drive to undermine the central government and foreign involvement.

The regime's acts of repression against the Kurdish population began to boomerang against Baghdad. In early 1976, spontaneous clashes between Kurdish citizens and Iraqi Army and police forces broke out against the backdrop of opposition to the forced displacement of the Kurdish population. It is well possible that clashes of this type, which intensified over time, moved the government to stop the displacement policy in July of that year. In this climate, political groups resolved to wage the Kurdish struggle began to reorganize. The first group to do so was Jalal Talabani's group, the Patriotic Union of Kurdistan (PUK), the establishment of which was announced by Radio Damascus in July 1975. Talabani had not played a central role in the last war nor had he been involved in the failed alliance with Iran and the consequences thereof. Hence, he could now disclaim responsibility for this fiasco and exploit the ensuing political vacuum to realize his dream of leading the movement—a dream that had been denied him as long as Barzani held the stage. The PUK base was in Damascus, where it presented itself as a party with a leftist-radical ideology. However, although it censured the KDP for its "rightist" and "tribal" policies that had led to the collapse of the rebellion, it actually promoted the same objectives as the KDP: the destruction of the dictatorial regime of the Baath, the establishment of a democratic regime in Iraq, and the application of "genuine autonomy" for the Kurds.[34]

For a number of reasons, the situation of the KDP was much more tricky than that of the PUK: the blot of failure that stained it; fierce internal criticism;

Barzani's disappearance from the scene causing the temporary absence of a patron; the dispersion of the party leadership and members in Iran, throughout Iraq, and in Europe; and internal bickering about the path to be followed. It therefore is no wonder that in the initial stages of reorganization, the KDP split into several factions. The most important of these were the KDP Interim Leadership, headed by Barzani's two sons, Idris and Mas'ud, and the KDP Preparation Committee, headed by Mahmud 'Uthman. Idris and Mas'ud, who accompanied Barzani throughout his political career and joined him in exile in Iran following the collapse of the insurgency in 1975, returned to Iraq shortly thereafter and attempted to follow in their father's footsteps. Of the two, Mas'ud was the more natural and active leader. At the age of sixteen, he abandoned his studies and joined the Peshmerga. At the age of twenty, he became head of the Parastin.

As to the state of affairs in the party in early 1976, KDP émigrés and Barzani supporters in Europe set about reorganizing the KDP Interim Leadership, which eventually became the dominant KDP faction.[35] With time, the Kurdish diaspora eventually came to play a growing role in galvanizing Western support for the Kurdish cause. Acknowledging past mistakes, the KDP Interim Leadership committed itself to democratizing party procedures, making a joint effort with Kurds from other countries to achieve genuine autonomy within the Iraqi framework. The group completed the preliminary stages of this enterprise in November 1979, when it held its Ninth Congress near Reza'iyeh in Iran and adopted the name of KDP. The congress determined the party's new strategy and chose Idris as party leader. In practice, however, Idris headed the party together with Mas'ud.

Parallel to these attempts at reorganization outside Iraq, the PUK and the KDP of Idris and Mas'ud strove to consolidate their hold in Kurdistan itself. The PUK spearheaded these efforts and, in time, managed to consolidate its hold in the Sulaymaniyya region, Talabani's traditional area of activity. The KDP came on the scene at a later stage, when it began to reorganize in the Badinan area. The two brothers endeavored to regain leadership over the entire Kurdish people, but failed to replicate their father's achievements. Idris died of a heart attack in 1987 at the age of forty-two while Mas'ud, two years younger, continued to hold onto power.[36] However, Mas'ud had to contend with a rival camp headed by Talabani that he has never been able to contain or defeat. As a result, Iraqi Kurdistan was divided into two camps after the passing of Mulla Mustafa Barzani. At the head of one faction stood the traditional leadership of the Barzanis while Talabani headed the more urban and educated camp. The failure of the Kurdish war of 1974–1975, the lackluster leadership of Barzani's sons, the difficult postwar conditions in Iraqi Kurdistan, and the demand for new leadership all paved the way for the rise of the Talabani camp. The conflict between the two camps was fought on many fronts and entailed an intergenerational struggle in which the Talabani camp represented a generally younger group.

The PUK and the KDP began small-scale guerrilla operations. As time went by, both claimed impressive—albeit difficult to verify and probably highly over-rated—successes. Of disastrous consequence for the Kurds was the intense power struggle that erupted between the KDP and the PUK as well as between them and fragments of other Kurdish parties. In the initial years of the reorganization effort, more energy was devoted to settling accounts among the parties themselves than to waging a struggle against the regime.

Despite past experience, the two parties were once again forced to rely on the support of external players, which did in fact contribute greatly to the movement's recovery. With Iran's temporary withdrawal from the scene, Syria hastened to use the Kurdish card to strike at Baghdad. In January 1975, while the war was still raging in Kurdistan, Baghdad indirectly accused Damascus of actively supporting the Kurds. Due to the bilateral problems mentioned above, the aid increased as a function of the deterioration of relations between the two countries. Damascus granted refuge as well as financial and military aid to Talabani's group and supported its propaganda efforts. It helped him infiltrate Iraq and consolidate himself there. However, the Syrian backing had one notable limitation: it was a function that hinged on the nature of relations between the two countries. Therefore, when Baghdad and Damascus initiated reconciliation talks in December 1977–January 1978, Damascus ordered Talabani to cease his activities and engage in a direct dialogue with the Baghdad government. But as reconciliation talks yielded nothing and relations between Baghdad and Damascus remained strained, Syrian aid to Talabani continued unabated.

Turkey scrupulously respected its security agreements with Iraq, preventing as far as possible any activities within its territory on the part of Iraqi Kurds. It followed this policy because of its generally good relations with Iraq and its fears of the spillover effect of Kurdish activities in Iraq onto the Kurds in Turkey. However, when there were major differences between Iraq and Turkey, as was the case in 1978 regarding Turkey's oil debt to Baghdad, Turkey turned a blind eye to Kurdish activities beyond its borders. Turkey and Iraq refrained from using the Kurdish card against each other, which may explain the relatively close cooperation that prevailed between the KDP and Kurdish opposition groups in Turkey at the time. This was especially true following the emergence of the PKK in Turkey and its anti-Turkish activities, which began in 1984.

As for Iran, so long as the shah was in power, he scrupulously implemented Iran's part in the Algiers Agreement and refrained from supporting the Kurds against the Iraqi government. But a real turning point came with Ayatollah Khomeini's rise to power and the establishment of the Islamic Republic of Iran in February 1979. The delicate balance of power between Iraq and Iran changed overnight. Initially, Khomeini sought to destabilize the "heretic" Baathi regime by way of what he considered his natural allies; namely, the Shi'is of Iraq. He soon realized, however, that whatever appeal he might have held for them was not translatable into political action because of the extreme weakness of the Shi'is. Hence, like his predecessor, Khomeini also reverted to the Kurds with a view toward destabilizing the Baath—and this, despite the inherent contradiction between Shi'i Iran and the Sunni Kurds as well as between the Iranian religious worldview and the relatively secular Kurdish national movement. The emerging alliance was all the more puzzling in view of the fact that the Iranian Kurds themselves were then up in arms against the Islamic Republic.

In clear defiance of the Algiers Agreement, Khomeini set about inciting the Iraqi Kurds against their government. The Kurdish group chosen for this task was the KDP of Barazani's sons, Idris and Mas'ud. In November 1979, Iran allowed the KDP to hold its Ninth Congress on Iranian soil. In February 1980 Radio Tehran started broadcasting reports in the name of the KDP, and in April it quoted a telegram confirming the party's support of the Islamic Revolution in Iran. Then in May the clandestine radio station Voice of Iraqi Kurdistan, which had been the main vehicle for mobilizing the Kurds, renewed its broadcasts after an interval of five years, apparently under Iranian auspices.

The Baath regime's initial reaction was to play the Kurdish card as well, with the twofold aim of pacifying nonbelligerent Iraqi Kurds and at the same time inciting Iranian Kurds against their government. In December 1979, Baghdad announced the Legislative Council Law, a revised edition of the March 1974 Legislative Council Law, which provided for the establishment of an elected legislative council for the Kurds. The regime presented the move as an important leap forward toward the realization of Kurdish aspirations for autonomy because, for the first time since 1974, members of the council were to be elected by the Kurds and not appointed by the government. The Kurdish opposition, however, was far more skeptical about the regime's real motives. First of all, the very wording of the law was problematic, evading as it did sensitive terms like *Kurds* and *Kurdistan* and using in their stead neutral ones such as *inhabitants of the autonomous region*. Second, since the council could be summoned and dismissed by a republican decree, it was de facto under the president's thumb. Even worse, members of the council were actually required to be Baathists: on assuming office, every member would be called on to swear allegiance to the principles of the Baathi July 1968 Revolution.[37] The Iraqi government's second move was to support Iranian Kurds who became embroiled in a rebellion after thirty years of relative quiet. Not only did Baghdad provide them with financial and military assistance, but it also went so far as to urge them to "liberate Iranian Kurdistan" and "to achieve its independence."[38] However, as it turned out, the war that Iran and Iraq were fighting by proxy was but a prelude to the direct and full-scale war that erupted in September 1980.

Notes

1. Ahmad Hasan al-Bakr described his situation as if he were a prisoner in his own country. Interview with an ex-Baathi official, Aljazeera, 2 June 2008.

2. The discussion of Saddam's rise to power is beyond the scope of this book. I will refer to its consequences in the relevant sections.

3. Iraq increased its military expenditures sixfold, from $800 million in 1972 to $5 billion in 1979. Abbas al-Nasrawi, "Economic Consequences of the Iraq-Iran War," *Third World Quarterly* 8, no. 3 (1986): 869–895.

4. *R. Iran Courier*, 16 June 1975, cited in *Daily Report*, 17 June 1975.

5. Because of the war with Iran, Iraq did not host, as initially planned, the conference of the Non-Aligned Movement in 1982.

6. Niccolò Machiavelli, *The Prince* (Harmondsworth: Penguin Books, 1971), p. 48.

7. *Pesh Merga* (Helsinki), August 1975.

8. Ofra Bengio, *The Kurdish Revolution in Iraq* (in Hebrew) (Tel Aviv: Hakkibutz Hameuhad, 1989), p. 170.

9. Chris Kutschera, *Le mouvement national kurde* (Paris: Flammarion, 1970), p. 331. Bedir Khan was the ruler of the principality of Botan until the mid-nineteenth century. He is considered the father of Kurdish nationalism.

10. Martin van Bruinessen, *Agha, Shaikh and State: The Social and Political Structures of Kurdistan* (London: Zed Books, 1992), p. 240.

11. Loqman's son Saywan Barzani told me how he had escaped such a fate. Saywan Barzani, interviewed by the author, Paris, 21 September 2008.

12. Quil Lawrence, *Invisible Nation: How the Kurds' Quest for Statehood Is Shaping Iraq and the Middle East* (New York: Walker; distributed by Macmillan, 2008), p. 31.

13. Radio Baghdad, Voice of the Masses, 2 February 1987, cited in *Daily Report*, 3 February 1987.

14. In an interview with Zubeyda Barwari, a former Kurdish refugee in Iran, she told me that the Iranian authorities had isolated them from other Kurds. Zubeyda Barwari. interviewed by the author, Paris, 20 September 2008.

15. *Amnesty International Report, 1975–1976* (London: Amnesty International, 1976), pp. 183–187.

16. Machiavelli, *The Prince*, p. 48.

17. Howard Adelman, "Humanitarian Intervention: The Case of the Kurds," *International Journal of Refugee Law* 4, no. 1 (1992): 7.

18. *Washington Post*, cited in *Ma'ariv*, 22 March 1976.

19. Ibid.

20. *The Times* (London, daily), 27 July 1976.

21. Ibid. On another occasion, he provided more specific details about the plan: the transfer from the borders would be "20 kms deep," the army would be "stationed in the region," and roads would be constructed in the mountains. Saddam Husayn, "Khandaq Wahid Am Khandaqan," in *Al-Thawra wal-Nazra al-Jadida* (Baghdad: Dar al-Hurriyya lil-Tiba'a, 1981) pp. 34–35

22. Bengio, *The Kurdish Revolution*, p. 172.

23. Camillia Fawaz el-Solh, "Migration and the Selectivity of Change: Egyptian Peasant Women in Iraq," *Peuples Méditerranéens*, no. 31–32 (1985): 243.

24. *Pesh Merga*, August–December 1976.

25. Mirella Galletti, *Le relazioni tra Italia e Kurdistan* (Roma: Istituto per l'Oriente C.A. Nallino, 2001), p. 218. Anthony McDermott mentions £750. Anthony McDermott, "The 1975 Crisis," Minority Rights Group Report no. 23 (London: Minority Rights Group, 1977), p. 20.

26. *Al-Jumhuriyya* (Baghdad, daily), 13 January 1975.

27. Ismet Sheriff Vanly, "Kurdistan in Iraq," in *A People Without a Country: The*

Kurds and Kurdistan, ed. Gérard Chaliand (London: Zed Press, 1980), p. 200; S. J. Laizer, *Martyrs, Traitors, and Patriots: Kurdistan After the Gulf War* (London: Zed Books, 1996), p. 165.

28. In early 1976, Baghdad expropriated 566,000 dunams in the autonomous area and established 160 agricultural collectives. Iraqi News Agency, 11 March 1976, cited in BBC, 11 March 1976.

29. In June 1975, landownership in the autonomous area was limited to 40–120 dunams per landowner. Middle East News Agency, 2 June 1975, cited in *Daily Report*, 5 June 1975.

30. Denize Natali, *The Kurdish Quasi-State* (Syracuse: Syracuse University Press, 2010), p. 2.

31. Iraqi News Agency, 2 September 1976, cited in *Daily Report*, 2 September 1976.

32. *Al-Thawra* (Baghdad, daily), 23 February, 22 March 1979.

33. Arab Report and Record, 1–15 May 1975.

34. "The main political parties in Iraqi Kurdistan were hardly marked off from each other by specific class interests or ideological differences." Michael Leezenberg, "Urbanization, Privatization, and Patronage: The Political Economy of Iraqi Kurdistan," in *The Kurds: Nationalism and Politics*, eds. Faleh A. Jabar and Dawod Hosham (London: Saqi, 2006), pp. 164–165.

35. According to Edmund Ghareeb, it began to organize in November 1975 and operate in May 1976. Edmund Ghareeb, *The Kurdish Question in Iraq* (Syracuse: Syracuse University Press, 1981), p. 182.

36. In 1999 Mas'ud made Nechirvan, Idris's thirty-three-year-old son, his right-hand man by appointing him prime minister of Kurdistan—the Barzani faction.

37. *Al-Thawra*, 6 December 1979, 17 March 1980.

38. "You must plan . . . to liberate Iran's Kurdistan and to achieve its independence." Radio Baghdad, 22 April 1980, cited in *Daily Report*, 24 April 1980.

Part 2

Caught in the Crossfire, 1980–1998

We are preparing the Kurdish movement to accept independence at the appropriate time. We therefore want the partition of Iraq into several small states—Shi'i, Sunni, and Kurdish.
> —Nawshirwan Mustafa, *Le Monde,* 16 April 1987

As an expression of the will of the great Iraqi people, the brave armed forces . . . in response to the treason of this stray clique . . . carried out the Anfal operation under the supervision of staff lieutenant General Sultan Hashim Ahmad. . . . This is a struggle admired by the entire world, the struggle of leader Saddam Husayn's people, Arabs and Kurds, who placed themselves in the service of the homeland.
> —Radio Baghdad, 19 March 1988,
> cited in *Daily Report,* 21 March 1988

10

"One War Begets Another": The Iran-Iraq War

Conventional wisdom has it that the main reason for the eight-year war launched by Iraq against Iran in September 1980 was Iraq's fear of the repercussions of the Islamic Revolution in Iran on its own Shi'i population and its need to take preemptive measures to forestall a similar upheaval in Iraq.[1] I challenge this alleged truism and present the following arguments instead.

First, Iraq had developed a position of strength and self-confidence, rather than fear and weakness. Indeed, though the conflict between the two countries was of long standing, Iraq had never felt strong enough to challenge Iran on the battlefield—as it did in 1980. Second, while the internal Shi'i problem might have been a source of deep concern for Baghdad, it was not sufficient, in and of itself, to drive the country to war. The most that can be said is it was an important catalyst. It is significant, however, that in the long run Iraqi propaganda used the Shi'i argument as the main justification for the war. And, third, if one were to point out the single internal Iraqi problem with the greatest impact on the country's conflict with Iran, it would be the Kurdish problem. Not only was it intimately bound up with the root cause of the war, but it also provided an immediate casus belli, as I explain later in this chapter. In addition, shortly after the outbreak of the Iran-Iraq War, this intractable problem developed into a war within a war and the two wars became inextricably intertwined.[2]

For a better understanding of Iraq's motives for initiating the war against Iran, it is instructive to take a close look at President Saddam Hussein's speech of 17 September 1980, which paved the way to war. Aside from routine anti-Zionist and anti-imperialist rhetoric, the greater part of the speech was devoted to the Kurdish problem, the 1975 Algiers Agreement with Iran, and their implied connection to the approaching war. Significantly, Saddam never mentioned a Shi'i problem nor did he suggest it was in any way connected to it. Indeed, this line of argument would surface much later, when Iraq was on the defensive. Analyzing the background of the Algiers Agreement, Saddam explained in an apologetic vein that Iraq had to sign the agreement because the army was facing an impossible situation in its fight against the Kurds, mainly due to a lack of ammunition, which had reached the point where "the air force had only three heavy bombs left." Saddam termed the decision to sign the agreement a "courageous" one since it was made "to safeguard sovereignty when the rifle and the sword alone [could] not achieve the objective." Furthermore, he maintained that the decision had "saved Iraq from real dangers which were threatening its unity, security, and future." Saddam then expounded the main points of the agreement, saying that Iraq had agreed that the thalweg line become the border in the Shatt al-Arab in exchange for an Iranian commitment "to refrain from giving military and any other kind of aid to the mercenary renegade gang in the northern part of the homeland." However, on the establishment of the new regime in Iran, he asserted, "the heads of the mercenary mutiny returned to Iran to use it as a springboard to threaten Iraq's unity and national security with the support of the ruling authorities." Accordingly, "since the rulers of Iran have violated this agreement by blatantly and deliberately intervening in Iraq's domestic affairs by backing and financing, as did the shah before them, the leaders of the mutiny . . . I announce before you that we consider the 6th March 1975 agreement to be abrogated from one side also." The bottom line of the whole speech was that "today's Iraq is more capable of carrying out its tasks" (i.e., of safeguarding its sovereignty over the Shatt al-Arab).[3]

Clearly, the Algiers Agreement, of which Saddam had been the main architect, weighed heavily on him and the impulse to rectify it was a central driving force behind the war. Support for this thesis can be found in a biography of Saddam published shortly after the beginning of the war. The biographer, Fuad Matar, states that Iraq's decision to go to war "can be said to have been taken from the day that the Algiers Agreement was signed on 6 March 1975." He further reveals that

> Saddam Hussein, who was vice-president at the time, was obliged to accept the agreement so that he could have a breathing space in which to build a strong army . . . an army which could one day take on the Shah's army in case the [Iraqi] territory [i.e., Khuzestan] and sovereignty over the Shatt al-Arab could not be restored through diplomatic means.[4]

The fact that the entire book was written under Saddam's inspiration, if not dictation, and that it was released very close in time to the outbreak of the war, lends much verisimilitude to this version.

As to the Kurds, they also were driven by an urge to avenge the consequences of the Algiers Agreement. However, as had already happened in the past, they found it easier to forge alliances with outside forces, rather than rally their own forces and present a unified stand vis-à-vis the government. In any case, the two main Kurdish parties, the KDP and the PUK, posed a real challenge to Baghdad.[5] Both claimed to represent the authentic Kurdish national movement; both sought to capitalize on the war to strengthen their hold in the north and force the government to grant meaningful autonomy to the Kurds; and both formed alliances with a number of parties to achieve these goals.[6] The alliances forged by the KDP and the PUK reflected the bitter rivalry between them and helped deepen the rift even further. Internally, the KDP allied itself with two groups from opposite extremes: the Iraqi Communist Party and the Shi'i fundamentalist party al-Da'wa.[7] If its alliance with the Communist Party was the natural outgrowth of their long-standing cooperation, collaboration with al-Da'wa was new and at times quite awkward for the KDP. Never in the past had a Kurdish party joined forces with a Shi'i or any other Islamic party. Even here, the physical, ideological, and political gulf between the two seemed too wide to bridge. While the Kurds spoke in national terms, al-Da'wa spoke in religious ones. While the former strove for Kurdish autonomy, the latter strove for an Islamic republic. Nevertheless, after the outbreak of the war, links were established between the two groups mainly at the instigation of Iran.

Indeed, this touches on a key point in this discussion. In spite of what the KDP itself considered as Iran's betrayal of 1975, it nevertheless revived its relations with that country. This stance could by no means be explained by naïveté, but rather by sheer necessity. In its drive to avenge the Algiers Agreement, the KDP could not have found a better ally than Ayatollah Khomeini. Even more important was the fact that an alliance with Iran was the KDP's only option since Syria had already "adopted" its rival, the PUK, and Turkey was deeply hostile to Kurdish national aspirations not only in Turkey but in neighboring countries as well. Paradoxically, painful as past relations with Iran might have been, these relations nevertheless provided some basis from which to resume them. Still, there were inherent dangers in the revived ties. One was that the KDP might lose the little independence it had achieved and become a pliant tool in the hands of Iran. Indeed, the relations of dependency that actually developed went a long way toward explaining both the KDP's assistance to Iran in fighting Iranian Kurds and its cooperation with al-Da'wa.[8] The second, and graver, danger was that Iran would once again turn its back on the KDP in exchange for a better deal with Iraq.

It was this anomalous situation that the PUK set out to redress, only to find itself caught in a vicious circle. Over eight years of war, the PUK changed alliances at least three times: first with Syria; then the Iraqi government; and, finally, Iran. Thus, in October 1986, the PUK concluded an agreement on economic, political, and military cooperation with the Iranian government, stipulating that it would press the fight against the Iraqi regime until Saddam was toppled and that it would not sign unilateral deals with Baghdad. Iran also agreed to provide the PUK with arms, financial support, and medical aid. Another outcome was that the PUK was urged to make its peace with the KDP at the instigation of Iran.[9] In changing sides so often, the PUK was motivated by its rivalry with the KDP, by pragmatism, and by the sheer need to survive. At the same time, this approach pointed to the severe constraints under which the Kurdish movement as a whole was acting.

Mutual Threat Perceptions

Shortly after the Kurdish collapse in 1975, Saddam boasted of "beating the collaborator enclave . . . in the high mountains (*a'ali al-jibal*)"; he nevertheless made a clear distinction between the Barzani clan and "our people in Kurdistan," whose loyalty he sought to gain by various means.[10] The outbreak of the war with Iran provided an opportunity for testing this loyalty. Yet if Saddam hoped that the war would help galvanize Iraqi national feelings among the Kurds, he was totally mistaken. Not only were they reluctant to contribute to the Iraqi war effort, but they also sought to capitalize on the war in order to weaken the central government, strengthen Kurdish national feelings, and achieve genuine autonomy.

Indeed, while the Baathi regime perceived the war as a means to vindicate the Algiers Agreement, the Kurds regarded it as an opportunity to vindicate their own part in the agreement. Developments during the eight-year war provided ample evidence of this thesis. Firstly, the Kurdish north was more restive than any other part of the country, becoming the center of almost all opposition groups, be they Kurds, Communists, or Shi'is. Secondly, at times this restiveness turned into a popular uprising, which the Kurds termed *intifada*.[11] Most worrisome, from the Iraqi point of view, was the fact that certain Kurdish groups went so far as to assist Iran in its offensive against Iraq.

The level of intensity of the Kurdish resistance reflected the various stages in the Iran-Iraq War: when the external war escalated, the internal miniwar escalated too. Generally speaking, Kurdish antiregime activities took two forms: popular resistance alongside guerrilla fighting. The two were not necessarily coordinated or even propelled by the same causes. While the war was still raging inside Iranian territory and the Iraqi Army proved to be the stronger, the Kurdish population challenged it mainly through passive resistance such as reluctance to serve in the Iraqi Army or the popular army, namely the Baath Party militia (*al-jaysh al-sha'bi*), which became greatly inflated during the war and served as the main buttress of internal security. However, no sooner had the military situation changed than Kurdish opposition became more active. Concurrently with the spring 1982 Iraqi setbacks at Khorramshahr in Iran, severe disturbances, described as a popular uprising by the Kurds, engulfed the entire Kurdish north. Altogether 12,000 people, including students from northern towns such as Sulaymaniyya, Erbil, and Duhok, were reported to have taken part in demonstrations and strikes.[12] Similar uprisings recurred in April–May 1984, September 1985, and May–June 1987. These, seemingly spontaneous, occurrences were said to have been spurred on by the regime's weakness or, alternatively, by the ruthless methods it had applied against the Kurds. In fact, so strong had the pressure become that the Baath Party was forced to exempt Kurds from compulsory military service and permit them to serve on a voluntary basis.[13] Saddam expressed his indignation regarding this situation when he stated, "It is shameful that the Arabs should defend the soil of Kurdistan while Iraqi sons of Kurdistan stand by watching them."[14]

The organized Kurdish opposition attempted to ride the crest of popular resistance to increase its own pressure on the government. Thus, in July 1983, the Peshmerga of the KDP joined hands with Iranian forces in their attack on Hajj 'Umran, a small Iraqi Kurdish town on the Iranian border. In October of the same year, Peshmerga forces again assisted the Iranian Army in its attempt to occupy Penjwin, another Kurdish border town near Sulaymaniyya. Faced with these constraints and in line with its policy of divide and rule, the Baath approached Talabani, the KDP's rival, in 1982 in the hope that he would do part of the job for Baghdad. However, the promise of large-scale autonomy with which the Baath lured the PUK evaporated once the cease-fire agreement between them had been signed in October 1983. Indeed, Baghdad's cynicism came to light even during the negotiations, when eleven PUK supporters, including Jalal Talabani's brother and two nieces, were executed.[15] Thus, the cease-fire that lasted about a year harmed only the Kurdish national movement since it split the Kurdish camp and provided the government with a much-needed breathing space, paralyzing the PUK itself. However, it took one year for Talabani to call for the cessation of the cease-fire and the renewal of the struggle for autonomy.

The most sustained Kurdish pressure against the government took place during 1985–1988. For the first time since 1975 a modus vivendi was established between the KDP and the PUK, enabling each to initiate separate guerrilla actions against government establishments and forces without the threat of an attack from the rear by the rival party. What is more, by 1987 a certain modus operandi had been established between the two, with the active encouragement of Iran. Thus, together with four other smaller groups, they formed the Iraqi Kurdish Front, with the declared aim of fighting for self-determination. Although in the final analysis this rapprochement was not of great consequence, it nonetheless gave the impression of unity so coveted by the Kurdish population. Both the KDP and the PUK employed guerrilla tactics to harass military convoys and attack government posts and buildings, including those within Kurdish towns which as a rule were under government control.[16] Similarly, they kidnapped foreign nationals and menaced strategic highways and other strategic facilities such as the Iraqi oil pipeline to Turkey. Over and above all of this, both parties deepened their cooperation with Iran. In November 1986 the KDP and the PUK participated in a conference of all Iraqi opposition groups, which was sponsored by Iran and aimed at coordinating anti-Iraqi activities. In October 1987 the PUK and Iranian forces carried out a joint attempt, which failed, to sabotage oil facilities in Kirkuk. By contrast, an earlier operation of March 1987 resulted in the Iranian capture of strategic heights in an area controlling the Hajj 'Umran-Rawanduz axis on the Iraqi-Iranian border. Finally, in March 1988 the PUK and Iran joined hands in the seizure of Halabja, a small town on the Iraqi-Iranian border.

Regarding their declared political goals, the Kurds continued for the most part to stick to that of a meaningful autonomy. However, in the spring of 1987 an important change occurred when the PUK declared its intention to fight for an independent Kurdistan. In retrospect, the Kurdish challenge had indeed failed to achieve any of its goals, but this is not to say that it was insignificant or not powerful enough to feed Baghdad's threat perceptions. In order to appreciate its real impact, it should be put in the proper context of time and place. From the Iraqi point of view, the most serious aspect of this challenge was a military-strategic one. First, the Kurdish opposition joined hands with the Iranian Army, precisely on those occasions when the Iraqi Army was hard-pressed in other sectors; for example, in the spring of 1986 after the fall of al-Faw into Iranian hands, or in the spring of 1987 almost simultaneously with the fierce Iranian offensive on Basra. The Kurdish threat was doubly menacing as it could divert the Iraqi Army's attention from the main battle zone and, even worse, bring about the separation of the Kurdish areas from the rest of the country. A no less severe strategic problem was the fact that between 1982 and 1985 Iraq's only viable oil pipeline was the one crossing Kurdish territory into Turkey, which meant that any Kurdish act of sabotage could have been fatal for Iraq.

On a number of occasions and echoing as it were the Kurdish threat, Iraqi officials raised the specter of the partition of Iraq into three statelets (*duwaylat*): Sunni, Shi'i, and Kurdish.[17] While this line of indoctrination was aimed at increasing the motivation of the Iraqi soldiers and enlisting Arab and international support for Iraq's cause, it betrayed at the same time the Iraqi government's deep-seated fears regarding the eventuality of partition. No doubt the Kurdish north constituted Iraq's Achilles' heel for, together with Syria and Iran, it formed an arc of forces hostile to Iraq. Neither were historical memories of much comfort: indeed, between the sixteenth and twentieth centuries this same area had changed hands between the Ottoman and Persian empires a number of times. In this context, declarations such as those by the PUK regarding the partition of Iraq could not fail to leave their impact on the Baath. As a matter of fact, the Kurds brought to bear severe psychological pressures on a regime that was conducting two separate wars at one and the same time.

In spite of its great vulnerability, the Baath Party was far better equipped to cope with the situation than was the Kurdish movement. The regime had all the military, political, and economic resources in hand as well as a range of policies that it could adapt to changing situations. During the first three years of the war, the regime sought to strike a fine balance between fighting Kurdish opposition and encouraging a sense of Iraqi patriotism among Kurdish citizens, or at least keeping them within the Iraqi consensus. However, as the war escalated, the Baath put more and more emphasis on the first strategy, ending up by treating the Kurdish population as sheer enemies.

Anticipating trouble from the Kurdish population, the regime held elections to the Kurdish legislative council just three days before launching the war on Iran; that is, on 19 September 1980. In essence, Baghdad attempted to use elections as leverage to mobilize Kurdish support for the approaching war and to dissuade the Kurds from supporting the Kurdish opposition and its ally Iran. In another move in June 1982, a Kurd, Taha Muhyi-al-Din Ma'ruf, was co-opted to the RCC, the highest legislative and executive body in the state—for the first time since the Baath's advent to power. On the face of it, this gesture represented a far-reaching concession to the Kurdish national movement, which until then the Baath had been reluctant to grant. But as in the case of the legislative council, here too, the regime made sure to empty the gesture of any real content. It should be noted that by 1982 the RCC had already lost much of its power, which came to be concentrated more and more in the hands of the president. Besides, Ma'ruf, who was also the vice-president, held ceremonial rather than real power. Coming as it did shortly after the Kurdish popular uprising in the spring of 1982, the co-option of a Kurd served as a barometer of the regime's deep sense of unease about the Kurdish problem. Occasionally, the Iraqi government adopted popular welfare measures: despite the war it announced the continuation of development activities in the north, distributed televisions to 20,000 families in Sulaymaniyya as well as land to Kurdish clerics, and held a festival for Kurdish art and culture.[18]

The regime also appealed to the Kurdish sense of Iraqi nationalism. It is well known that Baathi ideology had deeply antagonized Kurdish nationalist feelings, both by viewing Kurdistan as part of the Arab homeland[19] and by the implied threat of turning the Kurds into an insignificant minority once pan-Arabism was implemented.[20] It is true that, in the early 1980s, the chances for Iraq to unite with another Arab country appeared more remote than ever. Still, this did not allay the Kurds' fears of such an eventuality. The regime was quick to realize that if the Kurds were to contribute to the war effort, they should have a symbol or an ideal with which they could identify such as Kurdish autonomy in Iraq. Iraqi patriotism was more likely to appeal to the Kurds, who throughout their long struggle for autonomy had invariably stated that such an autonomy should be implemented within the framework of the Iraqi state. This induced the Baath to shift the center of gravity from pan-Arabism to Iraqi nationalism (*wataniyya*).[21]

Alongside such moves, the regime also suppressed all forms or expressions of Kurdish nationalism and culture. As shown in Chapter 8, the most blatant example was the relocation of Sulaymaniyya University from Sulaymaniyya to Erbil as early as 1981.[22] Long considered the stronghold of Kurdish nationalism, Sulaymaniyya had routinely been bypassed by the regime. In 1974 the Baath chose a more docile and amenable Erbil as "capital" and seat of the Kurdish legislative and executive councils of the autonomous region. Now that the war was raging, and it was feared that the campus at Sulaymaniyya would turn into a hub of Kurdish national resistance, they moved it to Erbil, where they could better control the situation. At the same time, the authorities closed the Kurdish academy and dispersed the Kurdish men of letters.

The Baath Counter-Alliances

In an attempt to counter the Iranian-Kurdish alliance, the Baath sought to ally itself with an outside power—Turkey. Fearing a spillover effect on its own Kurds, Turkey had cooperated with Iraq in curbing Kurdish guerrilla activities along their common border since the mid-1970s. With the outbreak of war and the loosening of Baathi control of the common Iraqi-Turkish border, cooperation between the two countries became even more vital, especially for Iraq. In May 1983, two Turkish brigades penetrated some twelve miles into Iraqi territory in hot pursuit of Turkish and Iraqi Kurdish guerrillas that, according to Kurdish sources, resulted in the capture and killing of several hundred Kurds.[23] This operation, which took place with tacit Iraqi consent, was to become the cornerstone or model of future relations between the two countries during the Iran-Iraq War. In October 1984 Iraq and Turkey signed a formal agreement, allowing each country to penetrate the other's border in pursuit of insurgents. Given the circumstances, the agreement could not be interpreted as anything other than an Iraqi appeal for help from Turkey. As such, it deepened Iraq's dependence on an external power for the control of the Kurdish north, which had begun to assume the characteristics of a no-man's-land. Yet in spite of the dangers inherent in such a situation, Iraq much preferred this to the possibility of the north falling into Kurdish or Iranian hands. Baghdad's calculations turned out to be right, as Turkey adhered fully to the spirit and the letter of the agreement. By the end of the war, Turkish planes or units had penetrated at least three times into Iraqi territory in an attempt to curb Iraqi Kurdish activities near the border.[24] At the same time, Turkey never abused its power to infringe on Iraq's sovereignty.

As important as Turkish assistance to Iraq was considered to be, it could by no means be a substitute for Iraq's military presence in the area. While at the beginning of the war Iraq's main efforts and military units were concentrated in the central and southern sectors, by the end of the war two of its seven army corps were stationed in the north: the First Army Corps along the Iraqi-Iranian border in Kurdistan and the Fifth Army Corps in the heart of Iraqi Kurdistan. Ironically Erbil, the capital of the autonomous region, served as the headquarters for this corps. Indeed, the task of the Iraqi Army in this sector was much more complex and delicate than in any other part of the country because it had to tackle four potential challenges at one and the same time: Iranian offensives from across the border (with KDP or PUK forces, or both, serving as guides in the difficult terrain); guerrilla activities inside Iraqi Kurdistan (by either the KDP, the PUK, the Communists, al-Da'wa, or other small groups); a Kurdish population that was growing increasingly restive; and the need to defend vital strategic assets. The seriousness of the challenge could be gathered from the fact that already in mid-1986 the president's office directed military and Baath Party commands in the autonomous region "to continue and intensify the blockades on the villages and the areas that are prohibited for security reasons." According to these directives, "it is completely prohibited for food and other supplies to reach there."[25] Similarly, elite units of the Republican Guard had to be rushed to the area in March 1987 to help stem the Iranian offensive and discipline the restive population.

Notwithstanding the superiority of the Iraqi war machine, the army found it quite difficult to cope with the military challenge in Kurdistan, mainly because of the ruggedness of the region and the difficulty of using tanks in mountainous areas but also owing to the deep-rooted reluctance on the part of Iraqi Arab soldiers to fight a guerrilla war. To compensate for such disadvantages and because the regime no longer had any allies among the Kurdish opposition parties after 1985, Baghdad mobilized Kurds for the dual task of fighting their own brethren and helping stem the Iranian offensive.

When negotiations with Talabani failed, Baghdad started mobilizing Yezidi Kurds. The Yezidis' special troops (*mafariz khassa*) were to be organized in small units of fifty each, "which [are] easier to control." In addition to fighting "terrorists," the larger overall aim was to "break the center of power and influence of the sect's leaders who consider the loyalty of their members along sectarian and racist lines," and "to inject in them Arab national feelings."[26]

More importantly, the Baath recruited the Kurds to what was initially the light battalions (*al-afwaj al-khafifa*) and later the battalions for national defense (*afwaj al-difa' al-watani*). The highly paid *afwaj*, which numbered about 250,000 men,[27] had the advantage of having a close acquaintance with the area and the population in addition to being well trained in guerrilla fighting. Thus, in a number of instances, the *afwaj* helped the Iraqi Army reconquer the high mountains that Iran had occupied with the help of Kurdish guerrillas of the KDP or PUK, or both.[28] Ironically, then, such encounters turned out to be a fratricidal war between Iraqi Kurds who were fighting someone else's wars.

Still Baghdad could not entrust the *afwaj* with the task of breaking the Kurdish popular uprising for, in quite a few instances, they "defected . . . [to the] enemy." The lack of trust in the *afwaj* was conveyed clearly in a Baathi document that forbade handing over Kurdish "terrorists" to this body, only allowing them to be turned over to the "security" forces.[29]

Anfal: Baghdad's Pyrrhic Victory

Two Baath onslaughts on the Kurds were to become etched in the collective Kurdish memory: the Anfal campaign and the massacre in Halabja.[30] Chemical weapons were used in large quantities in both attacks, with the aim of terrifying the population and destroying Kurdistan. The political discourse reflected these extreme measures. Thus, the very choice of the name Anfal (spoils), which is based on the eighth sura of the Quran, points to this extremism. Saddam, who most probably coined the name, sought on the one hand Islamic legitimization of his deeds and on the other a model for the punishment so vividly described in that sura. A few extracts from this quranic text include: "I shall cast into the unbelievers' hearts terror; so smite above the necks, and smite every finger of them" (8:12). "O God if this be indeed the truth from Thee, then rain down upon us stones out of heaven" (8:32). "The unbelievers will be mustered into Gehenna, that God may distinguish the corrupt from the good, and place the corrupt one upon another, and so heap them up all together" (8:36–37). "It is not for any prophet to have prisoners until he make wide slaughter in the land" (8:67).[31] Indeed, the verses that mention stones from the sky and heaping of bodies figuratively bespeak the outcome of the use of chemical weapons against the Kurds. Documents recovered after the collapse of the Baath in 2003 went even further than the public discourse in delegitimizing the Kurds.[32] According to one document, members of the *afwaj* were advised that "the Peshmerga are infidels and they shall be treated as such. You shall take any Peshmerga's property that you may seize while fighting them. Their wives are lawfully yours (*halal*), as are their sheep and cattle."[33] Taken together, these documents illustrate how systematic, well-planned, and encompassing the campaigns were. The language used is cold blooded and harsh.

The turning point in Baghdad's campaign against the Kurds was the appointment on 29 March 1987 of the president's cousin, 'Ali Hasan al-Majid, as absolute ruler of the north "in order to protect security and order and guarantee stability." Opening with the words "in the name of the people" to give greater legitimacy to this move, the decree granted al-Majid "authority over all the state's civil, military and security apparatuses."[34] Taking advantage of the emergency situation, Baghdad's strongman in Kurdistan moved to break the Kurdish rebellion once and for all. The onslaught he unleashed on them justifies Talabani's calling it "genocide . . . in Iraqi Kurdistan."[35]

In April 1987 following limited Iranian success in capturing certain strategic heights close to Sulaymaniyya,[36] al-Majid unleashed the most severe punitive campaign against the Kurdish population since the beginning of the war—the worst manifestation of which was the use of chemical weapons. His orders aimed among other things at crushing the rebels, completely destroying the Kurdish countryside, and Arabizing strategic areas such as Kirkuk.[37]

The first major chemical attack on the Kurds took place in April 1987 in the villages of Balisan and Shaykh Wassan. In reaction, the residents of the Kani Ashqan quarter in Halabja staged antigovernment demonstrations. Al-Majid's reprisal was particularly harsh:

The commander of the First Army Corps issued an order as requested by Comrade 'Ali Hasan al-Majid to execute the wounded civilians . . . to use earth movers and bulldozers to excise the Kani Ashkan neighborhood, to let the Security, Police and the Army take care of any gatherings . . . and to destroy with tanks and bulldozers any house from which fire is opened.[38]

A few days later, al-Majid informed Baath Party leaders of the following plan:

We will start attacking [the Pershmerga resistance] everywhere . . . then we will surround them in a small pocket and attack them with chemical weapons. I will not attack them with chemicals just one day, but I will continue to attack them with chemicals for fifteen days. . . . I will do it, with the help of God. I will defeat them and follow them to Iran.[39]

Another document issued shortly afterward detailed the bombing of various Kurdish villages causing, among other things, the blinding of thirty people—a clear indication of the use of chemical weapons. The same document revealed that certain members of the *afwaj* threatened that if their villages were to be "eliminated," they would join the "saboteurs."[40] The detailed plan came to light in the directives issued a few days later to the military forces deployed in Kurdistan by the Baath Northern Bureau, headed by al-Majid:

In view of the fact that the officially announced deadline for the amalgamation of these villages expires on 21 June 1987, we have decided . . . [that] 1. all the villages in which the saboteurs (*mukharribin*)—the agents of Iran [i.e., the PUK], the offspring of treason (*salili al-khiyana*) [i.e. the KDP], and similar traitors to Iraq—are still to be found shall be regarded as prohibited for security reasons. 2. The presence of human beings and animals is completely prohibited in these areas, and [these] shall be regarded as operational zones in which [the troops] can open fire at will, without any restrictions, unless otherwise instructed by our headquarters. . . . 4. The Corps Commands shall carry out random bombardments, using artillery, helicopters and aircraft all times of the day or night in order to kill the largest number of persons present in those prohibited areas. . . . 5. All persons captured in those villages shall be detained because of their presence there, and they shall be interrogated by the security services and those between the ages of 15 and 70 must be executed after any useful information has been obtained from them.[41]

Indeed, from the testimony of Kurdish survivors, it was apparent that one of the principal purposes of the Anfal campaign was to kill all adult males of military service age who had been captured in rural Iraqi Kurdistan. Firing squads massacred them by the tens of thousands.[42] In order to make it impossible for families to find refuge in other parts of Kurdistan, a secret order from the Northern Bureau called on the arrest of all families that arrived in towns or complexes (*mujamma'at sakaniyya*) of prohibited areas.[43]

The fate of the Kurds who did not live in the prohibited areas was not more enviable. For example, two orders called for the deportation of family members of saboteurs; they were divested of their Iraqi nationality and of their movable and immovable property.[44] Another document listed the names of mothers of Kurdish deserters. These sixty- to eighty-year-old women were stripped of their Iraqi nationality and deported.[45] As to the fate of the deportees, one document mentioned that, of 1,500 families, some 450 found refuge in Iran. The rest were moved to government-built *mujamma' sakani* that, ironically, the document named "the quarter of steadfastness (*hayy al-sumud*)."[46] All of this was a mere prologue to the Anfal campaign, however.

Saddam gave the green light to the Anfal campaign, which was carried out in eight stages from February to September 1988. On 13 March he visited the region, at the beginning of what would turn out to be a murderous campaign. It was also Saddam who decided on the use of chemical weapons. According to high-ranking military officers, the political, not the military, command decided on the use of such weapons against the Kurds.[47] In the top-secret memorandum Saddam issued in January 1988, one month before the beginning of the campaign, he gave his consent to "the execution of the condemned (*al-mudanin*)."[48] Other directives followed suit. For example, one directive called for treating family members of saboteurs as saboteurs and to execute a village mayor (*mukhtar*) if five or more such families were to be found in his village. Interestingly, the same document enjoined men of religion to expose (*ta'riya*) the saboteurs and their leadership.[49]

As time went by, even the language of the orders became harsher. An order from the First Army Corps, issued on 25 May 1988, stated the following:

> The information we received makes clear that there are villages and separate houses in the prohibited areas which were covered by the *Anfal operation* but have so far not been destroyed as required. It was decided to speed up the destruction and elimination of all the villages and scattered houses as soon as possible, and to give this matter top priority within a time frame not exceeding 10 June 1988.[50] (emphasis added)

Another top-secret document of June 1988 revealed clearly and unequivocally the army's use "during March 1988 of chemical weapons" in the attacks against the villages of Siwan and Balkajar. It further noted the collaboration between the "terrorists" and Iran, as well as the former's attempts to unite their ranks, and suggested various methods to forestall these attempts. It also warned of the use of identity cards issued by the *afwaj* to help the "terrorists" in their fight against the government.[51]

All in all the Anfal campaign, which targeted Kurdish villages albeit not the towns, included the destruction of hundreds of villages situated in strategic areas; the transfer (*tarhil*) of between 100,000 and 500,000 Kurds from the heart of Kurdistan to remote areas near the Jordanian or Saudi borders or, at best, to Kurdish areas more readily controlled by the regime such as Erbil; and the sporadic gassing of Kurdish villages with chemical weapons.[52] The Iraqi media cynically described these campaigns in superlative terms, applying phrases such as "the heroic Anfal operation," "the eternal Anfal operation," "an historic victory," "a brilliant victory," or "the chain of victorious military epics." Furthermore, it described them as "the best gift to our [Kurdish] masses who are celebrating Nowruz." In addition, Baghdad organized demonstrations and cables of support for the campaign.[53]

Though not considered part of the Anfal campaign, the chemical attack on the town of Halabja became the symbol of the Kurdish struggle for survival, much more so than the Anfal campaign itself.

The Halabja Massacre

"The Hiroshima of the Kurds" is what the Kurds termed the Iraqi Army's chemical attack on the Kurdish border town of Halabja on 16 March 1988, in which *circa* 3,200 civilians of all ages were killed or wounded in one day.[54] The timing of the attack was both tragic and ironic. It was in March 1970 that the Baathi regime acknowledged the Kurds' right to autonomy. In March 1975, the Kurds lost the war for a meaningful autonomy in the aftermath of the Algiers Agreement. And in March 1988, the Kurds started a new war for their very survival.

The chemical attack on Halabja, which had a population of *circa* 60,000, was carried out shortly after a joint attack by Peshmerga forces of the PUK and Iran had succeeded in driving the Iraqi Army from that town and occupying it. Accordingly, the most obvious rationale for this action could have been that the Iraqi Army was panic stricken and, fearing that the joint Iranian-Kurdish forces would make further advances into Iraqi Kurdistan, felt justified in taking a preemptive measure. A no less likely explanation could be the urge to avenge Kurdish cooperation with Iran, which in Iraqi eyes turned the Kurds into a fifth column.[55] While such feelings must have played an important part in Iraq's response, there is no doubt that the action was also motivated by more coldblooded calculations. The use of chemical weapons was not new for Iraq, which had already used them in 1983–1984 and in 1986 to stem the Iranian offensive.[56] What was new this time was that events were recorded by reporters brought to the scene by the Iranians, thus giving it worldwide publicity so it could no longer be ignored.[57] Moreover, unlike other such attacks, it was aimed at a large town populated by Iraq's own civilian population and it could not be regarded as a purely preemptive measure like the case against Iran in the past.

To understand this departure from past practices, one must put the attack on Halabja in the wider context of the Iran-Iraq War. Indeed simultaneously with the Iranian offensive in Kurdistan, a ferocious "war of the cities" was taking place between the two countries, a war initiated by Iraq and aimed both at breaking the morale of the Iranians and preempting a new Iranian offensive in the south. Thus, using chemical weapons at Halabja was meant as a warning, not just to the Kurds but also to the Iranians. To fuel Iranian fears, Iraq used chemical weapons against Iranian villages shortly after the attack on Halabja.[58] A few days later, an Iraqi spokesman warned that Iraq might "select a number of major Iranian cities as targets for chemical weapons."[59] Certainly what prompted Iraq to use such weaponry was not only that its use was very effective, but also that it did not carry a high risk since earlier usage had gone unpunished.

That a sophisticated war of nerves was behind the attack on Halabja could also be gleaned from Baghdad's reaction to Iranian accusations against Iraq for its use of chemical weapons. As in previous cases the Iraqi government neither admitted nor denied the accusations, but did emphasize its "determination to defend itself with all possible means."[60] For his part, the Iraqi defense minister 'Adnan Khayrallah Talfah threatened, after the fall of Halabja, to use "all means to defend Iraqi territory."[61] By adopting such a stance, Iraq only helped to increase Iranian apprehension about the possible use of chemical arms against its civilian population. Iran itself contributed to the mounting panic by launching a massive propaganda campaign against Iraq. On 1 April 1988, Radio Tehran warned of a chemical attack, emphasizing that "by resorting to these inhumane methods" Baghdad hoped to stop Iranian resistance.[62] Iranian fears never materialized, but the impact on civilian morale was seemingly enormous. Indeed, one can argue that Halabja proved to be a turning point in the long war. Also in early April, the last Iranian offensive was stopped in Kurdistan as the Iraqi Army managed to drive back the joint Iranian and PUK forces from the strategic area of Qara Dagh in the Sulaymaniyya region, close to the Darbandikhan dam. Two weeks later Iraq succeeded in reoccupying Faw in the south, which ushered the way to further Iraqi successes and, finally, to the Iranian acceptance of a cease-fire on 18 July. It may well be that the Halabja massacre had simply been the last straw. In any case, chemical weapons proved to be effective.

For the Kurds who had become as it were cannon fodder for the warring parties, the Halabja massacre was devastating. Against this background, Talabani's declarations about a Kurdish republic or a federal system within Iraq sounded out of touch with reality.[63] Iran and the Kurdish leadership attempted to rally world opinion against the Iraqi government. However, at that stage (March–April 1988), the international community was still united in its fear of a possible Iranian breakthrough toward the Gulf states and, viewing Iraq as the primary barrier to Iranian aggression, did not wish to weaken or antagonize Baghdad. Like Emile Zola's *J'Accuse*, Joost Hilterman points an accusing finger at the United States:

> Evidence shows that the U.S., fully aware it was Iraq that had gassed Halabja, accused Iran of being at least partly responsible, and then instructed its diplomats to propagate Iran's partial culpability. . . . This ploy, while successful in

getting the Iraqis off the hook, had an important consequence: the Iraqis saw another green light and took immediate advantage. Using gas tactically on the first day of every Anfal stage, they were able to gather up and methodically kill tens of thousands of Kurds.[64]

It was only at the beginning of June 1988, when it had become absolutely clear that the Iranian threat was over and that Iraq was about to win the war, that certain circles in the West became more outspoken in their criticism of the use of chemical weapons against the Kurds. Though not condemning Iraq outright, United Nations Secretary-General Javier Perez de Cuellar did cite "considerable and most serious evidence" that Iraq had used chemical weapons in Halabja.[65] Another symbolic gesture was the reception of Talabani during a visit to the United States the same month. The United States had always been careful not to initiate a move that could be interpreted as encouragement to Kurdish separatist tendencies in order not to antagonize Iraq—or Turkey or Iran. In line with this, the United States made it clear that all it was concerned about was the humanitarian aspect of the problem; namely, the need to stop Iraq from further use of banned chemical weapons. But for all its mildness, this stance provoked a swift reaction from Baghdad, which cancelled a meeting scheduled for 16 June between the Iraqi foreign minister Tariq 'Aziz and the US secretary of state George Shultz. The Senate Committee on Foreign Relations nonetheless passed a resolution on 21 June, condemning the use of chemical weapons by Iraq. But such gestures were too little, too late for the Kurds.

A Final Solution?

On 19 July 1988, just one day after Iran had agreed in principle to a cease-fire, Baghdad launched a large-scale campaign against the Kurds, this time including the KDP-controlled areas.[66] The attack went on uninterruptedly for six weeks.[67] The timing of the onslaught, which was termed *khatimat al-anfal* (the final Anfal), once again illustrated how closely the internal and external problems were intertwined. Beyond its symbolism (i.e., the Baath's advent to power twenty years earlier), the timing was of considerable advantage to Baghdad. Tied down by their own declaration in favor of a cease-fire agreement with Iran and loath to jeopardize it, the Iranians were not expected to rush to the Kurds' help. The cease-fire ultimately came into force on 20 August. Indeed, Iran had no qualms about breaching the agreement signed with the PUK in October 1986, which stipulated that neither party would sign a unilateral deal with Baghdad.[68] Caught by surprise, and left to their own fate by their ally Iran, the Kurds were not expected to put up much resistance to a victorious army that was now free to send reinforcements to the two army corps already stationed in the area. No less important was the fact that world attention remained focused on the issue of a cease-fire between the belligerent sides and had less interest in secondary issues.

Fifteen battalions and between 30,000 and 60,000 troops (the numbers vary, depending on the sources) of the First and Fifth Army Corps and the Republican Guard took part in the offensive, making use of airplanes, helicopters, and tanks.[69] Like earlier ones, this offensive also had three main goals: to wipe out the bases of the Kurdish guerrillas in all of Kurdistan, to terrorize the Kurdish civilian population in such a way as to discourage future support of the opposition, and to facilitate the transfer of restive groups to areas where the regime would have tighter control over them. The Kurds, on their part, were convinced that the government had embarked "on a campaign of annihilation, a final solution" to the Kurdish problem.[70] The extent and ferocity of the onslaught became known only in early September 1988, when news began to trickle out from the closed area to reach the outside world. According to various reports, by that time 100,000 to 120,000 Kurds had already fled to Turkey for fear of chemical warfare. Many of Iraqi Kurdistan's villages no longer existed—some asserted that 70 percent to 80 percent had been wiped out.[71] Kurds from larger towns were being deported, often to concentration camps in the southern Iraqi desert, to prevent them from forming a majority in their own region.[72] The Senate Committee on Foreign Relations issued a report on 21 September, in which it accused the Iraqi Army of having used chemical weapons against Iraqi Kurds beginning on 25 August and in violation of international law, "inflicting casualties on civilians in the thousands and possibly in the hundreds of thousands."[73] It further charged Iraq with implementing a policy designed to depopulate Kurdistan, the main tactic of which was "to destroy villages and deport survivors to other areas of Iraq where they [could] be watched closely by military authorities." On 22 September, the House Committee on Foreign Affairs called for sanctions against Iraq because of its use of chemical weapons. A few days earlier the European Parliament had condemned Iraq for the use of chemical weapons in an attempt to "exterminate" thousands of Kurdish civilians, and called on the twelve member states of the European Community to immediately suspend all weapons deliveries to Iraq as well as the export of materials used in the manufacture of chemical weapons.[74] Still, no sanctions were imposed on Iraq—not even by the United States.

Iraq's reaction to the uproar was to categorically deny the use of chemical weapons. At the same time, it did not admit any investigation committees into the area, claiming that this would amount to interference in Iraq's internal affairs. Nevertheless, in November 1988 while on a visit to France, the progovernment Kurdish vice-president Ma'ruf admitted outright the use of chemical weapons in Halabja.[75] Baghdad's next move was to mobilize internal support for the regime.[76] Taking advantage of US criticism, it launched a large-scale anti-American propaganda campaign reminiscent of earlier days, including mass rallies, anti-American articles in the government-controlled press attacking the

"American Knesset," and a series of other anti-American gestures. No doubt, the regime needed the United States as a diversion and a safety valve during the problematic postwar period. Moreover, Iraq sought to utilize the anti-American campaign as a focal point for rallying Arab support to its cause.

Iraq also had to contend with the exodus of the Kurds to Turkey, which it blamed on the harassment of the Kurdish population by the guerrillas and on Mulla Mustafa Bazani's son, Mas'ud, who had "staged" the exodus to mislead world public opinion.[77] Faced with pressure from the host country (i.e., Turkey, which was as weary of the Kurds as Iraq itself), the Iraqi government issued an amnesty for all Iraqi Kurds on 6 September 1988, inside and outside Iraq, with the exclusion of Talabani, who was accused of having betrayed previous agreements with the government.[78]

The refugees faced a major dilemma: to remain in Turkey, which did not recognize the existence of Kurdish nationhood; to go to Iran, which had betrayed them; or to return to Iraq, which might slaughter them as it had their brethren. Neither could their leadership be of any help in solving the dilemma or in attenuating their plight because it had itself lost its way. As to the goal of autonomy, for which so many Kurdish lives had been sacrificed, it appeared further removed than ever. The most that the Kurds could hope for at that stage was sheer survival. The following statement by a repentant Kurdish opposition leader, Hoshyar Zebari, member of the KDP Central Committee at the time (and, after the 2003 Iraq War, Iraq's foreign minister), speaks for itself: "President Saddam Husayn is a merciful man. Had he been otherwise, he would have exterminated us in retaliation for our behavior and betrayal of Iraq."[79]

The Kurds lost another round in their long struggle. The causes of the Kurdish defeat were not difficult to detect: some of them were the result of built-in constraints, others the immediate outcome of the Iran-Iraq War. As to the latter, the Kurdish movement had clearly and unequivocally tied its fate to that of Iran. Iran's "semidefeat" thus had an immediate impact on the Kurds. This is not to say, of course, that had Iran been the victorious party, the movement's lot would have been any better. The Iran-Iraq War marked a departure from the movement's habitual stance in that it called into question the territorial integrity of Iraq while allying itself with an active enemy, not merely a hostile neighbor as had been the case in the past. This, in turn, provoked the most extreme measures ever taken by any Iraqi government against its own population. Beyond its moral and human implications, the use of chemical weapons on civilian Kurds had a disastrous impact on the movement for it found itself totally helpless against a weapon that threatened the very existence of the Kurds.

On the face of it, the Baath once again emerged victorious, succeeding as it did in safeguarding the integrity of the state, extending its control throughout the north, breaking the backbone of the Kurdish national movement, instilling fear in the population, and depopulating the area. Yet the methods applied to safeguard the integrity of the state made the integration of the Kurds into the body polity more difficult than ever before. Accordingly, the longed-for goal of creating an Iraqi nation also suffered a blow. By adopting a policy of violence (so characteristic of Iraqi politics), the Baath Party may have sown the seeds of its own downfall; in the past, such victories repeatedly proved to be both shaky and counterproductive. Furthermore, the Baath Party also was acting under its own constraints, the most salient of which was the Gordian knot between the internal Kurdish dilemma and the country's external problems. So long as Iraq's external problems were not solved, there was little chance that the Kurdish card would not be used against it. But herein, too, lay the Kurds' tragedy: they had no choice but to rely on external forces that were liable to drop them at will. In addition, while Iraq's Arab civilian population remained far removed from this war, the Kurdish civilian population paid the full price. Above all, while the movement time and again proved its ability to weaken or harm Iraqi governments, it was much less effective in turning these "triumphs" into assets for the Kurds themselves. In sum, the Kurdish national movement and successive Iraqi regimes were each caught within its own vicious circle, unable to break it.

The Fallout of the Iran-Iraq War

The situation of the Kurds after the Iran-Iraq War in many respects resembled that of the Kurds after the collapse of the Kurdish rebellion in March 1975. In both cases, Iran, the major supporter of the Kurdish national movement, stopped providing aid for political reasons, thus dealing the movement a fatal blow. In each, there was an exodus of Kurdish refugees (to Iran in the first case and to Turkey in the second). The Kurds feared the retaliation of the Baathi authorities, which indeed seized the opportunity not only to crush the rebellion and extend their control over the Kurdish region, but also to introduce changes in the infrastructure and the social fabric of the area that would make any new revolt impossible. However, for all the similarities, the change in Kurdistan this time was much more thorough, systematic, and drastic, at times making it appear irreversible. It seemed that the eruption of the Kurdish rebellion during the Iran-Iraq War convinced Baghdad to adopt a much stricter policy than before.

Immediately after the collapse of the Kurdish movement in the autumn of 1988, the Baathi regime began a large-scale relocation of Kurds reportedly residing at a distance of 30–60 kilometers from the Syrian, Turkish, and Iranian borders.[80] Analyzing the ideological sources of population transfer in general, Joseph Schechla maintains that transfer policies, once thought to belong to the past, reemerged with greater force in the second half of the twentieth century. He emphasizes that the consequences of internal expulsion may be more dismal than those of cross-border expulsion because of "customary deference to the state's right to 'non-interference' in its domestic affairs."[81] Indeed, the two waves of Kurdish transfers—in 1975 and 1988–1989—which drastically changed the human landscape of Kurdistan, went almost unnoticed because of that very premise; namely, noninterference in Iraq's domestic affairs.

Initially, Baghdad denied having taken such action; however, a darker picture began to emerge, first from indirect reports in the Iraqi press and then directly from Iraqi officials. Initially, the officials claimed that both Kurds and Arabs who lived along the Iranian border had been moved in compensation for their suffering during the war or as the information minister Latif Nusayyif al-Jasim put it, "they have spent many years not having a life at all."[82] Later on officials argued that villagers had been relocated from remote areas to the center to enable the government to provide them with the services and facilities of modern life. In this vein Saddam contended, "if they remain in those distant mountains . . . we cannot reach or protect them under such difficult circumstances. They also cannot live a decent and stable life or improve their economic conditions. We want another standard of living for them. This is the whole truth."[83] Behind this seemingly humanitarian language lay the real motive, which according to Tariq 'Aziz was to establish a 30-kilometer-deep security belt empty of any population.[84] 'Aziz freely admitted the government's decision to "change the demographic situation" and to deport Kurds from different parts of Kurdistan. He presented two opposite justifications for the move: to bring modernity to the Kurdish villagers and to curb the assistance they extended to the Kurdish guerrillas.[85] The second explanation was closer to the truth as the villagers had provided the main logistical support for the rebellion. Thus, according to one informant, the Peshmerga had ordered each family to buy one weapon: "It was like a law, and the people agreed with this because they saw it was necessary. The armed civilians would join the Peshmerga in the defense of their villages. They were referred to as the 'backing force.' All the villages had this type of civil defense unit."[86]

Baghdad's policy thus pursued the following aims: to prevent Kurdish villagers from giving logistical support to the guerrillas; to cut the lifeline to Iran and Syria of Kurdish guerrillas who had their headquarters near the borders; to put the population of the border areas under close surveillance by moving them to more accessible locales; and, finally, to divide Kurdish loyalties and disrupt social structures so as to make it more difficult for the Kurds to mobilize against the regime. Conceding the lack of loyalty of the Kurds in those areas Saddam said, "We have decided that they should be moved to enable them to get rid of this dualism in personality. At night, they are blackmailed by the rebels, during the day, they say that they are with the government . . . therefore this area has remained in trouble."[87]

The 1989 transfer program was different from that of 1975 in various respects. First, it encompassed not only Kurdish villages, but also towns. Second, it involved razing all structures in areas included in the plan. And third, the population was transferred mostly within the Kurdish area itself, and not to the

Shi'i south as in 1975. The first phase of the plan called for creating the infrastructure for cluster settlements (*tajammu'at sakaniyya*) or "modern towns," mainly in the governorates of Erbil and Sulaymaniyya. In Erbil, there reportedly were twenty such settlements.[88] This part of the plan seemed to have been completed by April 1989, when Saddam paid three visits to the area, probably in an attempt to convince the Kurds to move to the new settlements voluntarily. Simultaneously, the government announced various incentives such as the decision in April to provide free housing,[89] a plot of agricultural land, and between 1,500 and 3,000 Iraqi dinars for constructing new houses. Townspeople were given the higher sum, but even this was hardly an incentive or compensation because the cost of building a house was estimated at 5,000–10,000 dinars.[90]

The resettlement program began at the end of April 1989 with the inauguration of the "new Saddamiyyat Halabja" to replace the old Halabja, which Iraqi forces had leveled to the ground following the chemical attack.[91] Named after Saddam and inaugurated on his birthday, the new town was 32 kilometers from the border inside the Sulaymaniyya governorate[92] and remained under the watchful eye of a nearby military camp.[93] This was a vivid example of the Baath's hardened cynicism. The government then proceeded to destroy other villages and towns, including Surdash, Talabani's headquarters.[94] The strongest resistance was put up by the inhabitants of Qal'a Diza who had been ordered to leave their town by 18 June 1989. Of the town's 70,000 inhabitants, only 1,000 families left. Earlier in April, when the senior Kurdish religious leader Muhammad Delgaii came to Baghdad to persuade Saddam to change the plan, he was jailed. The authorities then offered an indemnity of 10,000 dinars to the town's residents,[95] but even this sum did not convince them to relocate. In the face of continuing resistance, the authorities decided to evacuate them by force, which reportedly included the use of tanks. A secret document, dated 23 June, stressed the following: "The deportation of Qal'a Diza district has been completed today. The equipment of division 24 has begun destroying (*tahdim*) the houses."[96]

As to the fate of other places, most of them were leveled to the ground though some remained intact so as to enable the government to move to the second stage of the plan; namely, Arabizing the region by populating it with Iraqi Arabs or even with Egyptians.[97] A presidential decree announced the move in a subtle way: an Iraqi who was not an inhabitant of the autonomous region was permitted to buy land for housing in that region in addition to his original place of residence.[98]

Regarding the number of deportees, Ja'far 'Abd al-Karim al-Barzanji, then governor of Sulaymaniyya and a strong supporter of the regime, stated that 595,000 families had been resettled by August 1989.[99] *Al-Jumhuriyya* reported that 134,000 houses would be built in the new towns in the north before the end of the year.[100] And *The Economist* claimed that 1,500,000 Kurds had been relocated.[101] There were also conflicting reports regarding the number of villages involved. In January 1990, the government announced its intention to reduce the number of villages, which had reached 12,500, in order to overcome the problem of the dispersal of villages over a large area—without mentioning the Kurds, of course.[102] For their part, Kurdish sources maintained that 4,000 villages had already been destroyed since 1975.[103] A visiting reporter said the area had been turned into a desert.[104]

At the same time and in an attempt to belittle the role of the Kurds in Iraq, officials initiated what might be termed a "campaign of demographic disinformation." For example, the new speaker of the National Assembly of Iraq, Saʿdun Hammadi, stated that the Kurds represented less than 15 percent of the total Iraqi population.[105] Later, he lowered this percentage even further to 12 percent, stating that Kurds numbered 2 million in a population of 17 million and that they were the fourth largest Kurdish community in the world (i.e., after that of Syria).[106] These assertions, which were cited repeatedly, indicated either wishful thinking on the part of the government or a reflection of its future plans. In 1985, the lowest estimate of the Iraqi Kurdish population put it at 3.0 million and the highest at 4.3 million. The number of Kurdish speakers was estimated at 3.39 million, or 22 percent of the total population.[107]

The regime's resettlement efforts were accompanied by measures designed to spread its control over the north. The Iraqi Army, with two of its nine corps stationed in strategic areas, took control of what used to be the Kurdish liberated zone and the newly depopulated zone. A non-Iraqi journalist who visited the area said the army had total control.[108] Renewed efforts were also made to expand the Baath Party in the Kurdish area. Paradoxically, while party activity was significantly weakened in other parts of Iraq, it expanded in the Kurdish area. The man who carried out this policy was a Shiʿi, Hasan ʿAli al-ʿAmiri, an RCC and Regional Command member who assumed the office of secretary-general of the Baath Northern Bureau around April 1989. At the same time, the regime apparently became disillusioned with its Kurdish allies who proved unreliable and ineffective. Various pro-Iraqi Kurdish personalities and groupings were purged, including two long-standing Kurdish ministers who were deprived of their portfolios, so that the cabinet was left with only four Kurdish ministers.

On 9 September 1989, the regime generated much publicity for the elections to the legislative assembly of the Kurdish autonomous region. Saddam and other officials contended that the Kurds had "one and a half rights [to vote]" as they were entitled to vote in elections to the National Assembly in Baghdad as well as to the Kurdish legislative assembly.[109] However, it was doubtful whether the elections to the sixth assembly were any freer than the previous five had been and whether representatives of different political currents could actually be elected. Many of the candidates, perhaps the majority, were Baathis. There was actually a contradiction in terms: Kurds, who were supposed to represent the Kurdish nation, became tools for spreading a pan-Arab ideology. Candidates also had to prove that they had contributed to the war effort against Iran, or participated in the popular army, or in the auxiliary Kurdish forces that had been used against the Kurdish population and guerrillas. The Kurdish opposition in exile called the elections a farce, and even Kurds inside Iraq dared criticize both the elections and Kurdish autonomy in general. Reflecting this criticism, Saddam said at the swearing-in ceremony on 17 October, "Whoever wants to settle down and voice his own ideas on how to apply the autonomy better than we do, let him come forward." But he said that he would not grant privileges "to the misled and the deviants" who had brought the Iranians to Halabja and "almost gave them al-Sulaymaniyya." Probably reacting to criticism of the assembly's limited powers, Saddam told members, "When you work better . . . you encourage us to consider how to improve your powers." However, he warned them to exercise their powers carefully and not to amend them unless they "accorded with Saddam Husayn's instructions."[110]

The Kuwaiti daily *Al-Siyasa* described the Kurdish autonomy in Iraq as "the Hyde Park" of the Arab world.[111] Iraqi officials also stressed the superior status of the Kurds in Iraq as compared to other countries, especially Iran. Yet the social and economic misery brought on by the regime's ruthless policies was unprecedented in Iraq as well as in neighboring countries. Saddam explained that "since some of our sons in the Kurdistan region . . . got used to living by their guns," it was extremely important to teach them to live by their work and bring stability to the area.[112] The Kurdish movement became all but paralyzed after the government campaign in the north where guerrilla activities almost stopped. Leaders and many rank-and-file members of the various groups fled abroad with their families. They were dispersed in many countries: in Turkey (with 50,000–60,000 refugees), Iran, and Syria; and in a number of European countries, especially West Germany, Great Britain, and France. What changed the picture overnight was the use of chemical weapons against Kurdish civilians. Kurdish leaders admitted that fear of this weapon had reached the level of "mass psychosis."[113] It forced them to change their tactics. Instead of the traditional guerrilla operations inside Kurdistan, which could turn their families into victims of chemical attacks, Kurdish leaders considered using hit-and-run operations by well-trained commandos against Iraqi military installations, oil installations, and other targets as well as terrorist attacks on government officials and members of the army and security forces in central and southern Iraq.[114] This plan did not come to fruition, however, as the Kurdish movement in Iraq on the whole refrained from terrorist attacks. In addition, the guerrillas' access to Kurdistan became more and more difficult. Turkey would not permit attacks from across its border. Iran, which could have welcomed the revival of Kurdish action, was reluctant to jeopardize a fragile cease-fire. Syria did not use the Kurdish card against Iraq to the fullest, despite Iraq's extensive support for Syria's enemies in Lebanon. But it was ultimately the security belt that most severely undermined the Kurdish position.

Faced with these difficulties the Kurdish opposition, belatedly awakening to the importance of political activism abroad, attempted to mobilize world public opinion to stop both the mass deportations and Western military aid to Iraq. But beyond propaganda achievements, such as the first international Paris Conference on the Kurds held in October 1989, political gains were at that point next to nil. Ridiculing those Kurds "who have chosen to knock on the doors of Paris, Washington, and London," Saddam said that even if they continued to do so for a thousand years, they would never achieve their aims. "We are not afraid of five or six persons who speak to the press," he mocked.[115] Indeed, the Kurdish opposition did not present much of a challenge at that juncture, either at home or abroad. But neither was the government any closer to its declared aim of molding the entire population into an Iraqi nation. The government had gained physical control over the Kurds, but at the price of raising a spiritual and emotional divide that further nurtured a separate Kurdish national identity. As Hilterman states, the Kurds

> have sought to parlay the Halabja and Anfal tragedies into the foundations of their hoped-for state. . . . It is out of such deep emotions and national traumas that identities are forged or reinforced and, sometimes, that nations are born. These are certainly the factors that have given rise to the Kurds' strong sense of entitlement today.[116]

Notes

1. The title of this chapter is taken from Sa'd al-Bazzaz, *Harb Talid Ukhra* ('Amman: al-Ahliyya lil-Nashr wal-Tawzi', 1992).
2. Support for this view is found in Kendal Nezan, "The European Perspective," in *Kurdish Identity: Human Rights and Political Status*, eds. Carole A. O'Leary and Charles G. MacDonald (Gainesville: University Press of Florida, 2007), p. 237. Nezan attributes all the wars that ensued in Iraq to the Algiers Agreement and the abandonment of the Kurds.
3. For the speech, see Radio Baghdad, 17 September 1980, cited in BBC, 19 September 1980.
4. Fuad Matar, *Saddam Hussein, the Man and the Cause, and the Future* (Beirut: Third World Center, 1981), p. 12. It should be noted that Saddam was not vice-president of Iraq, as Matar suggests, but vice-chairman of the Revolutionary Command Council.
5. For details on other groups, see Martin van Bruinessen, "The Kurds Between Iran and Iraq," *Middle East Report*, no. 141 (1986): 22–26.
6. By 1987, the two parties accounted for about 20,000–25,000 persons. *Al-Majalla*, 21–26 December 1987; *The Independent*, 17 March, cited *in Al-Tayyar al-Jadid* (London, weekly), 27 March 1987.
7. On al-Da'wa, see Hanna Batatu, "Iraq's Underground Shi'a Movements: Characteristics, Causes and Prospects," *Middle East Journal* 35, no. 4 (1981): 578–594.
8. Van Bruinessen, "The Kurds," pp. 16–17.
9. Human Rights Watch, *Genocide in Iraq*, 1 July 1993, www.hrw.org.
10. Saddam Husayn, "Khandaq Wahid Am Khandaqan," in *Al-Thawra wal-Nazra al-Jadida* (Baghdad: Dar al-Hurriyya lil-Tiba'a, 1981) pp. 25–28.
11. *'Iraq al-Ghadd* (London, biweekly), 18 June 1987.
12. *The Guardian* (London, daily), 2 August 1982.

13. *Al-Thawra* (Baghdad, daily), 21 November 1984; *Al-Majalla* (London, weekly), 11 March 1987.

14. *Al-Thawra*, 25 October 1983.

15. Ofra Bengio, "Iraq," in *Middle East Contemporary Survey (MECS)*, vol. 9 (1984–1985), Itamar Rabinovich, Haim Shaked, eds. (Tel Aviv: Tel Aviv University, 1987), p. 471. The PUK later claimed that the regime had executed 1,400 of its members between 1976 and 1983.

16. At one point they claimed to have separately killed *circa* 450 soldiers. *The Guardian* (London, daily), 14, 23 February 1985; *The Times* (London, daily), 3 May 1985.

17. See, for example, Defense Minister 'Adnan Khayrallah Talfah who said that Iran's aim was "to divide Iraq into three weak sectarian statelets." *Al-Tadamun* (Baghdad, weekly), 20 February 1988.

18. *Al-Thawra*, 13 April 1980. In 1979, Baghdad distributed color television sets and cash donations to 32,000 Kurdish families residing in the new villages. *Baghdad Observer* (Baghdad, daily), 4 May 1979.

19. *Nidal al-Ba'th fi Sabil al-Wahda, al-Hurriyya wal-Ishtirakiyya* (Beirut, 1963–1965), part I, p. 175.

20. Muhammad Talab Hilal, "A Study of Al-Jazeera Province from an Ethnic, Social and Political Aspect," in Jawad Mella, *Al-Siyasa al-Isti'mariyya li-Hizb al-Ba'th al-Suri fi Gharb* [Western] *Kurdistan* (London: Kurdistan National Congress, 2004), pp. 63–227.

21. *Al-Thawra*, 26 January 1983.

22. Sulaymaniyya University was first established in 1968. After its relocation it was reestablished in 1992.

23. *The Economist* (London, weekly), 18 June 1983. For a different version, see van Bruinessen, "The Kurds," pp. 24–26.

24. Michael M. Gunter, "The Kurdish Problem in Turkey," *Middle East Journal* 42, no. 3 (1988): 396–397.

25. Document, Middle East Watch, 14 August 1986.

26. Document, Middle East Watch, 21 November 1985.

27. Human Rights Watch, *Genocide in Iraq*, http://www.hrw.org/reports/1993/iraqanfal/ANFAL1.htm; Faleh Abd al-Jabbar, "Why the Uprisings Failed," *Middle East Report*, no. 176 (1992): 2–14. The Kurdish auxiliaries had different names, including *jahafil al-difa' al-watani*, *quwwat salah-al-din*, and the pejorative *juhush*.

28. For the horrors committed by the *afwaj* against other Kurds, see Human Rights Watch, *Genocide in Iraq*, http://www.hrw.org/reports/1993/iraqanfal/ANFAL1.htm.

29. Document, Middle East Watch, 9 April 1988.

30. The best description of these onslaughts can be found in Kanan Makiya, *Cruelty and Silence: War, Tyranny, Uprising, and the Arab World* (London: Penguin Books, 1993); Joost R. Hilterman, *A Poisonous Affair* (New York: Cambridge University Press, 2007); and, most importantly, Human Rights Watch, *Genocide in Iraq*, http://www.hrw.org/reports/1993/iraqanfal/ANFAL3.htm.

31. Translation of the verses is by Arthur J. Arberry, *The Koran Interpreted* (London: Allen & Unwin, 1955).

32. In this chapter, I document only samples of these documents that do, however, reflect the general tenor of the Baathi words and deeds. I received some of the documents from Duhok University.

33. Human Rights Watch, *Genocide in Iraq*, http://www.hrw.org/reports/1993/iraqanfal/ANFAL5.htm. Indeed the *afwaj* looted the abandoned villages mercilessly before bulldozing and burning them to the ground.

34. Document, Middle East Watch, 29 March 1987.

35. *Le Monde* (Paris, daily), 19 March, cited in *Daily Report*, 24 March 1988. As early as 1978, Senator William Proxmire (D-WI) repeatedly maintained that the Kurdish situation in Iraq was "a vivid evidence of the need for the genocide convention." Lokman I. Meho, *The Kurdish Question in U.S. Foreign Policy: A Documentary Sourcebook* (Westport, CT: Praeger, 2004), p. 33.

36. *The Guardian*, 2 May 1987.

37. With regard to Arabization, I came across one document that stated that Arabs living in the provinces would be included in the Ta'mim governorate and would receive land and a financial grant (no details), Document Middle East Watch, 16 June 1987.

38. Document, Middle East Watch, 14 May 1987.

39. Human Rights Watch, *Genocide in Iraq,* www.hrw.org/reports/1993/iraq anfal/APPENDIXA.htm (accessed 19 July 2010).

40. Document, Middle East Watch, 11 June 1987.

41. Document, Middle East Watch, 23 June 1987.

42. Human Rights Watch, *Genocide in Iraq,* http://www.hrw.org/reports/1993/iraqanfal/ANFAL2.htm.

43. Document, Middle East Watch, 10 April–May 1988. The *mujamma'at* were villages to which surviving Kurds were transferred; they were described as concentration camps by the Kurds.

44. Document, Middle East Watch, 9 July, 15 September 1987.

45. Document, Middle East Watch, 15 September 1987.

46. Document, Middle East Watch, 23 May 1987.

47. Pesach Malovany, *The Wars of Modern Babylon* (in Hebrew) (Tel Aviv: Ma'arakhot, 2009), pp. 387–389.

48. Document, Middle East Watch, 26 April 1988.

49. Document, Middle East Watch, 19 April 1988.

50. Document, Middle East Watch, 31 May 1988.

51. Document, Middle East Watch, 26 June 1988.

52. Ibid. See also *International Herald Tribune* (Paris and Zurich, daily), 12 May 1987; *Financial Times*, 4 September 1987; *New York Times*, 22 September 1987; *Le Monde*, 23 October 1987; *Amnesty International Report, 1988* (London: Amnesty International, 1988).

53. For example, *Al-Jumhuriyya* (Baghdad, daily), 22, 24, 26, 27 March 1988; *Al-Qadisiyya* (Baghdad, daily), 21, 22 March 1988.

54. The first newspapers to report this, albeit belatedly, were: *International Herald Tribune*, 21 March 1988; *Times*, 22 March 1988, cited in *Daily Report*, 23 March 1988; *New York Times* (New York, daily), 24 March 1988, 22 June 1988; *Financial Times* (London, daily), 2 April 1988; *Le Monde* (Paris, daily), 8 April 1988. For a detailed discussion, see Joost R. Hilterman, *A Poisonous Affair* (New York: Cambridge University Press, 2007). The number of dead was verified by Middle East Watch. Human Rights Watch, *Genocide in Iraq,* http://www.hrw.org/reports/1993/iraqanfal/ANFAL3.htm. Iraq used mustard gas, tabun, VX (nerve agent), and sarin in that attack.

55. Hilterman maintained that the "the Reagan administration had three distinct opportunities to intervene and successfully extract an Iraqi commitment to refrain from further chemical weapons use": in 1983–1984, after Halabja in March 1988, and following the Badinan attacks in August 1988. Hilterman, *A Poisonous Affair*, p. 235.

56. Ibid. Hilterman claimed that "documents show that the CIA, for example, had forewarning of impending air attacks [in 1988] involving chemical weapons," ibid., p. 238; Bengio, "Iraq," in *MECS 1983–1984*, p. 465; Bengio, "Iraq," in *MECS 1986*, p. 366. Foreign Minister Tariq 'Aziz admitted the use of chemical weapons against the

Iranian Army. *Der Spiegel*, 14 November 1988, cited in *Daily Report*, 15 November 1988.

57. For a detailed description of the affair, see Human Rights Watch, *Genocide in Iraq*, http://www.hrw.org/reports/1993/iraqanfal/ANFAL3.htm.

58. *Le Monde*, 24 March 1988.

59. *Al-Ra'y*, 29 March 1988, cited in *Daily Report*, 29 March 1988.

60. *Al-Thawra* (international edition), 28 March 1988.

61. *Le Monde*, 24 March 1988.

62. Radio Tehran, 31 March1988, cited in *Daily Report*, 1 April 1988.

63. *Le Monde*, 19 March 1988.

64. Hilterman, *A Poisonous Affair*, pp. 239–240.

65. *New York Times*, as quoted by United States Information Service Wireless File, 14 June 1988.

66. In Baathi jargon, "the terrorists of Barzani's group first branch." Document Middle East Watch, 12 December 1988.

67. *Le Monde*, 8 September 1988.

68. Human Rights Watch, *Genocide in Iraq*, http://www.hrw.org/reports/1993/iraqanfal/ANFAL1.htm.

69. United States Information Service Wireless File, 16 August 1988; *International Herald Tribune*, 1, 3–4 September 1988; *New York Times*, 1 September 1988; *Middle East International*, 9 September 1988. For a detailed description, see Human Rights Watch, *Genocide in Iraq*, http://www.hrw.org/reports/1993/iraqanfal/ANFAL10.htm. This source claimed that 200,000 Iraqi troops had been involved.

70. This contention was repeated by Senator Al Gore (D-TN) in September 1988. Lokman I. Meho, *The Kurdish Question in U.S. Foreign Policy*, p. 57.

71. "According to a study by the Ministry of Reconstruction and Development of the Kurdish government, a total of 4,049 villages were destroyed, while only 673 were spared in the three governorates of Erbil, Duhok, and Suleymaniyeh. This study does not include the province of Kirkuk, where several hundred more villages were destroyed." Kendal Nezan, *Le Monde Diplomatique*, March 1998.

72. Talabani claimed that by March 1988, 1.5 million Kurds had been displaced. *The Guardian*, 24 March 1988; *Financial Times*, 1, 7 September 1988; *Le Monde*, 6, 7 September 1988; US Information Service Wireless File, 7 September 1988; *New York Times*, as quoted by the US Information Service Wireless File, 9 September 1988.

73. David McDowall, *A Modern History of the Kurds* (London: I. B. Tauris, 2004), p. 367; George Black and Human Rights Watch, *Genocide in Iraq: The Anfal Campaign Against the Kurds* (Washington, DC: Human Rights Watch, 1993) p. 27.

74. *Financial Times*, 19 September 1988.

75. *Le Monde*, 10 November 1988.

76. It was no coincidence that shortly after the end of the war, Baghdad published a book on the Barzanis' collaboration with Israel and Iran and their treason against Iraq. Fadil Barrak, *Mustafa al-Barzani: Al-Ustura wal-Haqiqa* (Baghdad: Dar al-Shu'un al-Thaqafiyya al-'Amma, 1989).

77. *Der Spiegel*, 14 November 1988, cited in *Daily Report*, 15 November 1988.

78. Baghdad claimed that by 21 September 1988, 40,613 Kurds had returned to Iraq. Radio Baghdad, 21 September 1988, cited in *Daily Report*, 22 September 1988.

79. *Al-Dustur* (London, daily), 10 October 1988.

80. *The Middle East* (London, monthly), July 1989.

81. Joseph Schechla, "Ideological Roots of Population Transfer," *Third World Quarterly* 14, no. 2 (June 1993): 239–275, www.jstor.org/pss/3992567.

82. *Al-Tadamun*, 28 August 1989; Joseph Schechla, "Ideological Roots of Population Transfer."

83. Iraqi News Agency, 17 October 1989, cited in *Daily Report*, 19 October 1989.

84. *Al-Musawwar* (Cairo, weekly), 14 July 1989.

85. *Der Spiegel*, 14 November 1988, cited in *Daily Report*, 15 November 1988.

86. Human Rights Watch, *Genocide in Iraq*, http://www.hrw.org/reports/1993/iraqanfal/ANFAL5.htm.

87. Iraqi News Agency, 17 October 1989, cited in *Daily Report*, 19 October 1989.

88. *Le Monde*, 22 July 1989.

89. *Al-Thawra*, 10 June 1989.

90. *Le Monde*, 21 September 1989.

91. Human Rights Watch, *Genocide in Iraq*, http://www.hrw.org/reports/1993/iraqanfal/ANFAL3.htm.

92. *Al-Siyasa* (Kuwait, daily), 12 August 1989.

93. *Le Monde*, 22 July 1989.

94. *Financial Times* (London, daily), 15 June 1989; *Le Monde*, 21 September 1989.

95. Tariq 'Aziz to *al-Musawwar*, 14 July 1989.

96. Document 8, Middle East Watch; *Financial Times*, 15 June 1989; *The Economist*, 24 June 1989. A citizen of Qal'a Diza described to me the horrors of this displacement. At the age of seventeen, he had to build a house for the rest of his family since his father and brother had been taken to the army. Ilan Israel, interviewed by the author in Tel Aviv, 9 February 2011.

97. *The Middle East*, July 1989.

98. Document, Middle East Watch, 20 September 1989.

99. *Al-Siyasa*, 12 August 1989.

100. *Al-Jumhuriyya* (Baghdad, daily), 11 July 1989.

101. *The Economist*, 24 June 1989.

102. *Al-Qadisiyya* (Baghdad, daily), 26 January 1989.

103. *The Economist*, 24 June 1989; *Le Monde* 22 July 1989.

104. *Le Monde*, 21 September 1989. See also Human Rights Watch, *Genocide in Iraq*, http://www.hrw.org/reports/1993/iraqanfal/.

105. *Al-Dustur* (London, daily), 29 May 1989.

106. *Al-Musawwar*, 15 September 1989.

107. Erhard Franz, *Kurden und Kurdentum* (Hamburg: Deutsches Orient-Institut, 1986), p. 12.

108. *Le Monde*, 21 September 1989.

109. *Al-Musawwar*, 15 September 1989.

110. Iraqi News Agency, 17 October 1989, cited in *Daily Report*, 19 October 1989.

111. *Al-Siyasa*, 7 September 1989.

112. *Al-Thawra*, 2 August 1989.

113. *Le Monde*, 21 September 1989.

114. *The Middle East*, February 1989; *Le Monde*, 21 September 1989.

115. Iraqi News Agency, 17 October 1989, cited in *Daily Report*, 19 October 1989.

116. Hilterman, *A Poisonous Affair*, pp. 226–227.

11

Rising from the Ashes

The Kurds paid a heavy price for their long involvement in wars during the twentieth century. The only exception was the 1991 Gulf War, which the United States and its allies launched after Iraq's invasion of Kuwait in August 1990.[1] This war provided the Kurds with the opportunity to break out of the vicious circle of paying the price of each new war. Initially, it seemed that history was going to repeat itself since the Kurds rebelled against the Baathi regime shortly after the cease-fire in February 1991 in what they came to term the intifada (*rapareen*). As in the past, the regime crushed the uprising by force. But then a sudden change took place.

The Kurdish Intifada

On 4 March 1991, shortly after the outbreak of the Shi'i intifada in the south, a similar uprising took place in the Kurdish north, but without prior coordination.[2] Jalal Talabani asserted that the intifada was spontaneous.[3] In fact, the Kurdish movement began preparing the ground for an uprising immediately after Iraq's occupation of Kuwait.[4] The Kurds' task was made easier by the government's pressing need to reduce its forces in the north in order to reinforce the Kuwaiti front.

Months before the uprising, the Tigris River became the main crossing point into Iraq for Kurdish guerrillas and activists from Syria. The Iraqi military intelligence informed Saddam Hussein that the leadership of the PUK had "distributed heavy and light arms as well as protective masks against chemical weapons to its saboteurs."[5] Even before the uprising began, progovernment Kurdish auxiliaries began to join the Kurdish movement so that by mid-March some 60,000 soldiers had reportedly changed sides, bringing along their military equipment—mainly booty taken from the army.[6]

As in the south, the vacuum created in the Kurdish region as the upshot of the cease-fire agreement between Iraq and the US-led coalition prompted the quick spread of an uprising throughout Kurdistan. Emboldened by initial successes, Kurdish leaders took an unprecedented step when they captured Kurdistan's main cities, formerly garrisoned by the Iraqi Army. Within days Sulaymaniyya, Erbil, and Duhok fell to Kurdish fighters as did the oil city of Kirkuk, which had been the major source of contention between the Kurds and the government since the early 1970s. This spectacular success can be attributed mainly to the government's urgent need to withdraw forces from northern Iraq to protect Baghdad and put down the Shi'i rebellion.[7]

The Kurdish euphoria of March 1991 did not last into April. Surrounded on all sides by internal and external enemies, the Baath Party pulled itself together as it tried to win at least the internal war. Herein lies a paradox: it is quite possible that the very eruption of the uprising helped unite the Sunni part of the population around the ruling elite and strengthened its cohesiveness since any alternative regime might have jeopardized the privileged status of the Sunnis.

As to the intriguing question of how the regime weathered the crisis, the most obvious answer is that it had superior force and organizational skills, to say nothing of its long experience in repressing any dissent. The mobilization of Saddam's ruling family was remarkable. As early as 6 March 1991, Saddam's tough cousin Hasan 'Ali al-Majid was appointed minister of the interior, an act that in itself could instill fear in the opposition. Another cousin became governor of al-Ta'mim (formally Kirkuk) while Saddam's brothers and other cousins came to play an important role in suppressing the uprising. Furthermore, a secret decree granted members of the RCC and the regional command of the Baath Party the same powers as those of the president when he meted out "reward and punishment" as he quelled the uprising.[8] The government also mobilized former generals and appointed six high-ranking officers as governors of rebellious provinces.

The relative weakness of the insurgents, who lacked organizational, tactical, and political coordination, must be weighed against the determination of the Baath.[9] Furthermore, the regime's task was greatly facilitated by Iran's qualified support of the opposition and the allies' vacillation between a desire to see the Baath ousted from power and fear of the breakup of Iraq. The approval of the allies for the Iraqi government's use of helicopters was critical to the Baathi success in crushing the uprising. Besides its military importance, it was also of great political significance as it signaled to both the Baath and Saddam that the United States did not wish them to fall—on the contrary, it wanted them to defeat the opposition. These signals reportedly discouraged high-ranking military officers from joining the uprising in an attempt to oust the Baath.[10]

Aware of its inability to handle two uprisings simultaneously, the regime chose to first crush the Shi'i revolt. This misled the Kurds into believing that the regime was too weak to mount an operation against them. The victory festivals lasted almost to the end of March 1991, when Talabani, who began to assume the mantle of Kurdish national hero, returned triumphantly to Kurdistan after two years in exile. But just as quickly as the victory had been so was the defeat that followed.

Having achieved relative quiet in the south, the government could now divert most of its energy to the Kurdish region. By early April 1991, the defeated and demoralized Kurds began an unprecedented exodus of nearly 2 million people. The regime did not directly provoke the flight, but its 1988 use of chemical weapons against the Kurds without doubt encouraged their flight. The Iraqi Army's extensive use of phosphorus shells was probably designed to spread terror and panic among the Kurds who mistook them for chemical bombs.[11] As late as June 1991, the First Army Corps issued a secret order calling for the killing of any "armed or unarmed" Kurd who insulted a soldier or defied the curfew order in Sulaymaniyya as well as of any soldier who left his post or lost his weapon.[12] The Kurds' flight served Iraq's immediate and long-term goals: robbing the guerrillas of all logistical support and changing Iraq's demographic balance in favor of the Arabs, a long-standing Baathi goal.[13]

Ironically, soon afterward, Iraq's government began autonomy negotiations with the Kurds, motivated by the need to ease international pressure, gain time, and split the opposition. For its part, the Kurdish leadership went to the negotiating table to try to recoup at least something from the debacle. The first round of talks were held with Talabani, but they ended in deadlock. Later on Mas'ud Barzani took the lead, but by February 1992 this channel had also come to naught. The inherent, mutual lack of confidence was a major stumbling block. Another was the opposition from within the Kurdish camp to any deal with Baghdad. However, the major impediment was the dramatic change of the status of Iraqi Kurdistan.

A Window of Opportunity for the Kurds

The turning point in the status of Kurdistan took place, paradoxically enough, at one of the most difficult points in Kurdish history: in the wake of the suppression of their uprising in the spring of 1991; the flight of about half of the Kurdish population to the Turkish and Iranian borders (the mass exodus called *rakeerden*);[14] and their resultant economic, social, and political dislocation. Indeed, the turning point was marked by a series of unique developments: the central government's loss of control over Iraqi Kurdistan; the crystallization of a genuine, Kurdish autonomous rule in a region that came to be known as the Kurdistan Regional Government; and the attainment by the Kurds of some international recognition.

In fact, it was the Kurdish exodus that contributed most to the internationalization of the Kurdish issue and the growing visibility of the Kurds. Faced with the terrible catastrophe that had befallen the refugees and the refusal of the neighboring states—Turkey, Iran, and Syria—to grant them entry, the allies were forced to intervene. The safety or no-fly zone that the allies set up in April 1991 was to become the nucleus for the Kurdish entity. Ironically, Turkey's president Turgut Özal played a central role in introducing this idea, which was eventually to become a nightmare for the Turks.[15] Indeed, according to an internal report "following the Gulf War and under President Turgut Özal's personal initiative, Ankara launched totally new relations with the Iraqi Kurdish movement."[16]

To translate the idea of a no-fly zone into action, an international force of 20,000 troops from eleven countries was dispatched to the region, in what became known as "Operation Provide Comfort."[17] The refugees were settled temporarily in camps, then returned to their place of origin. The United Nations also provided the necessary means for survival and safety, and humanitarian aid groups and nongovernmental organizations (NGOs) became active in the region. After the withdrawal of the Iraqi troops in July, the allies formed a rapid deployment force of 5,000 troops, based in Incirlik, Turkey, to intervene in case of Iraqi acts of reprisal. On top of this, Baghdad was forced to agree to the humiliating demand that its air force not act beyond the thirty-sixth parallel, the so-called no-fly zone over Kurdish territories that was enforced by coalition fighter jets.

In retrospect, it seems that the Kurdish catastrophe served as a catalyst for a more assertive stance. Yet a closer analysis must also take into account the importance of changing internal, regional, and international circumstances. On the international level, the redrawing of the map of Eastern Europe and of the former Soviet Union created a more favorable atmosphere for some Kurdish demands in Iraq. This mood was reinforced by disclosures concerning the Baathi policy of genocide against the Kurds in the preceding decade and by a growing awareness of the continuous threat that the Iraqi regime posed, not only to the Kurds, but to neighboring countries—especially to Kuwait. This international perception elevated the Kurds, once again, to the redoubtable status of a particularly effective tool against Iraqi expansionist designs. In addition, the Iraqi regime's misguided policies toward the Kurds in the aftermath of the Gulf War contributed significantly to the Kurdish determination to achieve self-rule. Ultimately, seventy-plus years of intermittent struggle galvanized the Kurdish national movement and consolidated its viability at a critical stage in its history.

Baghdad's Strategy in Kurdistan Backfires

Starvation, chaos, and a divide-and-rule policy encouraging fratricide were the three main guidelines followed by the Iraqi regime in Kurdistan after the Kurdish uprising was crushed. In October 1991, Baghdad imposed an economic blockade on the region on the assumption that this, combined with the ongoing international sanctions and the Kurds' economic dependence on the center, would bring them to their knees. Similar results were expected as an upshot of the administrative and political withdrawal of the regime from Kurdistan and of a well-tested, divide-and-rule strategy vis-à-vis the Kurdish leadership. The absence of the central government from Iraqi Kurdistan was expected to bring about such chaos in the area that the regime would be perceived as a savior not only by the Kurds themselves but also, and more importantly, by neighboring countries who might fear the impact of such developments on their own Kurdish populations. In fact, the regime hoped that Iraq's neighbors would take over its task by containing the Kurds in Iraq and curbing their national aspirations. It also hoped to exhaust Kurdish aspirations through acts of sabotage—performed by proxy since the Iraqi Air Force was prohibited from entering the Kurdish no-fly zone.

Combined with the ongoing external blockade, the internal blockade that the regime had initiated was expected to place the Kurds at the government's mercy, weakening their leadership and bringing it to the negotiating table in a markedly inferior position. An already poverty-stricken Kurdistan faced the harsh consequences of a double embargo, which was reducing the food supplies by 60 percent and fuel supplies by 80 percent. Food prices soared to two or three times higher than those in Baghdad while materials for construction projects were twelve times more expensive. The scarcity of oil all but crippled the few extant industrial projects in the area, reducing them by 90 percent.[18] Essential to this policy was the psychological pressure that the regime brought to bear on civil servants, demanding that they leave Kurdistan for government-controlled areas. When most of them rejected this demand, Baghdad cut off their salaries, along with payments to government pensioners. Some 300,000 civil servants were deprived of their income while the supply of water and sanitation was severely curtailed in government services, especially in health care.[19] The readiness of the civil servants and the population as a whole to endure such hardships was indeed a barometer of the crystallization of Kurdish nationalism.

More surprising was the regime's decision at the end of 1991 to withdraw all of its military forces from the area and station them outside the no-fly zone. In a rare reference to the Kurdish problem, in all probability prompted by criticism of this move, Saddam explained, "They wanted to maintain the bleeding in the north. . . . We said: let us withdraw the army and the state bodies because state employees cannot perform their duty when things have reached such a lowly level." On another occasion he declared, "We told the army to leave for some time. . . . Your people will then cry for the army's help and will call on it to rescue them."[20] What Saddam had omitted to mention, however, was the fact that ground forces without air support were ineffective in the mountainous Kurdistani terrain and could themselves become an easy target for Kurdish guerrilla forces. In an attempt to fill this military vacuum, the regime sponsored scores of acts of sabotage with the help of Kurdish collaborators, aimed not only at the Kurds, but also at UN personnel and representatives of humanitarian organizations with the aim of halting outside support for the Kurds. The most spectacular of these was a failed attempt on the life of Danielle Mitterrand, wife of French president François Mitterrand, on a tour of Kurdistan in early July 1992.[21]

Baghdad also attempted to drive a wedge between the two Kurdish camps of Barzani's son Mas'ud and Talabani, but this time quite unsuccessfully. All in all, the regime's strategy in Kurdistan proved a total failure. Far from producing the anticipated chaos, its policy turned into a springboard for advancing the Kurdish national cause.

Winds of Change: Kurdish Self-Rule

After years of severe repression verging on genocide, the Kurds were only too eager to fill the vacuum left by the central government and lay the administrative foundations for self-rule. The relatively free elections for the Kurdish legislature, held on 19 May 1992, were part of this endeavor. In theory the Iraqi Kurds had their own elected assembly since 1974, but in practice the members of the assembly had all been government nominees. This time, several factors combined to facilitate genuine elections: the administrative vacuum left by the regime; the need to attain the goodwill of the West by holding elections along democratic lines; the military umbrella provided for the success of such a move; and, finally, the fact that the cause of democracy and free elections was genuinely upheld by several Kurdish political groupings as the only guarantee against yet another government-nominated legislature.

Eight parties competed for the 105 parliamentary seats in elections supervised by international observers and described on the whole as "free and honest." Significantly, only the two major parties, the KDP and PUK, managed to secure seats. Since the results were close—50.22 percent for the KDP and 49.78 percent for the PUK—they decided to divide up 100 of the seats equally between them, with the 5 remaining seats awarded to a coalition of parties representing the Christian minority, 4 of which went to the Assyrian Movement.[22] No seats were allocated to the Turkoman minority because, as Talabani explained, they were outside of the area controlled by the Kurds. Concurrent elections were held for the office of president with Mas'ud gaining a slight lead over Talabani, the other major candidate. A second round of presidential elections to decide the contest did not take place and the office of president was not activated.

The elections in Iraqi Kurdistan greatly alarmed not only the Iraqi regime, but also neighboring countries that feared a spillover effect within their own Kurdish populations. The Iraqi regime ridiculed the elections as a "farce," denounced them as a plot to split up Iraq, and declared them "illegitimate" and "unconstitutional" inasmuch as the Kurdish legislative assembly, which was sponsored by the regime, was still functioning. In fact the very name the Kurds chose for their legislature, the Kurdistan National Assembly (*al-majlis al-watani al-kurdistani*), spoke volumes about their intention to turn it into a symbol of Kurdish nationalism.

The Kurdish elections were important because they conferred a measure of legitimacy on the Kurdish leadership, canceled out minor Kurdish groupings, and provided a basis for setting up a Kurdish administration. The Kurdistan National Assembly held its first meeting on 4 June 1992, followed by the formation of a Kurdish cabinet. The cabinet literally became the government of the region (*hukuma iqlimiyya*) and was formed under the chairmanship of Fu'ad Ma'sum of the PUK. It included fifteen other ministers, including a minister for military affairs in charge of the Kurdish military, the Peshmerga. Later in September, three Kurdish governors were appointed to the three Kurdish provinces, Erbil (the seat of the assembly), Sulaymaniyya, and Duhok. Concurrently, a number of other, important steps were taken. Employees' salaries became the responsibility of the Kurdish government. A court of appeals was established in November 1992. And the educational system, which had been neglected for years, received a significant impetus when 25 percent of the budget was earmarked for it: by the end of 1992, 1,100 schools, with Kurdish as the language of instruction, were in operation—as were three universities and a military college.[23] On the political level, unlike the single leadership of Mulla Mustafa Barzani in the 1960s and early 1970s, a dual leadership emerged of Mas'ud and Talabani. Although neither had the stature of Mulla Mustafa Barzani, together they managed to create a more or less functioning leadership team—at least for a short time. The overall impression created was one of greater cohesion within the Kurdish national movement than during the preceding ten years and the beginning of coalescence of a central Kurdish government.

Reformulating Kurdish national goals was the most important item on the Kurdish political agenda after the elections. Until the Gulf War the declared aim of the Kurdish mainstream had been autonomy but, in 1992 after much deliberation, it was elevated to that of federation.[24] A decision in early October 1992 by the Kurdistan National Assembly expressed the unanimous commitment of Iraqi Kurdistan "to determine its fate and define its legal relationship with the central authority at this stage of history on the basis of the federation (*al-ittihad al-fidirali*) within a democratic parliamentary Iraq."[25] The adoption of this formula by the entire Kurdish movement constituted a compromise between Talabani, who had championed the cause of an independent Kurdistan since 1988, and the more moderate Mas'ud Barzani, who had adopted autonomy as his goal. Indeed, the choice of federation expressed the Kurds' exasperation with the autonomy formula, which had been used by the regime as a cover for suppressing them.

No sooner was the idea of federation raised than it aroused the antagonism of the Baghdad regime, which viewed it as an act of separatism, while neighboring countries regarded it as a Pandora's box that threatened to open up at their own doorstep. So alarming did this development appear that it prompted a tripartite Syrian-Turkish-Iranian meeting in November 1992, aimed at curbing Kurdish ambitions. The Kurds themselves, aware of the need to tread cautiously, issued ambiguous statements as to their intention to remain part of the Iraqi state on the one hand, and their right to self-determination on the other.

Another development that marked a clear departure from the past was a degree of international recognition gained by the Kurds. In the past, no Kurdish leader or official had been permitted to meet openly with Western officials on the grounds that the Kurdish issue was a humanitarian, not a political, problem. Behind this pretext, of course, lay the West's fear of antagonizing Iraq and alarming Turkey and Iran. In 1992, however, Talabani, Mas'ud Barzani, and other Kurdish officials became personae gratae in several Western capitals, including: London, where they held talks with Prime Minister John Major in February 1992; Paris, where they met with President François Mitterrand in August; and Washington, DC, where they conferred with Secretary of State James Baker, together with three Iraqi opposition groups, also in August. Part and parcel of this development was the Kurdish leadership's broad access to the international media—including the Arab media. Another measure of this changing attitude was the introduction, in April 1992, of daily broadcasts in Kurdish by Voice of America.

The West, however, remained ambiguous in its attitude toward the Kurds. On the one hand, the three leading wartime coalition partners—the United States, Great Britain, and France—needed the Kurds to keep the pressure on the Iraqi regime and destabilize it. The official reception accorded to the Kurdish leaders was therefore designed to signal to the regime that the West was clearly pledging its political support to the Iraqi opposition. For example, following a meeting with Mitterrand on 19 August 1992, Talabani quoted the French president as being supportive of "the Kurdish people's rights within the framework of a federation in a united and democratic Iraq."[26] Still, the term *united* reflected Western fears of a partitioning of Iraq, which accounted for a continued adherence to the traditional support for the Kurds on only a humanitarian basis. Following the visit to Kurdistan—the first of its kind—by Mitterrand's wife and the French minister of health Bernard Kouchner in early July, a statement by the French government cautioned against interpreting the "humanitarian move" of Danielle Mitterrand as an official French political position.[27] While such ambiguity was far from reassuring to the Kurds, the very facts that pro-Kurdish activists in the West were becoming more outspoken and that the Kurdish leaders had succeeded in breaking the silence concerning the Kurds were important achievements in themselves.

Formidable Odds Against Kurdish Self-Rule

Important as these achievements may have been, they were also fragile. Internally, though Kurdish national identity had been considerably strengthened as a reaction to Baghdad's repressive policies especially in the previous decade,[28] at times it was still overshadowed by local and tribal loyalties. Furthermore, the years of state-imposed Arabization policies had had their effect. With Arabic as the previous language of instruction in Kurdistan and the key to social and political mobility, the Kurdish language—the primary symbol of national identity—was yet to emerge as a unifying factor. On the economic level, the internal embargo imposed by the government highlighted the economic vulnerability of landlocked Kurdistan and its total dependence on the regime's or neighboring countries' goodwill. The economic constraints inherent in this geopolitical situation could in fact thwart any aspiration for independence that the Kurds might harbor. Kurdish officials themselves acknowledged that Kurdistan's main problem was economic and that the regime in Baghdad knew only too well how to exacerbate it.

No less damaging were the deteriorating relations with the leftist Turkish Kurdish party, the Kurdistan Workers' Party (Partiya Karkerên Kurdistan, or PKK), which illustrated the underlying dilemmas and complex political constraints faced by the Kurds.[29] In 1983 the KDP and the PKK signed a cooperation agreement aimed at fighting both Iraq and Turkey.[30] The next year, Mas'ud Barzani and PKK leader Abdullah Öcalan met in Damascus for the first, and apparently only, time.[31] However, by the 1990s their interests had diverged. The PKK exploited the vacuum left by Baghdad in Iraqi Kurdistan to set up bases in remote mountain areas near the Iraqi-Iranian-Turkish border, areas in which the Iraqi Kurds lacked the power to intervene or had no foothold.[32] These bases were used by 5,000 PKK activists, supported by the Iraqi regime, to launch attacks against Turkey and simultaneously weaken the Iraqi Kurds.[33] Secret documents obtained by the latter in 1991 unequivocally proved PKK's cooperation with Baghdad against them.[34] The PKK was accused of blocking the vital access roads between Iraqi Kurdistan and Turkey "to prevent supplies and foodstuffs from reaching Iraqi Kurdistan."[35] According to the Iraqi Kurds, this act amounted to a third economic blockade against Iraqi Kurdistan since Turkey had become their sole economic lifeline.

This development increased the Iraqi Kurds' dependence on Turkey and impelled them to accept its dictates, even at the expense of Kurdish loyalties. At Turkey's instigation, Iraqi Kurdish forces launched a large-scale attack against the PKK in early October 1992 with the aim of forcing it to leave the border areas and move to the center of Iraqi Kurdistan.[36] This pattern of one country using another country's Kurdish community as a lever against its own Kurds and against the rival country, and the Kurdish groups' dilemma of having to choose between their immediate interests and overall national goals, constituted a built-in political constraint that militated against the Kurdish cause. Transborder cooperation thus cut both ways since it harmed the Kurdish cause in Iraq and Turkey as well as the governments of both countries.

Ironically, achieving the Iraqi Kurdish goals appeared to be conditional on their success in thwarting the goals of the PKK. Conceivably, the fact that the attacks on the PKK coincided with the Iraqi Kurdish declaration regarding a federation in Iraq was no coincidence. The Iraqi Kurds, probably hoping to gain Turkey's tacit support for their autonomy—an idea that frightened Turkey as much as it did Iraq, if not more so—were willing to pay the only price that might appease the Turkish government; namely, cooperation in combating the PKK. In this, the Iraqi Kurds were also motivated by their own desire to regain control of the remote border areas and eliminate the pro-Iraqi presence. However, the process exacted a heavy price from them. Under the pretext of fighting the PKK, Turkish forces, estimated at 15,000 troops, penetrated an area of nearly 25 square kilometers in northern Kurdistan in mid-October, including areas not known for harboring PKK guerrilla forces. Kurdish spokesmen complained, "We feel that this is against us and not against the PKK and that it is to establish some form of [Turkish] presence here."[37]

This episode also illustrated the complex regional situation in which the Kurds operated. As mentioned above, with the end of the Gulf War, Turkey emerged as the Iraqi Kurds' main lifeline. Turkey issued diplomatic passports to Mas'ud Barzani and Talabani to enable them to travel abroad; Mas'ud Barzani noted that since 1991 Turkey had been the Kurds' only window to the outside world.[38] Kurdish officials had open access to high-ranking Turkish officials, including the president and prime minister. In this, Turkey was motivated by a desire to control the area; prevent spillover effects among its own Kurdish population; and, most of all, frustrate any conception or plan for the emergence of an independent Kurdistan in northern Iraq. It was this fear that prompted the tripartite talks in November 1992 between Turkey, Syria, and Iran. That Iraq was excluded from the talks was of little consolation to the Kurds. Instead of confronting one state—Iraq—the Kurds now had to contend with four states.

The idea of a separate Kurdish state was not more palatable to the West— the other arbiter of the Kurdish fate. Though concerned about Saddam's schemes, including his continuous threats against Kuwait, the allies were even more worried about a possible partitioning of Iraq. The broad consensus against altering existing borders was motivated by fear of further chaos in the region and by an unwillingness to antagonize other states in the region as well as by a tendency to view colonial borders as sacred. This was another major stumbling block in the path of a Kurdish entity. Not a single country or international body extended recognition to the Kurdish government or established diplomatic relations with it. Moreover, the little economic and military support that the Kurds received from the allies was entirely a function of the latter's position vis-à-vis

Iraq. For all its achievements, the Kurdish entity thus remained at the mercy of powerful external forces.

Notes

1. Discussion of the Iraqi invasion of Kuwait and the resulting Gulf War is outside the scope of this study. It is referred to in connection with the Kurdish subject only.

2. For the intifada and its aftermath, see Ofra Bengio, "Iraq's Shi'a and Kurdish Communities: From Resentment to Revolt," in *Iraq's Road to War*, eds. Amatzia Baram and Barry Rubin (New York: St. Martin's Press, 1993), pp. 51–66; US Senate Committee on Foreign Relations, *Civil War in Iraq* (Washington, DC: May 1991); Najib al-Salihi, *Al-zilzal* (London: Mu'assasat al- Rafid lil-Nashr wal-Tawzi', 1998); and Bashir 'Ala', *Kuntu Tabiban li-Saddam* (Cairo: Dar al-Shuruq, 2006), pp. 154–170.

3. According to Jalal Talabani, the leadership of the Kurds did not order the uprising: "The Peshmerga were outside the towns and only later did we decide to support the demonstrators." *Wochenpresse* (Vienna), 11 April 1991, cited in *Daily Report*, 16 April 1991.

4. The Iraqi opposition groups met in Syria in December 1990 and decided to act toward the downfall of the Baath and in support of the United States in the forthcoming war. Document, Middle East Watch, 22 January 1991.

5. Document, Middle East Watch, 22 January 1991.

6. Agence France Presse, 12 March 1990, cited in *Daily Report*, 18 March 1990.

7. *New York Times* (New York, daily), 13 March 1991; *Al-'Alam* (London, weekly), 6 April 1991; US Senate Committee on Foreign Relations, *Civil War in Iraq*, p. 1.

8. Document, Middle East Watch, 9 March 1991.

9. Faleh Abd al-Jabbar, "Why the Uprisings Failed," *Middle East Report*, no. 176 (1992): 12.

10. US Senate Committee on Foreign Relations, *Civil War in Iraq*, p. 15.

11. Commenting on the causes of the "quick collapse" of the Kurdish rebellion, *Al-Jumhuriyya* reported that the rebels had not fought for a just cause, had been supported by foreign countries, and had antagonized the Arab citizens of the cities they occupied. *Al-Jumhuriyya* (Baghdad, daily), 15 April 1991.

12. Document, Middle East Watch, 12 June 1991.

13. US Senate Committee on Foreign Relations, *Civil War in Iraq*, p. 10. Western journalists were told this by the Kurdish refugees. Iraqi forces also reportedly "staged" chemical attacks. *Ha'aretz* (Tel Aviv, daily), 15 April 1991.

14. Kevin McKiernan, *The Kurds* (New York: St. Martin's Press, 2006), p. 54.

15. Kemal Kirişci and Gareth M. Winrow, *The Kurdish Question and Turkey* (London: Routledge Curzon, 2004), p. 159.

16. Ismet G. Imset, *The PKK: A Report on Separatist Violence in Turkey* (Ankara: Turkish Daily News Publications, 1992), p. 195.

17. Kirişci and Winrow, *The Kurdish Question*, p. 160.

18. *International Herald Tribune* (Paris and Zurich, daily), 2 April 1992; *Financial Times* (London, daily), 9 July 1992; *The Economist* (London, weekly), 11 July 1992. Reports in April indicated that an indigenous oil company named Kurdoil had begun extracting oil in Koysanjak. *2000 Ikibine Doğru*, 5 April 1992, cited in *Daily Report*, 23 April 1992; *Al-Sharq al-Awsat*, 8 April 1992, cited in *Daily Report*, 10 April 1992.

19. *New York Times*, 6 February 1992; Kurdistan Voice of Unification, 17 May 1992, cited in *Daily Report*, 18 May 1992.

20. *Al-Thawra* (Baghdad, daily), 12 March 1992; *Al-Jumhuriyya* (Baghdad, daily), 24 November 1992.

21. *International Herald Tribune*, 7 July 1992.

22. On the elections and their aftermath, see Agence France Press, 22 May 1992, cited in *Daily Report*, 26 May 1992; *Le Monde*, 24–25 May 1992; James M. Prince, "A Kurdish State in Iraq?" *Current History* 92 (1993): 17–22.

23. United States Information Service, Wireless File, 14 December 1992.

24. Interestingly, the Turkish PKK began to toy with this idea in 1990. Imset, *The PKK*, p. 231.

25. Voice of the People of Kurdistan, 5 October 1992, cited in *Daily Report*, 7 October 1992. Another Kurdish source emphasized that the decision was part of the Kurds' right to "self-determination." *Al-Manar al-Kurdi* (London), November 1992.

26. *Le Monde*, 21 August 1992.

27. *Le Monde*, 9 July 1992.

28. For a discussion of these policies, see *New York Times Magazine*, 3 January 1993; and Kanan Makiya, *Cruelty and Silence: War, Tyranny, Uprising, and the Arab World* (London: Penguin Books, 1993).

29. For a firsthand discussion of these relations see Imset, *The PKK*, pp. 180–209.

30. Ibid., p. 181.

31. Michael Gunter, *The Kurds and the Future of Turkey* (Houndmills: Macmillan, 1997), p. 116.

32. For a detailed discussion see ibid., pp. 115–125.

33. *Middle East International*, 23 October 1992.

34. Imset, *The PKK*, pp. 189–190.

35. Voice of the People of Kurdistan, 8 October 1992, cited in *Daily Report*, 9 October 1992.

36. See details in Jonathan C. Randal, *After Such Knowledge, What Forgiveness? My Encounters with Kurdistan* (Boulder, CO: Westview Press, 1999), pp. 236–242.

37. Agence France Press, 1 November 1992, cited in *Daily Report*, 2 November 1992; *The Independent* (London, daily), 6 November 1992; *Al-Manar al-Kurdi*, November 1992. For the relationship between the PKK and the Kurds of Iraq, see Hazir Teimourian, "Turkey: The Challenge of the Kurdistan Workers' Party," *Jane's Intelligence Review* 5, no. 1 (1993): 29–32.

38. Kirişci and Winrow, *The Kurdish Question*, pp. 162–163.

12

The Birth Pangs of Kurdish Self-Rule

The Kurdish euphoria of the early months of self-rule gradually gave way to a more levelheaded view of the formidable obstacles in the way of a nascent experiment. Yet the balance of power with Baghdad allowed at least for its survival.[1] By far the most salient feature of the Kurdish administration was the dual leadership of the KDP and the PUK, which made decisionmaking extremely cumbersome since it was contingent on the approval of both parties. Worse still, loyalty to either of the parties could at times override allegiance to the Kurdish national movement or hamper democratic evolution. As one observer put it, "After their 1992 election victory, both parties have been active in creating extensive patronage networks at the cost of developing a more democratic polity."[2] In fact some scholars regarded this as the legacy of intertribal rivalries in Kurdish society.[3] Another attributed these networks to "the division between the rural and urban areas, and between the Bahdini and Sorani regions."[4]

Between Unity and Fratricide

A key issue was the relationship between Jalal Talabani and Mas'ud Barzani. Since neither of them had managed to secure a majority in the presidential elections of 1992, they now settled for an unofficial division of power. Talabani, who was the more eloquent and cosmopolitan, and more of a diplomat, became increasingly responsible for developing new channels for the Kurds abroad and for mobilizing international opinion for their cause. Mas'ud Barzani, a more home-oriented leader, concentrated his activities on domestic concerns. The cooperation between the two parties was clearly demonstrated by Talabani's attendance at the Eleventh KDP Congress, which took place in Erbil in August 1993, and reelected Mas'ud Barzani as its president. In his speech, Talabani

209

said he hoped that the congress "would serve the objectives of our ally, the KDP," and promote "people's gains in liberated Kurdistan."[5] Another token of unity was the return of Mulla Mustafa Barzani's remains from his grave in Iran for burial in Iraqi Kurdistan on 6 October 1993. One observer described the triumphal procession as "the closest thing to a national holiday" as Kurds gathered in every city and village of the Kurdish region to celebrate.[6]

Initially, the modus vivendi between the two leaders reflected positively on their parties and prompted smaller groups to unite with either the KDP or the PUK. Thus, the Kurdistan Socialist Party announced its reunion with the PUK on 10 February 1993, following a fourteen-year separation. Similarly on 28 July, the Kurdistan Unity Party, headed by Sami 'Abd al-Rahman, announced its union with the KDP. The merger of the guerrilla armies and the Peshmerga under a unified command was also moving forward.[7] Similarly, KDP and PUK unions representing students, workers, and peasants (excluding women) reportedly also merged.[8]

These initial positive developments were jeopardized by the sudden flare-up of hostilities between the PUK and the al-Haraka al-Islamiyya fi Kurdistan or Islamic Movement of (Iraqi) Kurdistan (IMK) in October 1993, which threatened to engulf the entire Kurdish camp. In 1987 the Islamic movement, a relatively new organization in Iraqi Kurdistan, was established under the leadership of Mulla 'Uthman 'Abd al-'Aziz and with Iranian support. It was composed of three factions: that of 'Abd al-'Aziz, the most moderate faction and closest to the general Kurdish movement; that of 'Ali Babir (or Bapir), a radical group with links both to Iran and to the Baathi regime; and that of Mulla Krekar (Najm al-Din Faraj), with strong ties to Afghanistan. Then in 2001, 'Ali Babir and Mulla Krekar founded Ansar al-Islam, which would challenge both the Kurdistan Regional Government (KRG) and the United States. Mas'ud Barzani's cousin, Shaikh Muhammad Khalid of the Naqshbandiyya Sufi order, was at the head of another group, the Kurdish Hezbollah, which was supported by Iran and said to be associated with the IMK.[9]

According to the PUK, which published a book containing documents belonging to the IMK, the movement had established fifty-one military bases inside Iraqi Kurdistan and put them at the disposal of the Iranian Army. Besides Iran, the movement also received financial support from Pakistan, Afghanistan, Saudi Arabia, Algeria, Tunisia, and Lebanon, totaling a monthly financial backing of $1.57 million. According to the PUK, repeated attempts to include the IMK in the Kurdish cabinet and to unite the movement's militia with the Kurdish military joint command were rejected by the movement. Moreover, the PUK accused the movement of seeking to establish a government of its own within the Kurdish regime by erecting prisons and military checkpoints on public roads, imposing taxes, and even interfering with the school curricula. The movement was also accused of instigating armed clashes with the PUK.[10]

Following the waves of unrest in October 1993, which resulted in fifty deaths on both sides, representatives of the two groups met in early November to settle their differences.[11] However, fighting resumed in December. So serious were these clashes, that they engulfed large areas of Kurdistan, including Erbil and Sulaymaniyya, leaving 72 people dead and 250 injured.[12] By the end of 1993, the PUK announced the capture of all the Islamic movement's bases in Kurdistan, the detention of 'Abd al-'Aziz, the arrest of 200 members of the group, and the confiscation of its arms.

The clash between the PUK and the Islamic movement was significant in that it brought to light a radical Islamic group, which constituted a new phenomenon in Iraqi Kurdistan and became a tool in the hands of Iran in its fight against the Kurdish entity. After several years of relative peace among the Kurdish factions, these clashes once more highlighted the difficulty of forming a united Kurdish movement. There was also a real fear that internal fighting would endanger the Kurdish cause at the international level.

The most serious implication was that the conflict engulfed the two main groups, the KDP and the PUK, as the former attempted to intervene between the two hostile parties—the PUK and the Islamic movement. At one point, Mas'ud Barzani even expressed his indignation over the fact that his mediation efforts had not been acted on, blaming the PUK for initiating the December 1993 fighting in breach of the agreement it had reached with the Islamic movement on 25 December. "Regrettably," Mas'ud Barzani said, "we heard about fresh clashes even before the ink on the agreement had dried. Does this not show disrespect for our decisions and agreements and disregard for our national interests?" Later on, Mas'ud Barzani reportedly gave refuge to 'Abd al-'Aziz.[13]

In an attempt to contain the conflict and simplify the decisionmaking process in the Kurdish camp, a "strategic agreement" was signed on 20 December 1993 between Mas'ud Barzani and Talabani. The agreement put special emphasis on the fact that the success of the Kurdish administration and the continued international awareness of the Kurdish issue depended on "preserving the unity of the Kurdish ranks." The following main points were negotiated:

1. The two parties will join the parliament and the government as equals, and important decisions will be made by mutual agreement.
2. Political and organizational "monopolies" will be banned in the region.
3. Resorting to violence and weapons to resolve differences will be banned completely.
4. Neither party will ally itself with a third party against the other.
5. The parties will agree on a single, joint and flexible policy toward neighboring countries especially Turkey, Iran, and Syria.[14]

The agreement only served to highlight the profound differences and rivalries still existing between the two parties so that a renewed flare-up of hostilities was merely a question of time.

After long years of warfare against Baghdad, the KDP and PUK turned against each other, and the internal fighting went on intermittently until 1997. A fresh outbreak of violence erupted in May 1994, engulfing most areas of the autonomous region. This time the conflict, which was described as the worst in thirty years, involved the KDP and the PUK as well as the IMK and other smaller groups.[15]

The hostilities, which started on 1 May 1994, were triggered by a dispute over land in the area of Qal'a Diza, north of Sulaymaniyya.[16] Clashes broke out between the Peshmerga of the KDP, PUK, and IMK in all the large cities and smaller towns of Kurdistan, including Sulaymaniyya, Duhok, and Erbil, the seat of the Kurdish parliament and government. The warring parties, which included 6,000 Peshmerga fighters on both sides, used both light and heavy weapons. In early May 1994, the PUK took control of the parliament and government buildings in Erbil. The city became a particular focus of contention when Talabani's forces took control of the city in early 1995. Subsequent military and diplomatic attempts by the KDP to expel the Talabani forces from the city failed. According to Amnesty International, all sides committed serious human rights violations, including the torture and execution of prisoners.[17]

Exacerbating the situation even further was the fact that during the fiercest fighting in May 1994, Talabani went to Syria and was thus unable to restrain his men, even if he had been willing to do so. Indeed, the situation often seemed beyond the control of the leadership. Even though Talabani managed to enter Kurdistan in early June and agreed with Mas'ud Barzani on a cease-fire, the fighting continued.

The extent of the fighting was reflected by the rise in casualties at the end of 1995; it had already reached *circa* 2,000 dead after the first flare-up in May 1994.[18] An already poor economic situation continued to deteriorate: in addition to the double embargo imposed by the UN and Baghdad, the Kurdish population now had to cope with an internal embargo imposed by the warring parties against each other.[19] Worst of all was the political impact. Whatever level of democracy and unity had been achieved in the previous two years with the establishment of a Kurdish legislature and government was effaced with one stroke. The occupation of the parliament by the PUK, which Mas'ud Barzani described as a military coup d'état,[20] paralyzed both the parliament and cabinet. Ministers and officials reverted to narrowly partisan activities.

One striking example was provided by the Ministry of Peshmerga (i.e., defense). Jabbar Farman, the Peshmerga minister and a PUK member, admitted that the fighting had destroyed the unity of his ministry, splitting it into two warring parties. Farman left his ministerial job and joined the PUK in a move against the KDP. "Every minister," he said, "works for his party as if he were not a minister." He further remarked that the fighting had prompted many citizens to arm themselves.[21] The hostilities split the region into ever more conspicuous spheres of influence: the KDP controlled the northern area along the Turkish border; the PUK controlled the urban areas and the eastern province of Sulaymaniyya as well as the city of Erbil; and the IMK took control of some areas in the east and the south near the Iranian border.[22] The fighting went hand in hand with a fierce propaganda war, even among the Kurdish communities abroad, thus damaging the prospects for Kurdish unity even further. The Kurdish population itself was deeply frustrated by its leadership and by the setback that the experiment of Kurdish self-rule had suffered while its enemies were only too eager to exploit the conflict.

Roots of the Conflict

Theoreticians of conflicts attribute civil wars to a combination of frustration, opportunity (including access to finances), and a weak common identity.[23] The Kurdish civil war fits this model only to a certain extent. Indeed, its most serious cause was the lack of a strong Kurdish national movement that could override primordial, tribal, and local loyalties. The power struggle between Kurdish groups, particularly between the KDP and the PUK, was thus both a symptom and a cause of the absence of a strong national movement. Personal rivalries also played an important part in the conflict. Thus, up until 1975, Talabani had been resigned to the fact that Mulla Mustafa Barzani was leading the movement. However, after the failure of the rebellion, he came to see himself as the movement's legitimate leader. This led to a clash with the Barzanis and the KDP. Deep down, the old religious rivalries between the Barzanis and Talabanis must also have played a role. It should be remembered that they belonged to rival Sufi orders: the Barzanis to the Naqshbandiyya and the Talabanis to the Qadiriyya.[24] It was only after the outbreak of hostilities that the Kurds themselves as well as outside observers began to fathom the depth of the rivalry and discuss its underlying causes and implications for the future.

Nuri Talabani, a Kurdish intellectual, traced the crisis back to an ineffectual Kurdish parliament and cabinet, both of which were being manipulated by the KDP and PUK, and thus, instead of unifying the Kurds, became involved in the struggle for power between the two rivals. Nuri Talabani pointed out a number of failures of the Kurdistan Regional Government:

1. The Peshmerga forces of the KDP and PUK had actually never been unified, but continued to receive orders from both the KDP and the PUK leadership.
2. Instead of sharing information under the auspices of the Ministry of Culture and Information, the KDP and PUK continued to operate their own radio and television stations.

3. Parliament did not promulgate a constitution for the region (*iqlim*), in spite of increasing political pressure following the adoption of a model of rule in October 1992.
4. The government did not purge the administrative apparatus of the Iraqi regime's Kurdish "agents," some of whom had infiltrated the ranks of the Kurdish political parties.
5. The government did not end the widespread phenomenon of Kurdish civilians arming themselves.
6. A population census was not carried out to form the basis for upcoming elections, due in 1995.
7. The government did not revise a previous decision that granted equal powers to the prime minister and his deputy, who belonged to the two different parties, thus making it impossible for one to carry out any decision without the consent of the other.[25]

This balancing policy had, by Mas'ud Barzani's and Talabani's own admission, paralyzed decisionmaking and increased the rivalry between them. Not only ministers, but also most members of parliament joined their own parties' militias.[26] Another problem was the electoral threshold of 7 percent, which excluded important political groups from the democratic process, especially religious movements that were on the rise owing to the support of Iran and Saudi Arabia. Groups without parliamentary representation began to look for alliances with either of the two large parties in order to gain political clout.[27] The KDP and PUK were only too eager to bring as many of these groups as possible under their sphere of influence. Rather than build unity, however, these alliances led to further factionalism and rivalry.

Particularly striking were the relations between the KDP, the PUK, and the IMK. The KDP, which initially served as a mediator between the other two, ended up forming an alliance with the IMK.[28] This alliance had far-reaching implications for the KDP-PUK-IMK conflict as the IMK became an active partner of the KDP in the latter's fight against the PUK. Barzani rejected the PUK's demand that the KDP end its alliance with the IMK and blamed the PUK for "persisting in its tyranny and imposing its unilateral hegemony over the regions under its control."[29] No less serious was the PUK accusation that both the KDP and the IMK had received support from Iran in the fight against the PUK. It is quite possible that the tripartite cooperation between the KDP, the IMK, and Iran was cemented by Mas'ud Barzani's cousin, Shaikh Muhammad Khalid.[30] However, Mas'ud Barzani denied having received any support from Iran, although he was reported to have visited Tehran in October 1994.[31] The tripartite conflict thus served to highlight the deep-rooted problems facing the autonomous region.

The geographical divide into spheres of influence added fuel to the KDP-PUK feud and had debilitating consequences for the Kurdish national movement as a whole. The sphere of influence of the KDP was in the northern part of Kurdistan that borders Turkey while that of the PUK lay in the central and eastern regions that border Iran. This old geographical division of power assumed growing economic, political, and strategic significance with the establishment of the no-fly zone in the north. As Turkey became the gateway and the only lifeline to Kurdistan, the KDP, which controlled roads of about 100 kilometers in the area bordering on Turkey, came to hold a pivotal role. The KDP decided on who could enter the area and supervised all financial transactions conducted in the region. Indeed, the KDP controlled the main source of hard currency for Iraqi Kurdistan since it collected custom fees on goods crossing the main Ibrahim al-Khalil border point in Zakho. Mas'ud Barzani stated that custom posts constituted Kurdistan's major source of income. The nearly 700 Turkish trucks carrying goods to Iraq that crossed the area daily indeed constituted a significant boost to the KDP's economic and political powers.[32] In this respect, the situation of the KDP fit the model mentioned earlier—it boosted the opportunity (i.e., the finances). This put the PUK at a serious disadvantage vis-à-vis the KDP because it seriously limited its independent ties with the outside world. No less serious was the fact that this geographical configuration deprived the PUK of an important source of income, which the KDP was reluctant to share, thus adding another source of friction between the two. And as if this internal war were not enough in itself, another war erupted across the border with the Turkish PKK.

Iraqi Kurds vs. Turkish Kurds

The PKK remained the major source of friction between the Kurds of Iraq and the Kurds of Turkey because this organization was likely to use Iraqi Kurdistan as a base from which to launch attacks against Turkey.[33] Aware of this, Talabani attempted to mediate between the PKK and Turkey; and, in March 1993, the PKK declared its willingness to stop hostilities against Turkey. Two months later, however, the PKK once again initiated activities against Turkey. In June 1993, faced with this new complication, Talabani hastened to declare that the Iraqi Kurdish leadership would remain committed to preventing hostile acts against Turkey. Likewise, Mas'ud Barzani visited Turkey in June to discuss these issues.[34] The Kurdish leadership denounced the 1993 PKK attacks against Turkish consulates in Europe and called on the PKK to stop all use of "violence" and "terrorist methods."[35] In another gesture of goodwill, Talabani reportedly called on Turkey to occupy Kirkuk in cooperation with the Kurds in order to control oil installations there.[36]

As to the KDP, it had developed a common interest with Turkey in containing the PKK. The KDP's sphere of influence bordered on Turkey and it suffered as a result of the armed conflict between Turkey and the PKK. Speaking of his party's problems with the PKK, Barzani asserted that it was the KDP that had brought the PKK to Iraqi Kurdistan and had enabled it to build bases there in 1982.[37] Later on, however, he accused the PKK of seriously hampering the Kurdish experiment by seeking to "further aggravate the situation" in Iraqi Kurdistan, "flagrantly" interfering in the region's internal affairs, turning the area into a springboard for attacks against Turkey, and obstructing the reconstruction of villages in the areas bordering on Turkey.[38]

In August 1995, the growing rivalry between the Kurds of Iraq and the Kurds of Turkey erupted into open fighting between the KDP and PKK, adding another dimension to the intra-Kurdish conflict.[39] This rivalry had its roots in the tacit alliance that had been developing since 1992 between Turkey and the KDP, and in a parallel relationship between the PUK and the PKK. The Turkish incursion into Iraqi Kurdistan in March 1995, discussed below, seemed to have further solidified these alliances. While the operation was in progress, Barzani was invited to Turkey to discuss future provisions for the security of the Kurdish enclave in northern Iraq. Turkey reportedly was considering arming and paying the guerrillas of the KDP, whose territory was adjacent to the 330-kilometer border with Turkey, to help keep the PKK out of the area. This elicited an angry response by the leader of the PKK Abdullah Öcalan, who accused the KDP of directing the Turkish units toward PKK positions and warned them not to join the "enemy" as this "would be the end of them."[40] Unimpressed by this threat, the KDP took further steps to stop PKK infiltration into Iraqi Kurdistan in April 1995. According to one of the KDP leaders, Nechirvan Barzani (Mulla Mustafa Barzani's grandson) and his group deployed some 200 men near Zakho "to prevent the PKK from advancing from that strategically important gate" toward its previously established strongholds.[41] Öcalan's warning, however, was borne out on 25–26 August 1995, when his guerrillas launched simultaneous surprise attacks against "about 20 administrative and civilian sites" such as KDP offices and villages. The fighting, which spread to Zakho, 'Amadiyya, and 'Aqra, resulted in the deaths of nearly thirty people and hundreds wounded.[42] The motives behind these attacks, the PKK explained, were both to lure the Turkish Army into northern Iraq, where it would get bogged down, and to wreck the Turkish-brokered accord between the KDP and PUK that was signed on 11 August. Öcalan stated that the aim of the move had been to put an end to "an act of treason which has been going on for 30 years by the forces of South Kurdistan" by building relations between Iraqi Kurds and Turkey. The PKK's action, he said, was part of a general plan to establish "a democratic federal Kurdish state."[43]

The move sparked intermittent fighting between the PKK and KDP, which lasted until mid-December 1995 at which time Öcalan called for a cease-fire.[44] The violence, first initiated by the PKK, was subsequently escalated by the KDP. During three major rounds of fighting between September and November, the KDP set out not only to retaliate for the August attack, but also to "purge" the Kurdish areas under its influence from the "filth" of PKK terrorists.[45] The KDP was motivated both by its alliance with Turkey and by its perception of the PKK as constituting a threat to the very existence of the KDP since the two competed for influence in the same area and for the support of the Kurdish population. In addition, the unchecked presence of the PKK elicited repeated Turkish incursions into Iraq, which has a particularly detrimental effect on the Iraqi Kurdish cause—at least in the eyes of the KDP. The PKK also formed alliances that were detrimental to the KDP: the latter blamed Syria and Iran for instigating the PKK attack in August and blamed the PUK for allowing the PKK to provide military training in PUK-controlled areas.[46] By the end of 1995, the KDP had succeeded in ejecting the PKK from most of northern Kurdistan, in particular from its stronghold near the Iraqi-Turkish-Iranian border. Still, one successful round of fighting did not imply a decisive victory.

To summarize, the fighting between the KDP and PKK constituted yet another dimension of the complex Kurdish drama while at the same time shifting the focus away from the rivalry between the KDP and PUK. The endemic Kurdish rivalry once again proved to be the Kurds' worst enemy at the same time as the various Kurdish factions continued to be as prone as ever to manipulation by outside elements.

Baghdad Faces an Abnormal Situation

Al-Thawra called the relationship between the Kurdish "autonomous region" and Baghdad "the abnormal situation" (*al-wad' al-shadhdh*), thus harking back to the Iraqi term for the British Mandate (1920–1932) when the Iraqi government was the country's titular ruler and the British government its actual ruler. However, *Al-Thawra* also expressed the profound conviction that this "abnormal situation," which was a consequence of imperialism and military threats, would eventually be defused.[47] The newspaper's direct reference to this expression did illustrate Baghdad's helplessness regarding the situation in Kurdistan and its inability to regain control of the area.

While Baghdad insisted that Kurdistan had been and would always be an integral part of the Iraqi state, the Kurds sought to bolster the idea of a federal state. In presenting federalism as an ideal solution, the Kurds had to contend with opposition not only from their potential partners among the Iraqi Shi'is, but also from neighboring countries. Attempting to allay these fears Talabani, who had become the moving force behind the idea of federalism, stressed that federalism "came to unite countries, not to divide them"; that "it did not diminish the rights of the central state"; and that the Kurdish people affirmed "the unity of Iraq, of both Kurds and Arabs, within a modern federal system." In brief, that federalism was a suitable solution for Iraq. As for the other parts of Kurdistan, it was left to the local Kurds to decide on their course of action. Iraqi

Kurds did not wish to separate from Iraq, nor did they demand a Kurdish state, but rather a democratic Iraq and a federalism like that of the United States, Canada, Belgium, and Switzerland.[48]

Though the Kurds were cautious in displaying their national emblem and did not fly their flags or issue Kurdish stamps at this stage, they did use the Kurdish anthem on different occasions. But both the KDP and the PUK flew their own flags, respectively a yellow and a green flag.[49]

Even so Talabani's explanations could not fool Baghdad, which tried to forestall the emergence of an independent entity, irrespective of the official status it adopted. Baghdad raised the specter of separatism under the guise of federalism and warned the Kurds against relying on US support. Meanwhile it sought to tarnish the image of the Kurdish leadership, especially of Talabani, whom it accused of treason and of acting as an agent for Israel. In an article entitled "Shalom," published following a visit to Kurdistan by Israeli journalist Ron Ben Yishay in February 1993, an Iraqi newspaper described Talabani as an opportunist willing "to sell the honey of Kurdistan to its enemies."[50]

Concurrently, however, Baghdad made several attempts to draw the Kurds back to the negotiating table by playing on the differences between the Barzani and the Talabani camps, or to regain control of the region. Talabani disclosed that the Iraqi government had sent him unofficial delegations, requesting that a dialogue be reopened "on the basis of recognition of the current situation in Iraqi Kurdistan." He asserted, however, that the Kurds would not resume negotiations with Baghdad as long as Saddam Hussein remained in power and as long as democracy was not established. For his part Mas'ud Barzani disclosed that Baghdad had sent the Kurdish Communist Makram Talabani (no relation to Jalal Talabani) as mediator in February 1993, but that the Kurds had refused to engage in such a dialogue. Makram Talabani was sent again in July—with the same result.[51]

In line with its policy of the stick and the carrot (*al-tarhib wal-targhib*), Baghdad's approach went hand in hand with steps aiming to starve the region and bring the Kurds to their knees. The most serious measure, which complemented the economic embargo enforced on the Kurds by Baghdad in 1992, was the withdrawal of the foreign printed banknotes of 25 Iraqi dinars that was announced in early May 1993. This was especially harmful to the Kurds, as Baghdad sealed off Kurdistan from the rest of the country in order to prevent Kurds from exchanging their notes before the expiration date of the old currency.[52] Mas'ud Barzani claimed that, as a result of the withdrawal of the old dinar, the Kurds had lost half of the 1 billion dinars circulating in Kurdistan.[53]

The Kurdish government described the move as "a new economic war against Kurdistan." As for Talabani, he blamed Baghdad for "seeking to separate Kurdistan from Iraq," after isolating it politically by withdrawing utilities and administrative services from the area.[54] The Kurds thus continued to suffer from adverse economic conditions: a soaring inflation running at 100 percent annually, severe unemployment affecting 80 percent of the population, and a lack of basic commodities.[55] In August 1993, Baghdad took further punitive steps by cutting electricity from Mosul to the Badinan area (Duhok and Zakho), leaving the population without electric power for the remainder of the year.[56] Yet surprising as it may seem, the Kurds and Baghdad did carry out important economic transactions: the Kurds sold wheat crops to the central government while Baghdad sold gasoline to the Kurds.[57]

Baghdad attempted to unsettle the KRG through acts of sabotage against Kurds and foreign aid workers as well as by inciting Iraqi Arabs against them. Iraqi forces also carried out occasional attacks, particularly on villages in the Kurdish area, including burning agricultural lands.[58] In the final analysis, Baghdad failed to dislodge the KRG, but it did pin its hopes on intra-Kurdish fighting to do the job.

Baghdad's reaction to the internal war in Kurdistan was mixed. On the one hand, the Baath Party was more than happy to allow the Kurds themselves to destabilize the autonomous government, which it found so menacing. On the other hand, it feared that the situation in the north would get out of hand to the point that it would prompt Turkey and Iran to increase their influence in the region, even to the extent of bringing chunks of Kurdish territory under their control. Iraq massed troops in the region to demonstrate its hold on Kurdistan, but never activated them in the field. Iraq also tried to reactivate Kurdish tribal forces, and reportedly trained some 5,000 of them outside the Kurdish autonomous region.[59] As in the past, Baghdad carried on its sabotage activities and proxy attacks on journalists and UN personnel working in the area and continued to impose an internal economic embargo on the region. On the whole, however, the Iraqi government remained quite powerless against developments in Iraqi Kurdistan. Its calls for the return of Kurdistan "to the lap of the homeland"[60] (an appeal reminiscent of the discourse on Kuwait) succeeded only in accentuating its helplessness.

The Changing Role of Iraq's Neighboring Countries

"We are an island surrounded by hostile countries"[61] was Talabani's description of the geopolitical constraints under which the Iraqi Kurds were operating. Though it was their unwillingness to see the emergence of a Kurdish state in their midst that united Iraq, Iran, Turkey, and Syria, they differed on practically everything else—a fact that was crucial to the survival of the Kurds. The four countries were unable to formulate a common policy either because they were embroiled in mutual conflicts, or because each sought to use the vacuum in Iraqi Kurdistan for its own ends, or because they held different views about the implications of the situation in Iraqi Kurdistan for their own Kurdish populations. Each was thus left to its own devices.

In its policy toward Iraqi Kurdistan, Iran was motivated by fears that Kurdish autonomy would put down roots. Iran's main vehicle for obstructing this was the IMK, which it had helped establish and had ever since provided with material support.[62] In this it was also motivated by its rivalry with Saudi Arabia, which had attempted to infiltrate Iraqi Kurdistan by supporting Islamic groups.[63] At the same time Iran also reestablished its ties with the KDP, thus in a way reviving the informal alliance that had existed in the 1960s and early 1970s. Even if it did not actually instigate the clashes between the PUK, IMK, and KDP in the Sulaymaniyya region, Iran probably supported the latter two against the PUK.[64] The PUK accused Iran of providing bases for the IMK and KDP inside Iran and along the border and of supplying them with light weapons, ammunition, food, military experts, and troops "in the form of Pasdaran [the Iranian Revolutionary Guards] dressed in Kurdish traditional clothing." Above all, the PUK accused Iran of supporting the KDP and IMK by carrying out cross-border raids into the area during the inter-Kurdish fighting.[65] According to *Al-Sharq al-Awsat*, the Iranian Pasdaran was actively involved in the fighting in 1994. *Middle East International* also claimed that the bodies of six Iranian Pasdaran fighters were found after a clash that resulted in the deaths of 150 IMK warriors.[66]

A further complication arose because of the Kurdistan Democratic Party of Iran (KDPI), an opposition party with bases in the PUK sphere of influence. According to Talabani, PUK-Iranian relations soured because the PUK had not agreed to expel the Iranian Kurdish forces from the area under its control and was willing only to prevent them from launching military operations against Iran. Iran reacted, he added, by inciting the IMK and KDP against the PUK.[67]

Indeed, Iran initiated direct attacks along the Iraqi-Iranian border in Iraqi Kurdistan, as had been the case in 1993, causing among other things the displacement of several hundred Kurds.[68] Iran's official explanation was that the attacks had been carried out in response to activities of the KDPI, with its bases in Iraqi Kurdistan. Though both the PUK and KDPI denied these claims, Iran had in any case used the attacks to kill two birds with one stone. As the KRG began to stabilize, and as none of the other neighboring countries (namely, Turkey, Syria, and Iraq) was willing to take serious steps to stop its entrenchment in Iraq, Iran took the initiative to carry out direct military attacks, eventually inciting the Kurdish Islamic Party against the PUK.

In between these border skirmishes, Iraqi Kurdish and Iranian officials met twice, in May 1993 in Iran and in July in Iraqi Kurdistan, to discuss the situation along the border. During the second meeting, Iranian officials pressed Mas'ud Barzani and Talabani to hand over the Kurdish leaders of the KDPI; to disarm their members; and, finally, to hound them out of their territory. The KRG refused to comply with these conditions, but it did convince the Kurdish Iranian party to move its headquarters away from the border with Iran.[69] In general, the relations between the Iraqi and Iranian Kurdish parties were better than those between the former and the Turkish PKK. Nevertheless, the fact that the KDPI had its head-quarters in Iraqi Kurdistan complicated the situation even further.

To sum up, Iran's objectives in the Kurdish matrix were numerous: to harass the KDPI based in Iraqi Kurdistan; to strengthen and consolidate Kurdish Islamist groupings in order to increase Iran's political clout in Iraqi Kurdistan; and, most importantly, to pit Kurdish groups against each other, thereby preventing the consolidation of an autonomous Kurdish government.

Relations between the Kurds and Syria were also quite complicated. Syria had supported the PUK since 1975.[70] As Talabani said, "We maintain a special relationship with Syria. . . . Syria's assistance has enabled us to achieve much." It was further disclosed that Talabani had an office in Damascus and had published articles and books "in total conflict with its [Syria's] position." Referring to more direct support in the past, Talabani said, "I would not exaggerate if I said that our presence in the house of [Iraq's vice-president] 'Izzat Ibrahim al-Duri in the liberated city of Irbil [Erbil] bears Syria's fingerprints."[71] In its support for the Kurds, Damascus had been motivated by its enmity toward Iraq as well as its need to "export" its own Kurdish problem by supporting both the PUK and the PKK.[72]

Syria too grew wary of independent Kurdish activities, however, and tried to contain the Kurds by incorporating them into the Iraqi opposition operating in Syria and by coordinating activities with Turkey and Iran. In the aftermath of the meeting in June 1993, Syrian foreign minister Faruq al-Shar' described the situation in Kurdistan as "chaotic."[73] In addition, Syria had closed its border with Iraqi Kurdistan at the end of 1992 and was reluctant to reopen it. Talabani tried to placate Syria during several visits there, but with little success since Syria remained suspicious of Kurdish attempts to secede from Iraq. Unlike Iran, however, it did not go so far as to use military force.

Turkey's Pivotal Role

The Turkish stance toward the KRG remained crucial to its survival. But as in the past, it also remained ambivalent. Being the Kurds' only lifeline to the outside world, this role enabled Turkey to increase its pressure on the Kurds and contain them more effectively than the other parties could. In its policy toward the Kurds, Turkey was motivated by conflicting considerations. It hoped to use Iraqi Kurds against the Turkish Kurdish PKK, with its bases in Iraq, while it feared the implications of such a Kurdish entity for its own Kurds. Having incurred heavy losses because of the closure of the Iraqi oil pipeline after the invasion of Kuwait, Turkey considered reopening the pipeline and reestablishing relations with Iraq—a potentially fatal move for the Kurds. In the final analysis, however, Turkey gave in to the pressure from its Western allies not to take such a step and to further extend the mandate of the air cover to protect the Kurds in Incirlik.

All of this, however, did not prevent Turkey from launching a series of military attacks against Iraqi Kurdistan, which went on intermittently from 1992 until reaching a peak in 1995. While Turkey claimed that the attacks were directed against PKK bases, Iraqi Kurdish sources insisted that the attacks actually targeted Iraqi Kurds.[74] The Kurdish representative in France, Muhammad Isma'il, summed up the Turkish position, saying that Turkey had granted $13 million in humanitarian aid to the Iraqi Kurds while paradoxically continuing to bomb Kurdish areas.[75]

On 20 March 1995, the eve of the Kurdish New Year of Nowruz, the Turkish Army launched a major incursion into Iraqi Kurdistan. Code-named Operation Steel, it was the largest such invasion by Turkey since the establishment of the KRG. In fact, it constituted Turkey's most substantial military involvement in a foreign country in nearly twenty years.[76] The operation, which lasted six weeks, involved *circa* 35,000 Turkish troops that were deployed in a zone stretching 220 kilometers along the Turkish-Iraqi border and 40 kilometers into Iraqi territory. Targeting 2,400–2,800 Turkish Kurdish fighters from the PKK its aim, in the words of the Turkish prime minister Tansu Çiller, was "to cleanse that zone and uproot the PKK, whose operations are directed against our innocent population."[77] Most observers believe that proof that the Turks ultimately failed to achieve their main target—namely, uprooting the PKK—was provided, inter alia, by the fact that the operation was repeated on a smaller scale by the Turkish Army in June and October 1995.[78]

The Turkish incursions highlighted the complex situation that prevailed in Iraqi Kurdistan after the 1991 Gulf War and revealed the vulnerability of both the Iraqi Kurds and the Baghdad government itself. The establishment of PKK bases in northern Kurdistan demonstrated the power vacuum that had developed there, which neither Baghdad nor the KRG could fill. The central government's writ on Iraqi Kurdistan had all but disappeared in 1992. However, the KDP, in whose area of influence the PKK had established itself, was too weak to prevent this development. The presence of the PKK posed a challenge to the KDP. One important contributing factor to the entrenchment of the PKK was the bitter struggle for power between the KDP and the PUK. Stressing this point Turkish foreign minister Erdal İnönü expressed the hope that, following the Turkish operation, the two parties would realize that it was in their best interest to reach an understanding that would enable them to control the area more effectively. Turkey, he promised, would help them stave off PKK hegemony in their area.[79] Some reports claimed that Turkey had notified Iraq in advance of the projected incursions. Even if this was indeed the case the operations, which had initially been merely awkward for Baghdad, became more and more alarming as time went by. This can be inferred from the fact that initial reports in the Iraqi press were low-keyed, if they were publicized at all. Thus, for example, even though it did report on the spring operation, *Al-Qadisiyya*, the publication of Iraq's military establishment, did not mention that it had been carried out inside Iraqi territory. Radio Baghdad and the Iraqi News Agency, while more forthright in reporting the details of the operation as having taken place "in a dear part of northern Iraq" and condemning it as "a flagrant violation of Iraq's sovereignty and international law," indirectly admitted Baghdad's inability to either fill the "security and authority vacuum in northern Iraq" or stop Turkey from infringing on Iraq's sovereignty.[80] Iraq's fear mounted significantly, alongside growing speculations in the international press that Turkey might retain its military forces in the area permanently. These fears were heightened by visits of Turkish foreign ministry teams to northern Iraq aiming, at least in Baghdad's view, to establish closer cooperation between the Iraqi Kurdish "traitors" and the invading Turkish forces and thus "guarantee the security of Turkish borders."[81] Turkey's military and political moves in the area prompted Baghdad to seek the help of the UN Security Council and mobilize Arab and international pressure to induce Turkey to remove its forces from the area. Iraq put forward the following arguments: Turkey had encroached on Iraq's sovereignty, territorial integrity, and airspace, thereby violating both the UN Charter and international law; it had exploited the abnormal situation in northern Iraq, for which the United States and Great Britain, not Iraq, were to blame; and it had employed double standards when dealing with the Kurds, viewing its own Kurdish citizens, who were affiliated with the PKK, as terrorists while at the same time cooperating with what Baghdad termed "terrorist Iraqi Kurdish groups."[82] Accordingly, Iraq demanded the immediate and complete withdrawal of Turkish forces.

Although Turkey had pulled back the bulk of its forces by the end of April, as a result of international rather than Iraqi pressure, Baghdad was far from reassured about Turkey's intentions. Turkish president Süleyman Demirel's remarks of early May 1995, suggesting that the border with Iraq be altered to enable Turkey to better defend itself against PKK incursions, were particularly alarming. Demirel even appeared to be reviving Turkey's long-standing territorial claim to the former Ottoman province of Mosul in northern Iraq.[83] A prompt statement by Prime Minister Çiller that Turkey had no designs on Iraqi territory failed to dispel Iraqi anxiety since she also asserted that the Turkish Army would reenter Iraq if Turkey deemed it necessary. It appears that in challenging the territorial integrity of Kuwait in 1990, Iraq had set a precedent for others—that is, its own Kurds and its erstwhile ally, Turkey—to challenge its own territorial integrity.

Reaching Out to the Outside World

The Kurds' grave geopolitical constraints prompted them to search for allies in the region and in international arenas. As long as the KDP and the PUK appeared to be working in tandem, the KRG did seem to gain some support. However, when civil strife flared up, the Kurds lost much of the sympathy and good-will they had gained in the aftermath of the genocidal wars.

Kuwait, which stood to lose from even the slightest bolstering of Baghdad, was a potential ally of the Kurds. Accordingly, Talabani visited Kuwait on 8 March 1993 declaring that "the two fraternal people of Iraq and Kuwait," who were both suffering from Saddam's "despicable dictatorship," continued to be major allies against him. In August of the same year, a delegation of the Kuwaiti foreign ministry visited the KRG to confer with both Talabani and Barzani and declared Kuwait's intention to grant the Kurds $3 million in humanitarian aid.[84] Baghdad reacted by describing the move as a serious threat, adding that it reserved for itself the right to react at the appropriate time.[85]

Meanwhile, the Kurds attempted to reach out to the Arab world by sending representatives to countries such as Saudi Arabia and Qatar. Simultaneously, they also called for a Kurdish-Arab dialogue among intellectuals to discuss the relationship between the two nations; in particular, the silence of Arab intellectuals after the Halabja massacre. No such dialogue took place at that stage, however, and most Arab countries remained suspicious of the Kurds' secessionist tendencies. It was on these grounds that Egypt refused to welcome Kurdish leaders in Cairo.[86]

Talabani also attempted to send signals to Israel. At the beginning of 1993 he called on world Jewry to support the Kurdish cause, an appeal made through a *Yedi'ot Aharonot* article by a reporter who had visited Kurdistan. On another occasion when interviewed about the presence of Israeli experts in Iraqi Kurdistan, Talabani refuted these "rumors," at the same time asserting that it was the Kurds' legitimate right to have relations with Israel just as Egypt or the Palestinians did.[87] Officially, Israel neither denied nor confirmed such rumors.

The Kurds' most concerted efforts were directed at the international community, especially the allies—the United States, Great Britain, and France. However, all political aspirations of the Kurds met with a cool response from these countries, which continued to regard the problem as purely humanitarian. On the one hand, they sought to use the Iraqi Kurds as a tool for weakening Saddam and keeping up the pressure against him, but on the other they wanted to keep the Kurds too weak to jeopardize Iraqi unity or have a "negative" influence on Kurds elsewhere in the region, especially in Turkey. The allies were also concerned lest the situation deteriorate and require intervention as was the case in Bosnia.

The Kurdish leadership thus became concerned mainly with allaying the fears of the allies. At the end of April 1993, Barzani and Talabani (together with representatives of opposition parties) visited Washington, DC, where they were received by Vice President Al Gore, Secretary of State Warren Christopher, and National Security Adviser Anthony Lake.[88] However, they only managed to secure a promise that the allies would continue to provide air cover from Incirlik in Turkey. Barzani and Talabani also paid a visit to the Netherlands, Belgium, and France, where they were received by President François Mitterrand. How-ever, as in the US case, beyond the promise of continuing to provide air cover in Incirlik, which was due to expire at the end of June 1993, no other support was pledged.[89] In May of the same year, the French president's wife Danielle Mitterrand, who was a long-time supporter of the Kurds and received a human rights award from Barzani in Washington, attempted to mobilize support for the Kurds at the UN. She publicly voiced the idea of an independent Kurdish state. Hers, however, remained a solitary voice.[90] Neither was the Kurds' own conduct in this crucial time of any help.

Because of the internecine conflict raging within the Kurdish region, the Kurds risked losing any national support they gained after the establishment of the autonomous government.[91] Both the UN workers (*ca.* 300 people) and the members of humanitarian aid groups (*ca.* twenty-eight groups) found it in-creasingly risky to remain in the conflict areas, so much so that some actually left Kurdistan or threatened to leave it. The stance of the Western allies—the United States, Great Britain, and France—which had helped establish the Kur-dish autonomous government in the first place, was ambivalent at the very least. As long as their policy toward Baghdad remained unchanged, they wished to hold on to the Kurdish card against it. Only a relatively united Kurdish gov-ernment could serve their policy toward Baghdad. But they were unwilling to get involved in the fighting or to commit more troops to the troubled area. The United States on its part did not remain altogether aloof, so that the pressure it exerted on the parties apparently prompted a temporary halt in the fighting.

France's approach was even more ambivalent. Paris was the weakest link in the tripartite alliance against Baghdad, as it sought to gradually lift the em-bargo imposed by the UN. It was, however, the same French government that initiated in mid-July 1994 under the auspices of President Mitterrand a media-tion process between the PUK and the KDP. It is possible that the initiative was a result of the personal involvement of the president's wife in support of the Kurds. France's declared commitment to issues of human rights, and ongoing contacts with Kurdish leaders especially between Talabani and the French gov-ernment, led to a degree of sympathy in France for the Kurdish cause.[92] Tala-bani explained that France had no history of conflict with the Kurds, unlike Great Britain that had supported the Iraqi government against the Kurds during the British Mandate in Iraq in the 1920s.[93] While French involvement in the mediation efforts was important for internationalizing the Kurdish issue, it in-advertently exposed an inherent weakness, namely, the reliance on external powers to pacify the warring parties, which cast doubts on the Kurdish move-ment's internal cohesion and on its ability to capitalize on the crisis in Iraq. By their fractiousness the Kurds proved themselves unable to play their own cards right, at least at this stage. Just as they excelled in harming the other side, the Kurds also excelled in harming their own cause.[94] Still, the worst was yet to come—in the next phase of the civil war.

Notes

1. For a detailed discussion of this period see, Gareth R. V. Stansfield, *Iraqi Kurdistan: Political Development and Emergent Democracy* (London: Routledge Curzon, 2003).

2. Michael Leezenberg, "Urbanization, Privatization, and Patronage: The Political Economy of Iraqi Kurdistan," in *The Kurds: Nationalism and Politics*, eds. Faleh A. Jabar and Dawod Hosham (London: Saqi, 2006), pp. 164–165.

3. See, for example, Hanna Yousif Freij, "Tribal Identity and Alliance Behaviour Among Factions of the Kurdish National Movement in Iraq," *Nationalism and Ethnic Politics* 3, no. 3 (1997): 86–110; and Hussein Tahiri, *The Structure of Kurdish Society and the Struggle for a Kurdish State* (Costa Mesa, CA: Mazda, 2007), pp. 308–309.

4. Stansfield, *Iraqi Kurdistan*, p. 93.

5. Voice of the People of Kurdistan, 17 August 1993, cited in *Daily Report*, 19 August 1993.

6. David Korn, "The Last Years of Mustafa Barzani," *Middle East Quarterly* 1, no. 2 (1994): 13.

7. By the end of the year, the guerrilla army numbered 36,000. *The Economist* (London, weekly), 6 February 1993; *New York Times* (New York, daily), 21 January 1994.

8. Two Kurdish activists, interviewed by the author, April 1994.

9. Martin van Bruinessen, "The Kurds and Islam," Islamic Area Studies Project Working Paper no. 13 (Tokyo: 1999).

10. *Watha'iq al-Idana* (Damascus: Manshurat al-Ittihad al-Watani al-Kurdistani, 1994), pp. 5–24, 241.

11. Agence France Press, 9 December 1993, cited in *Daily Report*, 27, 28 December 1993.

12. Voice of Iraqi Kurdistan, 25, 26 December 1993, cited in *Daily Report*, 27, 28 December 1993; Agence France Press, 29 December 1993, cited in *Daily Report*, 29, 30 December 1993.

13. Voice of Iraqi Kurdistan, 24, 27 December 1993, cited in *Daily Report*, 27, 28 December 1993; *New York Times*, 21 January 1994. Another source suggested that the PUK had handed 'Abd al-'Aziz to the KDP. Stansfield, *Iraqi Kurdistan*, p. 97.

14. Voice of the People of Kurdistan, 24 December 1993, cited in *Daily Report*, 27 December 1993.

15. *Al-Wasat* (London, weekly), 16–23 May 1994.

16. *Al-Sharq al-Awsat* (London, daily), 5 May 1994.

17. Voice of Iraqi Kurdistan, 22 May 1994, cited in *Daily Report*, 24 May 1994; *Al-Hayat* (London, daily), 26 May 1994; *Middle East International* (London, biweekly), 27 June 1994; *Al-Sharq al-Awsat*, 27 May 1994; Agence France Press, 4 June 1994, cited in *Daily Report*, 6 June 1994; United States Information Service, Wireless File, 28 June 1994; *Nida' al-Rafidayn* (Damascus, biweekly), 16 September 1994.

18. *Le Monde* (Paris, daily), 2 August 1995; *The Middle East*, April, November 1995, claimed that the number of dead had already reached 3,000.

19. *Al-Hayat*, 7 June 1994.

20. Ibid.

21. *Nida' al Rafidayn*, 16 September 1994.

22. United States Information Service, Wireless File, 28 June 1994.

23. Mirjam E. Sørli, Nils Petter Gleditsch, and Håvard Strand, "Why Is There So Much Conflict in the Middle East?" *Journal of Conflict Resolution* 49, no. 1 (2005): 145.

24. Van Bruinessen, "The Kurds and Islam."

25. *Al-Hayat*, 7 June 1994.

26. *Al-Hayat*, 5, 8, 26, 29 June 1994.

27. *Al-Hayat*, 18 June 1994.

28. Voice of Iraqi Kurdistan, 6 January 1994, cited in *Daily Report*, 7 January 1994.

29. Voice of Iraqi Kurdistan, 25 August 1994, cited in *Daily Report*, 26 August 1994.

30. *Middle East International*, 27 May 1994; *Al-Sharq al-Awsat*, 31 May 1994; Iraqi News Agency, 15 June 1994, cited in *Daily Report*, 15 June 1994.

31. *Al-Hayat*, 5 June 1994; *Babil* (Baghdad, daily), October 1994.

32. *Al-Safir*, 2, 3 August 1994, cited in *Daily Report*, 10 August 1994; *Al-Hayat*, 1, 30 October 1994.

33. For the escalation in PKK-Turkish relations in the early 1990s, see Ismet G. Imset, *The PKK: A Report on Separatist Violence in Turkey* (Ankara: Turkish Daily News Publications, 1992), pp. 233–298.

34. *Turkish Daily News*, 11 June 1993, cited in *Daily Report*, 21 June 1993; *Baghdad*, 18 June 1993; Voice of Iraqi Kurdistan, 25 June 1993, cited in *Daily Report*, 30 June 1993.

35. For a discussion of PKK violence, see Hamit Bozarslan, *Violence in the Middle East* (Princeton: Marcus Wiener, 2004), pp. 43–57.

36. Voice of the Iraqi People, 19 August 1993, cited in *Daily Report*, 20 August 1993.

37. On KDP-PKK relations, see Imset, *The PKK*, pp. 180–187.

38. *Al-Sharq al-Awsat*, 30 April 1994; *Al-Safir*, 2 August, cited in *Daily Report*, 10 August 1994.

39. Nevertheless as someone observed, "even in their worst days at leadership level, the grassroots of both movements have cooperated extensively." Imset, *The PKK*, p. 180.

40. *Mideast Mirror*, 7 April 1995. For further details, see Michael Gunter, *The Kurds and the Future of Turkey* (Houndmills: Macmillan, 1997), pp. 115–125.

41. Agence France Press, 28 April 1995, cited in *Daily Report*, 28 April 1995.

42. Voice of Iraqi Kurdistan, 26 August 1995, cited in *Daily Report*, 29 August 1995; Voice of the People of Kurdistan, 28 August 1995, cited in *Daily Report*, 29 August 1995; *Al-Hayat*, 29 August 1995.

43. *Al-Hayat*, 29 August 1995; Agence France Press, 29 August 1995, cited in *Daily Report*, 30 August 1995.

44. On 10 December 1995, the PKK announced a cease-fire brought about in part through the mediatory efforts of Dawood Baghestani, the permanent UN representative at the Organisation for Security and Co-operation in Europe. See Gunter, *The Kurds*, p. 124.

45. Voice of Iraqi Kurdistan, 23 October, 5 December 1995, cited in *Daily Report*, 24 October, 6 December 1995.

46. Agence France Press, 2 September 1995, cited in *Daily Report*, 7 September 1995; Voice of Iraqi Kurdistan, 6 September 1995, cited in *Daily Report*, 7 September 1995.

47. *Al-Thawra*, 30 May 1993.

48. Kuwaiti News Agency, 11 February 1993, cited in *Daily Report*, 12 February 1993; *Al-Sharq al-Awsat*, 19 February 1993, cited in *Daily Report*, 23 February 1993; Voice of the People of Kurdistan, 10 March 1993, cited in *Daily Report*, 11 March 1993; *Al-Hawadith*, 26 March 1993, cited in Joint Publication Research Services, 18 May 1993.

49. *New York Times*, 21 January 1994; Kurdish exile, interviewed by the author, April 1994.

50. *Al-Thawra*, 10 February 1993; *Babil*, 13 February 1993.

51. Radio Cairo, Voice of America, 13 March 1993, cited in *Daily Report*, 15 March

1993; *Al-Sharq al-Awsat*, 21 May 1993, cited in *Daily Report*, 25 May 1993; *Akhbar al-Usbu'*, 8 July 1993, cited in *Daily Report*, 9 July 1993.

52. Agence France Press, 6 May 1993, cited in *Daily Report*, 7 May 1993.

53. *Al-Sharq al-Awsat*, 21 May 1993, cited in *Daily Report*, 25 May 1993.

54. Voice of the People of Kurdistan, 12 May 1993, cited in *Daily Report*, 13 May 1993; *Le Monde*, 14 May 1993, cited in *Daily Report*, 18 May 1993.

55. *Le Monde*, 18 June 1993; *New York Times*, 21 January 1994.

56. *Fédération internationale des ligues des Droits de l'Homme*, Report no. 178 (October 1993), p. 26; *New York Times*, 21 January 1994.

57. *Fédération internationale*, p. 36; Agence France Press, 15 August 1993, cited in *Daily Report*, 16 August 1993.

58. For example, *Fédération internationale*, p. 37; Voice of the Iraqi People, 21 May, 1993, cited in *Daily Report*, 24 May 1993; Voice of the People of Kurdistan, 17 March, 11 July 1993, cited in *Daily Report*, 18 March, 13 July 1993.

59. *Al-Sharq al-Awsat*, 11 April 1994.

60. *Alif Ba'* (Baghdad, weekly), 11 May 1994.

61. *Al-Shira'* (Beirut, daily), 13 December 1993, cited in *Daily Report*, 17 December 1993.

62. *Le Monde*, 14 June 1994.

63. Van Bruinessen, "The Kurds and Islam."

64. *Middle East International*, 27 May 1994.

65. *Al-Hayat*, 26, 27 May, 8 June 1994. See also Talabani to *Al-Sharq al-Awsat*, 27 May 1994.

66. *Middle East International*, 27 May 1994; *Al-Sharq al-Awsat*, 31 May 1994.

67. *Al-Safir*, 3 August 1994, cited in *Daily Report*, 10 August 1994.

68. *Fédération internationale*, pp. 20–24; Agence France Press, 9 May 1993; Voice of the People of Kurdistan, 15 August, 3 September 1993, cited in *Daily Report*, 16 August, 3 September 1993; Agence France Press, 24 August 1993, cited in *Daily Report*, 25 August 1993.

69. *Libération*, 29 July 1993, cited in *Daily Report*, 3 August 1993.

70. For a general discussion of Syria's position on the Kurds of Iraq, see Jordi Tejel, *Syria's Kurds: History, Politics and Society* (London: Routledge, 2009), especially chaps. 3, 4.

71. *Al-Hayat*, 16 December 1993, cited in *Daily Report*, 21 December 1993.

72. Michael Collins Dunn, "The Arab World and the Kurds," in *Kurdish Identity: Human Rights and Political Status*, eds. Charles G. MacDonald and Carole A. O'Leary (Gainesville: University Press of Florida, 2007), pp. 231–235.

73. *Al-Hayat*, 22 June 1993, cited in *Daily Report*, 30 June 1993.

74. Imset maintained that the villages hit by Turkish warplanes "have always been those of the KDP, including Barzan." Imset, *The PKK*, p. 180. See also Jonathan Randal, *After Such Knowledge, What Forgiveness? My Encounters with Kurdistan* (Boulder, CO: Westview Press, 1999), p. 240.

75. *Le Monde*, 15 December 1993.

76. See Kemal Kirişci, "Turkey and the Safe Haven in Northern Iraq," *Journal of South Asian and Middle Eastern Studies* 19, no. 3 (1996): 21–39.

77. *Le Monde*, 22 March 1995.

78. Radio Monte Carlo, 30 March 1995, cited in *Daily Report*, 31 March 1995; *The Middle East*, April 1995; Agence France Press, 26 April 1995, cited in *Daily Report*, 28 April 1995.

79. *Le Monde*, 9 April 1995.

80. Radio Baghdad, 26 March 1995, cited in *Daily Report*, 28 March 1995; Iraqi News Agency, 29 March 1995, cited in *Daily Report*, 30 March 1995.

81. Iraqi News Agency, 8 April, 2 May 1995, cited in *Daily Report*, 10 April, 2 May 1995.

82. Iraqi News Agency, 8, 9 April 1995, cited in *Daily Report*, 10, 11 April 1995.

83. *Al-Sharq al-Awsat*, 3 May 1995; Iraqi News Agency, 3 May 1995, cited in *Daily Report*, 4 May 1995; *Mideast Mirror*, 10 May 1995; *Middle East International*, 12 May 1995.

84. *Baghdad*, 27 August 1993.

85. Iraqi News Agency, 25 August 1993, cited in *Daily Report*, 26 August 1993.

86. *Al-Shira'*, 13 December 1993, cited in *Daily Report*, 17 December 1993. See also *Ara' 'Arabiyya Hawla al-Qadiyya al-Kurdiyya* (Damascus: al-Ittihad al-Watani al-Kurdistani, 1993).

87. *Al-Shira'*, 13 December 1993, cited in *Daily Report*, 17 December 1993.

88. *New York Times*, 3 May 1993.

89. *Le Monde*, 25 May 1993.

90. *Baghdad*, 21 May 1993; *Le Monde*, 6 November 1993.

91. Randal, *After Such Knowledge*, pp. 292–293.

92. Kendal Nezan, "The European Perspective," in *Kurdish Identity: Human Rights and Political Status*, eds. Charles G. MacDonald and Carole A. O'Leary (Gainesville: University Press of Florida, 2007), p. 140.

93. *Al-Safir*, 3 August 1994, cited in *Daily Report*, 10 August 1994.

94. Stansfield, for one, thinks that the 1990s were not a squandered opportunity, but may be seen as a decade of political development. Stansfield, *Iraqi Kurdistan*, p. 95.

13
Uncivil War in Kurdistan

Analyzing the impact of civil wars, Michael Howard asserts, "for the United States the nation was molded by the war of independence and united by the result of civil war."[1] Paul Collier puts it differently, "To the extent that civil war has a political rationale it is a catalyst for social progress." The other side of the coin, however, is described as "development in reverse."[2] Charles Tilly argues that "war makes states" and that there is "interdependence of war making and state making."[3] This model may have suited the Kurdish case in Iraq, but only in part. War became part and parcel of the existence of the Kurds in Iraq due to their protracted struggle against Baghdad, against the PKK, and among themselves. However, these ongoing wars had an ambiguous effect on the crystallization of the Kurdish national movement and on its state building. On one hand, the wars with Baghdad wreaked havoc on the Kurdish region and impeded its social and economic development; on the other hand, they served to sharpen feelings of Kurdish identity. By the same token, fighting the PKK did ensure the survival of the KRG for a while, but at the same time it also harmed the cause of the Kurdish national movement in Greater Kurdistan. As to the inter-Kurdish war, its immediate effect seemed to be purely negative. Only after the warring parties began to settle their differences could they divert their attention and energies to the task of nation building. In fact the most difficult undertaking for the Kurdish leaderships was fighting on two fronts simultaneously: first, on the military battlefield; and, second, for the soul of the people.

When the fighting in Iraqi Kurdistan degenerated into a full-fledged civil war in 1996, few Kurds were able to take a positive view of its outcome. Yet in the eyes of an outside observer, the civil war could and should be judged by its long-term consequences. The question was whether the American Civil War could serve as a model for the KRG.

Awkward Alliances and Strange Bedfellows

Mas'ud Barzani, leader of the KDP, took the world by surprise when in late August 1996 he called on the Iraqi Army to help in his struggle against the rival Kurdish party, the PUK. The move was widely perceived as a betrayal, both of the Kurdish people and of their US supporters, and as a lack of foresight that verged on political suicide. Barzani's action once again reshuffled the cards in Iraqi Kurdistan and raised a number of questions as to the motives behind this move. In what ways did it change the rules of the game in the KRG? What was its impact on local, regional, and international players? And might there perhaps be a more logical interpretation of his maneuver—different from the one suggested above?

Surprising as it might have appeared to outsiders, Barzani's act had in fact been brewing for quite some time. It was rooted in the situation prevailing in the KRG after the end of the Gulf War, in the rivalries and alliances that had developed since then, and in the fact that the region had turned into a testing ground for various internal and external forces. The two main internal players, the KDP and the PUK, sought to capitalize on the vacuum created in Iraqi Kurdistan by the Iraqi Army's withdrawal in 1991. The aim of the KDP and PUK was not to establish a united Kurdistan, but for each to enlarge its respective sphere of influence and ultimately become the sole power in the region.[4] This rivalry underpinned the fighting that continued intermittently between May 1994 and the end of 1995 when a cease-fire was brokered between the two sides. But the brief respite, which only lasted until the summer of 1996, was exploited by all players to forge new alliances or strengthen existing ones in order to improve their positions in the anticipated encounter. These alliances reflected the geographic, economic, and political concerns of the different players.

It should be noted that, in addition to the KDP, the PUK and their different supporters among the tribes and Iraqi Kurdish political groups, three other forces held entrenched positions in Iraqi Kurdistan: (1) the PKK with its stronghold within the KDP's sphere of influence, which reportedly controlled twelve permanent and twenty-one mobile training camps as well as 4,500–5,000 guerrillas;[5] (2) the Kurdistan Democratic Party of Iran, which was based near the Iranian border inside the areas of influence of both the KDP and the PUK; and (3) the Iraqi National Congress (INC), an alliance of several Iraqi opposition groups supported by the United States and based mainly in the PUK sphere of influence. Roughly speaking, since one must take into consideration the many nuances at play, the two camps were aligned as follows at the beginning of the flare-up in the summer of 1996: on the one hand, the KDP, Turkey, Iraq, and the KDPI; on the other, the PUK, Iran, the INC, and the PKK. Syria maintained the role of an aloof broker throughout whereas the US position was fraught with dilemmas.

The tacit alliance between Turkey and the KDP, which was nonetheless an ongoing source of friction, was based on shared geographical borders, economic interests, the passage of merchandise, and common enmity or rivalry with the PKK. Less understandable was the relationship that developed between the KDP and the Baathi regime, especially in view of the genocidal war conducted throughout the 1980s by the Baath against the Kurds in general and the Barzanis in particular. Hence, one could conclude that the alliance between the Baath and the KDP was cemented by the latter's deep enmity toward the PUK. Ever since his thwarted autonomy talks with the Baath in 1991, Barzani was reported to have held intermittent secret negotiations with Baghdad.[6]

The PUK publicly accused the KDP of "collaborating" with Baghdad as early as March 1996. It claimed that Barzani had held a "long" meeting with the Iraqi oil minister, 'Amir Rashid, who was traveling to Turkey through Kurdish-held areas in northern Iraq. According to the PUK, "this meeting was the culmination of coordination and secret two-year-long meetings between Saddam Husayn's regime and the KDP, and its treachery can no longer be hidden."[7] Kurdish and Arab sources in Kurdistan were quoted as saying that some sixty experts from the oil ministry had been in Duhok province on an unspecified date to inspect the section of the oil pipeline to Turkey that passed through a KDP-controlled area. The KDP, however, denied having held any talks with the oil minister or any other officials.[8] Whatever the truth of this specific report, the fact is that it touched on the most important factor in the triangle of relations between the KDP, Turkey, and Iraq—the oil pipeline, which all three had an interest in reactivating. The KDP, which according to Jalal Talabani already controlled 70 percent of the region's revenues (mainly fees from the passage of oil tankers and merchandise),[9] was expected to significantly increase its income with the reopening of the pipeline. It therefore perhaps was no coincidence that the KDP supported Baghdad's May 1996 oil accord with the UN—the oil-for-food program[10]—and expressed its desire to provide all the assistance necessary to implement it, "especially repairing and operating the pumping station in the Zakho area and repairing and operating the part of the pipeline that runs through the areas under our control."[11] Furthermore, Mas'ud Barzani came out publicly in favor of a "political solution" with Baghdad, including with Saddam Hussein, saying he was ready to go to Baghdad should talks be held on "the Kurdish people's future."[12]

As Barzani was tacitly moving toward an understanding, or even an alliance with Iraq, Talabani was drawing closer to Iran, though in a less outspoken manner. As in the past, Iran was seeking to strengthen its influence in Kurdistan by mediating between the two conflicting parties. For this reason, a delegation of forty-seven Iranians was sent to the region in early January 1996, but it reportedly failed to move the parties to reach an agreement.[13] Meanwhile, Iran also started broadcasting Kurdish programs in northern Iraq "to propagate the fundamentals of Islam . . . and counter foreign propaganda."[14]

Iran's actions aroused concern in Washington; in April, a US delegation headed by Robert Deutsch, the State Department's director of northern Gulf affairs, was sent to the KRG to mediate between the KDP and PUK. But like Iran, the United States also failed in its mission.

The fragile cease-fire between the KDP and PUK was broken in mid-June by a skirmish involving the KDP and the Surchi tribe, which had apparently changed sides and became allied with the PUK. The situation was further complicated by a Turkish attack, involving 6,000 troops, on PKK bases in northern Iraq in late June and a 2,000-troop Iranian offensive at the end of July against the bases of the KDPI. It was the latter incident that brought matters to a head. The war of words between the KDP and the PUK continued to escalate, with the PUK accusing the KDP of obtaining heavy weapons from Baghdad and colluding with Iraq against its Kurdish brethren. The KDP accused the PUK of asking Iranian troops to fight the KDPI, thereby infringing on the KDP's sphere of influence, and of obtaining heavy weapons from Iran.[15] Attempts by both the KDP and the PUK to bring about US involvement in the affair led nowhere.[16] The United States was aware of the inroads that both Iraq and Iran had made in Iraqi Kurdistan, but at that point was reluctant to take any step other than holding further talks in the United States with Kurdish officials from both factions.[17]

Signs of Baghdad's tilt toward the KDP, which surfaced occasionally throughout the year 1996, became quite obvious before the flare-up when the government published a KDP statement accusing Iran of collaborating with the PUK and waging war against Iraqi Kurdistan. A similar statement by the deputy prime minister Tariq 'Aziz was made public at the same time.[18]

Seen from a bird's-eye view, the situation in Iraqi Kurdistan on the eve of the flare-up could be described as moving in three concentric circles. At the center were the local powers, the KDP and the PUK, which attempted to increase their respective spheres of influence through alliances with stronger regional powers—the KDP with Turkey and Iraq, and the PUK with Iran and Syria. Forces in the wider circle were regional powers that tried to exploit the vacuum created by the infighting of local Kurdish groups—either to fight their own Kurdish minorities or to keep the others in check. Turkey attempted to use the KDP to enlarge its sphere of influence in Iraqi Kurdistan; to fight its enemy, the Turkish PKK; and to hold Iran in check. Through its alliance with the PUK, Iran sought to battle the Iranian KDPI; enlarge its sphere of influence in Iraqi Kurdistan; weaken Baghdad; and even limit US influence in Kurdistan. Baghdad on the other hand, through its alliance with the KDP, endeavored to regain control of Kurdistan; contain Iran and the PUK, which was in Iran's orbit; and challenge the United States. And finally, in the outer circle, stood the United States (and to a lesser extent Great Britain), whose main interest was to contain the local and regional powers in order to prevent renewed fighting, which could draw the United States into an unwelcome conflict particularly on the eve of its presidential elections.

Baghdad as a Proxy in the Kurdish Infighting

In September 1996 the KDP managed to dislodge its rival, the PUK, from its two strongholds in the Erbil and Sulaymaniyya provinces, becoming the sole ruler of Iraqi Kurdistan for one month.[19] The ease and swiftness of this victory could by no means be attributed to military prowess. It was the result of a political stratagem: the marriage of convenience between Mas'ud Barzani and Saddam, which moved the Iraqi Army to Erbil on 31 August to fight the KDP's war.[20] It must be noted, however, that the KDP was the stronger of the two: in 1993 the International Institute for Strategic Studies' Military Balance Report estimated that the KDP had 25,000 active Peshmerga and 30,000 reserves, compared to 12,000 active Peshmerga and 6,000 reserves in the PUK.[21] This was indeed another ironic turn of history, as the central government's army was called on to fight a war by proxy, in support of one Kurdish group against another, thus breaking the traditional pattern in which Kurdish groups were used as proxies to fight for one state as against another or against a rival Kurdish group.

The battle for Erbil, capital of the Kurdish autonomous region, lasted some fifteen hours, starting at dawn on 31 August 1996 and ending by 9 P.M. of the same day. There were conflicting reports regarding the size of the Iraqi military forces that took part in the offensive. Although Barzani initially attempted to deny their participation and then to belittle them, they apparently comprised some 30,000 soldiers of the Republican Guard elite forces, between 200 and 400 tanks, and the First and Fifth Army Corps, which were stationed in Iraqi Kurdistan before their withdrawal from the area in 1991.[22] Even if these numbers were inflated, the sight of a few Iraqi tanks in Erbil was enough to break the morale of the PUK, which indeed did not put up much of a fight.[23] The war for Erbil resulted in the flight of the PUK forces from the city, the imprisonment of some 2,000 of its members and supporters, including Fu'ad Ma'sum, a PUK member and the former prime minister of Iraqi Kurdistan (1992–1993). Another PUK member, Kosrat Rasul, proved his leadership skills by organizing the evacuation of PUK members from Erbil, thus preventing greater losses to the party.[24] Talabani's wife, Hero, was also caught in the crossfire, but managed to flee from Erbil in time. Hero, a political activist, was one of the few female Kurds who was a member of the 1992 parliament. She also helped create a PUK unit of female Peshmerga.[25]

As to the casualties, a PUK spokesman mentioned the fictitious number of 15,000 dead while a more neutral source gave an estimate of 100.[26] The umbrella group of the Iraqi opposition, the INC, later claimed that 96 of its members had been murdered by Iraqi troops when their ammunition ran out during the defense of their camp at Qushtepe, 22 kilometers southeast of Erbil.[27]

With the fall of Erbil into the hands of the KDP, the inter-Kurdish conflict came full circle: the reoccupation in 1996 of the city, which had first been captured by the forces of Talabani in early 1995. The fall of Erbil opened the way for the occupation of the rest of Talabani's sphere of influence, culminating in the fall of Sulaymaniyya, the traditional stronghold of the PUK, on 9 September 1996. The PUK's hopes of a US involvement tipping the balance in its favor did not materialize. The ambivalence of the United States, which began with muscle flexing far from the battleground, ended with a "declaration of unwillingness to be involved in internal Kurdish wars,"[28] leaving the PUK in the lurch.

Fears of Iraqi troops (which probably did not advance beyond Erbil), combined with their despair over the US stance, ultimately convinced Talabani to abandon Sulaymaniyya without a fight and leave for Iran at once, together with his supporters. As in earlier wars, Kurdish civilians paid a heavy price: nearly 50,000 Kurds, associated in one way or another with the PUK, were also forced to flee, causing them abject misery.[29] Indeed, this was a worldwide phenomenon, as shown by a World Bank report: while at the beginning of the twentieth century about 90 percent of all war victims were soldiers, in the 1990s, 90 percent were civilians.[30]

After the fall of Sulaymaniyya, Talabani proclaimed that the PUK had lost two battles, though not the war: "In guerrilla warfare you can always win or lose control of the cities. The important thing is to keep your forces."[31] Indeed, just one month later, the PUK initiated another round of fighting with Iranian support; it lasted ten days from 13 October to 23 October. Nullifying some of the KDP's short-lived achievements the PUK regained control of Sulaymaniyya and other important towns, including Koysanjak, Rawanduz, and Dokan, but left Erbil in the hands of the KDP. By 23 October, when a cease-fire was achieved between the two parties, Sulaymaniyya province had fallen into PUK hands while Duhok and Erbil provinces remained under the control of the KDP.

Meanwhile, in another ironic twist in the complex set of ties in the region, the KDP was reported to have attempted to mend fences with Iran at the same time as the PUK was holding secret contacts with Baghdad.[32] Baghdad, for its part, reportedly began putting out feelers to Iran in an attempt to reach an understanding on the Kurdish issue.[33]

Baghdad's Sweet, Short Victory

The first round of fighting in Kurdistan turned out to be Baghdad's most important achievement in six years. Qualifying it as a "sweet victory," Saddam explained, "what was very sweet in this battle was the fact that the armed forces carried out their duties together with brothers who followed the same path, against brothers who followed the opposite course in the autonomous region."[34]

Barzani's call for Iraqi military assistance was viewed in Baghdad as an ideal opportunity to reverse the traumatic events that had severed Kurdistan from the body of Iraq in 1991. It had both national and territorial implications: returning the Kurds to the Iraqi national fold and bringing the Kurdistan region back under state control. On the military level, although the participation and achievement of the army was limited, it was nonetheless an important boost to morale after years of paralysis and of the army's inability to set foot in Iraqi Kurdistan. On the regional level Iraq took the initiative again, after nearly six years, during which period the three countries bordering on Kurdistan—Turkey, Iran, and Syria—had turned it into their own backyard, to the near exclusion of Baghdad. Iraq also managed to gain the support of most Arab countries on the issue of its territorial integrity versus a US, Turkish, and Iranian infringement of it.

In returning openly to Kurdistan Baghdad had to tread carefully, balancing its desire to present the incident as the legitimate action of a sovereign state on its own territory with the need to prevent a Western military response in Kurdistan, which might deepen foreign involvement there. Following the occupation of Erbil, Baghdad publicized Barzani's letter of 22 August 1996 that sought the Iraqi Army's support in putting an end to the Talabani-Iranian conspiracy, as well as a later letter thanking the Iraqi leadership for the army's help.[35] Iraq thus presented the action not as its own initiative, but as a response to a call for help by Iraqi patriots fighting against treason. Mas'ud Barzani sought to describe the occupation of Erbil as having been accomplished almost single-handedly by his own forces, saying that "the Iraqi army did not enter Erbil, except for a matter of minutes, then it withdrew."[36] Baghdad, however, sought to describe the operation—which it code-named Al-Mutawakkil 'Ala Allah (relying on God)—as a great and heroic feat of the Iraqi Army, whose goals were to liberate Erbil from the traitors, "restore stability and security to northern Iraq," and "maintain national sovereignty there."[37] Similarly, when Baghdad announced the withdrawal of its forces shortly after the occupation of Erbil, it also initiated a series of actions to signal that the central government was there to stay. One symbolic move was raising the Iraqi flag. Of more serious consequence for the Kurds, especially those opposing Baghdad, was the return of the security forces to Erbil on the heels of the army.[38] Other much-publicized measures included the traditional general amnesty for all Kurds, and the lifting of the embargo on Kurdistan, declared on 11 September 1996, signifying, among others, the renewal of oil supply and the resumption of transportation to that area.

Following the occupation of Sulaymaniyya, *Al-Thawra* published a cartoon showing a map of Iraq with the slogan "God is One, Iraq is One, and Saddam is the leader."[39] Indeed, Iraqi unity was Baghdad's most important argument for mobilizing support for its actions at home, in the Arab world, and in international forums. In trumpeting the slogan or argument for Iraqi unity, Baghdad sought to capitalize on the built-in contradictions that characterized the regional and international players' stance on the Kurdish issue. On the one hand, they wished to use the Kurdish card to weaken the Baathi regime; on the other, they were adamantly opposed to the emergence of an independent Kurdish entity or to a fragmentation of Iraq, which might have spillover effects on many countries of the region. Interestingly, it was not only Baghdad that championed the motif of Iraqi unity. Mas'ud Barzani justified his agreement with Baghdad on the same grounds; namely, the need to put an end to "a violation of Iraqi national sovereignty." When asked whether the hoisting of Iraqi flags in Erbil meant an end to the federation project raised a few years earlier, he answered, "Even when we attain federation, the central flag will remain. . . . We love our flag, the flag of Kurdistan, very much. But we have not seceded."[40]

Thus the arguments for Iraqi sovereignty and territorial integrity were the most important weapons in Baghdad's propaganda arsenal. Iraq maintained that, while both Iran and the United States had infringed on the sovereignty of another country, the Iraqi actions were perfectly legitimate within Iraqi boundaries.[41]

The Kurdistan episode was of great importance to Baghdad: it scored points against the United States, contained the Iranian advance in Iraqi Kurdistan, and allowed the central government to establish only a brief foothold in Kurdistan. However, Iraq's position in Kurdistan subsequently suffered a setback, following the cease-fire between the KDP and the PUK and their return to the negotiating table under US-Turkish auspices. Sweet as Baghdad's victory was, it was also short-lived.

The United States Mediates Between the Kurdish Warring Parties

The war in Kurdistan, the involvement of Baghdad, and the approaching US presidential elections of November 1996 created an increasing number of dilemmas for President William J. Clinton's administration. The United States wished to use the Kurdish card to contain Baghdad, but did not want to get involved in intra-Kurdish fighting. Similarly the United States sought to weaken, or even unseat, Saddam's regime, but it also feared the possible breakup of the state. Though it wished to keep as low a profile as possible in Iraq because of the elections, the United States could not remain idle in the face of the challenges posed by Baghdad. Its stance on the Kurdish-Kurdish war reflected these dilemmas, resulting in further ambiguities on the Kurdish issue.

Because the United States was perhaps the only player not to thrive on intra-Kurdish conflicts, its main policy line was to try to mediate between the warring parties, which it did with some degree of success for a few months. Indeed, it was engaged in this endeavor on the very eve of the renewed flare-up.[42] The KDP, for its part, used the US inaction vis-à-vis the Iranian advance into Kurdistan to explain its own sudden volte-face. Barzani said that he had asked for US support "ten times" before approaching Baghdad.[43]

Once fighting had begun, the US administration decided to respond, but at a minimum political and military cost. It launched forty-four missiles against Iraqi installations, but none in Kurdistan. The missiles seemed to have solved one of the US dilemmas: it sent a message to Baghdad without involving the US Army in ground fighting, a move that could have had disastrous consequences.

As it turned out, the US show of force did not affect the fighting; it did not check the KDP's advance on the ground nor did it turn the tide later on. Furthermore, it elicited criticism from most of the Arab countries, and both Turkey and Saudi Arabia refused to allow the United States to launch the missiles from their territories. Fearing a loss of influence and seeking to maintain quiet in the area, especially before the elections, the United States once again reverted to mediation. On 18 September 1996, Mas'ud Barzani was called to Ankara for talks with Robert Pelletreau, US assistant secretary of state for Near Eastern affairs, probably with the preliminary intention of checking Barzani's drift toward Saddam. In return, Mas'ud Barzani was reputed to have demanded some kind of US involvement in the north.[44]

When the tide turned in the fighting, the United States was moved to act more vigorously and on 23 October managed to broker a cease-fire between the two Kurdish parties. The mediation talks, held in Ankara with the participation of US, Turkish, and Kurdish representatives, led to the formulation of a ten-point agreement announced on 31 October. The KDP, however, agreed to only the following five points: abiding by the cease-fire; the return of civil services in the KRG; an exchange of prisoners; halting the mutual media campaigns; and demarcating the cease-fire line in accordance with the lines in place on the night of 23 October. The KDP was reluctant to agree on the distribution of revenue or to desist from allowing the PKK to act from Iraqi territory against Turkey. The PUK, however, did announce its acceptance of the entire ten-point statement, "despite its reservations about some of these resolutions."[45]

Even more curious was the US move to establish a "peace-monitoring" force of 400 local Turkomans and Assyrians in October 1996. Financed by the United States, this force was entrusted with the task of supervising the cease-fire between the KDP and the PUK, but it remained idle when fighting once again erupted between the Kurdish groups.[46]

Mas'ud Barzani's Volte-Face Reconsidered

Shocking as Mas'ud Barzani's alliance with Baghdad appears, it must be placed in its historical context and analyzed against the backdrop of developments following the end of the Gulf War. Historically speaking, changing alliances had been part and parcel of Kurdish politics from the time of the Ottoman and Persian empires. If there was a change in the historic pattern, it lay in the fact that the Kurds had called on a central government to help them against another Kurdish faction.

Furthermore, the minimal, covert US support of the early 1970s had turned into substantial, albeit half-hearted, assistance in the 1990s. Barzani's "betrayal" of the United States should also be seen against the backdrop of the US "betrayal" of the Kurds in 1975 when it suddenly ended its clandestine aid to the Kurds, which led to the collapse of the rebellion against Baghdad.[47]

Considerations of realpolitik were not lacking either. Barzani had probably reached the conclusion that under no circumstances would the United States support a Kurdish independent entity and that moreover a US-Baghdad reconciliation was only a question of time as indicated by the oil-for-food agreement. Hence, prior to the lifting of sanctions, a KDP alliance with a weakened central government could serve various ends: obtain the support of Baghdad against its Kurdish rival, thus regaining the monopoly on power in Kurdistan as had been the case in 1970–1975; forestall a military action against the Kurds by Baghdad once its hands were untied; and serve notice to the United States that the KDP had learned from past experience and would not be a mere tool in the hands of others.

As it turned out, tactically speaking, Barzani's moves were not altogether mistaken from his perspective: the KDP gained control of Erbil, maintained its hold on the income of Iraqi Kurdistan,[48] and shored up its bargaining powers vis-à-vis the other actors. Years later, however, Barzani admitted that the civil war "was wrong, and it will not [be repeated]; therefore, we apologize to the people of Kurdistan."[49] He further stated in an apologetic vein that the move was not directed against the PUK, but against "Iranian intervention."[50] It may be too early to judge, but fifteen years without such friendly fire in Iraqi Kurdistan could mean that the civil war was a sobering experience for the Kurds that translated into an opportunity for greater unity.

Notes

1. Michael Howard, "War and Nations," in *Nationalism*, eds. John Hutchinson and Anthony D. Smith (Oxford: Oxford University Press, 1994), p. 235.

2. Paul Collier, *Breaking the Conflict Trap: Civil War and Development Policy* (Washington, DC: World Bank; New York: Oxford University Press, 2003), p. 19 and chap. 1.

3. Charles Tilly, "War Making and State Making as Organized Crime," in *Bringing the State Back In*, eds. Peter B. Evans, Dietrich Rueschemeyer, and Theda Skocpol (Cambridge: Cambridge University Press, 1985), p. 170.

4. The warring parties used mechanisms employed by states; namely, "eliminating or neutralizing their rivals" inside their territories. Tilly, "War Making," p. 181.

5. *Al-Sharq al-Awsat* (London, daily), 14 September 1996. Until 1984, the PKK used KDP camps. However, following Turkish attacks on these camps in that year, the KDP asked the PKK to leave; therefore, the Turkish group began establishing its own camps in Iraq. Ismet G. Imset, *The PKK: A Report on Separatist Violence in Turkey* (Ankara: Turkish Daily News Publications, 1992), p. 185.

6. *Le Monde*, 26 August 1996.

7. Agence France Press, 5 March 1996, cited in *Daily Report*, 6 March 1996.

8. *Mideast Mirror*, 4 March 1996; *Al-Hayat* (London, daily), 7 March 1996; *Al-Watan al-'Arabi* (Cairo, weekly), 12 April 1996; *Al-Sharq al-Awsat* (London, daily), 4 May 1996.

9. Voice of the People of Kurdistan, 31 January 1996, cited in *Daily Report*, 1 February 1996.

10. Under the program, Iraq was able to sell Iraqi oil after it had been forbidden to do so because of the sanctions imposed on it after the invasion of Kuwait in 1990. Most of the revenues were supposed to be used to purchase humanitarian supplies.

11. Voice of Iraqi Kurdistan, 2 May 1996, cited in *Daily Report*, 23 May 1996.

12. *Hürriyet*, 6 June 1996, cited in *Daily Report*, 20 June 1996.

13. Middle East News Agency, 13 January 1996, cited in *Daily Report*, 17 January 1996.

14. Agence France Press, 18 February 1996, cited in *Daily Report*, 23 February 1996.

15. This was also mentioned by Marion Farouk-Sluglett and Peter Sluglett, *Iraq Since 1958: From Revolution to Dictatorship*, 3rd ed. (London: I. B. Tauris, 2001), p. 299.

16. Even as the meeting was taking place, Barzani had already made the deal with Baghdad. Gareth R. V. Stansfield, *Iraqi Kurdistan: Political Development and Emergent Democracy* (New York: Routledge Curzon, 2003), p. 98.

17. US State Department and Kurdish officials, interviewed by the author, Washington, DC, 7, 8 August 1996.

18. *Alif Ba'* (Baghdad, weekly), 28 August 1996.

19. For a graphic description of this war, see Quil Lawrence, *Invisible Nation: How the Kurds' Quest for Statehood Is Shaping Iraq and the Middle East* (New York: Walker; distributed by Macmillan, 2008), pp. 63–132.

20. In its propaganda, the PUK referred to the KDP as "the 31 August party." Hussein Tahiri, *The Structure of Kurdish Society and the Struggle for a Kurdish State* (Costa Mesa, CA: Mazda, 2007), p. 281.

21. Quoted by Anthony H. Cordesman, *Iran and Iraq: The Threat from the Northern Gulf* (Boulder, CO: Westview Press, 1994), pp. 229–230.

22. *Jerusalem Post* (Jerusalem, daily), 1 September 1996; *Financial Times* (London, daily), 2 September 1996; Voice of the People of Kurdistan, 3 September 1996, cited in BBC, 5 September 1996; *The Economist* (London, weekly) 16 September 1996; *Al-Wasat* (London, weekly), 16 September 1996.

23. In an interview, Talabani said that he had lost "several tanks that were in the cities." Radio Monte Carlo, 2 September 1996, cited in *Daily Report*.

24. Stansfield, *Iraqi Kurdistan*, p. 98.

25. Lawrence, *Invisible Nation*, p. 82.

26. A PUK spokesman quoted in *L'Unità*, 3 September 1996, cited in *Daily Report*; *Le Monde* (Paris, daily), 3 September 1996; on 4 September 1996, *International Herald Tribune* (Paris and Zurich, daily) quoted an eyewitness as saying that 1,000–2,000 people had died in Erbil.

27. *Middle East International* (London, biweekly), 6 September 1996.

28. US assistant secretary of state for Near Eastern affairs, Robert Pelletreau, maintained, "We have no commitment to them against their own bad judgment if the party invites Saddam Husayn in." *Mideast Mirror*, 26 September 1996.

29. *Financial Times*, 16 September 1996.

30. Collier, *Breaking the Conflict Trap*, p. 16.

31. *Financial Times*, 16 September 1996.

32. *Mideast Mirror*, 11 November 1996.

33. *Middle East International*, 8 November 1996.

34. Iraqi TV, 18 November 1996, cited in *Daily Report*.

35. *Alif Ba'*, 4 September 1996.

36. *Al-Sharq al-Awsat*, 26 September 1996, cited in *Daily Report,* 2 October 1996.

37. Iraqi News Agency, 2 September 1996, cited in BBC, 3 September 1996.

38. *Le Monde*, 3, 14 September 1996; Talabani said that they dressed as Kurds. *Al-Majalla* (London, weekly), 6 October 1996.

39. *Al-Thawra* (Baghdad, daily), 11 September 1996.

40. Voice of Iraqi Kurdistan, 5 September 1996, cited in *Daily Report*.

41. See, for example, Iraqi News Agency, 2, 3 September 1996, cited in *Daily Report*; *Al-Qadisiyya* (Baghdad, daily), 7 September 1996.

42. *Al-Wasat* (London, weekly), 9 September 1996.

43. *Al-Sharq al-Awsat*, 21 September 1996. The bottom line for the two Kurdish representatives in Washington, Hoshyar Zebari of the KDP and Barham Salih of the PUK, was that the United States should broker peace between the two or in some way venture to stop the fighting. Hoshyar Zebari, KDP representative in Washington, and Barham Salih, PUK representative in Washington, interviewed by the author, Washington, DC, 7–8 August 1996.

44. *Mideast Mirror*, 26 September 1996.

45. *Al-Sharq al-Awsat*, 1 November 1996; Voice of Iraqi Kurdistan, 1 November 1996, cited in *Daily Report*; Voice of the People of Kurdistan, 2 November 1996, cited in *Daily Report*.

46. As to the Turkomans, not only did they fail to make peace with the Kurds, but they also failed to maintain it among themselves. There were several groupings and conflicting trends among them; for example, the rival factions of the Turkomans of Kirkuk and those of Erbil that had been formed in 1995.

47. A KDP official justified the move by, among other things, the earlier US stance toward the Kurds. KDP official, interviewed by the author, Ankara, 23 October 1996.

48. Michael Gunter estimated revenues at $150,000 per day. Michael Gunter, *The Kurds and the Future of Turkey* (Houndmills: Macmillan, 1997), p. 117. *Al-Majalla*, 5 October 1997, estimated them at $1 million.

49. Kurdish Media, 4 June 2010, www.kurdishmedia.com.

50. Lawrence, *Invisible Nation*, p. 87.

Part 3

A Kurdish Entity
in the Making, 1998–2010

Iraq is like a big ship for all Iraqis—Arabs and Kurds. We will not allow anyone to drill a hole in that ship lest it break and sink.
　　　　　—Saddam Hussein, *Los Angeles Times*, 20 April 1979

Oh foes who watch us, the nation whose language is Kurdish is alive / It cannot be defeated by makers of weapons of any time / Let no one say the Kurds are dead, the Kurds are alive / The Kurds are alive and their flag will never fall. —the Kurdish anthem

14

The Foreign Relations Imbroglio

In an interview with an Arab newspaper in December 2000 Mas'ud Barzani stated that, although the KDP was committed to the unity and territorial integrity of Iraq, this should take the form of a federation that leaves only foreign policy, national defense, and financial affairs in the hands of the central government.[1] Yet even in those areas, the Kurds had already taken some independent steps. Nowhere was this more conspicuous than in the field of foreign relations, thus raising the stakes for all regional and international players.

One of the important tools for nation building and state building by aspiring secessionists is the ability to conduct foreign relations independently of the state. Indeed, the classic definition of a *state* includes "the capacity to enter into relations with other states."[2] In the Kurdish case, the very contact with the outside world was so crucial to the processes of nation and state building that I have opted to discuss the foreign arena before the domestic one. Whether intentionally or not, Kurdish nation building received a tremendous boost from outside forces: from Baghdad's relentless wars against the Kurds; from Turkey's provision of a lifeline in the critical period of state building; and from other players, especially the United States, and their initial role as mediators, followed by the mobilization of the Kurds for the war against the Baath in 2003.

For a number of reasons, Kurdish ties with the outside world were quite complex: the KRG was not a state; multiple outside players were involved; the field of international relations was largely uncharted territory; and there were contradictory impulses because of rivalries with other Kurds in Greater Kurdistan on the one hand and the impulse of pan-Kurdism on the other. Yet certain factors helped the Kurds in their endeavor—among others, the regionalization and internationalization of the Kurdish issue in the aftermath of the Iran-Iraq War and the Gulf War. Accordingly while most of the relations between the Kurds and outside parties were covert until the early 1990s because neither the Kurds nor their partners were willing to publicize these ties, from that time onward, semi-official contacts were held openly with various states. One explanation for this lies in the stance of the Kurds themselves. For all their disunity, they did learn how to avail themselves of the international media and make their cause known to the outside world, especially following the Halabja and Anfal massacres. The role of the Kurdish diaspora in this domain was crucial.[3]

Similarly, the Kurds took advantage of Baghdad's misguided invasion of Kuwait to advance their own agenda of a federative state, hoping that the international atmosphere would eventually become more supportive on this issue. They also took their first tentative steps in the field of diplomacy and international relations. Thus, the international sanctions against Baghdad forced the Kurds to pursue diplomatic contacts with the UN missions and agencies, which began relating to the Kurdish emissaries as "true representatives of their own people."[4] A US diplomat, Francis J. Ricciardone, assessed that "as non-state practitioners in international relations Kurdish organizations now [2000] enjoy greater influence, access, credibility, and meaningful international relations than does the regime."[5] Admittedly, as shown in this chapter, warlike activities remained part of Kurdish foreign policy making, but in time this part would be more than balanced out by political-diplomatic activities. As Hamit Bozarslan observes, "Within a single decade [the 1990s] a general process of pacification supplanted the general trend of violence and rebellion."[6]

The other side of the coin was the change in stance of various regional and international players, including the United States, Great Britain, France, and Russia, which sought to contain Baghdad via the KRG. But with the Kurds fighting one another, the KRG could hardly take on such a role; hence, the hectic mediating activities by external players. This was indeed one of the positive, albeit unintended, consequences of the Kurdish civil war—the fact that it helped upgrade relations with outside powers. The mediators began, willy-nilly, to regard their Kurdish interlocutors as representatives of a Kurdish entity and not of an Iraqi state with which some countries had no diplomatic relations since the Gulf War. In fact since the establishment of the KRG, the KDP (as well as the PUK) had representations in "the European countries, North America, and neighboring Arab countries."[7] These representatives, whose initial task was to facilitate mediation efforts, began in time to engage in wider diplomatic missions on behalf of the KRG, thus adding another important dimension to Kurdish state building. In other words, the KRG established foreign relations inch by inch, using mediation as a springboard.

The Peace Brokers

The late 1990s witnessed intensive efforts by various governments to mediate between the warring Iraqi Kurdish parties. This unusual development seemed puzzling at first glance since none of the mediators involved took the Iraqi Kurdish cause to heart. However, closer analysis reveals that the mediation efforts were in effect meant to carry on the war against Iraq by using the Kurdish card through diplomatic means. The mediators had certain general aims in common, though they differed on the specifics. All sought to utilize mediation as a tool to contain the situation in Kurdistan; maintain influence over the Kurdish parties; neutralize the influence of rival mediators; keep Baghdad weak; and, at the same time, prevent the establishment of a strong and independent Kurdish entity. One important difference, however, involved the United States and Turkey, which on the whole saw eye to eye on the Kurdish issue and initially even coordinated their mediation efforts. Even so, they were far apart in their views of the Kurdish-Iraqi relationship: while Turkey encouraged the Kurdish factions to negotiate with Baghdad, the United States came out strongly against such negotiations.[8] This gap hinted at a deeper difference; namely, Turkey's readiness to cooperate with Saddam Hussein's regime and ultimately accept his regaining control of the area, in contrast to the US position that was adamantly opposed to Saddam's return to the Kurdish region. For Turkey, the worst-case scenario was the dismemberment of Iraq.

The mediation dynamics followed a specific pattern. After each flare-up in hostilities, mediators would rush in to broker a cease-fire, which would be observed for a short period and then be followed by a renewed round of fighting and mediation efforts. The parties involved in the process competed over the role of mediator while attempting to torpedo even the slightest success achieved by a rival mediator. A case in point is the US demand of July 1995 that the Kurds put a halt to the ongoing dialogue with Iran aimed at negotiating peace between the parties and instead hold such talks in Europe under US auspices.[9] A particularly salient example of mediation and countermediation was the US-sponsored peace conference in Drogheda, Ireland, 9–11 August 1995, in which the KDP, the PUK, the INC, and Turkey participated—the latter as an observer. No sooner had an agreement been reached than the parties initiated another round of fighting. The KDP blamed Iran and Syria for instigating the offensive in order to disrupt all US and Turkish attempts at mediation. However, it unhesitatingly consented to take part in a later mediation effort by Iran itself.

To be sure, both the KDP and PUK provided the mediators with ample opportunities to do their job, alternately as peace brokers and as peace breakers. The irony of the situation was that only through intracommunal fighting, so detrimental to their national cause, could the KDP and PUK maintain a measure of international interest in the Kurdish issue.

The Bridge of Amity Between Baghdad and the KRG

The treatment of the Kurds as a separate entity was nowhere more evident than in the Iraqi central government's stance on the Kurdish problem. In this sense,

Baghdad's political discourse is most revealing. It depicted its participation in the 1996 war for Erbil as a direct response to Barzani's request, which is indeed quite bizarre. A sovereign state would not normally ask its citizens for permission to act on its own territory. Neither would it relate to one section of its population as partners, on a par with the central government. No less strange was the central government's involvement in mediation efforts between factions that it had fought to the death with only shortly before.

From the start, attempts at mediation by different countries were a cause of great concern to Baghdad. The last thing that it wished for was reconciliation between the Kurds, which might consolidate the autonomous status of Kurdistan. Another worrisome aspect of the situation was the ease with which various states, most of them sworn enemies of Iraq, manipulated the Kurds while heightening their respective influence in Iraqi Kurdistan without the central government being able to stop them.

Equally perturbing were the widely held notions regarding the creation of an Iraqi federate state. In light of the fact that the Kurds had achieved one major step toward federalism and in light of the volatile situation, this fear had now become quite tangible. The almost daily US and British air attacks in the no-fly zone in the Kurdish north heightened the Baath regime's anxiety regarding the future of the region. While Baghdad had de facto lost control of the area as far back as 1992, it feared that such a ubiquitous Western presence in the region would help lead to its final severance from the rest of the country or, alternatively, help covetous neighbors (especially Turkey) increase their control over the area. Baghdad also feared that Iraqi Kurdistan would become a springboard for toppling the Baath. Additionally, the strategic importance of the region was heightened by the international embargo against Iraq, turning it into a lifeline for the rest of the country because of its proximity to Turkey and the outside world.

Iraq's helplessness vis-à-vis the diplomatic and political developments in Kurdistan were reflected in its response to the mediation efforts. After each round of mediation, Baghdad would warn the Kurds anew, condemning the mediator involved and vowing to redress the situation, only to end up taking no action at all. Iraq was especially incensed at the United States' interference in Kurdish affairs, which it cited as the "main cause for the destruction and misery of our Kurdish people." Following the US mediation attempt of January 1995, for example, Baghdad warned the Kurdish leaders, whom it depicted as "swimming against the national aspirations of Iraqi Kurds," that they "will certainly drown if they do not come to their senses and escape the quagmire of the foreigner."[10] Baghdad further urged its Kurdish citizens to "learn the right lesson and stop playing this filthy game in which the U.S. uses them as a cheap card in its political bargaining."[11] The Washington summit of September 1998, discussed below, was another slap in Baghdad's face. Warning the Kurdish parties of US machinations and of the possibility that the United States would betray them as it had done with the late Mulla Mustafa Barzani, Baghdad called on them to break free of the evils of the United States and to engage in a dialogue with it instead.[12]

With regard to Turkey, in April 1995 Iraq demanded its one-time ally to stop its negotiations with "traitors," "thieves," and "assassins." It blamed the "chaotic situation" on Turkey itself for having taken "an active" part in fomenting it by becoming an "obedient tool" of the United States. While warning Turkey of the likely consequences of its mistaken policies, Baghdad called on Turkey to reinstate the historical ties between the two countries.[13]

Similarly, Baghdad depicted Iran's mediation as interference in Iraqi internal affairs and as an example of that country's policies of "treachery, deception and hypocrisy." Iran, for its part, justified its attempts at mediation as necessary to prevent spillover from the intra-Kurdish fighting into Iranian territory and to stop "foreign forces" from interfering in the affairs of the region. Rubbing salt in Iraq's wounds it ascribed the "real roots of the crisis" to "the Iraqi regime's inability to impose its sovereignty over all Iraqi territory."[14]

This blunt truth pointed to the deep changes experienced in the region since the Gulf War and their far-reaching implications. Kurdistan was now beyond the regime's control and subject to manipulation against Baghdad by an array of foreign forces, a situation that threatened to turn into a fait accompli that would be difficult to reverse. That Iraqi Kurdistan had in a sense become an extended no-man's-land raised the question of whether a return to the status quo ante was still possible. The countries in the region, especially Turkey, Iran, and Syria, for their part, had learned to their dismay that the Kurdish card could easily become a double-edged sword. Aware of this they reiterated, probably sincerely, that they were opposed to the fragmentation of Iraq, although their interventionist policies inevitably contributed to precisely this prospect.

Having failed to dissuade other countries to stop their mediation efforts, Baghdad reverted to the same mediation method, but without much success. As the no-fly zone imposed on parts of the Kurdish region prevented Iraq from effectively using force to bring Kurdistan back into the fold, Baghdad adopted subtler means to reduce its losses there. Thus, it sought to keep all channels of communication open to both the KDP and the PUK. Although it had tilted heavily toward the KDP, even supporting it in its fight against the PUK in 1996, from 1997 onward it adopted a more evenhanded approach and initiated a dialogue with the PUK as well. According to one source, the regime dispatched the head of the Iraqi military intelligence (*istikhbarat*), Rafi' Dahham al-Tikriti, to hold talks with Jalal Talabani at his stronghold in Sulaymaniyya. Baghdad was also reported to have provided light arms to the PUK, expecting a weakening of the faction's relations with Iran in return as well as an end to its support of the Iraqi opposition in its area of influence.[15] The PUK, for its part, accepted Baghdad's overtures inter alia in order to neutralize the regime's support of the KDP. The fear of both Jalal Talabani and the Iraqi authorities about the growing influence of Turkey in Kurdistan, and the ties that both maintained with the Turkish PKK, formed a renewed platform for dialogue between Baghdad and the PUK.[16]

Baghdad's next move was to encourage a dialogue between itself and the two parties by mobilizing Egypt to the task, but to little avail. Indeed, it was ironic that Iraq should ask such a distant player to do the job. This was another sign of the changing times, indicating the regionalization and internationalization of the Kurdish issue as well as Baghdad's endeavors to bring Kurdistan back into the central government's fold by fair means or foul.

In another ironic twist of history, at the end of 1997 the central government called on representatives of the KDP and PUK to come to Baghdad for peace talks to be held under the auspices of Iraq itself.[17] Had Iraq abandoned its divide-and-rule policy or its support for the KDP? Not necessarily. But it needed to promote the thesis that it had disseminated after it lost control of Kurdistan; namely, that only Baghdad could broker peace between the warring parties and that only the return of Kurdistan to the Iraqi fold could guarantee peace to the Kurds and security to the countries of the region.

In one of his conciliatory speeches, Saddam acknowledged that "our Kurdish people" had suffered greatly, but were now in a convalescence period. Therefore, "we should treat our Kurdish people as if they were like gold and diamond[s]."[18] Baghdad concurrently released the information that it was supplying Iraqi Kurdistan with oil on a regular basis.[19] It also announced that in the previous five years it had supplied 8 million textbooks to schools in Kurdistan, emphasizing that under Saddam's rule the Kurdish language had flourished to an unprecedented degree.[20] On another level, the government-controlled newspapers *Al-Jumhuriyya* and *Babil* called for the convention of an all-Kurdish congress in Baghdad in order to put an end to the "abnormal" situation in the north and bring Kurdistan back into the fold.[21]

In May 1998, the deputy premier Tariq 'Aziz revealed that the central government was in regular contact with the Kurds and that delegations of both the KDP and the PUK had been in Baghdad as recently as "last week." According to 'Aziz, relations were "normal" and Baghdad would have reached an agreement with the Kurds, had the United States not prevented the Kurds from doing so.[22] The KDP and the PUK also asserted repeatedly that (separate) contacts were taking place with the government, that neither of the parties was seeking separation (*infisal*) from Iraq, and that the best solution was that of a federation with the central government. On one occasion, Mas'ud Barzani declared that a dialogue with the Baath was "vital," for "in the final analysis our problem is with the government of Baghdad." Even if the Kurds disagreed with Baghdad, this did not mean that they would necessarily take up arms and fight, he stated.[23]

Clearly, the KDP was the major interlocutor with Baghdad since the relationship represented a continuation of the alliance of 1996. In addition, Mas'ud Barzani badly needed the dialogue in order to sustain the flourishing economic interaction between the two entities. This strategy served as a tool to balance the other interested parties in the region, especially Turkey and the United States, and to cultivate good relations as a contingency measure should Baghdad reassert control over the region. It was also meant to counterbalance the KDP's main rival, the PUK. A symbolic reflection of the KDP-Iraqi relations was a visit in November 2000 of a delegation of "Iraqi artists" to "Iraqi Kurdistan." A member of the delegation stated that 100 works by artists "from Iraqi governorates" would be exhibited "as a means to consolidating the bridge of amity between the two sides."[24]

While on the tactical level both the Kurds and Baghdad sought to leave the line of communications open between them, strategically speaking the two parties remained far apart. According to the speaker of the Iraqi National Assembly, Sa'dun Hammadi, the main stumbling block was that the Kurds were seeking "more than self-rule"; namely, federation with Iraq. "Any formula other than . . . self-rule will lead to partition and will be rejected," he asserted. "Iraq is a single entity, and will have only one authority, with the north enjoying self-rule."[25] For his part, Mas'ud Barzani revealed that, while the dialogue with Baghdad had proved successful on day-to-day matters, it had failed with regard to the issue of federation.[26]

These developments changed the nature of relations between the north and the center. Paradoxically, interdependence between the two parts of Iraq increased significantly. Since it no longer controlled the region, Baghdad was forced to depend on the Kurds, both for the flow of water—the PUK controlled the region in which the two major dams, Darbandikhan and Dokan, were located—and the flow of oil in the strategic pipeline to Turkey—located in the area controlled by the KDP. The Kurds, for their part, depended on Iraq for such necessities as electricity and commerce. All this gave further impetus to the notion of a federal Iraq—so cherished by the KDP and so feared by Baghdad.

In one respect, by the end of the twentieth century the Kurds of Iraq had attained the most enduring and tangible achievements of any Greater Kurdistan communities, having driven out the central government from most of Iraqi Kurdistan and established autonomous rule. However, they had yet to prove their ability at maintaining communal cohesion and nation building.

Iran and Turkey: Roles Reversed

In the early 1990s, a major shift took place in the roles played by Iran and Turkey in Iraqi Kurdistan. Iran had remained the Kurds' main lifeline to the outside world until then, but now Turkey assumed that role. Relations with Iran had been mostly covert, but with Turkey they became overt. And Iranian forces entered Iraqi Kurdistan to fight Iraq in the 1980s, but Turkish forces did the same to fight the Turkish Kurds in the 1990s. Unlike Iran, Turkey had an additional focus of interest in Iraqi Kurdistan—its historical claim to the province of Mosul and the Turkoman-Kirkuk issue.

The fact that Iran's role had become secondary in importance to that of Turkey did not mean that Iran had abandoned its efforts to promote its influence in the KRG, among other things through mediation. The internal Kurdish dialogue elicited concern in Iran that genuine reconciliation between the rival parties might strengthen the Kurdish national movement; weaken the Kurdish parties' dependence on Iran; and, ultimately, lead to the consolidation of the fragile autonomous entity that had been developing since 1992. Iran also feared that the United States would increase its hold on the region at it own expense.

Alarmed by the March 1995 Turkish operation in Iraqi Kurdistan and the growing influence of Turkey there, as well as by the increasing involvement of its archenemy the United States in the Kurdish issue, Iran summoned the leaders of the two warring parties, the KDP and the PUK, to Tehran in late March to press for a cessation of hostilities.

Another (unsuccessful) attempt at mediation by Iran was the reconvening in Tehran of representatives from both sides in February and March 1997. While warning the parties of the machinations of both the United States and Iraq, Iran declared itself to be an "impartial" and "reliable" mediator, willing to support the Kurdish cause.[27] But Iran's real agenda was different from its declared one: it was aimed at containing the United States in Iraqi Kurdistan, curbing the Turkish military interference, and preventing close relations between the KDP and Baghdad. Another attempt by Iran to mediate between the parties in 1998 also came to naught. As the Kurds began to move more clearly into the US orbit, Iran's misgivings increased. In an attempt to cut its losses, Iran increased its support for the various Kurdish Islamist groupings as well as for the PKK—the one-time ally of the PUK.[28] Ultimately, however, it could not stop the emerging alliance between the Kurds and the United States and was forced to contend with a different geostrategic map in Iraq.

Turkey, the Reluctant Builder of Iraqi Kurdistan

Turkey also had its worries regarding the burgeoning Kurdish entity to the south.[29] It was certainly opposed to a federative solution in Iraq, which risked becoming a model for its own Kurds.[30] Therefore, Turkey sought to increase its influence in the KRG by different means, including: mediation; economic transactions; mobilization of the Turkomans; and the occasional use of force, ostensibly against the PKK but with a hidden message to the KRG as well.[31] However, by turning itself into a lifeline for the KRG, Turkey paradoxically contributed most of all to its survival and, ultimately, to its success. For this reason, Turkey could be depicted as the reluctant builder of Iraqi Kurdistan.

From the start, Turkey styled itself as the main mediator between the KDP and the PUK, to the extent of designating its policy as "the Ankara peace process."[32] Indeed, the parties used conflict resolution terminology taken from other contexts, including phrases such as "confidence-building measures" or "the peace process," to describe their attempts to resolve conflicts.[33] It hence was Turkey, together with the United States, which brokered the October 1996 cease-fire between the KDP and the PUK.

In 1997 Turkey initiated three rounds of peace talks between the parties—in January, March, and May 1997—with the following off-the-record aims: keeping the two parties under Turkish control; minimizing the involvement of other local and regional players; and, most importantly, employing the two parties against the PKK with its established base in Iraqi Kurdistan. In short, the policy to be followed "would be one of commercial exchange, with the Kurds of both countries as the mutual commodity."[34] It was indeed the PKK threat that dictated Turkish involvement in the Iraqi Kurdish issue, not only through military incursions into Iraqi Kurdistan, but also through the alliances that Turkey had formed with the local Kurdish players. As Michael Gunter observes, Turkey's own Kurdish domestic issue had far-reaching implications on Turkey's extensive foreign relations as a whole.[35]

While posing as a neutral mediator by conducting the Ankara peace process with the KDP and the PUK, Turkey was concurrently also strengthening its ties with the KDP in order to better fight the PKK—a common enemy. This convergence of interests was tactical in nature and did not impact the long-term goal that diametrically put Turkey and the KDP against each other. While Turkey sought to break the Kurdish national movement in both countries, the KDP endeavored to reinforce it. And while Turkey sought to eliminate the PKK, the KDP merely wished to weaken it. In fact the KDP and the Kurds of Iraq in general were convinced that, if the PKK were to be eliminated, it would harm their own cause. The military cooperation between Turkey and the KDP against the PKK consequently had another side. Alongside the verbal and physical attacks, the KDP also provided secret support to the PKK.[36]

The Turkish tilt toward the KDP motivated the PUK at that stage to ally itself with the PKK and withdraw from the Ankara peace process, which it did in July 1997.[37] Nevertheless, the PUK did not cut its links with Turkey; Talabani visited Ankara in August. Talabani's tactic was to play as many cards as possible.

On 14 May 1997 concurrently with the mediation process, Turkey launched a military campaign against the PKK in Iraqi Kurdistan, deploying between 25,000 and 50,000 Turkish troops.[38] Operation Sledgehammer lasted more than a month and, according to Turkish sources, resulted in the destruction of twenty-seven PKK camps and the deaths of 2,500 PKK members.[39] Such an operation was not unusual as it was preceded by two similar major operations, in 1995 and 1996. However, the distinguishing factors were its size—it was the largest in scope and the most ambitious in nature since the establishment of the Turkish

Republic[40]—and the fact that Turkey, like Iraq before it, invoked the KDP call for help as a pretext for the operation.[41] Although the KDP did not admit having asked for Turkish intervention, its reaction a day after the onset of the operation was quite telling. Rather than condemning the operation as it had done on previous occasions, the KDP blamed the action on the PKK.[42] Moreover, it declared itself "indifferent to their [the PKK's] expulsion from Iraqi Kurdistan." The statement of the KDP's politburo further elaborated on the PKK's harmful activities in the KRG:

> The PKK's unjustified presence [in Iraqi Kurdistan], which has been imposed on our territory since 1991, has become an obstacle in the face of the Kurdistan government, as well as a source of annoyance and problems to our people, particularly the residents of areas that have been used by the PKK for their bases. This . . . has turned these areas into hotbeds of conflict and instability.[43]

The KDP further accused the PKK of not recognizing "the legitimate authority of Kurdistan," and of meddling in all administrative and social affairs in the area while collecting taxes and attacking its citizens.[44] Mas'ud Barzani later revealed that the PKK had concentrated most of its forces in Erbil, where it opened fifteen camps and "many secret homes." Barzani asserted that "this time" the KDP did not object to the Turkish intervention, asserting, however, that it was the PKK that "invited the Turkish army to intervene."[45] According to a Turkish military source "the operation will continue until Barzani says enough" because the KDP had attained complete authority in northern Iraq.[46]

Whether or not Mas'ud Barzani did in fact send an official request to Turkey to intervene in the conflict, as he had done in August 1996 with the Iraqi Army, was of secondary importance. More significant was the interdependence that had developed between Turkey and the KDP. The need to curb the PKK had been the main common denominator between the two for some time. Turkey needed the KDP for two important tasks: preventing the establishment of PKK bases inside Iraqi Kurdistan, which would give the PKK a convenient springboard for incursions into Turkey; and supporting the Turkish government in its pursuit of the PKK. The KDP needed Turkey for precisely the same reasons: to provide it with the necessary military support and, thus, prevent the PKK from infringing on KDP sovereignty in the area under its control; and, if necessary, to fight the PKK.

The KDP did feel threatened by the PKK's presence in the region, which encroached on the KDP's sphere of influence and was seen as an "alternative authority."[47] Undoubtedly, fighting the PKK was a price that the KDP had to pay for its relationship with Turkey. Demonizing the PKK was another.[48] As to the fighting itself, according to one source the KDP seemed to be doing "the bulk of the fighting" deep inside Iraq, with the Turks providing logistical and air support.[49] According to another, KDP forces served as guides for the Turkish forces in a region that the KDP knew intimately while the Turkish Air Force and ground forces did the actual fighting.[50]

Even as the operation was going on, Abdullah Öcalan, leader of the PKK, vehemently attacked the KDP "clique" for inviting the Turkish Army into Iraqi Kurdistan, warning that it would "pay dearly for its policy" and that the Turkish state would "have to deploy an army to protect the KDP."[51] For its part the PUK blamed the KDP for committing "high treason" by calling on the Turkish Army, and on 10 July 1997 announced its withdrawal from the Ankara talks with the KDP because of "Turkish interference in northern Iraq in favor of the KDP."[52]

Thus, the ad hoc KDP-Turkish alliance reinforced an equally tactical counteralliance between the PUK and the PKK so that the KDP accused the PUK of forty-four instances of cease-fire violations, committed together with the "Kurdish rebels" (the PKK).[53] Clearly, neither the PKK nor the PUK could accept the new situation as a fait accompli. The PKK feared that the entrenchment of the KDP with the support of Turkey would severely impede its freedom of action. The PUK, for its part, could not accept the cease-fire line of October 1996, which left it at a serious disadvantage territorially, politically, and economically. Its major task was therefore to try to redress the situation. The next major Turkish military operation in the fall of 1997 apparently enabled it to do so.

Operation Twilight, in which between 8,000 and 15,000 troops participated, was carried out between 24 September and 13 October 1997. According to one source, troops advanced some 60 kilometers into Iraqi territory.[54] A Turkish spokesman maintained that the operation was aimed at preventing PKK forces from regrouping in camps along the Turkish-Iraqi border, from where they had been expelled in the May operation. For its part, the KDP announced that simultaneously with the Turkish operation, its forces had launched "extensive attacks" against PKK bases in the Barvari and Mateen regions in northern Iraq.[55] Turkey and the KDP boasted of having killed 797 PKK members by mid-October and 3,000 since the beginning of the May operation.[56] Whatever the truth of these claims, the joint Turkish-KDP operation triggered another miniwar between the PUK and the KDP.

No sooner had the Turkish forces declared their pullout from Iraqi Kurdistan than the PUK initiated a large-scale offensive against the KDP. The PUK, however, did not gain much from this round of fighting. It neither succeeded in dislodging the KDP from the Erbil governorate nor in forcing the KDP to share revenues from customs duties on the shipment of merchandise between Turkey and Iraq. The issue of sharing revenues had become a major bone of contention; indeed, one observer termed it the "mother of customs" war.[57]

As previously with the Ankara peace process, the fighting made the complexity of the Kurdish issue more evident. On the one hand, the PUK reportedly was supported not only by the PKK, but also by Iran, which provided it with surface-to-surface Grad missiles to shell the Barzani headquarters at Salah al-Din.[58]

On the other hand, it blamed Turkey for giving massive support to the KDP by bombarding areas under PUK control with napalm, missiles, and conventional payloads.[59]

The trend toward improved relations between the KDP and the Turkish government was reinforced as a result of the dramatic capture of PKK leader Öcalan in February 1999 and the uncertainty surrounding the PKK's likely response. Öcalan's capture and an announcement by the PKK in August 1999 that it would withdraw its forces from Turkey on 1 September evoked fears that the PKK intended to turn Iraqi Kurdistan into its central base. Indeed, in July the PKK announced the founding of what it termed the "PKK's south" branch in northern Iraq (Hizb al-'Ummal al-Kurdistani Janub).[60] Particularly worrisome for the KDP was the fact that half of the PKK commandos were Iraqi Kurds who had joined the PKK because it was engaged in "an honorable struggle."[61]

As military operations against the PKK were going on, Turkey and the KDP also strengthened relations on other levels. Close relations between them were evidenced by extensive economic dealings, as shown in Chapters 15 and 16. In September 1999, a Turkish parliamentary delegation made a three-day visit to Iraqi Kurdistan at Barzani's invitation.[62] Similarly, Turkey turned a blind eye to a KDP announcement in November regarding the formation of a "new [Kurdish] government." Turkey's curious explanation was that the announcement was of no account since it did not represent a joint step by the KDP and the PUK and that historically Turkey had maintained a special relationship with the Barzanis, going back to the reign of Sultan Abdul Hamid and covering Mustafa Kemal's era up to the present.

Meetings between Turkish officials and KDP delegates visiting Turkey—inter alia to brief the government on various developments with regard to the Kurdish region and to coordinate certain activities—took place regularly in Ankara. Mas'ud Barzani visited Ankara and met with Turkish officials in October 2000 and May 2001. So confident of these relations had the KDP become that in March 2000 its representative's office in Ankara held a reception for the first time, marking the Kurdish festival of Nowruz. Representative Safeen Dizayee and the tourism minister of the "northern Iraqi region," Huseyin Fincare, welcomed the guests in Peshmerga uniforms.[63] However, no representatives from the Turkish Ministry of Foreign Affairs or the government attended the reception.[64]

By contrast, relations between the PUK and Turkey turned sour because the Turkish government suspected Talabani's group of sheltering members of the PKK and supporting them in their fight against Turkey.[65] Hence, the PUK had to tread carefully with regard to the PKK so as not to antagonize Turkey. The PUK representative in Ankara, Shazad Saib, announced that the movement had closed some of its bureaus in the areas under its control—bureaus known to have been "close to the PKK."[66] On the other hand, Talabani called on Turkey to ensure a fair trial for Öcalan[67] while protests against his capture were being held simultaneously in Sulaymaniyya.[68]

Another twist in the complex inter-Kurdish and Kurdish-Turkish relationship occurred shortly afterward. In March 2000, a PUK delegation visited Ankara at the invitation of the Turkish foreign minister, followed by a visit by another high-ranking PUK delegation seeking Turkish economic support. Talabani's visit to Ankara in July, and his meeting with then prime minister Bülent Ecevit to inform him of "the latest developments in Kurdistan," elicited this response from Ecevit: "Recently the institution headed by Talabani has begun to take more effective measures against the terrorist organization PKK. He gave detailed information to me concerning this issue. We appreciate this."[69]

Clearly, Talabani had reached the conclusion that, in order for him to improve the situation of the PUK and alter its balance of power with the KDP, he would have to ally himself with Turkey. The quid pro quo was to fight the PKK. Indeed, less than two months after Talabani's visit, intense clashes broke out between the PUK and the PKK, lasting until the end of 2000. Each party blamed the other for the violence. The extent of these clashes could be inferred from a PUK report claiming that the PUK had killed 120 PKK members in one attack.[70] During the course of 2000, the PUK therefore replaced the KDP as the militant foe of the PKK, presumably hoping to raise its political standing in Turkey.

To the Kurdish-Turkish complex another, most problematic issue was added, highlighting the fact that relations between Turkey and the KDP were not as idyllic as might at first appear. A major problem was the growing tension between the KDP and the Turkomans who were both supported by Turkey. Already in September 1996 a joint meeting between the Turkish military and the cabinet resulted in the decision to support the Turkomans and encourage them to demand their rights.[71] Indeed, the Turkomans epitomized the problems of being a minority within a minority and of their complex relationship with an outside player.

A case in point was the Turkoman Front, a political group that claimed that it represented 95 percent of Turkomans and had bureaus and headquarters stretching from Zakho to Kifri. It accused KDP officials of ignoring its "fraternal efforts" and of standing "against the Turkoman people's aims and aspirations."[72] The KDP denied that it had placed obstacles before Turkoman schools or "persecuted" the Turkomans in any way and insisted that the Turkomans enjoyed freedom of expression and movement; had their own schools, newspapers, radio, and television; and, above all, had a minister to represent them in the KDP-established cabinet.[73] The two parties initiated a dialogue in May 2000 to attempt to resolve outstanding problems. However, in July the KDP reportedly attacked the Turkoman Front headquarters in Erbil, killing two people and injuring six others. This led to charges from the Front that the KDP was seeking "to annihilate the 2.5 million-strong Turkoman population in Iraq" and that Barzani was worse than Saddam.[74] The Front called on Turkey to support the Turkomans against KDP repression, which Turkey promised to do.

Although the Turkoman Front greatly overestimated the size of the Turkoman population, the Turkomans were a power that the KDP had to reckon with—all the more so since Turkey backed them with a view toward counterbalancing the growing power of the KDP in the region. Moreover, the Turkomans tried to ally themselves with the PUK, on account of the two enemies they both confronted: the KDP and the Iraqi government, which was accused of increasingly persecuting Kurds and Turkomans in Kirkuk province adjacent to the Sulaymaniyya province under PUK control. The PUK and the Turkomans were also concerned with the alleged expulsion of Kurds and Turks from the oil-rich Kirkuk region and the settling of Palestinians in their stead. Talabani, calling attention to this policy, advocated reinforcing the Kurdish-Turkoman brotherhood to counter the threat. The situation was fraught with contradictions, however, since journalists and Palestinian officials in Iraq denied the report. Both the KDP and the PUK felt threatened by Turkey's increasing support of the Turkomans and by the policy of Turkification that Turkey was reportedly pursuing in the region.[75]

To sum up, the Kurds' relationship with Turkey in the late 1990s was more crucial and complicated than ever before. In a field study of the external threats to the KRG, Turkey was considered to be the most dangerous of the four states surrounding the Kurds.[76] Indeed concurrently with establishing working relations with the KDP, Turkey used all of its resources (political, diplomatic, and military) to impede the progress of the Kurdish national project in Iraq. Nevertheless, the KDP and later on the PUK managed to turn Turkey into a springboard for forging relations with the outside world and thus reinforcing their national project while, at the same time, waging a war by proxy against the PKK to gain Turkey's goodwill. All in all, the years 1991–2003 were but a prelude to the dramatic change in the Kurdish-Turkish equation as a result of the US-led Iraq War of 2003.

The Arab-Kurdish Nexus

Kurdish-Arab relations have always been intricate and it is not my intention to delve into their complexity, but rather to highlight some general points relating to the past two decades. In fact when analyzing the Kurdish-Arab relations in the 1990s, it is necessary to distinguish between the level of discourse and the level of politics. With regard to the first, the Kurds sharply criticized Arab intellectuals because they had expected them to show greater solidarity with the Kurdish cause, especially after the Halabja and Anfal massacres. In this sense, it might be said that the Kurds' relationship with the Arabs was more emotionally laden than those with the Turks and the Iranians. The Kurds were convinced that it was pan-Arab ideology that sought to delegitimize Kurdish nationality and that an Arab government had perpetrated the genocidal war.[77] In addition, the Kurds noted the similarities between their cause and the Palestinian one, with which the Arabs identified so wholeheartedly, stressing time and again that the Kurdish question was no less just.

Regarding the Arab attitude toward the Kurds, as of late it has become more ambiguous than ever. On the one hand there has been a tendency to ignore the Kurds and their unique identity, culture, and history, and on the other to magnify the threat emanating from them.[78] The Anfal and Halabja massacres represented one pole,[79] and the burgeoning autonomy the other. Indeed, the Arab tendency to deny or ignore Baghdad's genocidal war against the Kurds has remained, as shown in Chapter 15, a major sore point between Kurds and Arabs.[80]

The indifference regarding Anfal and Halabja left room for greater engagement with the Kurdish issue at the turn of the twenty-first century. Some Arab journalists have reported the developments in Iraqi Kurdistan quite objectively, sometimes even with an admiration verging on envy.[81] While identity issues governed Arab-Kurdish polemics, the Arabs' main concern was the changing balance of power on the ground and their feeling of weakness vis-à-vis the Kurds.

As to the political level, until well into the mid-1990s Arab governments kept aloof from the fate of the Kurds in Iraq. The one exception was the Libyan leader Muammar Qaddafi who consistently supported the Kurdish cause and even called for the Kurds' independence.[82] This bold stand, however, did not find an echo among other Arab governments. One could at most talk about Egyptian attempts to mediate between the KDP and the PUK.

In February 1997, Egypt invited a KDP delegation to an official visit to Cairo, the first such move since the first Baath rule in 1963 when Gamal 'Abd al-Nasser was involved in mediating between the Baathi government and the Kurds.[83] Then in May, Egypt hosted Talabani in Cairo and a month later even allowed the PUK to open an office there. However, attempts in May and September to bring the two parties to Cairo for talks failed. Surprising as the Egyptian role might appear, it seemed to have been motivated by the desire to have a slice of the Kurdish pie, by the need to curb Turkish involvement in Iraq, and by Baghdad's request to encourage talks between the parties.[84]

Egypt moved one step forward when it approved an unofficial initiative by an Egyptian academic organization to hold an Arab-Kurdish dialogue dealing with "historic relations between Arabs and Kurds" and "Kurdistan: Present and Future in the Context of a United Iraq" in Cairo on 27–28 May 1998. Delegations from both Kurdish parties participated in the discussions but, while the PUK delegation was headed by Talabani, the KDP was represented only by a lower-ranking official. The encounter, the first of its kind between Arabs and Kurds, ended with an appeal for reconciliation between the KDP and the PUK.[85] Some observers viewed the initiative as part of Egypt's efforts to counteract the deepening Turkish-Israeli alignment of the mid-1990s or, at the very least, to remove the Kurds from the Turkish orbit. The dialogue infuriated both Turkey and Iraq,[86] which in vain attempted to dissuade Egypt from holding the event. Anyway, beyond a certain recognition given to the two Kurdish parties, the mediation endeavors did not progress far.

The Kurds, for their part, notwithstanding their criticism of Arab governments, were anxious to develop relations with them. Thus, the KDP's overtures toward Syria, for instance, were evidenced by a three-day mourning period following the death of Syrian president Hafiz al-Asad in June 2000 and by Mas'ud Barzani's visit to Damascus in November for talks with President Bashar al-Asad. The two parties notably "affirmed" the need to bring about the lifting of the embargo on Iraq.[87] Attempts by the KDP to develop relations with the Arab states were also reflected in the establishment of the Arab-Kurdish Friendship Society in Erbil in March 2000.[88]

In addition to Syria, Mas'ud Barzani visited other Arab countries, including Libya, Egypt, Saudi Arabia, and Jordan, reiterating his message that the KDP was opposed to the sanctions against Iraq and committed to its unity and territorial integrity. However, he stressed, Iraqi unity should take the form of a federation.[89] Mas'ud Barzani's statements during his visits in Arab countries clearly aimed to ingratiate the KDP with Arab leaders and perhaps prepare the ground for the lifting of sanctions and for the possibility that Baghdad might clamp down on the Kurds. An additional motive for Barzani's visits was perhaps the need to counterbalance those of Talabani who frequently toured Arab capitals.

The visits of Barzani and Talabani were important, not in themselves, but rather because of their symbolic significance. These leaders were not welcomed as emissaries of the central government, but as ambassadors of their own Kurdish enclave. As such, it was in fact an implicit admission by Arab leaders of the failure of pan-Arab nationalism and of its aspiration to obliterate Kurdish nationalism.

The United States and the Kurds: Unlikely Allies?

If there is one factor that has forever changed the Kurds' fate in Iraq, it is the United States. The two wars launched by the United States against Iraq changed this seemingly axiomatic situation by forcing it to become more and more involved in the Kurdish issue. In time the Kurds, who were first viewed as a moral burden on the United States, became allies of sorts. The relationship between the Kurds and the United States in the 1990s and beyond could thus be seen as a case study of the interdependency that at times developed between a superpower and a "non-state client."[90] Initially, it seemed that the dependency was entirely one-sided: in favor of the United States. However, as time went by, the United States began to develop a certain dependence on Kurdish cooperation and goodwill. Yet as one US official admitted, the United States had no clear policy on the Kurds and should in fact not even have one because "we support the principle of Iraqi unity and territorial integrity."[91]

Though limited and problematic, the relationship the Kurds forged with the United States was nevertheless extremely significant. The transformation that these relations had undergone was indeed quite dramatic. Having courted the United States for thirty years or more in an attempt to gain even the slightest attention from it, the Kurds were cynically shunned by it.[92] Like Mulla Mustafa Barzani, Talabani also thought that the Kurds should position themselves high on the US agenda. In fact he came to Washington to plead the Kurdish case shortly after the Gulf War, but no official would meet with him.[93] However, by the mid-1990s the change was such that the United States began to openly engage the Kurds and even court them.

The US change of heart toward the Kurds went through two phases: the first after the attack on Halabja; and the second following the Iraqi invasion of Kuwait in 1990. The wide coverage of the Halabja massacre by the international media brought the Kurds much sympathy and humanitarian support from individuals, but little more. Thus, for example, Peter Galbraith, then a staff member for the Senate Foreign Relations Committee, was instrumental in the passage of the Prevention of Genocide Act of 1988, which actually called for the imposition of sanctions on Iraq.[94] The Ronald Reagan administration blocked the motion, however, and even approved $1 billion in loan guarantees for Iraq.[95] In fact, the White House and a number of US journalists and scholars blamed the chemical attack on Iran.[96]

Initially, the George H. W. Bush administration sought to follow in its predecessors' footsteps. In a document entitled "Guidelines for U.S.-Iraq Policy," the new administration declared its intention to improve diplomatic relations with Saddam's Iraq. Even though they described the human rights record of Iraq as "abysmal," Bush's foreign policy analysts concluded, "in no way should we associate ourselves with the 60-year Kurdish rebellion in Iraq or oppose Iraq's legitimate attempts to suppress it."[97] It was only after the Iraqi invasion of Kuwait that the United States gradually and cautiously began to change its stand vis-à-vis Halabja and the Kurds.[98] During the war over Kuwait, the administration used the Iraqi regime's chemical attacks against the Kurds as an important argument in its claim that its war against Iraq was a "just war." No doubt there was much cynicism in this move, but in the final analysis it did serve Kurdish interests.

Clearly, the change had to do with the entire US establishment; yet certain individuals played a pivotal role in it. As mentioned before, one of these was Galbraith, whose activities included lobbying for the Kurds in various US administrations; introducing Talabani and Barzani to the corridors of power in Washington where they had up until then been personae non gratae; helping bring the 14 tons of Baathi secret police documents captured by the Kurds in the aftermath of the uprising in March 1991 to the United States; and, finally, becoming the Iraqi Kurds' advocate in the media following the collapse of the March 1991 uprising and the flight of hundreds of thousands of Kurds to Turkey and Iran.[99]

The reasons for the United States' tilt toward the Kurds were discussed in Chapter 13. Here I elaborate on its dramatic consequences for the Kurds. Thanks to the US umbrella, the Kurds enjoyed real autonomy for the first time in Iraq's modern history. The Kurdish issue became internationalized and the Kurdish entity received a degree of legitimacy with the establishment of Kurdish diplomatic offices in Washington and other Western capitals—at a time (following the post-1990 sanctions) when Iraqi officials were banned. The internal Kurdish war of 1994–1996 could have detracted from this support, but fortunately for the Kurdish people the United States stepped in to mediate between their leaderships and thus became even more involved in the issue.

Initially the United States played the role of mediator between the warring Kurdish parties, but then began to engage the Kurds as partners of sorts. The first round of mediation took place in early January 1995, when a US official visited Iraqi Kurdistan to warn the KDP and the PUK against a protracted struggle. This was followed by the arrival on 25 January of a high-level joint US and Turkish delegation.[100]

In July 1995 the United States invited Talabani and Mas'ud Barzani to hold talks in Washington, but Mas'ud Barzani declined the invitation. This was indeed a sign of changing times: the United States, being willing to deal openly and officially with the Barzanis—a gesture that would have been unthinkable in the 1970s and 1980s—and Barzani declining the offer. Mas'ud Barzani's reluctance was perhaps due to his suspicion about US motives, and his unwillingness to compromise with Talabani and limit his options. The United States' second attempt at negotiations was initiated on 18 September 1996 when Mas'ud Barzani was called to Ankara for talks with the US assistant secretary of state for Near Eastern affairs Robert Pelletreau, probably with the preliminary intention of checking Mas'ud Barzani's drift toward Saddam. In return, Mas'ud Barzani was reputed to have demanded some kind of US involvement in the north.[101]

Another important turning point in the Kurdish-US relations was the mediation effort by the United States, which gained momentum from July 1998 onward, reflecting its policy toward Iraq. The United States was worried about the Baghdad-Kurdish dialogue and hoped to thwart it. In addition, it was concerned that the inter-Kurdish dialogue might develop independently of US influence.[102] The declarations by both the Iraqi regime and Kurdish groups on a possible reconciliation attracted US attention (as they were actually intended to do). Similarly, because the United States preferred to avoid launching a military attack on Iraq, the Kurdish card was essential for keeping up pressure on Baghdad. Last but not least, the US decision to unseat the regime by means of the opposition cast the Kurds, who would hold the key to its success, in a pivotal role.

Reconciliation between the parties, backed by the United States, was therefore a means toward the end of better control over the situation in Kurdistan and, thereby, in Iraq.

Before such a reconciliation could take place, however, the United States had to make its own peace with the KDP, which in 1996 had received support from Baghdad against the PUK and thus implicitly against the United States. Barzani was still unreceptive to US overtures, blaming the United States not only for having betrayed the Kurds in the past and for siding with the PUK, but also for lacking a clear policy on northern Iraq.[103] As a preliminary move, the United States dispatched a delegation to the KRG on 18 July 1998, headed by US deputy assistant secretary of state for Near Eastern affairs David Welch, along with a Turkish observer, for separate talks with the KDP and the PUK. Lasting four days, they culminated in an invitation to Talabani and Mas'ud Barzani to continue talks in Washington. But unlike earlier, Mas'ud Barzani now accepted the invitation, explaining that the United States had promised him that it would "continue protecting the people of northern Iraq against Baghdad," that the sanctions against Baghdad would not be lifted, and that US ties with Iraq would not be normalized. Mas'ud Barzani's decision seemed to have stemmed from his need to reduce his dependence on Turkey in order to deflect Turkish pressure to fight against the PKK operating out of northern Iraq.[104]

Not surprisingly, Baghdad condemned the US delegation's visit and the invitation to Washington as US interference in internal Iraqi affairs and submitted a letter of complaint to the UN.[105] Baghdad, however, could not stop Mas'ud Barzani, its one-time ally, from drifting into the US orbit. In contrast, Mas'ud Barzani had to deal more cautiously with Turkey, with which he had a closer partnership. He had reportedly signed an agreement with Turkey on 18 July 1998 to join forces in a counterattack against the PKK in northern Iraq[106] and was quoted by a Turkish newspaper as saying that the KDP would continue fighting the PKK, independently of whether it received support from Turkey or not.[107] Moreover, en route to Washington in September, Mas'ud Barzani paid a three-day visit to Ankara for discussions with high-ranking Turkish officials, including the deputy prime minister Ecevit.[108] Turkey, probably fearing that it might lose the Kurdish chip when it was not invited to Washington, sought to preserve its influence by attempting to dissuade Barzani from tilting too far toward the United States.

The Washington summit opened on 14 September 1998 with separate meetings of Secretary of State Madeleine Albright with Mas'ud Barzani and Talabani, followed by a tripartite meeting. It was the first time that Mas'ud Barzani and Talabani had met in four years. After the tripartite meeting, Albright declared that they had "opened a new and hopeful chapter in their efforts to work together on behalf of their people," emphasizing that the "renewed spirit of reconciliation" would make it easier for the United States and others to help the Kurds. Albright disclosed that the joint meeting had taken place after six months of "working level talks" with the parties.[109] On 17 September, the summit concluded with an agreement between the two Kurdish groups and a tacit understanding between them and the William J. Clinton administration.[110]

While the agreement, signed by Talabani, Mas'ud Barzani, and Welch, confirmed "the territorial integrity and unity of Iraq," it also mentioned the Kurds' aspiration "that Iraq be reformed on a *federative* basis" (emphasis added). The choice of the word *aspiration* is telling because the United States was actually opposed to ethnic federalism in Iraq.[111] The main points of the agreement were: (1) the reestablishment of a unified administration and assembly, based on the results of the 1992 Kurdish elections; (2) provision of exclusive control of all revenues to the regional administration; (3) new regional elections; and (4) prohibition of the movement of "terrorists"; that is, denying sanctuary to the PKK "throughout the Iraqi Kurdistan region" and preventing the PKK "from destabilizing and undermining the peace or from violating the Turkish border."[112]

The agreement fixed a timetable according to which the better-funded KDP would begin to "extend appropriate financial assistance on a monthly basis" to the PUK, starting on 1 October 1998, and hold elections within a year. The agreement also called on the United States, Great Britain, Turkey, and the entire international community "to continue to exercise vigilance to protect and secure the Iraqi Kurdish region." This lay at the root of the most troublesome issue relating to the Kurds: Who would guarantee Kurdish autonomy? Following the summit, both Talabani and Mas'ud Barzani asserted that "the United States promised to deter Iraqi intervention, should it take place, and to remain 'committed to the Kurdish people's security.'"[113] Albright declared, rather tentatively, that the United States might respond if Saddam posed a "threat to the Iraqi people, including those in the north." A Kurdish official participating in the talks claimed that the United States' assurances were stronger in private; namely, that the United States would "protect you as we protect Kuwait," provided the Kurds adhered to the new agreement, kept Saddam's troops out of areas held by Kurds, and did not provoke Saddam merely to elicit US intervention.[114]

Whatever the participants' precise commitments, the Washington summit was extremely significant for internationalizing the Kurdish cause. Albright was the highest-ranking US official ever to have held talks openly with the Kurds. It was a far cry from the situation thirty years earlier when contacts were exclusively clandestine. Ever since the Gulf War, US contacts with the Kurds had been conducted in conjunction with other opposition groups. This time, the United States hosted the Kurds alone. Moreover, while Turkey had been involved in all previous US mediation efforts, this time the United States conducted them single-handedly.

The US efforts to bring about reconciliation between the KDP and PUK, and to generate a rapprochement between them and the exiled opposition groups, continued unabated in the years to come. The United States attempted to gain favor with the Kurds through symbolic gestures—such as marking the eleventh anniversary of the chemical attack on Halabja[115]—by the Congressional Human Rights Group and other US officials. This step contrasted sharply with the initial disregard of the Halbja affair in 1988, heralding a change in the US stance.

On the political level, then vice president Al Gore's meeting with Kurdish officials in Washington on 26 June 2000 provided another boost in the US official ties with the Kurds. Addressing the PUK and KDP representatives, Gore reaffirmed the US commitment to "the protection of the people of Iraqi Kurdistan" (and not people of "the north," as Albright had stated).[116] He also urged the parties to speed up the implementation of the 1998 Washington Agreement, which sought to normalize relations between the two. Talabani attended the meeting, but Mas'ud Barzani did not and sent his nephew and son-in-law Nechirvan Barzani, who headed the KDP-led regional government, instead. Mas'ud Barzani's absence was in all likelihood prompted by his distrust of US motives and intentions (i.e., the fact that Gore wished to use the Kurdish card to promote his candidacy for the presidency by issuing a challenge to Saddam); by his self-confidence, which allowed him the luxury not to attend such a meeting; and by his desire to leave the door open to Baghdad, and to disparage Talabani, signaling that Nechirvan was more than adequate as his counterpart.[117]

In fact realizing that the Kurds were the strongest, and perhaps also the most reliable, of the anti-Saddam opposition groups, the Clinton administration spent much effort to broker peace between the KDP and PUK. Indeed, the Kurds' potential for destabilizing Saddam would be realized as self-fulfilling prophecy by dint of their contribution to the Iraq War.

The Countdown to the 2003 US Invasion of Iraq

The event that gave the greatest push to Kurdish foreign policy making, and even endowed the Kurds with a degree of international stature, was the 2003 US-led Iraq War. Initially, the Kurds appeared reluctant to participate in the United States' grand design. Both the KDP and the PUK were skeptical of the US backing and of US efforts to unite the Iraqi opposition with a view toward toppling the Baath. In Talabani's view, the Kurds were not a party to the US efforts to topple Saddam. "Our negotiations with the Americans were focused on achieving reconciliation between the KDP and the PUK," he said, adding that "we refuse to be a party to any foreign conspiracy with this aim in mind."[118] The same point was reiterated by Mas'ud Barzani who also expressed reservations about the opposition outside Iraq. The opposition, he said, "should stay in Iraq because no opposition can be imposed on the Iraqi people from abroad."[119] Mas'ud Barzani further asserted that he would not allow "the Kurdish region to become a springboard for changing the regime, unless there are firm guarantees that Iraq's future will be pluralistic and democratic and that there will be a federal solution to the Kurdish issue."[120]

At this juncture, the Kurds were reluctant to support the US plan because they feared that the United States would betray them as it had done in the past. They did not want to turn Kurdistan into a base for opposition groups, which could complicate the Kurds' situation even further, and they wanted to leave the door open for a dialogue with Baghdad. Their tactic therefore was to participate in the opposition meetings organized by the United States in order to keep the channels of communication open while, at the same time, refusing to commit themselves to any plan that might endanger the Kurdish population and their own organizational well-being.

The Kurds' change of mind came after Al-Qaida's 11 September attacks in the United States, which proved to be a turning point in the history of Iraq as a whole and of the Kurds in particular. The United States' rather vague ideas regarding Iraq's future began to crystallize after that event, leading to the Iraq War in March 2003, which resulted in the ousting of the Baathi regime by the US-led coalition and the disintegration of Iraq's political, social, and economic system.

As early as November 2001 Barham Salih, head of the PUK government, was summoned to Washington to meet with Secretary of Defense Donald Rumsfeld.[121] This extraordinary invitation to the Pentagon sent a clear message to the Kurds that, this time, the United States was seriously considering driving out the Baath. What tipped the balance, however, was a secret meeting between Barzani, Talabani, and President George W. Bush in April 2002 that would have important implications for future Kurdish-US relations.[122]

These developments prompted the KDP and the PUK to bury their differences and start closing ranks or as Hoshyar Zebari, head of the KDP foreign relations, put it, "There are times when you must tidy your house before it gets blown up."[123] Eager to present a united front in advance of the anticipated war, the two parties took tangible steps toward reconciliation. They opened a window of opportunity that acted like a magic wand so that, within months, the Kurds accomplished what they had not managed to do in years. In September 2002, Barzani and Talabani hinted that they were willing to participate in a war against Baghdad, even though it meant risking the hard-won fruits of a ten-year autonomy period.[124] Cooperation between the Kurds and the United States increased, following the fighting that broke out at the end of 2002 between Kurdish forces and Ansar al-Islam, a Kurdish Islamist pro–Al-Qaida organization. Ansar al-Islam, which had established itself a year earlier in Iraqi Kurdistan, prompted the KDP and PUK to seek US help to fight it. Then, in a joint KDP-PUK decision reached on 15 February 2003, the two parties declared their intention to join the US invasion forces in the anticipated war against Iraq. By that time, some 3,000 Peshmergas had already been trained to work with US troops by the US Army's European Command in Hungary.[125]

Meanwhile in its drive to gain world support and Kurdish cooperation, the George W. Bush administration chose the Halabja massacre to justify and encapsulate the approaching war. On 14 March 2003 for the first time ever, President Bush received three Iraqi Kurds in the Oval Office of the White House to draw attention to the chemical weapons attack on Halabja fifteen years earlier. The next day, Bush's radio address began with the following words: "Good morning. This weekend marks a bitter anniversary for the people of Iraq. Fifteen years ago, Saddam Hussein's regime ordered a chemical weapons attack on a village in Iraq called Halabja." Finally on 16 March, Bush reminded the world that "on this very day 15 years ago, Saddam Hussein launched a chemical weapons attack on the Iraqi village of Halabja." It was followed by a White House message that "this weekend, we remember the victims of Saddam Hussein's heinous chemical weapons attack on the people of Halabja, a city in northern Iraq, and other villages attacked in the Al-Anfal campaign."[126] Cynical as the manipulation of the Halabja tragedy might have been, it did help bind the Bush administration more closely to the Kurds.

In the war itself, the Kurds played a unique and important role. It was the first time in the modern history of Iraq that they fought alongside a non-Muslim power and for a purpose beyond their own autonomy. The Kurds made their contribution—by no means a trifling one—not in secret, but in broad daylight. Without Kurdish help, the United States could not have opened a northern front simultaneously with the southern front opened by the coalition. Due to Turkey's last-minute decision not to allow the passage of US troops through its territory, the coalition had to launch the war without troops in Iraq's north. This put the burden of the ground fighting on the Kurdish Peshmerga. In most cases, Kurds played a major role in the ground battles while the United States provided air support and intelligence. The Kurds also departed from their habitual mode of fighting close to their strongholds in the mountains. They moved into the plain and occupied the two major northern cities of Mosul and Kirkuk.

The PUK, and to a certain extent also the KDP, proved their usefulness to the United States in another way, namely, by fighting their common enemy, the Ansar al-Islam, which the United States believed to have ties with Al-Qaida and perhaps even with the Baath. In the battles that followed the main war against Iraqi forces, US forces and PUK Peshmerga launched a combined air and ground assault to eject Ansar al-Islam from their village bases.[127] Indeed, the uniqueness of the Kurdish role lies precisely in the fact that the Kurds took part in the fighting at all. Neither the United States nor Great Britain invited other Iraqi opposition groups to do so.

The Kurdish performance during the war was an important Kurdish asset vis-à-vis Turkey. Kurds proved their mettle and their loyalty to the United States, two characteristics magnified by Turkey's policy that had left the United States in the lurch. The US stance toward the Kurds of Iraq had always been influenced by considerations about Turkish sensitivities. But given the wartime record of the Kurds as compared to that of Turkey, it became quite difficult for the United States to forsake the Kurds in order to satisfy Turkey.

To sum up, the war proved to be a golden opportunity for the Kurds to leave their mark on the domestic, regional, and international arena. From this position of strength, it became much easier for them to intensify initiatives toward nation building and to develop their national project.

Notes

1. *Al-Sharq al-Awsat* (London, daily), 6 December 2000.

2. Quoted in Gareth R. V. Stansfield, *Iraqi Kurdistan: Political Development and Emergent Democracy* (New York: Routledge Curzon, 2003), p. 14.

3. For the role of the diaspora in Europe, see Kendal Nezan, "The European Perspective," in *Kurdish Identity: Human Rights and Political Status*, eds. Charles G. MacDonald and Carole A. O'Leary (Gainesville: University Press of Florida, 2007), pp. 237–245.

4. Rend Rahim Francke, "Political Impact of Sanctions in Iraqi Kurdistan," in *Kurdish Identity: Human Rights and Political Status*, eds. Charles G. MacDonald and Carole A. O'Leary (Gainesville: University Press of Florida, 2007), p. 142.

5. Lokman I. Meho, *The Kurdish Question in U.S. Foreign Policy: A Documentary Sourcebook* (Westport, CT: Praeger, 2004), p. 543.

6. Hamit Bozarslan, *Violence in the Middle East* (Princeton: Marcus Wiener, 2004), p. 21.

7. Kurdistan TV International, 13 January 2000, cited in BBC.

8. *Financial Times* (London, daily), 27 July 1995.

9. *Al-Hayat* (London, daily), 23 July 1995.

10. *Al-'Iraq,* 4 February 1995, cited in *Daily Report,* 16 February 1995.

11. Iraqi News Agency, 29 July 1995, cited in *Daily Report,* 1 August 1995.

12. Iraqi News Agency, 22 October 1998, cited in *Daily Report; Al-Thawra* (Baghdad, daily), 30 October, 5 November 1998; *Al-'Iraq,* 26 January 1999, cited in *Daily Report.*

13. *Al-'Iraq* (Baghdad, daily), 11 February 1995; *Al-Qadisiyya* (Baghdad, daily), 23 April 1995.

14. Iraqi News Agency, 6 October 1995, cited in *Daily Report,* 10 October 1995; Voice of Iraqi Islamic Republic, 8 October 1995, cited in *Daily Report,* 10 October 1995.

15. *Al-Wasat* (London, weekly), 26 January 1998. The date of al-Tikriti's talks with Talabani is not known.

16. The most informative and knowledgeable book on the PKK is by the Turkish Kurd, Ismet G. Imset. *The PKK: A Report on Separatist Violence in Turkey* (Ankara: Turkish Daily News Publications, 1992), p. 205. See also David Romano, *The Kurdish Nationalist Movement: Opportunity, Mobilization and Identity* (Cambridge, UK: Cambridge University Press, 2008). chaps. 2–4.

17. *Al-Hayat,* 6 November 1997.

18. *Al-'Iraq,* 14 March 1998.

19. Iraqi News Agency, 10 March 1999, cited in BBC, 16 March 1999.

20. *Al-'Iraq,* 20 May 1999. The source did not specify whether these textbooks were in Arabic or Kurdish.

21. *Al-Jumhuriyya* (Baghdad, daily), 11 March 1998; *Babil,* 21 March 1998, cited in *Daily Report.*

22. *Al-Sharq al-Awsat*, 11 May 1998.

23. *Al-Khlaij* (online edition), 2 September 1999.

24. Kurdistan satellite TV, 23 November 2000, cited in BBC.

25. *Al-Sharq al-Awsat* (online edition), 25 April 1999.

26. *Al-Sharq al-Awsat*, 22 May 1999.

27. *Tehran Times*, 1 March 1997, cited in *Daily Report*.

28. Relations between Iran and the PKK were cemented in 1986. Imset, *The PKK*, p. 205. For Iran's occasional support to the PKK, see Michael Gunter, *The Kurds and the Future of Turkey* (Houndmills: Macmillan, 1997), pp. 94–97.

29. For a discussion of Turkish policy, see Gunter, *The Kurds*; and Wahram Betrosian, *Siyasat Turkiyya Tujah Kurdistan al-'Iraq wa Amerika* (Duhok: Duhok University, 2008).

30. Betrosian, *Siyasat Turkiyya*, p. 17.

31. The KDP and PUK often accused Turkey of "inflicting damage on Kurdish villages in northern Iraq" during operations against the PKK. Kemal Kirişci and Gareth M. Winrow, *The Kurdish Question and Turkey* (London: Routledge Curzon, 2004), p. 162.

32. Turkey was not interested in real peace between the parties, but in their cooperation against the PKK. Betrosian, *Siyasat Turkiyya*, p. 15.

33. Voice of Iraqi Kurdistan, 16 January, 9 March, 4 April 1997, cited in *Daily Report*; Voice of Iraqi Kurdistan, 17 January, 29 July 1997, cited in *Daily Report*.

34. Imset, *The PKK*, p. 188.

35. Gunter, *The Kurds*, pp. 89–92.

36. A Kurdish activist, personal communication with the author, 14 September 2010. The activist, who played the role of liaison between the KDP and PKK in the mid-1990s, told me that at times the KDP assisted PKK fighters who were surrounded by Turkish forces by providing them with Peshmerga uniforms. The KDP also tended wounded PKK in its hospital.

37. Reportedly, initial contacts between the PUK and PKK were forged by Ibrahim Ahmad in Europe. Telephone interview with a Kurdish activist, personal communication, October 2010.

38. *International Herald Tribune* (Paris and Zurich, daily), 19 May 1997; Agence France Press, 25 May 1997, cited in *Daily Report*, 29 May 1997; *Al-Wasat*, 26 May 1997; *Middle East International* (London, biweekly), 30 May 1997.

39. *Sabah*, 29 May 1997, cited in *Daily Report*; Anatolia, 10 June 1997, cited in *Daily Report*. Abdullah Öcalan, leader of the PKK, rejected the number of dead, saying that PKK losses by 27 May were only thirty dead, in contrast to 1,850 quoted by Turkey. Medya TV, 27 May 1997, cited in *Daily Report*. Turkish journalist Ismet G. Imset observed that the Turkish press routinely published inflated casualty figures for the sake of public opinion. Kevin McKiernan, *The Kurds* (New York: St. Martin's Press, 2006), p. 66.

40. Öcalan to Medya TV, 27 May 1997, cited in *Daily Report*.

41. *Le Monde* (Paris, daily), 22 May 1997.

42. For an interpretation of the conflict between the KDP and PKK as part of tribalism, see Hussein Tahiri, *The Structure of Kurdish Society and the Struggle for a Kurdish State* (Costa Mesa, CA: Mazda, 2007), pp. 263–309.

43. Voice of Iraqi Kurdistan, 15 May 1997, cited in *Daily Report*.

44. Ibid.

45. *Al-Nahar* (Beirut, daily), 4 June 1997, cited in *Daily Report*, 9 June 1997.

46. *Turkish Probe*, 30 May 1997.

47. Voice of Iraqi Kurdistan, 20 June 1997, cited in *Daily Report*.

48. Romano, *The Kurdish Nationalist Movement*, p. 125.

49. *Middle East International*, 30 May 1997.

50. *Le Monde*, 22 May 1997.

51. Medya TV, 27 May 1997.

52. Voice of Rebellious Iraq, 10 July 1997, cited in *Daily Report*; *Al-Safir*, 12 July 1997, cited in *Daily Report*; *Al-Shira'* (Beirut, weekly), 14 July 1997.

53. Islamic Republic News Agency, 23 September 1997, cited in *Daily Report*.

54. *International Herald Tribune*, 26 September 1997; Middle East Broadcasting Center Television, 27 September 1997, cited in *Daily Report*.

55. Islamic Republic News Agency, 27 September 1997, cited in *Daily Report*.

56. *Le Monde*, 14 October 1997.

57. *Al-Majalla* (London, weekly), 5 October 1997.

58. *Middle East International*, 21 October; *Babil*, 22 October 1997, cited in *Daily Report*.

59. Middle East Broadcasting Center TV, 25 October 1997, cited in *Daily Report*; *International Herald Tribune*, 10 November 1997.

60. *Al-Hayat*, 13 July 1999, cited in BBC, 15 July 1999.

61. Voice of Iraqi Kurdistan, 15 May 1999, cited in BBC; *Al-Wasat* (London, weekly), 1 November 1999.

62. Anatolia, 23 September 1999, cited in *Daily Report*, 26 September 1999.

63. Already in 1991, the KDP and the PUK had representatives in Ankara. Michael Gunter, "Turkey's New Neighbor, Kurdistan," in *The Future of Kurdistan in Iraq*, eds. Brendan O'Leary, John McGarry, and Khaled Salih (Philadelphia: University of Pennsylvania Press, 2005), p. 224.

64. Anatolia, 20 March 2000, cited in BBC.

65. Visiting the region years later, I saw a large gathering of PKK partisans.

66. Anatolia, 12 January 1999, cited in BBC, 14 January 1999.

67. Voice of the People of Kurdistan, 18 February 1999, cited in BBC, 20 February 1999.

68. *Ha'aretz* (Tel Aviv, daily), 22 February 1999 (quoting Associated Press).

69. Anatolia, 25 July 2000, cited in BBC.

70. KurdSat TV, 7 December 2000, cited in BBC.

71. Betrosian, *Siyasat Turkiyya*, pp. 20–21.

72. *Turkoman Eli* (Erbil), 22 March 2000, cited in BBC; Liam Anderson and Gareth Stansfield, *Crisis in Kirkuk: The Ethnopolitics of Conflict and Compromise* (Philadelphia: University of Pennsylvania Press, 2009), p. 126.

73. KDP satellite TV, 28 March 2000, cited in BBC.

74. Anatolia News Agency, 14 July 2000, cited in BBC.

75. *Al-Sharq al-Awsat*, 24 March 1997, cited in *Daily Report*, 26 March 1997; *Al-Millaf al-'Iraqi*, April, May, July 1997; Iraqi Broadcasting Corporation, 16 October 1997.

76. Raja'i Fayed, *Tahawwulat al-Shakhsiyya al-Kurdiyya nahwa al-Hadatha* (Duhok: Markaz al-Dirasat al-Kurdiyya wa Hifz al-Watha'iq, 2008), pp. 44–46.

77. For such delegitimization by the Syrian Baath, see Jordi Tejel, *Syria's Kurds: History, Politics and Society* (London: Routledge, 2009), pp. 56–62.

78. This was true also for Turks and Iranians.

79. See, for example, a scathing self-criticism on the Arab stance: Joe Stork and Sally Ethelston, "Politics and Media in the Arab World: An Interview with Hisham Milhem," *Middle East Report* 180 (1993): 16–19.

80. See Michael Gunter's observation that "many Arabs consider the Kurds traitors for having supported the United States in the 2003 war. On the other hand, many Kurds see the Arabs as chauvinists who oppose Kurdish rights." Michael Gunter, "Federalism and the Kurds of Iraq: The Solution or the Problem?" in *The Kurds: Na-*

tionalism and Politics, eds. Faleh A. Jabar and Dawod Hosham (London: Saqi, 2006), p. 231.

81. This was true especially for *Al-Hayat* and *Al-Sharq al-Awsat*.

82. Sabir ʿAli Ahmad, *Al-Qadhdhafi wal-Qadiyya al-Kurdiyya* (N.p.: Dar al-Multaqa lil-Nashr, 1991). During Turkish prime minister Necmettin Erbakan's visit to Libya in October 1996, Qaddafi went as far as to declare the following: "The state of Kurdistan should take its place in the spectrum of nations under the Middle Eastern sun." *New York Times* (New York, daily), 7 October 1996. Michael Gunter, "Qaddafi Reconsidered," *Research Note* 21, no.1 (2001).

83. *Al-Sharq al-Awsat*, 26 February 1997.

84. *Middle East International*, 16 May 1997; *Al-Wasat*, 16 June 1997.

85. For criticism of this dialogue, see *Suraqiyya* (London, weekly), 31 August 1998.

86. *Al-Hayat*, 22 May, 6 June 1998; *Mideast Mirror*, 27 May 1998; *Al-Sharq al-Awsat*, 2 June 1998, cited in *Daily Report*, 9 June 1998; *Al-Ittihad* (Abu Dhabi), 5 June 1998, cited in *Daily Report*.

87. Kurdistan satellite TV, 11 June 2000, cited in BBC; Radio Damascus, 21, 22 November 2000, cited in BBC.

88. *Al-Hayat*, 13 March 2000.

89. *Al-Sharq al-Awsat*, 6 December 2000, cited in *Mideast Mirror*.

90. This anthropological description may also be applied to the political realm:

> The patron-client relationship . . . may be defined as a special case of dyadic (two-person) ties involving a largely instrumental friendship in which an individual of higher socio-economic status (patron) uses his own influence and resources to provide protection or benefits, or both, for a person of lower status (client) who, for his part, reciprocates by offering general support and assistance, including personal services, to the patron.

James C. Scott, "Patron-client Politics and Political Change in Southeast Asia," *American Political Science Review* 66, no. 1 (1972): 91–113.

91. David Mack, "The United States Policy and the Iraqi Kurds," in *Kurdish Identity: Human Rights and Political Status*, eds. Charles G. MacDonald and Carole A. O'Leary (Gainesville: University Press of Florida, 2007), p. 117. In 1999 President William J. Clinton stated before the Congress that US policy was to aim at "a united, pluralistic, and democratic Iraq," but he did not mention federalism. Meho, *The Kurdish Question*, p. 624.

92. As to the American public, some had no idea who the Kurds were. When asked, some answered that a Kurd was a radio station, a musical group, or a language. McKiernan, *The Kurds*, p. 164.

93. Ibid., p. 49.

94. Peter Galbraith, *The End of Iraq: How American Incompetence Created a War Without End* (New York: Simon & Schuster, 2006), pp. 29–35.

95. Romano, *The Kurdish Nationalist Movement*, p. 202. He further quoted US congressman Paul Findley, who published an essay at the end of 1988 advocating good relations with Baghdad. Paul Findley, "The U.S. Stake in Good Relations with Baghdad," *Washington Report on Middle East Affairs* (December 1988): 15; Romano, *The Kurdish Nationalist Movement*, p. 203.

96. Khaled Salih, "Iraq and the Kurds: A Bibliographic Essay," *Digest of Middle East Studies* 4 (1995): 24–39.

97. Quoted in ibid. Later Senator Dennis DeConcini (D-AZ) criticized the George W. Bush administration's stance on the Kurdish issue, asking "what happened to principles?" Another senator, Alan Cranston (D-CA), followed suit by saying that "if Saddam is Hitler, then we must support the Kurd." Meho, *The Kurdish Question*, pp. 116–128, 149.

98. Jon Lee Anderson, "Mr. Big," *The New Yorker*, 5 February 2007, p. 53.

99. Peter Galbraith, "Saddam's Documents: A Report to the Committee on Foreign Relations United States Senate" (Washington, DC: Government Printing Office,1992), pp. 1–8.

100. Voice of the People of Kurdistan, 25 January 1995, cited in *Daily Report*, 26 January 1995.

101. *Mideast Mirror*, 26 September 1996.

102. On the beginning of indigenous rapprochement, see Chapter 15 of this volume and Stansfield, *Iraqi Kurdistan*, p. 100.

103. On the last point, see Barzani in *Turkish Daily News* (Ankara, daily), 7 August 1998.

104. Agence France Press, 20 July 1998, cited in *Daily Report*, 21 July 1998; *Turkish Daily News*, 7 August 1998; *Al-Wasat*, 14 September 1998.

105. Iraqi News Agency, 24 July 1998, cited in *Daily Report*.

106. Islamic Republic News Agency, 19 July 1998, cited in *Daily Report*.

107. *Turkish Daily News*, 7 August 1998.

108. Anatolia, 2 September 1998, cited in *Daily Report*, 3 September 1998; *Al-'Alam* (London, weekly), 5 September 1998.

109. Meho, *The Kurdish Question*, p. 525.

110. See Stansfield, *Iraqi Kurdistan*, pp. 100–102.

111. Rajiv Chandrasekaran, *Imperial Life in the Emerald City* (New York: Alfred A. Knopf, 2007), p. 242. After the 2003 Iraq War, the United States was reconciled to this idea.

112. *Al-Sharq al-Awsat* (Internet version), 19 September 1998; *Mideast Mirror*, 13 October 1998.

113. *Al-Ittihad* (Abu Dhabi), 19 September 1998, cited in *Daily Report*, 22 September 1998; *Al-Sharq al-Awsat*, 19 September 1998, cited in *Daily Report*.

114. Alan Makovsky, "Kurdish Agreement Signals New U.S. Commitment," *Policy Watch*, 29 September 1998.

115. Wireless File, 16 March 1999.

116. Kurdistan satellite TV (Salah al-Din), 27 June 2000, cited in BBC. According to the PUK, Gore promised protection to the "liberated" area of Kurdistan. KurdSat (Sulaymaniyya), 27 June 2000, cited in BBC.

117. The PUK quoted a KDP source as saying that Barzani did not want to meet with Talabani to discuss problems. *Kurdistani Nuwe* (online edition), 9 July 2000, cited in BBC.

118. *Al-Quds al-'Arabi* (London, daily), 22 September 1998.

119. *Al-Sharq al-Awsat* (online edition), 19 September 1998.

120. *Al-Sharq al-Awsat*, 22 May 1999.

121. McKiernan, *The Kurds*, p.179.

122. The information on the meeting was provided to an anonymous source by one of the participants.

123. *Time Europe*, 12 September 2002, p. 32.

124. In July 2002, however, the two parties rejected a CIA request to establish stations in Kurdistan.

125. *The Scotsman* (Edinburgh, daily), 15 February 2003.

126. Project Sheffield, "How the Forgotten City of Halabja Became the Launchpad for War on Iraq," http://projectsheffield.wordpress.com; See also BBC, 16 March 2003; *The Daily Telegraph* (London, daily), 17 March 2003. Earlier in March 2000, the Senate and Congress decided to commemorate Halabja and the Anfal campaign. Meho, *The Kurdish Question* p. 397.

127. For details, see Quil Lawrence, *Invisible Nation: How the Kurds' Quest for Statehood Is Shaping Iraq and the Middle East* (New York: Walker; distributed by Macmillan, 2008), pp. 170–181.

15

From Victims to Victors

The social scientist Miroslav Hroch observes that a national movement in a "small nation" develops in three main phases: phase A—the period of scholarly interest; phase B—the period of patriotic agitation; and phase C—the rise of a mass national movement. In the third phase, he suggests, "national consciousness has become the concern of the broad masses . . . and the national movement has a firm organizational structure extending over the whole territory."[1] This characterization only partly fits the Kurdish case because the intellectuals, who according to Hroch's theory would lead this development in phase A, came onto the scene quite late because of the formidable obstacles in their way. And even though by the end of the twentieth century a strong Kurdish national consciousness, as well as a firm organizational structure, had developed, these were separated into two distinct parts. Consequently, what became known as "Barzaniland" and "Talabaniland" gave rise to a fractured imagining of the nation.

By the turn of the twenty-first century, the Kurdish national project had begun to show signs of maturing, following the juxtaposition of various internal and external factors: the steady decline of the Baathi regime and the resulting weakening of the Iraqi state; the end of the Kurdish civil war and the slow normalization process that followed close on its heels; the convergence of interests, for the first time in modern history, between a superpower, the United States, and the Kurds; a gradual change in the international community's position on the sanctity of borders after the collapse of the Soviet Union; and, most importantly, the demise of the Baathi state in 2003.

One of the most important explanations for the rise of the Kurdish quasi-state was the steady decline of the Iraqi Baathi state in the 1990s. Indeed, after more than a decade in which Iraqi Kurdistan was outside the control of the central government, significant differences between that region and the center could be observed. Some of these differences were inherent while others were more transitory—the result of changing domestic, regional, and international circumstances.

One striking difference was that at a time when political activity in the center was all but frozen, the Kurdish region brimmed with it. Moreover, while in the center a single political party, the Baath, monopolized power, a host of parties, groups, and outside interests vied for influence within Iraqi Kurdistan and helped promote democracy in the region one way or another. One indication for this disparity was that while the media in the center were monopolized by the Baath, in the Kurdish north they were owned by several main parties, and thus more diversified. The Kurds also had unrestricted access to the Internet (if at all accessible) and to satellite television—media that Iraqis in the center and south could only dream of.[2]

Economically, the Kurds were better off than people in other parts of the country because implementation of the oil-for-food program instituted in 1996 was supervised by the UN. In fact, the UN program in Kurdistan—according to which the region was entitled to $130 million out of the $1 billion received by Iraq—was the largest in the world.[3] In addition, fifteen NGOs were actively involved in the process of rehabilitation.[4] The region's income also grew significantly as Iraqi Kurdistan became the major outlet for Iraqi trade and economic transactions with the outside world. According to one observer, the area was flourishing as never before.[5] The new balance of power went a long way toward explaining the Kurds' success in building a quasi-state.

Closer examination of the Kurdish scene reveals that, from the late 1990s onward, two simultaneous and complementary processes have taken place in Iraqi Kurdistan: on the one hand, slow reconciliation between the warring parties, which helped reinforce a culture of peace at the expense of a culture of confrontation in Kurdish society; on the other, intensive activity articulating a Kurdish nationalist discourse and the development of a system of symbols of nationalism and statehood. By the time the last Kurdish war against Baghdad broke out in 2003, the KRG had developed all the trappings of a quasi-state, which would be greatly boosted in the aftermath of the war. Although the political developments in post-Saddam Iraq are outside the scope of this book, this chapter tackles the process of Kurdish nation building as a continuum because by nature such processes do not stop at a specific moment and therefore must be explored over a longer period of time.

Kurdish Soul-Searching

A sine qua non for successful nation building is unity of purpose among the leading elites. For this to happen, different Kurdish groups needed to settle their differences, which had deepened during the civil war. Indeed, concurrently with mediation efforts by outside forces, the Kurds themselves took steps toward reconciliation. Meanwhile, a slower process of soul-searching was also taking place.

To the outside observer, Iraqi Kurdistan seemed a kaleidoscope of groupings, constantly shaping and reshaping alliances and rivalries. The main players in the region after the civil war remained the two leading parties, the KDP and the PUK, various Islamist groups, a leftist Communist group, Turkoman organizations, and the Turkish Kurdish Workers' Party. The main focus of this chapter, however, is on the two leading parties.

Relations between the KDP and the PUK continued to be tense, long after the end of the civil war; nevertheless, at no point did they revert to military violence as in 1994–1996. Confrontation was prevented, not by any sudden amity between the two, but more likely by popular pressure. For example, a prominent Kurdish figure involved in the mediation process, former secretary-general of the Iraqi Communist Party 'Aziz Muhammad, called on the parties to take responsibility, correct their ways, and stop blaming outside forces for their plight. In his view, had it not been for the fighting between the two Kurdish parties, Iraqi, Turkish, and Iranian intelligence would not have managed to infiltrate into Iraqi Kurdistan.[6]

For their part, the KDP and PUK seemed to have realized that fighting would not serve their interests and certainly not the Kurdish cause. Hence they initiated conciliatory moves while, at the same time, continuing to compete for the Kurds' minds and souls by boosting the Kurdish national project and improving the population's socioeconomic situation.

The year 1998 ushered in an era marked by intensive efforts for reconciliation between the KDP and the PUK—in marked contrast to the preceding four years. The initiative for "a real and comprehensive reconciliation" between the parties came from Jalal Talabani, who on 31 December 1997 had already sent a letter to Mas'ud Barzani appealing to him to put an end to the "Kurdization (*takrid*) of war in Kurdistan" and to act for the "unification of the government in the Kurdistan region."[7] Talabani's move came after a two-year period in which the rival KDP had held the upper hand militarily, politically, and economically. This superiority, and Talabani's futile attempts to overcome it by military means, undoubtedly convinced him to try to regain ground by peaceful overtures. Though suspicious of Talabani's real intentions, Mas'ud Barzani nevertheless reacted positively, if for no other reason than popular Kurdish pressure.

Until the beginning of 2000, relations between the KDP and the PUK proceeded along parallel lines. On one level, the two parties went through the motions of pursuing a dialogue, a reconciliation process, and the normalization of relations. On the other, rivalry and conflict continued unabated, though falling short of actual fighting. The reconciliation efforts, which according to a high-ranking official in the KDP began on 12 February 1998 with weekly meetings,[8] included an exchange of letters between Talabani and Mas'ud Barzani, prisoner swaps, confidence-building projects, joint moves in Europe and the United States, and coordinated activities of their respective foreign relations bureaus. The level of cooperation reached its highest point since the beginning of the civil war in 1994.[9]

In January 1999, Mas'ud Barzani and Talabani met near the KDP stronghold at Salah al-Din in Kurdistan. The meeting, the first in Iraqi Kurdistan after four years of hostilities, was aimed at preparing the ground for reconciliation between the two groups and unifying Kurdish ranks. One positive result was the decision to halt mutual hostile propaganda. Another was to transfer 60 million dinars from the KDP to the PUK as its share of the customs collected by the KDP on the transit of goods to and from Turkey.[10]

The two parties took a further step forward in April 2002 when they set up a "joint operation room" to deal with terrorism in the region; namely, fighting Ansar al-Islam.[11] Then on 8–9 September 2002, Mas'ud Barzani and Talabani held a meeting in Sari Rash in Kurdistan in which they signed a "historic agreement" to solve their differences, agreeing on a "democratic, federal Iraq." A few days later, on 23 September, the PUK and KDP published the draft of a joint, federal project, which drew immediate warnings from Turkish leaders who feared that a US military campaign in Iraq would encourage the Kurds to create an independent state there. Most importantly, on 4 October of the same year the Kurdistan National Assembly, which had been paralyzed for eight years, reconvened with the participation of both groups and their leaders. On that occasion, eleven members of the US Congress sent a joint message to Mas'ud Barzani, congratulating him on the move and reaffirming their support for the democratic experience in Iraqi Kurdistan. On 8 February 2003, in a final gesture of reconciliation, the KDP and PUK decided to open offices in each other's region.

To present a balanced picture it must be pointed out that, even though the peace process continued unabated, the two parties remained locked in a series of economic, political, and strategic disputes. The area under KDP control was better off than that of the PUK. The KDP controlled the two provinces of Duhok and Erbil, with an estimated 1.8 million people, while the PUK controlled the province of Sulaymaniyya, with an estimated 1.5 million inhabitants. The areas controlled by the KDP bordered on Turkey, which meant that the passage of goods and its revenue from customs was substantial (one estimate put it at $1 million a day).[12] Barzaniland was thus economically better off than Talabaniland. Transport routes were more developed and KDP officials received their salaries regularly, in contrast to the PUK officials who held demonstrations several times because they were financially less well off.[13]

Similarly the KRG continued, well into 2005, to evolve around two competing centers of gravity; that is, two governments, two parties, two leaders, two administrations, and two courts of appeal. This duality severely drained the region's resources, which entailed the doubling of administrative funding.[14] However, for all of the complex relationships between the two parties, they did manage to form a cohesive front against both their domestic and external enemies.

The most dangerous domestic enemies were the various Kurdish Islamist groups, the Kurdish Islamic Movement in particular.[15] Based in the Halabja region near the Iranian border, it was estimated to have 1,500–2,000 armed fighters. The movement expanded at the expense of both the Kurdish Communist Party and the KDP. Reportedly, the strengthening of the Islamists was a reaction to manifestations of corruption among KDP leaders who had amassed wealth overnight and built palaces for themselves while most officials in the Kurdish region subsisted on $10 to $20 a month.[16] Additional causes included the difficult socioeconomic situation in Kurdistan in the mid-1990s, which drove people into the arms of religion, and support for Islamist groups by both Iran and Saudi Arabia.[17] Accordingly, as Gareth Stansfield notes, "although it [Iraqi Kurdistan] remains comparatively secular compared to the rest of Iraq or immediate neighbors, a growing number of mosques and institutions have been built and organizations formed in Iraqi Kurdistan and religious conservatism in society has noticeably increased."[18] In any case, both the KDP and the PUK had to deal with a common enemy—Islamist groups—which made them close ranks.[19] This stood in sharp contrast with the mid-1990s, when an Islamist group was the main trigger for the flare-up of hostilities between the KDP and PUK (see Chapter 12).

The Islamists were accused of masterminding terrorism and planning acts of sabotage in various parts of Kurdistan. A member of one of the groups, the Islamic Unity Movement of Kurdistan (IUMK), confessed to planning the attacks.[20] In August 2000, for example, the KDP clashed with the militia of another group, Islamic Unification, killing twenty-one militants.[21] Numerous bombs and booby-trapped cars, for which Islamists were held responsible, exploded throughout 2000 in various parts of Kurdistan. Four years later, Ansar al-Islam set off explosives at KRG *'id al-adha* festivities, causing the death of more than 100 people, including that of Sami 'Abd al-Rahman and his son.[22]

Clearly, beyond the open struggle for power, the two sides (the KDP and PUK vs. the Islamists) engaged in a covert struggle over the direction that Kurdish nationalism would take and over the identity and orientation of the KRG. The Kurdish leadership had always boasted of its championship of secular nationalism and democracy.[23] Indeed, Faleh Jabar maintains that Kurdish nationalism was of an ethnic, secular brand that stood in contrast to the Islamic nationalism that gained ground in the Arab world.[24] Nevertheless, he too warns that Islamic nationalism might engulf the Kurds of Iraq.[25] Fighting the Islamists had become a joint endeavor of the KDP and PUK for winning the Kurds' support for a secular brand of nationalism and, at the same time, improving the image of the Kurds in the eyes of the United States and closing ranks with it on the eve of the 2003 Iraq War.

The process of reconciliation between the two rival factions (the KDP vs. the PUK) and their common fight against the Islamic agenda formed the cornerstone of a growing Kurdish cohesion. One important facet of this process was that after the outbreak of the 2003 war, the Kurds were able to present a relatively united front—in the Kurdish region itself and vis-à-vis the center and the various international players. This enabled them to extend their autonomous activities. Consequently, the region began to acquire the trappings of Kurdish statehood, which, though still fragile, will not be eradicated easily. In addition, the Kurds of Iraq also appeared to be more capable than before of playing by the geopolitical rules of realpolitik, both regionally and internationally.

Nation Building Against All Odds

In his analysis of Kurdish society, Hussein Tahiri contends that the most formidable obstacle to the emergence of Kurdish nationalism was tribalism, which was revitalized in the modern Kurdish polity and in various Kurdish parties. He states that "the tribal system has caused divisions in Kurdish society for centuries and prevented the Kurds from forming their own nation state."[26] Not everyone agrees with this sweeping generalization. For example, Hamit Bozarslan, another Kurdish scholar, maintains, "As late as the 1990s, the success of the Kurdish movement in Iraqi Kurdistan was due in part to the participation of the Kurdish tribes in the nationalist movement."[27] Bozarslan explains that the tribe could act as a national and as a transborder regional actor, and that a tribal chief could find in his tribe the resources that allowed him to become an actor in the national or the supranational sphere. He concludes that "Kurdish nationalist movements . . . had and still have to take tribes into consideration either as allies or as enemies."[28]

Even if Tahiri's observations were entirely correct, I argue that this truism was gradually eroded with the establishment of the KRG. A public opinion poll, conducted in Iraqi Kurdistan to gauge its citizens' loyalty, showed that allegiance to the KRG came first, followed by allegiance to the tribe and other symbols of identity, for example Iraq. Interestingly, allegiance to "Iraqiness" scored low points. In another question as to who was closer to the respondent, the Kurds of neighboring countries or the Arabs of Iraq, the majority opted for the Kurds, where among one group, the Kurds scored 100 percent.[29] These findings fit in with Martha and Richard Cottam's definition of a nation-state; that is, a "state in which the citizens of a country identify with the territorial unit as a political unit more strongly than any other politically relevant identity group." In their definition, "the nation is given primary loyalty" and "all other identities and their demands drop to the side when nationalism becomes salient."[30] These findings reinforce Stansfield's observation that "to all intents and purposes, the people of Kurdistan (or at least the Kurdish majority there), long distinct in their ethnic identity, have developed a vibrant Kurdish nationalism and few are willing to be labeled 'Iraqi' any longer."[31] This also fits the empirical observation of Denise Natali to the effect that

> what is significant is that the idea of liberty has changed. The stranger is no longer the imperialist but the Arab. . . . The idea of fatherland is no longer Iraq but Kurdistan. Kurdish nationalists also claimed that the Iraqi identity was formed of two parts, a Kurdish part and an Arab part, and that only the Arab part formed part of the greater Arab nation.[32]

Indeed, Kurdish nationalist feelings have for quite a long time been strong among the Kurdish rank and file. The following example reflects the general tone of these sentiments. A doctor assigned to the Kurdish region in 1958 relates the common conviction that Kurdish women were "never to stay empty, the more babies they delivered the better it was for the nation." They all wanted as many boys as possible because they believed that the male was destined to die before his time, in battle; therefore, there should be "one boy for Kurdistan and the rest for me." The doctor emphasizes that this stance was tantamount to a national policy.[33] Indeed, in the Iraqi Kurdish case, pressure for more maximalist goals was brought to bear from the grassroots to the top. Intellectuals and the population at large were seeking independence while the leadership maintained a far more cautious approach in stating the Kurds' final goal.[34] As one observer asserts, "many [Kurds] claim that the leadership of the KDP and PUK wasted the opportunity to secede from Iraq and move toward independence."[35] This is, in fact, the Kurdish politicians' greatest dilemma: if they state publicly that the Kurds' goal is independence, the surrounding countries might unite against them; but if they do not, they risk losing the support of their own people and might never achieve independence.

Even though the Kurdish political elite's declarations stopped short of full-fledged independence, they did manage to develop a unique kind of federation by 2003: while divided into two quasi-states, it was only loosely connected to Baghdad. This double-headed entity cultivated different structures and symbols of nationhood, which would be difficult to efface, even by the enemy from within—tribalism.

The Building Blocks of a Kurdish National Identity and Entity

As noted above, the framework of a separate Kurdish entity has been in the making from the early 1990s. It included a constitution, a parliament, a cabinet, and security forces—namely, the Peshmerga, Parastin, and Asayish—all of which became state symbols and functioned independently of Baghdad.[36] Even though the territorial and political frameworks for the Kurdish entity had yet to be settled with Baghdad, Kurdish state building and nation building proceeded apace, unhindered.

Evidence thereof was the establishment "of an academy to train officers in accordance with contemporary requirements"; of "police-gendarmerie" units to maintain law and order and control traffic; of a medical college for training doctors and other health personnel; and the printing of "Kurdistan stamps," featuring scenes of northern Iraqi Kurdistan and a portrait of the late Mulla Mustafa Barzani, founder of the KDP. Another important move was Mas'ud Barzani's decision to adopt the national anthem of the short-lived Kurdish Republic of Mahabad, established in Iran in 1946.[37] Its first part reads thus: "Oh foes who watch us, the nation whose language is Kurdish is alive / It cannot be defeated by makers of weapons of any time / Let no one say the Kurds are dead, the Kurds are alive / The Kurds are alive and their flag will never fall."[38]

Its adoption was part of a long-time project for articulating a Kurdish nationalist discourse, a system of nationalist symbols, as well as memory work. The horrors of the Halabja and Anfal massacres, from which almost no Kurdish family was spared, were the final catalyst for the crystallization of a Kurdish identity and entity. Instead of crushing the Kurds, as Saddam Hussein had hoped, these traumatic experiences served to etch in their minds a national identity separate from that of the Arabs of Iraq and reinforced their resolve to establish their own political entity and bring their cause to the attention of the world. According to one observer, the Halabja massacre was a formative event for Kurdish nation building, which moved from theory to practice.[39] Or, as Joost R. Hilterman puts it, "The Kurds' drive for greater autonomy today, and independence down the line when circumstances permit, predates Halabja and the Anfal, but these twin events gave the quest a renewed urgency: the Kurds simply cannot trust a central Iraqi government not to resort to similar tactics in the future."[40]

With time, the term *Anfal* became part and parcel of the Kurdish lexicon and discourse. Thus for example, a victim of the campaign was called *muanfal*; a new verb, *anfala*, entered the lexicon; and the attack itself was given a plural form, *anfalat*. The huge number of victims called for a special ministry to take care of the orphans, widows, and injured, which was hence called the ministry of the *muanfalin*.[41] As part of the memory work, a growing number of hymns and songs about Anfal were written and aired every year between February and April. One singer, Diyar Qaradaqi, even became known as the "Anfal singer."[42] Eventually, the KRG declared 14 April as the yearly anniversary to commemorate the Anfal massacre. It was the day in 1988 when the Iraqi government began its Anfal operations against the Kurds.

Mas'ud Barzani stated that the KRG had made this move "so that our people will not forget the crimes of Saddam's regime against the people of Kurdistan" and "in order to prevent further genocidal practices from happening against the Kurdistan people." Barzani pointed out, "Some people believe that the policy of genocide against the Kurdish people was part of the Iraq-Iran war, but we believe that war only played a factor in the facilitation of the Anfal Campaign."[43] On 14 April 2008, and on Kurdish insistence, the Iraqi parliament finally recognized Anfal as genocide.[44]

The traumatic events also provided the basis for the memory work within and outside of Iraqi Kurdistan because it was etched deeply in the individual and collective memory of the people of Kurdistan. The month of March became the focus of remembrance as it came to symbolize the Kurds' best and worst of times in modern history. Indeed, March is the month that opens the Kurdish Nowruz. It is the month when the leader of the modern Kurdish struggle, Mulla Mustafa Barzani, was born. And it is the month when the Kurds were granted autonomy under the Baathi regime in 1970. On the other hand, March also witnessed what proved to be the catastrophic Algiers Agreement; the collapse of the rebellion in 1975; and, worst of all, the Halabja massacre in 1988.

Thus, the Halabja massacre became the main symbol of the Kurds' memory work. The event was commemorated in different ways across the region. One such example was the ceremony held on 16 March 2002 when all activity in the Kurdish region came to a standstill at 11 A.M. to observe a five-minute silence in memory of those killed in Halabja fourteen years earlier. On the same occasion, Kurdistan TV displayed a black band throughout its broadcast. Vigils, performances, and exhibitions about the tragedy were organized across the region. The Chemistry Department at the University of Salah al-Din organized a seminar on the effects of chemical weapons. Thousands marched to the city of Halabja to lay wreaths on the graves of victims and were welcomed by surviving relatives. Gas masks and shells of chemical bombs—painted with question marks—were displayed at the entrance to the city. Kurdistan TV ran the story of a Kurdish woman who testified to the following: "I lost 120 of my relatives, who were in Halabja for a wedding. I'm the only one left."[45] In time, 16 March came to be commemorated among the Kurds in Greater Kurdistan and not just among the Kurds of Iraq. It was also observed in different countries around the world, illustrating the ability of the Kurds in the diaspora to bring the Kurdish cause to the attention of the world. Generally speaking, the existence of a large Kurdish diaspora in Europe (850,000) and the United States (about 20,000) served as a catalyst for internationalizing the Kurdish issue, arousing sympathy for the Kurdish plight in Iraq, and mobilizing support for their cause in those countries.[46]

Another project included the building of a monument and museum, inaugurated in Halabja in 2003.[47] The memorial, which included photographs, artifacts, poems, and a list of the victims' names, gave Halabja residents a place to honor their family members.[48] The inauguration of the Halabja Monument, just six months after the US invasion of Iraq in March 2003, received international media attention. Then secretary of state Colin Powell and other US dignitaries participated in the ceremony and were received by cheering crowds in the streets. As most of the victims of the attack had been buried in the village cemetery in Halabja, a memorial sculpture was erected there, too. Another project was the Center of Halabja Against *Anfalization* and Genocide of Kurds, which was established in 2002. At the same time, KurdSat TV also published the details of the Anfal campaigns on its website.[49] Later, when the permanent constitution of post-Saddam Iraq was drafted in 2005, the Kurds insisted that "the massacres of Halabja, Barzan, Anfal and the Fayli Kurds" be included in its preamble.[50]

The city of Sulaymaniyya created its own remembrance center in the Red Security compound, which under the Baath had housed the headquarters of internal security forces and the Directorate of General Security. The Kurds labeled it Red Security—red representing both the color of the building and of the blood of the people who were executed there. The compound consists of six buildings, including an administrative block and cells. Now a museum, its various displays commemorate the victims of the Anfal campaign. In one hall 182,000 shards of glass, the estimated number of Anfal victims, form a mosaic. The 5,000 light bulbs inside the building represent the estimated number of villages destroyed. Other exhibits contain photos of the chemical attacks in Halabja and of other atrocities, and mark the Kurdish resistance to the Saddam regime. Additional displays exhibit the equipment used to torture victims.[51] Also shown is a special room where Kurdish women were systematically raped.[52]

Kurdish individuals further contributed to this memory project by writing novels, poems, and history books on Halabja and Anfal. And as with the Jewish Holocaust, the Kurds have mobilized these events both for Kurdish identity building and to gain international support for their cause.

The Kurdish-Arab Divide on Halabja and Anfal

As mentioned before, the agonizing events of Halabja and Anfal helped bolster a distinct Kurdish identity and separated the Kurds from the Arabs who were perceived as supporting the perpetrators of the genocide and promoting its denial. The Arab stance on Halabja and Anfal was thus taken as a yardstick for testing Arab solidarity with the Kurds. A case in point was the scathing criticism leveled by the Kurdish poet and playwright Khalid Sulayman at Arab intellectuals for their silence or even denial of the Kurdish genocide: "The Arabs were conditioned to accept the idea of the *anfalization* of the Kurds by the Ba'th. Arab officials, intellectuals and even the general public were of the opinion that the campaign was nothing but an action to hold in check human groupings that did not fit the expectations of the Arab state" (emphasis added).[53] Similarly, an article on the KurdishMedia website vehemently attacked an Iraqi university professor, Mohammed Al Obaidi, described as a racist Arab intellectual for being "involved in the politics of denial of the Kurdish genocide," and called on him to apologize to the survivors of the Halabja massacre. The same article protested that there was not a single Kurdish research institute or Kurdology department in the entire Arab world.[54] In the same vein, another Kurdish journalist maintained that the Arabs suffered from a "Kurdish complex" and from Kurdophobia, adding that "Iraqi and Arab pens" used "organized terrorism" to harm the Kurds and their leadership.[55] Mas'ud Barzani, for his part, deplored the attitudes of the Arabs toward the Kurds when he wrote, "At all stages we have defended the Arab causes. But regrettably, when the Al-Anfal chemical attack targeted our villages, we did not hear any Arab voice defending the Kurdish people. We did not hear any official Arab condemnation of those unjust, inhuman measures against the Kurdistan people."[56] The head of the Kurdish government, Nechirvan Barzani, complained that not only did Arab countries not extend any support to the Kurds, but that certain Arab and Muslim countries also used this state of affairs as a cover for supporting Islamist terrorist groups.[57]

The stance on Halabja and Anfal did open a chasm between Kurds and Arabs on the emotional-intellectual level. It was a well-known fact that, but for a few exceptions, Arab intellectuals shied away from tackling Halabja and Anfal.[58] The leading intellectual Edward Said, for example, raised doubts about Saddam's use of chemical weapons against the Kurds.[59] Even the well-known Arab liberal Sa'd al-Din Ibrahim, who published a voluminous book on minorities in the Arab world in 1994, mentions Halabja in two laconic sentences. Furthermore, he does not even briefly recall the Anfal campaigns and the number of victims, despite the fact that Human Rights Watch had long before published its documented report on these campaigns.[60] In fact, the Iraqi exiled Shi'i intellectual Kanan Makiya argues in his book *Cruelty and Silence* that Arab intellectuals "chose silence when it came to the elimination of thousands of Kurdish villages by an Arab state."[61] Makiya's book thus became the most damning indictment against Arab intellectuals on this issue. Not unexpectedly, Arab intellectuals fought back. The Lebanese intellectual Fawwaz Trabulsi accuses Makiya of falsifying the truth; for example, by not mentioning the fact that Trabulsi had written about the Anfal back in 1989. At the same time, however, Trabulsi warns that "Iraqi Kurds have no need for the solidarity of Arab intellectuals if their aim is to secede from Iraq; they would need that solidarity rather to imagine new forms of Arab-Kurdish coexistence." Edward Said states that most of what Makiya had written was revolting, "based as it was on cowardly innuendo and false interpretation."[62] Still years later, an *Al-Hayat* commentator emphasizes that the Halabja affair did not leave its imprint on Arab consciousness and that, moreover, "Arab culture" either denied its existence altogether, or blamed it on Iran, using security considerations for its justification. As for the Anfal campaign, he maintains that it caused a rupture between the Arab and Kurdish social strata in Iraq, both culturally and socially.[63]

The Dissemination of Kurdish National Culture

The Kurds took various steps for reinforcing their Kurdish identity, especially in the realms of language, education, and culture. Because language was considered an important building block of nationalism, the Kurds made major strides forward in this domain. In his book *Nationalism and Language in Kurdistan, 1918–1985*, Amir Hassanpour emphasizes the lack of awareness of language inequality and of a universal declaration of linguistic rights in the world. In his opinion this was all the more important because of the policy of linguicide of the Kurdish language. Hassanpour also stresses that language was perceived as such a potent symbol of nationality that the very act of prohibiting it officially was the major reason for its survival.[64] Indeed, having been under constant threat of linguicide, the Kurdish language witnessed an unprecedented renaissance following the establishment of the KRG.

Both the written and the spoken language became the main tool of communication between people, in the media, and in the educational system. An important step forward was taken in 2005 when the Iraqi constitution recognized Kurdish as an official language, alongside Arabic.[65] Similarly, the ministry of education altered school curricula, translated Arabic textbooks into Kurdish, and added Kurdish culture and history to textbooks.[66] Although Kurdish became the official language in the entire Kurdish educational system, in certain domains, especially at higher levels of education, it lagged behind. Thus, for example, because of a lack of Kurdish textbooks, lecturers in medical schools were forced to use Arabic textbooks, which many Kurdish students could barely understand.[67] All in all, these changes bred a young Kurdish generation that knew little Arabic. This, in turn, opened up further gaps between Kurds and Arabs, bolstering the unique character of the Kurdish region.

The content of textbooks, especially history books, also underwent dramatic changes. Under the Baath, textbooks were replete with Saddam's pictures and pan-Arab, Baathi ideological indoctrination; in the KRG, little by little, Kurdish national heroes and Kurdish history took place of honor. A salient example of the Kurdish narrative in a Kurdish textbook was *Mejuy Nwe w Hawcharkh Poli Dwazdahami Amadayi Wejayi* (Contemporary and Modern History for the Grade Twelve High School).[68] Examining the emergence of the Ottoman Empire, the textbook states that the Ottomans had spread toward "Kurdistan and the Arab world." Clearly, the text separates Kurdistan from the Arab world while at the same time giving it an equivalent status. The textbook refers to the Safavids in a similar vein, claiming that "they moved to conquer the neighboring regions, including Kurdistan and Iraq." Once again Kurdistan is mentioned separately from Iraq. This distinction persists throughout the text, including from the last years of the Ottoman Empire up to the formation of the modern Iraqi state. When discussing the history of modern Iraq, the focus is once again on the history of Kurdistan—Iraq being mentioned as a side issue only. In line with this, the Barzanis, especially Mulla Mustafa, receive the lion's share in this narrative. The Barzanis, however, are positioned in a wider context, alongside the rebellions in Greater Kurdistan. Also discussed at length in the textbook are the Baathi policies of ethnic cleansing, deportation, displacement, and Baathification.[69] As expected, the Anfal campaign was added to school textbooks.[70]

Maria O'Shea puts this new trend in the context of rewriting Kurdish history, saying that as largely substate actors Kurds were often denied a role in official regional histories and suffered from the state-centered core-periphery perspective that informed much of academic history. Hence, she maintains, "The Kurdish nationalist movement seems to have now reached such a level of consciousness that a more complete history is sought to complete the 'imagining' of the Kurdish nation."[71]

Notwithstanding formidable obstacles, Kurdish literature also flourished. All in all, it witnessed a genuine revolution, from oral production not widely known abroad to a written corpus that found a place in world literature. The broad autonomy gained by the Kurds of Iraq after the Gulf War contributed greatly to the spread of written Kurdish, as more and more writers and poets shifted to writing in their mother tongue, whereas in the past they wrote in Arabic either because they were forced to or because the Arabic language seemed more "handy."[72] No less important was the activity of Kurdish intellectuals in the diaspora who contributed substantially to the spread of Kurdish literary works, particularly in Europe. Kurdish theater also began flourishing after a setback in the 1970s.[73]

As with most nascent national movements, poetry and literature were highly politicized and mobilized for the Kurdish cause. Poets like Sami Shoresh, Abdullah Pashew, and Sherko Bekas stress the motif of freedom and independence in their work. The poem "Storm Tide" by Bekas, a prominent modern Kurdish poet, reflects this:

> The tide said to the fisherman:
> There are many reasons
> why my waves are in a rage.
> The most important is
> that I am for the freedom of the fish
> And against the net[74]

The same trend is also noticeable in literature. One particularly noteworthy example is the novel *Jan-I Gal* (The Agony of People), published in Paris in 1994 as *Mal du peuple*, almost thirty years after it was written. Its author is no other than Ibrahim Ahmad, the Kurdish intellectual and leading political figure of the mid-1950s and 1960s. The original Kurdish text was banned under the Baath, but young people read it secretly. It can now be read openly in Iraq and was even made into a successful film.

In his novel, Ahmad combines literary motifs with ideological-political ones. The hero, Jwamer from Sulaymaniyya, was imprisoned for ten years because of his Kurdish patriotism (*Kurdayeti*). When he was finally released from prison, he discovered that his wife had been killed when giving birth to a child, who also died. This terrible news and the deplorable conditions in which the Kurds lived convinced Jwamer to join the National Army for Independence and continue the struggle for his people. Emphasizing the notion that the Kurds had been subservient to other nations throughout their history, Ahmad calls on them to break out of this vicious circle.

Denise Natali observes that as part of the politicization process anti-Arab sentiments began to creep into Kurdish literature: "In contrast to the colonial period, whereby Kurdish intellectuals criticized the backward Kurdish society and repressive colonialist regime, in the ethnicizing state, Iraqi state and anti-Arab themes became prominent in Kurdish nationalist literature."[75]

Another means for bolstering Kurdish identity was through archaeological projects and the preservation of antiquities. Recognizing the role of history and archaeology in Kurdish nationalism, Saddam suppressed both by prohibiting digs, censoring museum exhibits, and even destroying artifacts.[76] Clearly, Saddam's moves were aimed at suppressing Kurdish evidence of a cultural heritage distinct from that of other Iraqis. Accordingly, even though a study carried out under the Baath had catalogued more than 3,000 sites, fewer than 25 were excavated during Saddam's rule.[77] The KRG, which was involved in more urgent tasks at the time, started to pay serious attention to these issues only after the collapse of the Baathi regime. In this, it benefited from the expertise of foreign archaeologists—mainly Czech, German, and US—as the huge number of unexcavated treasures and the satisfactory security situation in the region held a special attraction for foreign archaeologists. Among the greatest pulls was Erbil's citadel, believed to be one of the oldest, continuously inhabited human settlements in the world and, according to some, about 8,000 years old.[78] Acknowledging its importance, the United Nations Educational, Scientific and Cultural Organization (UNESCO) financed preliminary studies about the possibility of renovating parts of the citadel. Indeed, by 2009 much progress had been made in its preservation and study.[79] Further progress was expected when a US delegation visited Erbil in 2010 to examine the possibility of establishing an archaeological institute and training archaeologists on-site. One indication for the changing status of the region in this field was the visit in March 2008 of a delegation from the Iraqi Ministry of Tourism and Archaeology "to find mechanisms of mutual cooperation with the regional Ministry of Tourism and Archaeology."[80] Clearly, Baghdad recognized the separate status of the Kurds—at least verbally.

The Social Factors in Nation Building

One of the main factors that assisted the Kurds in their nation-building project was a relatively open society and a relatively strong public opinion, which developed in spite of the existence of old and, as many would say, corrupt leaderships.[81] Indeed, there was lively and authentic participation by the population. People did not merely go to the polls in the first-ever elections in 1992, or in later ones, but formed pressure groups that forced the leadership to open up to and accommodate the demands from those not in the ruling elite.[82] Thus, for example, in June 2004 some 60,000 to 70,000 Kurds reportedly demonstrated in Sulaymaniyya, demanding—for the first time in decades—that the Kurdish *iqlim* be separated from the Iraqi central government and that Kirkuk become the capital of an independent Kurdistan. Simultaneous demonstrations in other cities pressed for the unification of the two parties and for a stronger stand on the issue of Kurdish independence.[83] The Kurdish public thus was much more radical and critical of its leadership.[84] It was probably such pressure that ultimately forced the leadership to unite forces in May 2006. Demonstrations, in which students, intellectuals, and the population at large participated, became part and parcel of political life in Iraqi Kurdistan, especially in Erbil, the political capital and in Sulaymaniyya, the cultural capital of the region. Such demonstrations opposed corruption, nepotism, difficult economic conditions, and deficiencies in the rule of law. The worst demonstration took place in Halabja in March 2006, when angry demonstrators burned down the memorial because they maintained that the leadership had exploited it for their own political purposes while neglecting the reconstruction of the town itself.[85] Strikes also became a common phenomenon in Iraqi Kurdistan.[86]

Another facet of the burgeoning civil society was the formation of NGOs, one of which was the Referendum Movement in Kurdistan (harakat al-istifta' fi Kurdistan), established in July 2004, which discovered that 98.6 percent of the Kurds supported independence.[87] With a view toward internationalizing the issue, it later sent a memorandum signed by 1.7 million Kurds to the UN, asking it to carry out a referendum of its own to verify this fact.[88] A Kurdish intellectual, Kamal Mazhar Ahmad, points out that the prevalent view among the Kurds was that their leadership did not insist strongly enough on self-determination. In other words, the leadership was more moderate than the Kurdish public.[89]

The proliferation of Kurdish media and Internet sites, which had started much earlier in Kurdistan than in the area under tight control of the Baathi regime, went a long way toward explaining the rapid growth of a Kurdish identity and the active involvement of the Kurdish public in national and political affairs. This new media involvement enabled them to interact virtually and freely with each other across previously impassable "national" boundaries.[90] It enhanced relations between Kurds within Iraqi Kurdistan and brought them into contact with Kurds in Greater Kurdistan, with the Kurdish diaspora, and with the world at large. The Kurdish media began enjoying an unprecedented boom, including numerous newspapers, periodicals, radio and television stations, and broadcasting satellites.[91] To give just a few examples, in 2002 there were no less than nineteen Kurdish television stations and dozens of periodicals.[92]

Interestingly, alongside the hegemonic discourse in the Kurdish media an alternative discourse developed in the newspapers and on Internet sites that was highly critical of the Kurdish government and its policies. The Kurdish-Media site, for example, which had been active since 1998, became a platform for airing grievances against the Kurdish government, demanding reforms, and criticizing the leadership for various misdeeds—especially for granting the Peshmerga too much power and too many economic benefits. The main assertions were that the Peshmerga's salaries were three times higher than those of other government employees, and that the formation of a unified Kurdish Army was being obstructed.[93] Even more important was the independent biweekly *Hawlati*, which was first published in 2000. *Hawlati*, the most popular newspaper in the KRG, kept a close watch on negative social and political issues, including corruption, nepotism, and the use of violence by the authorities.[94] These developments could be interpreted as a sign of weakness of the Kurdish polity. However, they could also be regarded as the manifestation of a budding democracy, indicating the existence of a vibrant society that dared challenge its leadership.

The relative openness in the Kurdish region had a clear impact on another aspect of social life: Kurdish women were better integrated in the political system than during the Baathi regime. It is noteworthy that in thirty-five years of Baathi life, there was only one woman minister, Su'ad Khalil Isma'il, and for only one year (1971–1972).[95] The KDP, although considered more traditional and tribal than its rival the PUK, had a woman minister of development and construction, Nasrin Barwari, in its cabinet in the year 2000.[96] Likewise, Barham Salih of the PUK notes that the Kurds could boast of the only woman judge in the Islamic world.[97] Going one step further, Talabani, the head of the PUK, promised that women from various regions of Kurdistan would be brought into the leadership of the party.[98] His wife Hero indubitably played an important role, as she held prominent positions in the KRG: she was a member of the first parliament elected in 1992; helped organize the PUK's company of female Peshmerga;[99] owned, among others, the KurdSat TV station and Khak Publishing Group; and was chairwoman of Kurdistan Save the Children.[100] Furthermore, she won the most votes in the June 2010 internal elections for the PUK leadership; namely, 1,070 out of a total 1,619, thus surpassing all male candidates. Interestingly, the total number of women elected to the leadership on that occasion was 9 (out of 33) or more than 25 percent.[101]

Another sign of the changing times was that women's NGOs proliferated in the region to the point that, by 2003, fifteen were active. It should be noted that one of the first to be established was an NGO that supported the victimized families of the Anfal campaign. Hero Talabani was one of its organizers.[102] Another indication of gradual change was then women were being able to drive, at least in the large cities, indicating a shift in what used to be a male-dominated society. Finally, the increasingly relevant role played by women in Kurdish society was symbolically reflected by the statue of a woman at the entrance to Zakho.[103]

Yet for all the progress, honor killing of women, female circumcision, polygamy, and general discrimination continued unabated.[104] One woman activist, Houzan Mahmoud, representative abroad of the Organisation of Women's Freedom in Iraq, complained that

> the current family status law upholds patriarchal, religious and conservative norms which discriminate against women. The government has totally failed to promote equality, women's rights and individual rights and freedoms. They insist on implementing Islamic Sharia law and recognizing ethnic, tribal and religious mores instead of a modern civil family law. Our basic problem is a ruling class which divides society on the basis of gender, religion and ethnicity and race.[105]

As to female representation in the echelons of power, although there were 37 women lawmakers in the 111-seat Kurdish parliament (33 percent), women activists claimed that the most senior posts were almost exclusively reserved for men. Moreover following regional elections in July 2009, the KRG dissolved the Ministry of Women's Affairs and reduced the number of ministerial posts from forty-two to nineteen. Women paid the price since there was only one woman minister in the new cabinet as opposed to three in the former one. Janar (Chinar) Sa'd 'Abdullah, the former minister of martyrs and Anfal affairs, who was replaced by a man in the new cabinet, said: "To have only one woman in the cabinet is an unfair share of power and it doesn't reflect our society. We should have a real voice in power."[106] Neither did the mobilization of Kurdish women for the national cause bring them the expected fruits as one scholar laments: "The praxis of the established bearers of the national cause may represent more of a fetter than enabler of liberation for both women and the nation."[107]

The Writing on the Wall

In his famous memorandum, written shortly before his death in 1933, King Faysal I warned of the extreme weakness of the Sunni rulers who had to rule over the Kurds, most of whom he said were "ignorant" and sought to secede from the state, as well as over an equally "ignorant" Shi'i majority, which opposed the Sunni government because of profound feelings of discrimination. These two, he maintained, severely handicapped the process of Iraq's state and nation building.[108] Eight decades later, the king's prescient perception has proved more valid than ever. Aware of the complex mosaic of Iraqi society, the king had employed moderate methods in his attempts to build an Iraqi nation-state. However, unlike him, Saddam, who assumed power forty years later, resorted to extreme violence and ruthlessness. Despite the fact that—at least in the first decade of the Baathi regime—the Iraqi state radiated strength, determination, and even a certain cohesion, beneath the surface deep rifts were opening that even Saddam could not ignore. Thus, like a prophet of doom, Saddam warned of the danger of Iraq splitting into three parts. On one occasion, he compared Iraq to a big ship shared by Arabs and Kurds and warned that he would not allow a hole to be drilled in its bottom, lest it sink.[109] On another occasion, he warned of the dangers of separatism and factionalism and promised to combat them by any means: "I support every effort leading to the prosperity of the region and against any plan, no matter how small it is, which assists separation or disunifies the Iraqis. Then I will draw my sword and fight it wherever it exists."[110]

This led to what Andreas Wimmer diagnoses as the problem of all societies and states in which a similar pattern of exclusivist nationalism existed. According to Wimmer, when elites are not prepared to include the entire population into the dominant nation representing the state, those who thereby become "minorities" are excluded from the benefits of political modernity and do not feel inclined to "embrace the project of nation-building through assimilation."[111] This in turn causes technocrats to rely on terror to control the population, which alienates the minorities even further. In Wimmer's view, the polity is compartmentalized at the end of this process into a series of ethnic groups whose members see themselves as separate communities, each of which shares a common political fate. In other words, what transpires is social isolation and political fragmentation along ethnic lines.

The Kurds of Iraq illustrate an interesting case whereby primordial loyalties were further enhanced by Baathi policies of compartmentalization as Wimmer's model suggests. Years of exclusionist policies, wars, and persecution verging on extermination deepened political fragmentation along ethnic lines, enhancing the nation-building process among the Kurds while significantly weakening all-Iraq nation building. Post-Saddam Iraq, which I discuss in Chapter 16, presents a different picture. In an ironic twist of history, Saddam, who had initiated the Kurdish autonomy and then reneged on it in a most brutal way, met his own death in a no less brutal way: death by hanging at the end of 2006. As to the state, in the absence of the man who did and undid it, Iraq took a revolutionary course. The Kurds were to fulfill a pivotal role in this process.

Notes

1. Miroslav Hroch, *Social Preconditions of National Revival in Europe: A Comparative Analysis of the Social Composition of Patriotic Groups Among the Smaller European Nations* (New York: Columbia University Press, 2000), pp. 22–23.

2. *Wall Street Journal* (online edition), 6 January 2000; Kurdistan TV International (Salah al-Din), 19 February 2000, cited in BBC; *Al-Sharq al-Awsat* (London, daily), 5 May 2000.

3. Stafford Clarry, "Iraqi Kurdistan: The Humanitarian Program," in *Kurdish Identity: Human Rights and Political Status*, eds. Charles G. MacDonald and Carole A. O'Leary (Gainesville: University Press of Florida, 2007), p.153.

4. *Al-Mushahid al-Siyasi* (London, weekly), 10 December 2000.

5. *Al-Sharq al-Awsat*, 5 May 2000.

6. *Al-Sharq al-Awsat*, 21 May 1998.

7. *Al-Sharq al-Awsat*, 4 January 1998.

8. *Al-Sharq al-Awsat*, 12 June 1998; Agence France Press, 20 July 1998, cited in *Daily Report*.

9. *Al-Sharq al-Awsat*, 8 February 1998; *Financial Times* (London, daily), 23 February 1998; Islamic Republic News Agency, 3 April 1998, cited in *Daily Report*; *Al-Wasat* (London, weekly), 6 April 1998.

10. *Al-Wasat* (London, weekly), 1 November 1999. The source of this report was a noted Kurdish analyst, Chris Kutschera, so in all likelihood the information is credible. By the end of the year, the sum granted to the PUK reached 110 million dinars. *Khebat*, 1, 3 December 1999, cited in BBC, 9 December 1999.

11. Two years later, however, Ansar al-Islam caused an explosion at KRG *'id al-adha* festivities that caused the death of more than 100 people, including that of Sami 'Abd al-Rahman and his son. Quil Lawrence, *Invisible Nation: How the Kurds' Quest for Statehood Is Shaping Iraq and the Middle East* (New York: Walker; distributed by Macmillan, 2008), pp. 237–238.

12. *Al-Wasat*, 1 November 1999.

13. Ibid.

14. One observer opined that the "the managed division of Kurdistan" had its positive sides. Gareth Stansfield, "Governing Kurdistan: The Strengths of Division," in *The Future of Kurdistan in Iraq*, eds. Brendan O'Leary, John McGarry, and Khaled Salih (Philadelphia: University of Pennsylvania Press, 2005), p. 214.

15. *Al-'Iraq* (Baghdad, daily), 2 February 2000.

16. *Al-Wasat*, 1 November 1999; Denise Natali, *The Kurdish Quasi-State* (Syracuse, NY: Syracuse University Press, 2010), p. 99.

17. Muhammad Kirmanj, an ardent anti-Islamist, told me that he forbade his wife to wear the scarf. Muhammad Kirmanj, KDP activist, interviewed by the author, Erbil, 30 April 2009.

18. Gareth R. V. Stansfield, "Finding a Dangerous Equilibrium: Internal Politics in Iraqi Kurdistan: Parties, Tribes and Ethnicity Reconsidered," in *The Kurds: Nationalism and Politics*, eds. Faleh A. Jabar and Dawod Hosham (London: Saqi, 2006), p. 267.

19. In 2001, the two parties cooperated to combat the "jund al-Islam" grouping. Wahram Betrosian, *Siyasat Turkiyya Tujah Kurdistan al-'Iraq wa Amerika* (Duhok: Duhok University, 2008), p. 24.

20. Kurdistan satellite TV, 10 March 2000, cited in BBC. The group denied the authenticity of the confession. Kurdistan satellite TV, 31 August 2000, cited in BBC.

21. The PKK also was said to have attacked an Islamist group, the Islamic Mujahidin Movement, and to have killed thirty of its members. Anatolia News Agency, 21 September 2000, cited in BBC.

22. Lawrence, *Invisible Nation*, pp. 237–238.

23. In 2002 Barham Salih, head of the PUK government, declared that Kurdistan would become "a beacon of democracy" in the region. Kevin McKiernan, *The Kurds: A People in Search of Their Homeland* (New York: St. Martin's Press), 2006, p. 178.

24. In May 2007, a signature-collecting campaign was initiated in support of the secularization of the constitution of the KRG. *Kurdish Globe*, 9 May 2007.

25. Faleh A. Jabar, "Arab Nationalism Versus Kurdish Nationalism: Reflections on Structural Parallels and Discontinuities," in *The Kurds: Nationalism and Politics*, eds. Faleh A. Jabar and Dawod Hosham (London: Saqi, 2006), p. 303.

26. Hussein Tahiri, *The Structure of Kurdish Society and the Struggle for a Kurdish State* (Costa Mesa, CA: Mazda, 2007), p. 344.

27. Hamit Bozarslan, "Tribal Asabiyya and Kurdish Politics: A Socio-historical Perspective," in *The Kurds: Nationalism and Politics*, eds. Faleh A. Jabar and Dawod Hosham (London: Saqi, 2006), pp. 133, 137.

28. Ibid., p. 136.

29. Raja'i Fayed, *Tahawwulat al-Shakhsiyya al-Kurdiyya nahwa al-Hadatha* (Duhok: Markaz al-Dirasat al-Kurdiyya wa Hifz al-Watha'iq, 2008), pp. 30, 43, 122.

30. Martha L. Cottam and Richard W. Cottam, *Nationalism and Politics: The Political Behavior of Nation States* (Boulder: Lynne Rienner, 2001), pp. 17, 195, 197. Quoted by Carole A. O'Leary, in *Kurdish Identity: Human Rights and Political Status*, eds. Charles G. MacDonald and Carole A. O'Leary (Gainesville: University Press of Florida, 2007), p. 172.

31. Stansfield, "Finding a Dangerous Equilibrium," pp. 264–265.

32. Denise Natali, *The Kurds and the State: Evolving National Identity in Iraq, Turkey, and Iran* (Syracuse: Syracuse University Press, 2005), p. 55.

33. Henry D. Astarjian, *The Struggle for Kirkuk* (Westport, CT: Praeger Security International, 2007), p. 78.

34. An unpublished essay by Sherko Kirmanj that compared the position of the political leaderships with that of intellectuals regarding independence showed that while the politicians had an ambivalent attitude toward independence, the intellectuals were all for it.

35. Stansfield, "Finding a Dangerous Equilibrium," p. 265.

36. For a thorough discussion of the development and functioning of these bodies, see Gareth R. V. Stansfield, *Iraqi Kurdistan: Political Development and Emergent Democracy* (New York: Routledge Curzon, 2003).

37. *Hürriyet*, 15 April, 9 May 1999, cited in *Daily Report; Al-Khalij*, 26 August 1999.

38. Kurdistan Regional Government, "Flag and National Anthem," www.krg.org.

39. *Al-Hayat*, 14 May 2006.

40. Joost R. Hilterman, "Halabja: The Politics of Memory," Open Democracy, 14 March 2008, www.opendemocracy.net.

41. In 2006 the minister was a woman, Janar Sa'd 'Abdullah.

42. Kurdish scholar Sherko Kirmanj, personal communication with the author, 30 October 2010.

43. *Kurdish Globe*, "Anfal Campaign Receives National Day of Remembrance," 18 April 2007, www.kurdishglobe.net.

44. *Kurdish Globe*, "Baghdad Recognizes Anfal as Genocide," 16 April 2008, www.kurdishglobe.net.

45. BBC News, 17 March 2002.

46. Institut Kurde de Paris, www.institute.org/en/kurdorama (accessed 15 September 2009).

47. Affinity Group on Documents and Confronting the Past Kurdistan Conference, 3–8 May 2006, pp. 3–4.

48. BBC News, "Kurdish Clash at Halabja Memorial," http://newsvote.bbc.co.uk.

49. www.kurdsat.tv/E_Direje.aspx?CoriWene=5&Cor=Aburi&Jimare=43 (accessed 25 October 2003).

50. Hilterman, "Halabja," p. 226.

51. Affinity Group on Documents and Confronting the Past Kurdistan Conference, pp. 3–4.

52. I was shown this room during a visit to the museum in May 2009.

53. Khalid Sulayman, *al-Hiwar al-Mutamddin*, 13 August 2005.

54. KurdishMedia.com, "Halabja: The Racism of So-called Arab Intellectuals Towards Lands and Kurdistan," January 2005.

55. *Al-Ahali* (Cairo, weekly), 7 June 2006.

56. BBC, "Kurdish President Barzani Interviewed on Kurdish, Iraqi Issues," 9 January 2006, www.krg.org.

57. *Al-Sharq al-Awsat* (London, daily), 1, 6 June 2006.

58. One of these few was Fawwaz Trabulsi who wrote about Anfal in 1989. Fawwaz Trabulsi, "On Being Silent: A Response to Kanan Makiya," *Middle East Report*, nos. 187–188 (1994): 61–63.

59. Khalid Sulayman, *Al-Hiwar al-Mutamddin*, 13 August 2005.

60. Sa'd al-Din Ibrahim, *Al-Milal wal-Nihal wal-A'raq: Humum al-Aqalliyyat fi al-Watan al'Arabi* (Cairo: Markaz Ibn Khaldun, 1994), p. 236.

61. Kanan Makiya, *Cruelty and Silence: War, Tyranny, Uprising, and the Arab World*. London: Penguin Books, 1993), p. 201.

62. Fawwaz Trabulsi, "On Being Silent," pp. 61–63; Edward Said, "Misinformation About Iraq," 28 November 2002, www.aliraqi.org/forums/showthread.php?t=15324.

63. *Al-Hayat*, 14 May 2006. Another serious accusation on the role of Arab intellectuals appeared earlier in the Egyptian periodical, *Akhbar al-Adab*, 24 November 2004. Ironically, Kuwait accused the media of fabricating lies to discredit Iraq; little did it know that it would be the next victim. Kuwaiti accusations are quoted in David Romano, *The Kurdish Nationalist Movement: Opportunity, Mobilization and Identity* (Cambridge, UK: Cambridge University Press, 2008), p. 202.

64. Amir Hassanpour, *Nationalism and Language in Kurdistan 1918–1985* (San Francisco: Mellen Research University Press, 1992), pp. 144–147.

65. Article 3 of the constitution provides that "Arabic is the official language, and together with it is the Kurdish language in the Kurdistan Region (*iqlim*)." *Al-Mustaqbal al-'Arabi* (Beirut, monthly), September 2005, no. 319.

66. Natali, *The Kurdish Quasi-State*, p. 91.

67. University professor Ahmed Alavde, interviewed by the author, 3 October 2010.

68. Kurdistan Regional Government, Ministry of Education 2008, 4th ed. (Lebanon: Al-Mustaqbal Press). I am indebted to Sherko Kirmanj for providing information on the textbooks.

69. Ibid., pp. 3–8, 53–89, 90–99, 100–113, 126, 176–183.

70. *Kurdish Globe*, "Anfal Campaign Receives National Day of Remembrance," 18 April 2007, www.kurdishglobe.net. Arguments on the Kurds' historical antiquity and historical rights can be also found in Mas'ud Barzani, *Al-Barzani wal-Haraka al-Kurdiyya al-Taharruriyya*, vol. 3 (Erbil, 2002), pp. 522–523.

71. Maria O'Shea, "Tying Down the Territory: Conceptions and Misconceptions of Early Kurdish History," in *The Kurds: Nationalism and Politics*, eds. Faleh A. Jabar and Dawod Hosham (London: Saqi, 2006), pp. 113, 125.

72. See interview with the Kurdish poet Khalat Ahmad, 25 December 2005, www.alarab.co.uk. Ahmad said that although Arabic literary works were being translated into Kurdish there was little interest among Arabs in publishing or translating Kurdish works.

73. *Al-Hayat*, 21 March 2006.

74. Sherko Bekas, "The Uprising," in *The Secret Diary of a Rose*, 2d ed., Reingard Mirza and Shirwan Mirza, trans. (Univeristy of Ottowa, 1998).

75. Natali, *The Kurds and the State*, p. 55.

76. www.archaeology.org/0607/abstracts/letter.html.

77. Radio Free Europe/Radio Liberty, "Iraq: Irbil's Kurds Live on a Hill of Undiscovered Treasures," 13 December 2005, www.rferl.org.

78. *Kurdish Globe*, "Erbil Eyes Archaeological Tourism," 25 November 2009, www.kurdishglobe.net.

79. Ibid.

80. *Aswat al-Iraq*, 3 March 2008, http://en.aswataliraq.info/?p=71650 (accessed 20 March 2008).

81. Corruption was the main factor militating against the solidarity between the Kurds and their leadership. Anonymous Kurdish intellectual, interviewed by the author, 1 July 2007.

82. Michael Leezenberg, however, belittled the importance of such organizations saying that "there have been various protest movements and organizations . . . but they faced an unequal battle." Michael Leezenberg, "Urbanization, Privatization, and Patronage: The Political Economy of Kurdistan," in *The Kurds: Nationalism and Politics*, eds. Faleh A. Jabar and Dawod Hosham (London: Saqi, 2006), p. 168.

83. *Al-Ahali*, 10 June 2004.

84. The head of the Kurdish government, Nechirvan Barzani, emphasized that democracy reigned in Iraqi Kurdistan, one aspect of which was freedom of expression. He further emphasized that he himself was severely criticized in the Kurdish media. *Al-Sharq al-Awsat*, 1 June 2006.

85. BBC News, "Kurdish Clash at Halabja Memorial," 16 March 2006, http://news.bbc.co.uk.

86. *Al-Ittihad* (Baghdad, weekly), 15 August 2005; *Al-Zaman* (London, daily), 21 August 2006.

87. *Al-Ittihad*, 15 August 2005.

88. "Country of Origin Information Iraq," Report of the United Nations High Commissioner for Refugees (October 2005), p. 75.

89. *Al-Watan al-'Arabi* (Paris, weekly), 30 December 2005.

90. Interestingly, Iraqi Arabs who found refuge in Kurdistan began to learn Kurdish. Sometimes the language for communication was English. *Al-Watan al-'Arabi*, 11 April 2007.

91. The Kurdish Ministry of Culture alone publishes sixteen periodicals. *Al-Hayat* (London, daily), 12 March 2006.

92. Kevin McKiernan, *The Kurds: A People in Search of Their Homeland* (New York: St. Martin's Press, 2006), p. 178.

93. KurdishMedia, 27 March, 4 April 2006; 6 January, 8 February 2007; www.kurdmedia.com.

94. For example, *Hawlati*, http://83.169.12.202/English.aspx (accessed March 2010).

95. Ofra Bengio, "Women in Iraq Between Tradition and Revolution," in *Women in the Middle East: Tradition and Change*, ed. Ofra Bengio (in Hebrew) (Tel Aviv: Moshe Dayan Center of Middle Eastern and African Studies, 2004), p. 100.

96. *Khebat* (online edition), 14 January 2000, cited in BBC.

97. McKiernan, *The Kurds*, p. 178.

98. *Kurdistani Nuwe* (Sulaymaniyya, Internet version), 15 November 2000, cited in BBC.

99. Lawrence, *Invisible Nation*, p. 82.

100. KurdishMedia, "Bloodline Instead of Merit: The Talabanis," 7 January 2007, www.kurdmedia.com.

101. "'Aqilat al-Talabani Tahsud Akthariyyat al-Aswat," www.akhbaar.org /wesima_articles/index-20100614-91811.html. A PUK member told me that in fact she had rigged the elections. Interviewed by the author on condition of anonymity.

102. Nazand Bagikhani, "Kurdish Women and National Identity," 11 August 2003, www.kurdmedia.com.

103. *Al-Hayat*, 5 November 2000. There also is a statue of a woman in a Duhok square.

104. Bagikhani, "Kurdish Women and National Identity."

105. *Hawlati*, 31 March 2010, http://83.169.12.202/English.aspx (accessed 15 April 2010).

106. *Al-Ta'akhi* (Baghdad, daily), 3 May 2007; Iraqi Crisis Report, "Glass Ceiling for Female Kurdish Politicians," no. 334, 29 April 2010, http://iwpr.net.

107. Bagikhani, "Kurdish Women and National Identity."

108. The memorandum appeared in 'Abd al-Razzaq al-Hasani, *Ta'rikh al-Wizarat al-'Iraqiyya*, part 3 (Sidon, Lebanon: Al-'Urfan Press, 1939), pp. 189–195.

109. *Los Angeles Times*, 20 April 1979. The image of Iraq as a "ship for everyone," and for which all must take responsibility, has become a common image in post-Saddam Iraq. See Aljazeera, 19 January 2006, on the program "ma wara' al-khabar."

110. Iraqi News Agency, 12 July 1982, cited in BBC, 14 July 1982.

111. Andreas Wimmer, *Nationalist Exclusion and Ethnic Conflict* (Cambridge: Cambridge University Press, 2002), p. 194.

16

The Great Leap Forward in Post-Saddam Iraq

The seven years that followed the collapse of the Baathi regime in the spring of 2003 may be called the Kurds' "seven good years," during which they managed to catapult themselves onto the center stage of Iraqi politics while, at the same time, energetically building their own entity. The demise of the Baathi state gave a real boost to Kurdish state building. At the same time it provided them with the opportunity, for the first time in Iraqi history, to play an important part in Iraq's state building. The Kurds have thus been engaged in two state-building projects, their own and that of the Iraqi state, since 2003. Although there seemed to be a contradiction between their role in the center and in the Kurdish region, the Kurds nevertheless have succeeded in finding a golden mean for acting simultaneously on both planes, without one harming the other.

The Kurds' Dual Role of State Building

Generally speaking, the Kurds have been more successful than the central government in the building project. For one thing, the peace process between the two Kurdish parties, in which they were engaged since the late 1990s, brought greater cohesion to their ranks by the beginning of the 2003 Iraq War. This in turn laid the groundwork for the post-Saddam era, during which the Kurdish region has been the most stable and war-free region in the country. Thus, while the central government started building a state almost from scratch after 2003, the Kurds had already been building their own state for nearly ten years, which gave them a significant advantage. And while the Iraq War ignited a Sunni-Shi'i strife in the center that reached the level of civil war, in the Kurdish region the war acted as a catalyst for greater cohesion among the Kurds. Their ability to rise above the Arab Shi'i-Sunni fray has shielded the Kurds to a great extent from the terrorist attacks that rocked the Arab part of the country. Similarly, unlike in the past when different Iraqi governments used the divide-and-rule formula to weaken the Kurds, such tactics became useless after the war since the Kurds present a unified front vis-à-vis the center, which for a time was itself in a state of collapse. Being the most organized militarily and the strongest economically, the Kurds have added their weight to the shaping of post-Saddam Iraq.

Since the mid-1990s Kurdish representation in Washington gave their leadership a head start over the other Iraqi players in their relations with the United States. In addition, the Kurds also made themselves indispensable to the US coalition during the Iraq War. Turkey's decision to not allow US forces to launch attacks against Iraq from the north was ably used by the Kurds. They played an important part in the US war effort in the north and, consequently, in the defeat of the Baath. This vital aid made them a trustworthy ally to the United States. Notwithstanding ups and downs in the relationship, the marriage of convenience between the Kurds and the United States has continued. Not only did the United States not have to send forces to maintain security in the KRG, but the Peshmerga also assisted US troops in fighting insurgents in other parts of Iraq. Unlike their Sunni and Shi'i partners in Baghdad, the Kurds strongly objected to what they perceived as an early withdrawal of US troops from Iraq. Jalal Talabani repeatedly warned against an early withdrawal as did the Iraqi chief of staff, the Kurd Babakr Zebari, who even asked the US troops to stay until 2020.[1] On the whole as Qobat Talabani, the Kurdish representative in Washington, stressed, the Kurds looked at the United States as a liberator and not as a conqueror; hence, their firm friendship toward the United States.

The relative strength of the Kurdish elite is another important factor that distinguishes them from the Sunnis and the Shi'is. Thus, in contrast to the rifts within the old Sunni and the newly emerging Shi'i elites, the Kurds paradoxically managed to maintain a fair degree of historical continuity. This was attained despite a number of episodes in the history of modern Iraq in which the Kurdish leadership or ranking community members were expelled from their homes and driven into exile. The elite that most embodied this continuity was the Barzani tribe, which has passed on the leadership mantle from generation to generation since the 1930s. The Barzanis have managed to resolve all crises while safeguarding their leadership role, if not over all the Kurds then at least over a significant portion of the population. This continuity can be attributed, among other things, to the personality and charisma of Mulla Mustafa Barzani and the cohesiveness of the Barzani tribe itself. This enabled the Barzanis to force competing tribes to the margins of leadership or to forge alliances with them and, thus, hold on to power. It is noteworthy that, although quite strong at times, the Talabani elite was less cohesive than the Barzani elite.

The fact that unlike other opposition groups, the Kurdish elites usually remained steadfast on the land of Iraqi Kurdistan—their decade-long experience with self-rule and the cohesiveness that they have displayed after the Iraq War—

has given them tremendous advantages over other Iraqi elites that came to the fore after the war. One example of this cohesiveness is that well before the December 2005 nationwide Iraqi elections, the decision was made to integrate the two Kurdish camps and present a single, joint list to the electorate. The list consisted of the two leading parties as well as the smaller parties—with the exclusion of the radical Islamists. These advantages, which were obviously projected onto all of Kurdish society, stem from the disparate experiences of the Kurdish elite as compared with the Sunnis and Shi'is. Not only has the Kurdish leadership been immune to purges or assassinations, but since the late 1990s the extent of cooperation between the belligerent factions also has progressed to the point of a meaningful modus vivendi. Indeed, the rapprochement reached a point where the KDP and PUK formed a joint list in the July 2009 elections to the Kurdish parliament. Interestingly their main challenge was the Change List (Gorran), headed by Nawshirwan Mustafa, a one-time member of the old PUK elite. This again illustrates the continuity distinguishing the Kurdish elite from the Sunni and Shi'i elites.

Another crucial advantage is that the Kurds have been allowed to maintain their irregular forces, the Peshmerga, which had joined forces with the coalition forces in minor skirmishes after the major battle in the spring of 2003 such as the capture of the city of Falluja, a center of Sunni resistance, in November 2004. Similarly, when the Iraqi police and national guard units in the city of Mosul collapsed in the face of an insurgent uprising in late 2004, Kurdish Peshmerga battalions led the counterattack alongside US military units. This support provided them with the justification to vehemently reject calls to dismantle the Peshmerga as part of a general plan to disband all the militias in Iraq.

While the Arab part of Iraq underwent an acute identity crisis, making it extremely difficult to normalize the internal relations between its two chief components—the Shi'i and Sunni—the Kurdish region presented a contrasting picture. It was characterized by relative stability; by the ability to act as an occasional mediator between Shi'is and Sunnis; by the important role it played in the central government in Baghdad; and, most importantly, by the creation of a Kurdish national identity, with symbols of independence that distinguished it from the Arab region of Iraq. Jalal Talabani, the Iraqi president since 2005, explained that for years the Kurds had enjoyed political rights and freedoms that had turned Iraqi Kurdistan into a model for the rest of the country.[2] Mas'ud Barzani, president of the KRG since 2005, for his part also claimed, "the success of the Kurdistan experiment is due to the culture of tolerance and the adoption of national conciliation in the region."[3] Certainly, the reconciliation talks between the KDP and the PUK did play an important role. However, this in itself would not have sufficed had the Kurdish national movement not reached critical mass and cohesion, enabling it to exploit the current favorable conditions to achieve its goals. In other words, pressure from below played an important role in the peacemaking process and in the Kurdish nation-building project.

While the Gulf War in 1991 cut the Kurds off from the center, the 2003 Iraq War brought them closer to it so that they became important players in the reshaping of post-Saddam Iraq. In one of his interviews, Mas'ud Barzani stated that, "after the fall of the [Baathi] regime, we the Kurds have safeguarded the unity of Iraq and to this day we are the main reason for Iraq's remaining unified."[4] As a matter of fact, the collapse of the Sunni center in Baghdad resulted in an unprecedented strengthening of the peripheries: factions residing in the outlying regions enhanced their positions at the expense of the central government and political forces from the periphery moved to Baghdad to become part of the new political elite. The Kurds epitomize this development. The systemic contradiction between the collapse of the Sunnis and the ascendancy of the periphery triggered a desperate attempt by the Sunnis to restore the status of the old Sunni center on the one hand, and to enhance the periphery's autonomy on the other. In fact, the weakness of the new center, despite US backing, contributes even further to the strengthening of the periphery.

The demise of the Baathi regime brought about another revolutionary change in the makeup of the government in Baghdad. For the first time in Iraqi history, two disenfranchised sections of society, the Kurds and the Shi'is, came together to forge an alliance that remained in force for three consecutive governments. This alliance signified the interdependence of the Kurds and the Shi'is, the dislodgement of the Sunni Arabs from their pivotal role in the state, and the newly acquired role of the Kurds as a balancing power between the Shi'is and the Sunnis. The Kurds' avowed secularism enabled them to rise above the Sunni-Shi'i sectarian war and, at times, to play the role of mediator. In fact, the Kurds ably used the Sunni-Shi'i strife to promote their own interests in the central government as well as in the KRG.

The leading role of the Kurds in the central government in Baghdad is manifested in various realms: vigorous participation in shaping the new constitution; an active role in the formation of governments; a mediatory role between rival parties in Baghdad; and the filling of key posts in the Iraqi center of power. The Kurds' bargaining leverage was already manifest in the interim constitution of March 2004, termed the Transitional Administrative Law. This law gave the Kurds de facto veto power over the permanent constitution since Article 61 stated that the permanent constitution would be "ratified if two-thirds of the voters in Iraq approve and if two-thirds of the voters in three or more governorates do not reject it."[5] Brendan O'Leary interprets this article as granting the Kurds the right of veto over the nature of the future federation. The law also recognizes Kurdish as an official language, alongside Arabic. But even though this right had already been granted to the Kurds by the Baath in March 1970, not everyone in Iraq was happy with the decision. One commentator remarked: "On what foundation did the legislators base themselves when they set the Kurdish language on the same level as Arabic? That is, with the mother tongue that the inhabitants of Iraq in their various communities and components have been speaking since the dawn of Islam?"[6]

As to the permanent constitution, which was approved in October 2005, the most important issues over which the Kurds managed to have a strong influence were the federative makeup of Iraq; the inclusion of controversial Clause 140, which called for a referendum over the disputed areas, chief among which was Kirkuk; and the toning down of the Islamic nature of the state through the declaration that Islam was *a* and not *the* foundation of the country's laws.[7] Herein lay the main problem because these issues have remained the main bone of contention between the Kurds and their partners in government.

By endorsing federalism the constitution in fact foreclosed the idea of a nation-state, which had been the founding concept of modern Iraq.[8] Little wonder, then, that the Sunnis rejected the idea of a federation and agreed to participate in the vote on the constitution only on condition that this issue would be reconsidered by the parliament that was to take office after the elections. In this context, it is interesting to note that the Sunnis felt comfortable accepting the idea of a federation between the Kurdish north and the rest of the country while they totally rejected the possibility that this arrangement would apply to the entire Shi'i region or any part of it.

The Kurds also have proved their competence as mediators between rival groupings in Iraq. When differences of opinion occurred regarding the constitution, the makeup of the government, or elections, it was the Kurds who put their weight behind resolving the disputes. For example, after the December 2005 elections, both Shi'i and Sunni leaders came to the Kurdish region to hold talks about the future government.[9] The same scenario was repeated in December 2010.[10] Taking pride in this new role, Barzani stated, "We [Kurds] had a prime role in the negotiation between the Sunnis and the Shiites." For his part Talabani declared, "The Kurds are fulfilling a true national role for the sake of preserving the unity of the state as a democratic, pluralistic, and unified Iraq, and will not, as was claimed after the fall of the previous regime, turn towards separatism."[11]

The Kurds' more crystallized objectives and orientation provided them with superior maneuverability and negotiating skills in the crucial moment when power was being redistributed in Baghdad. Hence, the Kurdish elite managed to secure a solid foothold in the Iraqi national government. Evidence of the sweeping change in their standing is the fact that five Kurdish leaders—including Mas'ud Barzani and Talabani—served on the Iraqi Governing Council, the provisional government of Iraq from 13 July 2003 to 1 June 2004. The council's ethnic and religious breakdown included thirteen Shi'is, five Sunni Arabs, and five Kurds, which meant that the latter two were put on an equal footing. Other important posts in Baghdad include that of president, which was filled by Talabani in two consecutive governments in April 2005 and December 2010;[12] that of foreign minister held by Hoshyar Zebari; and that of army chief of staff held by Babakr Zebari—the latter two since the establishment of the first Iraqi government in September 2003 and in the 2010 government. With regard to Babakr Zebari it is worth noting that the fact that he had quit the Iraqi Army in 1973 to serve in various command posts in the Peshmerga, most important during the 1991 intifada, did not prevent him from becoming Iraq's chief of staff. Another Kurdish role, of symbolic rather than practical importance, was that of the first two chief justices in Saddam Hussein's trial, both of whom were Kurds.

The Kurdish Bid for Self-Determination

On 11 December 2010 Mas'ud Barzani, the KRG president and the KDP leader, took the world by surprise at the opening session of the Thirteenth KDP Congress when he called for Kurdish self-determination. The boldness of the move was underscored by the presence of a number of guests whose interests would be directly affected by it: the Iraqi prime minister designate Nuri al-Maliki and the speaker of parliament Usama al-Nujayfi, Turkish and Iranian government representatives, and Kurdish delegates from neighboring countries. Surprisingly, Barzani's declaration went unchallenged by the non-Kurdish participants.[13] It is true that shortly afterward Mas'ud Barzani had to tone down his statement, but this did not detract from the Kurds' efforts to move forward.

Thus, simultaneously with their display of Iraqi patriotism and loyalty to the state, the Kurds continued to develop a separate Kurdish national identity in the Kurdish region that was based on independent state institutions. These parallel roles helped develop a kind of division of labor between Talabani, the president of Iraq, and Barzani, the president of the KRG. In the words of one observer, following the 2005 elections the PUK was forced to act in an "Iraqi" nationalist manner whereas the KDP moved toward a more "Kurdish" nationalist position.[14]

Although the Iraqi constitution speaks of a federal arrangement between the KRG and the other regions, in practice a quasi-state structure, rather than a more limited federative one, has developed in Kurdistan after the Iraq War. This is evidenced by the official terminology as well as by the language of the Kurdish media. For example, reporting on a meeting between President Mas'ud Barzani and a Baghdadi delegation, *Al-Ta'akhi* asserted that "decisions were taken to strengthen relations between the federal government and the government of the Kurdistan region."[15] With regard to terminology it should be noted, for example, that the Kurds made a point of using the term "the people of Kurdistan," which designated land and geography, rather than "the Kurdish people," which only referred to a group of people.

By the end of 2010, the KRG could boast of impressive achievements on the social, political, economic, and strategic levels, all of which serve to illustrate the degree of their independence from Baghdad. Politically speaking, in

May 2006 the Kurdish parliament voted for the unification of the KDP and PUK governments, a ceremony in which ambassadors from the United States, Great Britain, Russia, China, and even Iran participated.[16] The establishment of a single government enhanced the sense of unity among the Kurds, which also found expression on the symbolical level. During the period of harsh rivalry, each faction had adopted a distinct flag of its own—a yellow flag for the Barzanis and a green one for the Talabanis. After the reconciliation there was only one flag, the Kurdish banner flown in 1920 after the Treaty of Sèvres but suppressed later on in the Lausanne agreement in 1923. It should be noted that the Kurds refused to display the Saddam-era Iraqi flag, on which *Allah Akbar* (God is Great) was inscribed in Saddam's own handwriting, because they explained Saddam had committed genocide against the Kurds.[17] The Kurds later agreed to an Iraqi flag that did not have Saddam's handwriting inscribed on it.

Elections to the Kurdish parliament were held independently of the central government.[18] Thus, for example, the latest Kurdish elections took place in July 2009, while the general Iraqi elections (in which the Kurds also participated) took place in March 2010. The same departure marked the constitution. Indeed, the KRG had a draft constitution of its own that was endorsed by the Kurdish parliament in June 2009. Even though it has not yet been endorsed by the Kurdish people, it is interesting to analyze it, reflecting as it does the Kurds' general political aims.[19] In contrast to the highly controversial Iraqi constitution, which had been hastily drafted and endorsed in a short span of two years, the Kurdish constitution is less controversial, at least among the Kurds, since its creation required years of discussions and lengthy negotiations that lasted from 2002 until 2009.[20] The Kurdish constitution, which benefited from the advice of foreign constitutionalists and experts, is written in both Kurdish and Arabic.

One of the important clauses of the Kurdish constitution is Clause 7, which speaks about the right of "the people of Kurdistan-Iraq" to self-determination. Clause 2 lays claim to all the disputed areas as part of the "geographic and historic" Iraqi Kurdistan, including the province of Kirkuk and certain districts in three other provinces. However, it also states that the "political" borders of Iraqi Kurdistan would be determined by Article 140 of the Iraqi constitution. The Iraqi prime minister, Nuri al-Maliki, is reported to have opposed this clause, saying it hindered any real progress toward resolving the differences between Kurdistan and the federal government. And he even asked visiting US vice president Joe Biden in July 2009 to try to persuade Kurdish leaders to abrogate the constitution (see Map 16.1).[21]

Other clauses include proclaiming Kurdish and Arabic as the official languages in the region; having free tuition at all levels of education, including universities; keeping the Peshmerga as defense (*difa'iyya*) forces for protecting the region; allotting 30 percent of all parliamentary seats to women; and constitutionally determining the region's own flag, hymn, and national holiday (21 March), as well as the capital city, Erbil. It should be noted that the constitution

Map 16.1 Contested Areas in Northern Iraq

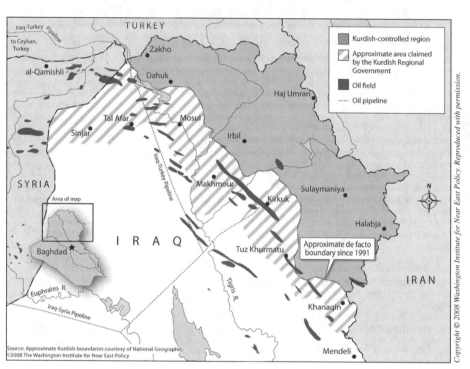

Source: Approximate Kurdish boundaries courtesy of National Geographic.
©2008 The Washington Institute for Near East Policy

regulates the official weekly gazette *Waqa'i' Kurdistan*, which started publications in 2009, and promulgated all new laws. It paralleled the Iraqi official gazette *Al-Waqa'i' al-'Iraqiyya.*

Also significant on the military level is the strengthening of the paramilitary force, the Peshmerga, which (together with the Kurdish security organization, Asayish) is the main body responsible for stability in the region.[22] The "green line" delimiting the borders of the Kurdistan region from the rest of Iraq continues to function as a real border, guarded by Peshmerga at the checkpoints.[23] Heading the Peshmerga force is the Ministry of Peshmerga Affairs, a euphemism for defense ministry. A Kurdish source maintained that cooperation with US troops has enhanced the training of the Peshmerga, thus justifying their depiction as a regular army. It maintained that, at least on the technical level, the Peshmerga possesses many of the characteristics of a regular army such as a well-defined internal hierarchy, symbolic and ceremonial systems, specialized training camps, and uniforms.[24] Estimates varied widely regarding the strength of the Peshmerga forces. However, the best estimate for 2010 seemed to have been that of the US Division-North, which estimated the Peshmerga forces at approximately 200,000, including the personnel that the KRG planned to pension off.[25]

In April 2009, the two branches of the Peshmerga (one loyal to the KDP and the other to the PUK) were officially united to be headed by minister Shaikh Ja'far Mustafa 'Ali. Yet many considered this move as merely a formal arrangement since the merger was far from complete.[26] Nevertheless, in spite of the differences within the KRG, all political parties seemed to have established common grounds for facing Baghdad, especially when they perceived that the special status of the Peshmerga was being questioned or when the interests of Iraqi Kurdistan came under threat.

In September 2006, the KRG established a Department of Foreign Relations at ministerial level, with a wide range of powers and responsibilities. However, in order not to antagonize the Arab partners in Baghdad, the KRG did not use the term *foreign minister*, but a euphemism and rather a clumsy one at that. It appeared, for example, on its official site as "the minister who leads the Kurdistan Regional Government Department of Foreign Relations." Falah Mustafa Bakir, who filled this post in the 2006 and 2009 governments, was described as "the chief architect of KRG foreign policy" because his department served as "the conduit between the KRG and the international community."[27] The Department of Foreign Relations is the main conduit between the KRG and offices maintained by foreign governments in Erbil. Many countries, including France, Germany, the Islamic Republic of Iran, the Russian Federation, and Turkey opened consulates general. In December 2010 Egypt became the first Arab country to open a consulate in Erbil, joining seventeen consulates from other countries. The Republic of Korea and Great Britain both maintain an embassy office in the region while Austria, the Czech Republic, Greece, and Italy have economic or trade offices. Japan, Denmark, the Netherlands, Spain, and Sweden appointed honorary consuls to the region, and the United States is represented by its regional reconstruction team.

As part and parcel of its policy of expanding international relations, the KRG has established representation in several countries, including the United States, Great Britain, France, Iran, the European Union, and surprisingly Baghdad itself. No less important is the fact that the KRG managed to send representatives to the UN as part of the Iraqi delegation. Members of the delegation attended the 63rd session of the UN General Assembly committee meetings in September 2008 and met with diplomats and UN officials with the support of the Iraqi Mission to the UN. This was the second time that the KRG was included in a visiting Iraqi delegation. The KRG delegation was led by Bakir and also Dilshad Miran, KRG representative to Baghdad.

Economically, the degree of independence that the Kurds have managed to achieve in post-Saddam Iraq has gone a long way toward explaining their success in other realms. While in the last years of Baathi rule reconstruction of the economy and of the infrastructure in the Arab part of Iraq was brought to a halt, it was accelerated in the Kurdish region. This trend has received a further boost in post-Saddam Iraq. In fact, underlying the swift changes in the Kurdish society and polity was a dynamic economy. For the first time in Kurdish history, two international airports (in Erbil and Sulaymaniyya) were built, constituting an important turning point for the Kurdish national project. The airports enabled the Kurds to at least partially overcome their dependence on the center caused by their lack of access to the sea and to broaden their external ties on an unprecedented scale. Thus, direct flights from different parts of the world to Erbil and Sulaymaniyya were at times even more frequent than flights to the capital of Baghdad. In 2009, there were eighty such direct flights per week.[28]

The relatively stable Kurdish region attracted many companies and entrepreneurs, most importantly in the oil industry. This trend received a boost in 2007 when the KRG passed a petroleum law under which it signed oil and gas exploration- and production-sharing agreements, binding for twenty-five years and worth $5 billion, with more than thirty-five foreign companies. Calling the contracts illegal, the oil ministry in Baghdad blacklisted the companies that had signed them. For his part, Ashti Hawrami, the KRG minister for natural resources, criticized the "outdated practices" of the federal oil ministry, which he said had spent some $8 billion over three years while still failing to increase production. Contrasting this with the KRG's achievements he stated, "In a short period of time we have managed to create some real opportunities for the benefit of all Iraqis."[29]

In October 2009 in reaction to Baghdad's criticism, the KRG suspended crude oil exports through the Iraqi government-controlled pipeline, which was pumping crude from the Kirkuk oil fields to Turkey's Mediterranean terminal of Ceyhan.[30] Concurrently, it set up three licensed oil refineries in the region. The KRG authorities admitted that there were also illegal refineries in Erbil, Sulaymaniyya, and Duhok.[31] Another project dealt with the conversion of reservoir gas to electricity, thereby solving a substantial part of the Kurdistan region's power needs.[32]

In an interview with Falah Mustafa Bakir, he stated that a free-market economy was being promoted as the driving force behind Kurdistan's economy. He further revealed that the KRG had licensed more than 160 projects, valued at more than $16 billion.[33] In 2004 the Kurdish region, which came to be called the "northern gateway for Iraq," launched the yearly Erbil international fair that attracted companies worldwide. The major companies active in the KRG are Turkish, Iranian, Chinese, Malaysian, Lebanese, Gulf Arab, US, European, and Australian.[34]

The *New York Times* maintains that Turkey is ahead of all other countries in projecting so-called soft power. Turkey asserts its influence not only through business, but also through culture and education. Reportedly about 15,000 Turks work in Erbil and other parts of the KRG, and more than 700 Turkish companies make up two-thirds of all foreign companies in the region. The twenty-six-lane checkpoint of Ibrahim Khalil, through which 1,500 trucks pass daily, brings Turkish building materials, clothes, furniture, food, and other materials that fill the shops in northern Iraq. Travel requirements were lifted, and the consulate in

Erbil issues as many as 300 visas a day. In addition, Turkey sponsors numerous cultural activities; for instance, it opened a branch of Bilkent University in Erbil. A Turkish religious movement operates nineteen schools in the region, with 5,500 students—Arabs, Turkmens, and Kurds. Turkey still keeps as many as 1,500 troops in the KRG, which enables it, as a senior US official put it, "to quite effectively strike" out at the Kurdish Turkish rebels.[35]

Kurdish cities have grown rapidly, with new high-rise buildings, up-to-date supermarkets, sports centers, and banks. In 2001 the KRG established an independent Kurdish Central Bank while the number of public and private sector banks has also mushroomed.[36] In 2008 the United States opened a university in Sulaymaniyya—not in Baghdad—which is telling both of the Bush administration's priorities and of the relative stability of the Kurdish region.[37] Altogether, by 2010 seven universities were operating in the KRG.

The Challenges Ahead

To balance this somewhat rosy picture, one must point out that the KRG still faces serious challenges, both internally and externally. On the home front, it needs to articulate a clear-cut vision regarding the future of the Kurds in Iraq. The idea of federalism that it adopted has not suited the aspirations and expectations of the Kurds, as shown by an impromptu referendum where the majority of Kurds supported independence.[38] Similarly, in the long run the two-pronged state building in the KRG and in Baghdad could collide and weaken the Kurdish project.

The democratizing experience remains a fledgling enterprise and the KRG has yet to turn it into a robust one while pretending to develop it into a model for the rest of Iraq. Freedom of expression is far from guaranteed, as journalists are quite frequently jailed or even killed. On the social level tribalism, nepotism, corruption, and sexism are rampant, and it is one of the KRG's greatest challenges to fight these social problems in order to establish a more progressive society and polity. Similarly, although the two rival camps of the KDP and PUK have taken important steps to unify the administration and governmental institutions, deep down rivalry and competition are very much alive.

In addition, the KRG has yet to settle differences with the Baghdad federal government over some major issues, including: the type of federation to be established in Iraq (i.e., the division of power between the region and the federal government); the distribution of resources; the right to sign oil deals with companies; and, most importantly, the chronic problem of Kirkuk and the territorial delineation of the KRG. The unyielding Kurdish stance with regard to the inclusion of the oil-rich district of Kirkuk in their region has been interpreted by Baghdad as a clear indication of their aspirations to achieve economic and, in the long run, political independence. Such fears even further exacerbate the problem.

Thus having been a major bone of contention between the Kurds and various Iraqi regimes, Kirkuk once again, and even more forcefully, has emerged as a major problem that could break the post-Saddam coalition governments and rip apart alliances with the Shi'is or the Sunnis.[39] On the whole, the Kurdish leaders' insistence on referring to Kirkuk as Quds al-Akrad, Jerusalem of the Kurds,[40] promises to turn it into another thorny problem, like Jerusalem.

Regionally speaking, although the KRG has successfully managed to contain its giant neighbors and even to develop strong economic relations with them, it still has to cope with ongoing challenges. Turkey, Iran, and Syria with their large Kurdish minorities remain extremely fearful of the possibility that the KRG could become a model for their own Kurds. Hence, they have done their best to prevent it from crossing the threshold toward strong autonomy. Meanwhile, the debate over Kirkuk has come to include Iraq's neighbors, chief among which is Turkey, which has threatened to interfere if the Kurds include it in their region. Mas'ud Barzani replied to the threat by stating that Kirkuk was "an Iraqi city with a Kurdish identity" and that, if Turkey interfered in Iraqi affairs, the Kurds of Iraq would interfere "for the benefit of 30 millions Kurds in Turkey."[41]

On the international level, although the Kurds have managed to achieve visibility in the outside world and to develop diplomatic and economic relations with various world countries, there is much left to be desired. They do not have permanent representatives of their own at the UN, nor does any state recognize their entity or their right to self-determination. In this sense, they are far behind the Palestinians.

All of these challenges notwithstanding, on balance the general trend seems more promising for the Kurds than at any time in the past. The weak national movement of the past century has become more robust as it embraces all walks of Kurdish society. The economy, which was in shambles, now flourishes despite considerable difficulties such as high unemployment. The younger generation has access to schools, colleges, and universities that teach in their mother tongue. Although democratic norms have yet to take root, they nonetheless have made some important strides forward. If relativity is a measure for success, then the Kurds have done well on all three levels: in comparison to their own situation only a decade earlier; in comparison to other Kurds in Greater Kurdistan; and, finally, in comparison to Arab Iraq.

In 2005 the Kurds launched an advertising campaign in the United States, called "Kurdistan—The Other Iraq," to attract tourists and investors to the region. It seems that the KRG has indeed become another Iraq.

Notes

1. Complete withdrawal of US troops was completed at the end of 2011.
2. *Al-Ittihad* (Baghdad, weekly), 27 January 2005.

3. *Al-Mada* (Baghdad, daily) 17 December 2006.

4. Al-'Arabiyya (TV channel), 9 April 2007.

5. Brendan O'Leary, "Power Sharing, Federation and Federacy," in *The Future of Kurdistan in Iraq*, eds. Brendan O'Leary, John McGarry, and Khaled Salih (Philadelphia: University of Pennsylvania Press, 2005), pp. 47–48.

6. Dahham Muhammad al-'Azzawi, "Al-Ihtilal al-Amriki wa-Mustaqbal al-Mas'ala al-Kurdiyya fi al-'Iraq," *Shu'un 'Arabiyya* 125 (2005): 188.

7. For an analysis of the constitution and the Kurdish role in drafting it, see Andrew Arato, *Constitution Making Under Occupation: The Politics of Imposed Revolution in Iraq* (New York: Columbia University Press, 2009), pp. 205–249.

8. Even though they did not say it in so many words, the founders and the leaders of the Iraqi state wanted it to be a sort of Arab nation-state.

9. At the same time, it is important to recall that the Kurds were the ones who began to challenge Ja'fari's candidacy to serve as prime minister after the December 2005 elections. The main reason was Ja'fari's opposition to Kurdish claims on Kirkuk.

10. The Egyptian foreign minister visited Kurdistan in December 2010 to open a consulate there and expressed his appreciation of President Mas'ud Barzani's initiative to help form a new Iraqi government. He said that the initiative "brought different Iraqi political forces closer to each other and led to the formation of a government of national-partnership that comprised all political forces in the country." See Kurdistan Regional Government, "Egypt's Foreign Minister Opens First Arab Consulate in Erbil," 29 December 2009, http://krg.org.

11. Unrepresented Nations and Peoples Organization, "Kurdistan: Identity Denied in the Iraqi Constitution," 3 March 2006, www.unpo.org; *Al-Usbu' al-'Arabi* (Beirut, weekly), 9 January 2006.

12. It should be stressed, however, that unlike in the Baathi period, the president in post-Saddam Iraq had symbolic rather than effective powers.

13. Ten days later, however, 'Abd al-Karim Zaydan, a professor of Islamic law, issued a fatwa (religious ruling) according to which it was permitted to kill anyone who called for the dismemberment of Iraq or called for the independence of Kurdistan. http://almoslim.net/node/138489 (accessed 12 January 2012).

14. Gareth R. V. Stansfield, "Finding a Dangerous Equilibrium: Internal Politics in Iraqi Kurdistan—Parties, Tribes and Ethnicity Reconsidered," in *The Kurds: Nationalism and Politics*, eds. Faleh A. Jabar and Dawod Hosham (London: Saqi, 2006), p. 261. Mas'ud Barzani was elected president of the KRG in 2005 by the Kurdish parliament and in 2009 in the KRG general elections.

15. *Al-Ta'akhi* (Baghdad, daily), 12 July 2007. It is like saying that the cities of Washington and Los Angeles decided to strengthen their relations. Qobat Talabani, Jalal Talabani's son and the Kurdistan delegate in the United States, stated that federalism was the minimum that the Kurds would agree to. *Al-Hawadith* (London, weekly), 9 September 2005.

16. *The Economist* (London, weekly), 13 May 2006. *Al-Hawadith*, 9 September 2005, reported that they had started opening embassies abroad.

17. Mas'ud Barzani was more outspoken than others about this decision. See *Al-Mada*, 4 September 2006. Another justification that he gave was that the constitution stipulated the introduction of a new flag. Barzani was willing to raise the flag that had been in use during the Qasim period. The Kurds look at this period as a golden era in comparison to the Baathi era. See *Al-Ahali* (Baghdad, weekly), 15 February 2006.

18. From 2005, the central government became known as the federal government.

19. For the full text, see Kurdistan Regional Government, "Draft Constitution," 22 June 2009, www.krg.org. The Kurdish constitution was controversial among Arab partners, who regarded it as paving the way for separatism. Hence the KRG was forced to cancel the referendum on the issue, which was scheduled to take place in August 2009, together with the elections in the region.

20. Erbil—Capital of Kurdistan, "Constitution, Federal Kurdistan Region-Iraq," www.erbil-capital.org.

21. *ABC News This Week with Christiane Amanpour*, "This Week Transcript: Exclusive: Vice President Joe Biden," 5 July 2009, abcnews.go.com.

22. Mas'ud Barzani referred to the Peshmerga as an organized army rather than a militia. *Al-Mushahid al-Siyasi* (London, weekly), 11 June 2006.

23. David Romano, *The Kurdish Nationalist Movement: Opportunity, Mobilization and Identity* (Cambridge: Cambridge University Press, 2008), p. 220; *Al-Sharq al-Awsat* (London, daily), 1 June 2006.

24. Kurd Net, "Who Are the Peshmerga? The Army of Kurdistan," 20 May 2010, www.ekurd.net.

25. *Defense Industry Daily*, "Iraqi Security Forces Order of Battle 2010–04," 12 April 2010, www.defenseindustrydaily.com.

26. Kurd Net, "Who Are the Peshmerga? The Army of Kurdistan."

27. Kurdistan Regional Government, "Minister Falah Mustafa Bakir—Head of the Department of Foreign Relations," 20 November 2009, www.krg.org.

28. www.ifpexpo.com/exhibition_overview.php?id=113 (accessed May 2009).

29. Kurdistan Regional Government, "Natural Resources Minister Urges Lawmakers to Pass Fair Transparent Revenue Sharing Law at UNAMI Conference," 25 April 2009, www.krg.org.

30. *APS Diplomat Operations in Oil Diplomacy*, 27 September 2010, quoted in The Free Library, "The KRG-RWE Agreements," www.thefreelibrary.com. Already in September 2006, the Kurdish government threatened separation from the state if it was not given a free hand in signing agreements of its own with companies willing to drill in the Kurdish area. *Al-Zaman* (London, daily), 23 October 2006.

31. *Al-Sharq al-Awsat* (English edition), "Iraqi Kurdistan Region Government Denies Crude Oil Smuggled to Iran," 14 July 2010, www.asharq-e.com. See the speech of Prime Minister Barham Salih at the London Trade and Investment Conference, Kurdistan Regional Government, "PM Salih's Speech at London Trade and Investment Conference," 17 June 2010, www.krg.org.

32. Kurdistan Regional Government, "Natural Resources Minister Urges Lawmakers to Pass Fair Transparent Revenue Sharing Law at UNAMI Conference."

33. *Kurdish Herald*, "Kurdistan's Economy: Its Potential and Its Challenges," 21 September 2009, www.krg.org.

34. *Al-Zaman*, 23 October 2006.

35. *New York Times* (New York, daily), 4 January 2011; and www.bilkenterbil.com/.

36. Several private banks were opened in 2006. Mariwan Hama-Saeed, "Kurdish Banks Slowly Win Trust," 4 May 2006, www.krg.org.

37. The foundation stone was laid by Talabani at the end of 2005. A sum of $250 million was earmarked for education in that region. *Al-Mada*, 13 December 2005.

38. According to *Al-Hawadith*, 9 September 2005, 95 percent of the Kurds were in favor of separation (*infisal*).

39. It is claimed that between the years 1991 and 2003, the Baath regime exiled 300,000 Kurds from the Kirkuk area and promulgated a law forbidding the teaching of

the Kurdish language in this area in order to Arabize it and pull out the rug from under Kurdish demands that the Kirkuk area be included in their autonomous zone. *Al-Siyasa al-Duwaliyya* (Cairo, quarterly), no. 162, October 2005, p. 73.

40. *Al-Watan al-'Arabi*, 14 March 2007.

41. Al-'Arabiyya, 9 April 2007.

Part 4

Conclusion

17

"No Friends but the Moutains" Reconsidered

For the greater part of the twentieth century the Kurds of Iraq staged rebellion after rebellion against the central government in Baghdad, while at other times they fought among themselves. Thus, the Kurds were perceived as the main destabilizing force in Iraq. This ongoing struggle witnessed many ups and downs—terrible defeats as well as more successful episodes. By the turn of the twentieth century, however, the Kurds of Iraq had managed for the first time in their history to become an entity—the Kurdistan region headed by the Kurdistan Regional Government (KRG). And after the Iraq War of 2003, the KRG became a quasi-state. It also became a model of stability and success for the rest of Iraq, which was being torn apart by civil war, fratricide, and chronic instability. Likewise, the KRG became a prototype for Kurds in three surrounding countries—Iran, Turkey, and Syria. In this book, I have attempted to answer the following questions: What turned the tide for the Kurds from their twentieth-century pattern of failing national endeavors? To what extent were the wars and civil strife a conduit to Kurdish nation building and state building? What caused the difference between the KRG and the rest of Iraq, and between the KRG and the Kurdish communities in the surrounding countries? What role did the Kurds play in the Iraqi state-building project?

The amazing story of the Kurdish revival in Iraq, following the genocidal war of 1988–1989, very much resembles that of the Jews following the Holocaust. Within the first four years after that war, the Kurds managed to launch an ambitious project for Kurdish nation building and state building, which competed with the all-Iraqi narrative. And although the Kurdish national project encountered enormous internal and external obstacles, the general trend was positive from the Kurds' point of view.

Notwithstanding the fact that the Kurdish national project began to take shape only after the 1991 Gulf War, its success was in fact achieved through the accumulated fruit of eighty-five years of ongoing struggle. As such, it consti-

315

tuted a challenge to the centralized nation-state of the post-Ottoman era into which the Kurds did not really fit. The Kurdish project thus threatened to undermine the geopolitical Iraqi order that had been established in the aftermath of World War I.

To understand the Kurdish feat at the turn of the twenty-first century, it must be considered in the general context of Iraq's structural problems, which only deepened over time. One of the most important hurdles was the fact that Iraq had been plagued, at different times and to different degrees, by competing national allegiances or identities: Iraqi territorial nationalism, pan-Arab nationalism, and Kurdish nationalism.[1] The existence of one territorial framework for nearly a century led to the development of an Iraqi local patriotism that distinguished Iraq from the neighboring Arab states, thus gradually eroding the allegiance to pan-Arabism even among its leading champions, the Arab Sunnis. It did not, however, blur the primordial identities and ties within Iraq. Neither did it strengthen Iraq's internal cohesion. Accordingly, from the end of World War I onward, there were ongoing identity clashes between all-Iraqi nationalism and Kurdish nationalism. The policies of the various governments in Baghdad, especially that of the Baath toward the Kurds, only served to exacerbate these clashes.

The longevity of the Baath regime, which remained in power for thirty-five years, allowed for experimentation with the Kurdish problem. The Baath adopted a wide range of well-tried strategies for solving this national minority problem. These ranged from pluralism to high-handed control; assimilation; transfer; and, ultimately, genocide. The implementation of pluralism, manifested by autonomy, seemed doomed to failure from the start—not only because the regime regarded autonomy as a tactical rather than a strategic solution, but also because Kurdish autonomy was diametrically opposed to the totalitarian system of government at the center. Indeed, under the slogan of autonomy, the Baath invoked the harshest measures ever taken by any Iraqi regime against the Kurds and their national movement.

If we were to evaluate the balance of power between the Baath and the Kurdish national movement at the end of the Iran-Iraq War in 1988, we would by necessity reach the conclusion that the Baath was the incontestable victor at that historical juncture. While the Iraqi Army became unprecedentedly strong, comprising about fifty divisions equipped with the most lethal weapons,[2] the Kurdish movement remained impoverished in terms of means, organization, and external relations. The Kurds thus failed to make headway as a political power in the international arena, remaining a mere item in newspaper headlines. Most importantly, the Baath succeeded in maintaining the state's territorial integrity while the Kurds moved further away from the goal of genuine autonomy.

However, the Baath's was but a Pyrrhic victory. Preserving the territorial integrity of the state came at a cost: the alienation of the Kurds from the Iraqi state and the bolstering of their separate national identity. Moreover, the various strategies used by the regime against the Kurds not only failed to enhance coexistence between the Baath and Kurds, but further deepened their mutual threat perceptions. Similarly, notwithstanding its extreme weakness, the Kurdish national movement still had one weapon in its arsenal; namely, the enmity between Iraq and its neighbors—Iran, Syria, and Kuwait. The Gordian knot between the Kurdish domestic problem and Iraq's external problems ensured that, whenever Iraq faced an external problem, the Kurdish national movement experienced a resurgence.

The Iraqi invasion of Kuwait in 1990 and the ensuing 1991 Gulf War make a case in point. As the state became extremely weakened by these developments, the Kurds took full advantage of this window of opportunity to advance their own project for state building. Indeed, the correlation between the decay of the Iraqi Baathi state on the one hand and the strengthening of the Kurds on the other has gone a long way to explain the huge transformations that Iraq's sociopolitical map has undergone over the past two decades.

The severe sanctions imposed on Iraq by the UN in the aftermath of the Gulf War gave a significant boost to the Kurds on both an ideological and a practical level. In 1992 for the first time in their history, the Kurds advanced the agenda of a federative state rather than mere autonomy, believing that the international atmosphere was ripe for granting tacit support to such a project. Concurrently the Kurds established an autonomous government, which began to assume all of the attributes of a separate entity that clearly distinguished it from the Iraqi state. Another crucial matter was the external aid that started pouring into the Kurdish region while the central government continued to be paralyzed by the embargo.[3]

The fall of the Baath in 2003, to which the Kurds contributed no small part, was another crucial historic turning point. It ushered in a new era in the history of the Kurdish quasi-state and of the Iraqi state itself, both of which could be depicted as states in the making. Indeed, the Kurdish project seemed to have a certain advantage over the Iraqi one. While the all-Iraqi national project had for some time been in a state of paralysis, the fortunes of the Kurdish national project appeared brighter than at any time in the past. The achievements of the Kurdish national project on the ground thus made it almost impossible to turn back the tide. With Baghdad lacking the air force to impose a military solution and with the Kurdish entity having become a robust quasi-state, it is difficult to see how the Iraqi state could go back to the twentieth-century model of a centralized unitary state. As the cards were being reshuffled, the vision of a nation-state went bankrupt in Iraq. Instead, there was an accelerating trend toward transforming Iraq into a quasi-binational state or a unique kind of federation in which the Kurdish region acquired more and more power.

The sweeping developments on the Kurdish scene reflected the crystal-lization of a more mature Kurdish ethnonationalism. In this the Kurds joined other ethnonational groups throughout the world, which became more assertive at the end of the Cold War and after the collapse of the Soviet Union. As far as the Kurds were concerned, another important transformation took place; that is, one in the Kurdish psyche. The Kurds began to free themselves of their own self-perception as an eternal victim lacking allies—a perception that was en-capsulated in the famous saying, "no friends but the mountains." The Kurds' more assertive stance had far-reaching implications in their policymaking, es-pecially the ability to develop autonomous relations with the outside world and to cultivate friends of sorts even from within their landlocked region.

Another important development on the Kurdish domestic scene was that, although Kurdish society continued to be plagued by tribalism, the Kurdish polity did manage to find a modus vivendi between the old framework of trib-alism and the newer one of nationalism. The case of the Iraqi Kurds proves that nation building can in fact coexist with tribalism, exactly as is the case with Arab states, where the political framework helps contain the negative impact of tribalism on nationalism. One such evidence of coexistence after the 2003 war was that the Kurds managed to present a unified front when facing Baghdad. This represented a clear departure from the past when the tribal card was ably used by different governments in Baghdad, as well as by other states, to weaken the Kurds and split their ranks.

Linked to this was the democratizing process that began in the KRG, a decade earlier than in the center of the country. As a matter of fact the process has been agonizing, marked by the struggle for power and a civil war that sapped the region's human and economic resources. It has also been marred by negative phenomena such as corruption, nepotism, clientelism, and partisanism. Still, there are signs that organizations of civil society have begun to have their say in the politics of the region. The education system, which received a huge boost, is another encouraging development from the Kurdish point of view. Is-lamism, which began making headway in the region, is still held in check com-pared to the Arab part of Iraq. The emergence of a third party, the Gorran, which competed successfully with the KDP and the PUK in the 2009 elections, also energized the democratic process as it energetically fought the negative phe-nomena mentioned above. Gorran's platform called for social justice; the insti-tutionalization of the separation of powers within the KRG; limitations on KDP and PUK powers over the government, the judicial system, and parliament; and fighting corruption.

On the regional level developments in the KRG have had far-reaching im-plications, not just for the Iraqi state itself, but also for the Kurds in Greater Kurdistan and the countries surrounding Iraq. The Kurdish experiment in Iraq has energized the other Kurdish communities, especially in Turkey where they too have started to press for a broad autonomy. Similarly, a number of Kurds from Greater Kurdistan came to join the KRG to learn from its experience and turn it into a springboard for their activities back home. Thus, transborder influences have become more manifest than ever. Altogether, there is a growing potential for changing the strategic configuration of Greater Kurdistan.

In addition, transstate influences between the four countries sharing greater Kurdistan present a mirror image of these developments. Strategies and tactics used by a certain state against its own Kurdish community have been emulated by the other states. These include denial of a Kurdish identity by prohibiting the use of the Kurdish language and the observation of unique Kurdish customs; the transfer of Kurds from their native soil to other areas; the formation of a security belt to prevent contact and support from one Kurdish community to another; and the use of brutal force with a view toward destroying the infrastructure of the region and frustrating the attempts to develop Kurdish nationalism. However, all of these policies have proved futile because they have only encouraged Kurdish nationalism, certainly in Iraqi Kurdistan.

To conclude, the juxtaposition of different domestic, regional, and international factors have made possible the Kurds' leap forward into post-Saddam Iraq. Their relative internal cohesion and the development of the Kurdish ethnie into a nation are the key to understanding this phenomenon. The collapse of the Iraqi nation-state model and the shift of emphasis from the struggle between the two Arab-Kurdish national movements to the Islamic Sunni-Shiʻi struggle were also crucial facilitating factors. The Kurds' strength has been highlighted against the weakness of the Arab part of Iraq, which has enabled them to fulfill a crucial role in Iraq's state building.

While World War I established the old Iraqi order, another war—more than seven decades later—helped undermine it. And while one great power, Britain, established the old order there was a need for another great power, the United States, to help shake it up. Certainly, the United States did not have such an agenda in mind. On the contrary, it kept emphasizing the need for preventing the dismemberment of Iraq and preserving its unity. However, its actions willy-nilly culminated in the exact opposite. It seems therefore that the far-reaching strategic changes in the region, which went hand in hand with the maturing of the Kurdish national movement, ultimately have been the enablers of a broad Kurdish autonomy.

The Kurdish poet Hazar eloquently describes the Kurdish predicament in the following words: "The Kurdish people is like a dervish. It spins around and around, searching for someone to lead it to the Garden of Eden." The Kurds' Garden of Eden is a state of their own. They have not reached that garden yet, but with the emergence of the Kurdish quasi-state in Iraq they are closer to it than at any time in the past century.

Notes

1. See Sherko Kirmanj, "The Construction of the Iraqi State and the Question of National Identity," PhD thesis, University of South Australia, 2010, pp. 1–18.

2. GlobalSecurity.org, "Iraqi Army," www.globalsecurity.org.

3. For a thorough discussion of the importance of external aid, see Denise Natali, *The Kurdish Quasi-State* (Syracuse, NY: Syracuse University Press, 2010).

Bibliography

Abd al-Jabbar, Faleh. "Why the Uprisings Failed." *Middle East Report*, no. 176 (1992): 12.

'Aflaq, Michel. *Nuqtat al-Bidaya*. Beirut: Al-Mu'assasa al-'Arabiyya lil-Dirasat wal-Nashr, 1974.

Adamson, David. *The Kurdish War*. London: Allen & Unwin, 1964.

Adelman, Howard. "Humanitarian Intervention: The Case of the Kurds." *International Journal of Refugee Law* 4, no. 1 (1992): 4–38.

Ahmad, Sabir 'Ali. *Al-Qadhdhafi wal-Qadiyya Al-Kurdiyya*. N.p.: Dar al-Multaqa lil-Nashr, 1991.

Amnesty International Report, 1975–1976. London: Amnesty International, 1976.

Anderson, Jon Lee. "Mr. Big." *The New Yorker*, 5 February 2007.

Anderson, Liam, and Gareth Stansfield. *Crisis in Kirkuk: The Ethnopolitics of Conflict and Compromise*. Philadelphia: University of Pennsylvania Press, 2009.

Andrews, David, ed. *The Lost Peoples of the Middle East*. Salisbury, NC: Documentary Publications, 1982.

Anonymous. *Dawr al-Jaysh al-'Iraqi Fi Harb Tishrin 1973*. Beirut: al-Mu'assasa al-'Arabiyya lil-Dirasat wal-Nashr, 1975.

———. *The Iraqi Army in the Yom Kippur War*. In Hebrew, Tel Aviv: Ma'arakhot, 1986.

———. "The War in Kurdistan." *Strategic Survey* 75, no. 1 (1974): 82–84.

———. *Ara' 'Arabiyya hawla al-Qadiyya al-Kurdiyya*. Damascus: Al-Ittihad al-Watani al-Kurdistani, 1993.

Arato, Andrew. *Constitution Making Under Occupation: The Politics of Imposed Revolution in Iraq*. New York: Columbia University Press, 2009.

Arberry, Arthur J. *The Koran Interpreted*. London: Allen & Unwin, 1955.

Asasard, Farid. *Al-Mas'ala al-Kurdiyya ba'd Qanun Idarat al-Dawla*. Cairo: Maktabat Madbuli, 2006.

Astarjian, Henry D. *The Struggle for Kirkuk*. Westport, CT: Praeger Security International, 2007.

Al-'Azzawi, Dahham Muhammad. "Al-Ihtilal al-Amriki wa-Mustaqbal al-Mas'ala al-Kurdiyya fi al-'Iraq." *Shu'un 'Arabiyya* 125 (2005): 174–198.

Baram, Amatzia, and Barry Rubin, eds. *Iraq's Road to War*. New York: St. Martin's Press, 1993.

Barir, Idan. "This Is Our Story: The Yezidi Cultural Movement and the Processes of a

Collective Identity Constructing Among the Yezidis in Kurdistan and the Diaspora." Master's thesis, Tel Aviv University, 2009 (in Hebrew).

Barrak, Fadil. *Mustafa al-Barzani: Al-Ustura wal-Haqiqa*. Baghdad: Dar al-Shu'un al-Thaqafiyya al-'Amma, 1989.

Barth, Fredrick. "Introduction." In *Ethnic Groups and Boundaries*, ed. Fredrick Barth. Long Grove, IL: Waveland Press, 1998, pp. 9–37.

Barzani, Mas'ud. *Al-Barzani wal-Haraka al-Kurdiyya al-Taharruriyya*, 3 vols. Erbil, 2002.

Barzani, Nechirvan. "Perspective of Nechirvan Barzani, Prime Minister, Kurdistan Regional Government." In *Kurdish Identity: Human Rights and Political Status*, eds. Charles G. MacDonald and Carole A. O'Leary (Gainesville: University Press of Florida, 2007), pp. 15–20.

Batatu, Hanna. "Iraq's Underground Shi'a Movements: Characteristics, Causes and Prospects." *Middle East Journal* 35, no. 4 (1981): 578–594.

———. *The Old Social Classes and the Revolutionary Movements of Iraq*. Princeton, NJ: Princeton University Press, 1978.

al-Bazzaz, Sa'd. *Harb Talid Ukhra*. Amman: Al-Ahliyya lil-Nashr wal-Tawzi', 1992.

Bengio, Ofra. "Iraq." In *Middle East Record (MER) 1968*, ed. Daniel Dishon (Jerusalem: Israel Universities Press, 1977), pp. 505–532.

———. "Iraq's Shi'a and Kurdish Communities: From Resentment to Revolt." In *Iraq's Road to War*, eds. Amatzia Baram and Barry Rubin (New York: St. Martin's Press, 1993), pp. 51–66.

———. *The Turkish-Israeli Relationship: Changing Ties of Middle Eastern Outsiders*. New York: Palgrave Macmillan, 2004.

———. "Women in Iraq Between Tradition and Revolution." In *Women in the Middle East: Between Tradition and Change*, ed. Ofra Bengio (in Hebrew) (Tel Aviv: Moshe Dayan Center of Middle Eastern and African Studies, 2004), pp. 95–109.

Benjamin, Charles. "The Kurdish Nonstate Nation." In *Nonstate Nations in International Politics*, ed. Judy S. Bertelsen (New York: Praeger Publishers, 1977), pp. 69–97.

Ben-Zvi, Varda. *Middle East Record 1969–1970*. Tel Aviv: Tel Aviv University, 1977.

Bertelsen, Judy S. "Introduction." In *Nonstate Nations in International Politics: Comparative System Analyses*, ed. Judy S. Bertelsen (New York: Praeger, 1977), pp. 1–5.

———. *Nonstate Nations in International Politics: Comparative System Analyses*. New York: Praeger, 1977.

Betrosian, Wahram. *Siyasat Turkiyya Tujah Kurdistan al-'Iraq wa Amerika*. Duhok: Duhok University, 2008.

Bilci, Mücahit. "Black Turks, White Turks: On the Three Requirements of Turkish Citizenship." *Insight Turkey* 11, no. 3 (2009): 23–35.

Black, George. *Genocide in Iraq: The Anfal Campaign Against the Kurds*. Washington, DC: Human Rights Watch, 1993.

Blau, Joyce. "Refinement and Oppression of Kurdish Language." In *The Kurds: Nationalism and Politics*, eds. Faleh A. Jabar and Dawod Hosham (London: Saqi, 2006), pp. 103–113.

Al-Botani, 'Abd al-Fattah 'Ali. *Dirasat wa Mabahith fi Ta'rikh al-Kurd wal-'Iraq al-Mu'asir*. Erbil: Hajji Hashim, 2007.

Bozarslan, Hamit. "Tribal Asabiyya and Kurdish Politics: A Socio-historical Perspective." In *The Kurds: Nationalism and Politics*, eds. Faleh A. Jabar and Dawod Hosham (London: Saqi, 2006), pp.130–147.

———. *Violence in the Middle East*. Princeton: Marcus Weiner, 2004.

Chaliand, Gérard, ed. *A People Without a Country: The Kurds and Kurdistan.* London: Zed Press, 1980.

Chandrasekaran, Rajiv. *Imperial Life in the Emerald City.* New York: Alfred A. Knopf, 2007.

Charountaki, Mariana. *The Kurds and US Foreign Policy: International Relations in the Middle East Since 1945.* London: Routledge, 2011.

Clarry, Stafford. "Iraqi Kurdistan: The Humanitarian Program." In *Kurdish Identity: Human Rights and Political Status,* eds. Charles G. MacDonald and Carole A. O'Leary (Gainesville: University Press of Florida, 2007), pp.149–155.

Collier, Paul. *Breaking the Conflict Trap: Civil War and Development Policy.* Washington, DC: World Bank; New York: Oxford University Press, 2003.

Confino, Michael, and Shimon Shamir, eds. *The U.S.S.R and the Middle East.* Jerusalem: Israel Universities Press, 1973.

Cordesman, Anthony H. *Iran and Iraq: The Threat from the Northern Gulf.* Boulder, CO: Westview Press, 1994.

Cottam, Martha L., and Richard W. Cottam. *Nationalism and Politics: The Political Behavior of Nation States.* Boulder: Lynne Rienner, 2001.

Dann, Uriel. "The Communist Movement in Iraq Since 1963." In *The U.S.S.R and the Middle East,* eds. Michael Confino and Shimon Shamir (Jerusalem: Israel Universities Press, 1973), pp. 377–395.

———. *Iraq Under Qassem: A Political History, 1958–1963.* New York: Praeger, 1969.

Davis, Eric. *Memories of State: Politics, History, and Collective Identity in Modern Iraq.* Berkeley: University of California Press, 2005.

Dinstein, Yoram, ed. *Models of Autonomy.* New Brunswick, NJ: Transaction Books, 1981.

Dishon, Daniel, ed. *Middle East Record (MER)1968.* Jerusalem: Israel Universities Press, 1977.

Dunn, Michael Collins. "The Arab World and the Kurds." In *Kurdish Identity: Human Rights and Political Status,* eds. Charles G. MacDonald and Carole A. O'Leary (Gainesville: University Press of Florida, 2007), pp. 231–237.

Al-Durra, Mahmud. *Al-Qadiyya al-Kurdiyya,* 2nd ed. Beirut: Dar al-Tali'a, 1996.

Edmonds, Cecil J. *Kurds, Turks and Arabs.* London: Oxford University Press, 1957.

Elazar, Daniel, ed. *Federalism and Political Integration.* Ramat-Gan, Israel: Turtledove, 1979.

Eppel, Michael. "The Demise of the Kurdish Emirates: The Impact of Ottoman Reforms and International Relations on Kurdistan During the First Half of the Nineteenth Century." *Middle Eastern Studies* 44, no. 2 (2008): 237–258.

———. *Iraq from Monarchy to Tyranny: From the Hashemites to the Rise of Saddam.* Gainesville: University Press of Florida, 2004.

Eskander, Saad B. "Fayli Kurds of Baghdad and the Ba'ath Regime." In *The Kurds: Nationalism and Politics,* eds. Faleh A. Jabar and Dawod Hosham (London: Saqi, 2006), pp. 180–203.

Evans, Peter B., Dietrich Rueschemeyer, and Theda Skocpol, eds. *Bringing the State Back In.* Cambridge: Cambridge University Press, 1985.

Eytan, Refa'el. *Raful: The Story of a Soldier.* With Dov Goldstein. In Hebrew, Tel Aviv: Sifriyat Ma'ariv, 1985.

Farhan, Dilshad Nu'man. *Mu'anat al-Kurd al-Izidiyyin fi Zill al-Hukumat al-'Iraqiyya 1921–2003.* Duhok: Duhok University, 2008.

Farouk-Sluglett, Marion, and Peter Sluglett. *Iraq Since 1958: From Revolution to Dictatorship,* 3rd ed. London: I. B. Tauris, 2001.

Fayed, Raja'i. *Tahawwulat al-Shakhsiyya al-Kurdiyya nahwa al-Hadatha.* Duhok: Markaz al-Dirasat al-Kurdiyya wa Hifz al-Watha'iq, 2008.

Fédération internationale des ligues des Droits de l'Homme. Report no. 178 (October 1993).

Findley, Paul. "The U.S. Stake in Good Relations with Baghdad." *Washington Report on Middle East Affairs* (December 1988).

Francke, Rend Rahim. "Political Impact of Sanctions in Iraqi Kurdistan." In *Kurdish Identity: Human Rights and Political Status*, eds. Charles G. MacDonald and Carole A. O'Leary (Gainesville: University Press of Florida, 2007), pp. 137–145.

Franz, Erhard. *Kurden und Kurdentum.* Hamburg: Deutsches Orient-Institut, 1986.

Friedlander, Robert A. "Autonomy and the Thirteen Colonies: Was the American Revolution Really Necessary?" In *Models of Autonomy*, ed. Yoram Dinstein (New Brunswick, NJ: Transaction Books, 1981), pp. 135–148.

Friedman, Robert O. *Soviet Policy Towards the Middle East Since 1970.* New York: Praeger, 1978.

Fuccarro, Nelida. *The Other Kurds: Yazidis in Colonial Iraq.* London: I. B. Tauris, 1999.

Fuller, Graham E., and Rend Rahim Francke. *The Arab Shi'a: The Forgotten Muslims.* New York: Palgrave, 2001.

Galbraith, Peter W. *The End of Iraq: How American Incompetence Created a War Without End.* New York: Simon & Schuster, 2006.

———. "Saddam's Documents: A Report to the Committee on Foreign Relations United States Senate." Washington, DC: US Government Printing Office, 1992.

Galletti, Mirella. *Le relazioni tra Italia e Kurdistan.* Rome: Istituto per l'Oriente C.A. Nallino, 2001.

Gantner, Serge. *The Kurdish National Movement.* In Hebrew, Tel Aviv: 'Am Hasefer, 1968.

———. "Le mouvement national kurde." *Orient*, nos. 32–33 (1964–1965): 29–120.

Ghareeb, Edmund. *The Kurdish Question in Iraq.* Syracuse, NY: Syracuse University Press, 1981.

Gunter, Michael. "Federalism and the Kurds of Iraq: The Solution or the Problem?" In *The Kurds: Nationalism and Politics*, eds. Faleh A. Jabar and Dawod Hosham (2006), pp. 231–258.

———. "The Kurdish Problem in Turkey." *Middle East Journal* 42, no. 3 (1988): 389–406.

———. *The Kurds of Iraq: Tragedy and Hope.* New York: St. Martin's Press, 1992.

———. *The Kurds and the Future of Turkey.* Houndmills: Macmillan, 1997.

———. "Qaddafi Reconsidered." *Journal of Conflict Studies, North America* (21 August 2001), http://journals.hil.unb.ca.

———. "Turkey's New Neighbor, Kurdistan." In *The Future of Kurdistan in Iraq*, eds. Brendan O'Leary, John McGarry, and Khaled Salih (Philadelphia: University of Pennsylvania Press, 2005), 219–232.

———. "United States Foreign Policy Toward the Kurds." *Orient* 40, no. 3 (1999): 427–437.

Halliday, Fred. "Can We Write a Modernist History of Kurdish Nationalism?" In *The Kurds: Nationalism and Politics*, eds. Faleh A. Jabar and Dawod Hosham (London: Saqi, 2006), pp. 11–21.

Hama-Saeed, Mariwan. "Kurdish Banks Slowly Win Trust." 4 May 2006. www.krg.org.

al-Hasani, 'Abd al-Razzaq. *Ta'rikh al-Wizarat al-'Iraqiyya*, part 3. Sidon, Lebanon: Al-'Urfan Press, 1939.

Hassanpour, Amir. *Nationalism and Language in Kurdistan 1918–1985.* San Francisco: Mellen Research University Press, 1992.

Hayim, Avraham. "The Shi'a in Iraq." *Hamizrah Hehadash* 19, no. 4 (1969): 346–348 (in Hebrew).

Hilterman, Joost R. "Halabja: The Politics of Memory." Open Democracy, 14 March 2008. www.opendemocracy.net.

———. *A Poisonous Affair*. New York: Cambridge University Press, 2007.

Al-Hirmizi, Arshad. *The Turkmen Reality in Iraq*. Istanbul: Kerkük Vakfı, 2005.

Hoffman, Stanley. *Primacy or World Order*. New York: McGraw-Hill, 1978.

Howard, Michael. "War and Nations." In *Nationalism*, eds. John Hutchinson and Anthony D. Smith (Oxford: Oxford University Press, 1994), pp. 254–258.

Hroch, Miroslav. *Social Preconditions of National Revival in Europe: A Comparative Analysis of the Social Composition of Patriotic Groups Among the Smaller European Nations*. New York: Columbia University Press, 2000.

Human Rights Watch. *Genocide in Iraq*. www.hrw.org.

Husayn, Saddam. "Khandaq Wahid Am Khandaqan." In *Al-Thawra wal-Nazra al-Jadida*. Baghdad: Dar al-Hurriyya lil-Tiba'a, 1981.

Hutchinson, John, and Anthony D. Smith, eds. *Nationalism*. Oxford: Oxford University Press, 1994.

Ibrahim, Ferhad. *Die Kurdische Nationalbewegung im Iraq*. Berlin: Klaus Schwarz Verlag, 1983.

Ibrahim, Sa'd al-Din. *Al-Milal wal-Nihal wal-A'raq: Humum al-Aqalliyyat fil-Watan al'Arabi*. Cairo: Markaz Ibn Khaldun, 1994.

Imset, Ismet G. *The PKK: A Report on Separatist Violence in Turkey*. Ankara: Turkish Daily News Publications, 1992.

Izady, Mehrdad R. *The Kurds: A Concise Handbook*. Washington, DC: Taylor & Francis, 1992.

Jabar, Faleh A., and Dawod Hosham, eds. *The Kurds: Nationalism and Politics*. London: Saqi, 2006.

Jawad, Sa'ad. *Iraq and the Kurdish Question, 1958–1970*. London: Ithaca Press, 1981.

Jwaideh, Wadie. *The Kurdish National Movement: Its Origins and Developments*. Syracuse, NY: Syracuse University Press, 2006.

Kelidar, Abbas. "Iraq: The Search for Stability." *Conflict Studies*, no. 59 (1975): 1–22.

Kelly, J. B. *Arabia, the Gulf, and the West*. London: Weidenfeld & Nicolson, 1980.

Khadduri, Majid. *Independent Iraq, 1932–1958: A Study in Iraqi Politics*. London: Oxford University Press, 1960.

———. *Republican Iraq: A Study in Iraqi Politics Since the Revolution of 1958*. London: Oxford University Press, 1969.

Kinnane, Derek. *The Kurds and Kurdistan*. London: Oxford University Press, 1964.

Kirişci, Kemal. "Turkey and the Safe Haven in Northern Iraq." *Journal of South Asian and Middle Eastern Studies* 19, no. 3 (1996): 21–39.

Kirişci, Kemal, and Gareth M. Winrow. *The Kurdish Question and Turkey*. London: Routledge Curzon, 2004.

Kirmanj, Sherko. "The Construction of the Iraqi State and the Question of National Identity." PhD thesis, University of South Australia, 2010.

Kissinger, Henry. *White House Years*. Boston: Little, Brown, 1979.

Korn, David. "The Last Years of Mustafa Barzani." *Middle East Quarterly* 1, no. 2 (1994): 13–27.

Kutschera, Chris. *Le mouvement national kurde*. Paris: Flammarion, 1970.

Laizer, S. J. *Martyrs, Traitors, and Patriots: Kurdistan After the Gulf War*. London: Zed Books, 1996.

Lambert, Peter J. "The United States and the Kurds: Case Studies on the United States Engagement." Master's thesis, Naval Postgraduate School, 1997.

Larteguy, Jean. *The Walls of Israel*. New York: M. Evans, 1969.

Lawrence, Quil. *Invisible Nation: How the Kurds' Quest for Statehood Is Shaping Iraq and the Middle East*. New York: Walker (distributed by Macmillan), 2008.

Leezenberg, Michael. "Urbanization, Privatization, and Patronage: The Political Economy of Iraqi Kurdistan." In *The Kurds: Nationalism and Politics*, eds. Faleh A. Jabar and Dawod Hosham (London: Saqi, 2006), pp. 151–180.

Lewis, Bernard. *The Emergence of Modern Turkey*. London: Oxford University Press, 1965.

Longrigg, Stephen H. *Iraq, 1900 to 1950: A Political, Social, and Economic History*. London: Oxford University Press, 1953.

Lortz, Michael G. "Willing to Face Death: A History of Kurdish Military Forces—The Peshmerga—From the Ottoman Empire to Present-day Iraq." Master's thesis, Florida State University, 2005.

MacDonald, Charles G., and Carole A. O'Leary, eds. *Kurdish Identity: Human Rights and Political Status*. Gainesville: University Press of Florida, 2007.

Machiavelli, Niccolò. *The Prince*. Harmondsworth: Penguin Books, 1971.

Mack, David. "The United States Policy and the Iraqi Kurds." In *Kurdish Identity: Human Rights and Political Status*, eds. Charles G. MacDonald and Carole A. O'Leary (Gainesville: University Press of Florida, 2007), pp. 117–119.

Makiya, Kanan. *Cruelty and Silence: War, Tyranny, Uprising, and the Arab World*. London: Penguin Books, 1993.

Makovsky, Alan. "Kurdish Agreement Signals New U.S. Commitment." *Policy Watch*, 29 September 1998.

Malovany, Pesach. *The Wars of Modern Babylon*. In Hebrew, Tel Aviv: Ma'arakhot, 2009.

Marr, Phebe. *The Modern History of Iraq*. Boulder, CO: Westview Press, 1985.

Al-Mas'udi, Abu al-Hasan 'Ali bin al-Husayn bin 'Ali. *Muruj al Dhahab*, vol. 3. Paris: L'imprimerie Nationale, 1918.

Matar, Fuad. *Saddam Hussein, the Man and the Cause, and the Future*. Beirut: Third World Center, 1981.

Matar, Salim. *Al-Dhat al-Jariha*. Beirut: al-Mu'assasa al-'Arabiyya lil-Dirasat wal-Nashr, 1997.

McDermott, Anthony. "The 1975 Crisis." Minority Rights Group Paper no. 23. 1977.

McDowall, David. *A Modern History of the Kurds*. London: I. B. Tauris, 2004.

McKiernan, Kevin. *The Kurds: A People in Search of Their Homeland*. New York: St. Martin's Press, 2006.

Meho, Lokman I. *The Kurdish Question in U.S. Foreign Policy: A Documentary Sourcebook*. Westport, CT: Praeger, 2004.

Meiselas, Susan. *Kurdistan: In the Shadow of History*. New York: Random House, 1997.

Mella, Jawad. *Al-Siyasa al-Isti'mariyya li-Hizb al-Ba'th al-Suri fi Gharb Kurdistan*. London: Kurdistan National Congress, 2004.

———. *Kurdistan and the Kurds: A Divided Homeland and a Nation Without State*. London: Western Kurdistan Association, 2005.

Al-Minhaj wal-Nizam al-Dakhili lil-Hizb al-Dimuqrati al-Kurdistani. Min Manshurat Pareti Dimuqrati Kurdistan, 1960.

Minorsky, Vladimir. "Kurds," in *Encyclopedia of Islam*, 1st ed. Leiden: Brill, 1927.

Mu'awwad, Adib. *Al-Akrad fi Lubnan wa-Suriyya*. 1945; reprint, Duhok: University of Duhok, 2008.

———. *Al-Qadiyya al-Kurdiyya*. Duhok: Duhok University, 2008.

Nakdimon, Shlomo. *Broken Hope: The Israeli-Kurdish Relations, 1963–1975*. In Hebrew, Tel Aviv: Yedi'ot Ahronot, 1996.

Al-Nasrawi, Abbas. "Economic Consequences of the Iraq-Iran War." *Third World Quarterly* 8, no. 3 (July 1986): 869–895.

Nasser, Munir H. "Iraq: Ethnic Minorities and Their Impact on Politics." *Journal of South Asian and Middle Eastern Studies* 8, no. 3 (1985): 22–37.

Natali, Denise. *The Kurds and the State: Evolving National Identity in Iraq, Turkey, and Iran*. Syracuse, NY: Syracuse University Press, 2005.

———. *The Kurdish Quasi-State*. Syracuse, NY: Syracuse University Press, 2010.

Nebez, Jemal. *The Kurds*. London: Western Kurdistan Association, 2004.

Neuberger, Benyamin. *National Self-Determination in Postcolonial Africa*. Boulder: Lynne Rienner, 1986.

Nezan, Kendal. "The European Perspective." In *Kurdish Identity: Human Rights and Political Status*, eds. Charles G. MacDonald and Carole A. O'Leary (Gainesville: University Press of Florida, 2007), pp. 237–246.

———. "The Kurds Under the Ottoman Empire." In *A People Without a Country: The Kurds and Kurdistan*, ed. Gérard Chaliand (London: Zed Press, 1980), pp. 113–130.

Nidal al-Ba'th fi Sabil al-Wahda, al-Hurriyya wal-Ishtirakiyya. Beirut: 1971.

Nikitine, Basile. *Les Kurdes: Étude sociologique et historique*. Paris: Éditions d'Aujourd'hui, 1965.

O'Leary, Brendan. "Power Sharing, Federation and Federacy." In *The Future of Kurdistan in Iraq*, eds. Brendan O'Leary, John McGarry, and Khaled Salih (Philadelphia: University of Pennsylvania Press, 2005), pp. 47–92.

O'Leary, Brendan, John McGarry, and Khaled Salih, eds. *The Future of Kurdistan in Iraq*. Philadelphia: University of Pennsylvania Press, 2005.

O'Leary, Carole A. "Communalism and the Future of Iraq." In *Kurdish Identity: Human Rights and Political Status*, eds. Charles G. MacDonald and Carole A. O'Leary (Gainesville: University Press of Florida, 2007), pp. 168–177.

O'Shea, Maria. "Tying Down the Territory: Conceptions and Misconceptions of Early Kurdish History." In *The Kurds: Nationalism and Politics*, eds. Faleh A. Jabar and Dawod Hosham (London: Saqi, 2006), pp. 113–130.

Penrose, Edith, and E. F. Penrose. *Iraq: International Relations and National Development*. London: Ernest Benn, 1978.

Petrosian, Wahram. *Siyasat Turkiyya tujah Kurdistan al-'Iraq wa-Amerika 1991–2003*. Duhok: University of Duhok, 2008.

Pipes, Daniel. "A Border Adrift: Origins of the Conflict." In *The Iran-Iraq War*, eds. Shirin Tahir-Kheli and Shaheen Ayubi (New York: Praeger, 1973), pp. 3–25.

Prince, James M. "A Kurdish State in Iraq?" *Current History* 92 (1993): 17–22.

Randal, Jonathan. *After Such Knowledge, What Forgiveness? My Encounters with Kurdistan*. Boulder, CO: Westview Press, 1999.

Raymond, Walter John. *Dictionary of Politics*. Lawrenceville, VA: Brunswick, 1992.

Report of the United Nations High Commissioner for Refugees (UNHCR), "Country of Origin Information Iraq," October 2005. http://www.unhcr.org.

Revolutionary Iraq 1968–1973. Report of the Eighth Regional Congress of the Arab Ba'th Socialist Party, Iraq, January 1974. Baghdad: October 1974.

Romano, David. *The Kurdish Nationalist Movement: Opportunity, Mobilization and Identity*. Cambridge, UK: Cambridge University Press, 2008.

Rubin, Avshalom H. "Abd al-Karim Qasim and the Kurds of Iraq: Centralization, Resistance and Revolt, 1958–1963." *Middle Eastern Studies* 43, no. 3 (2007): 352–382.

Said, Abdul Aziz. "Perspective of Abdul Said." In *Kurdish Identity: Human Rights and Political Status*, eds. Charles G. MacDonald and Carole A. O'Leary (Gainesville: University Press of Florida, 2007), pp. 30–35.

Said, Edward. "Misinformation About Iraq." allraqi, 28 November 2002, www .aliraqi.org.

Salih, Khaled. "Iraq and the Kurds: A Bibliographic Essay." *Digest of Middle East Studies* 4, no. 2 (1995): 24–39.

al-Salihi, Najib. *Al-Zilzal*. London: Mu'assasat al- Rafid lil-Nashr wal-Tawzi', 1998.

Schechla, Joseph. "Ideological Roots of Population Transfer." *Third World Quarterly* 14, no. 2 (1993): 239–275, www.jstor.org/pss/3992567.

Schmidt, Dana Adams. *Journey Among Brave Men*. Boston: Little, Brown, 1964.

Scott, James C. "Patron-client Politics and Political Change in Southeast Asia." *American Political Science Review* 66, no. 1 (1972): 91–113.

Segev, Shmu'el. *The Iranian Triangle*. In Hebrew, Tel Aviv: Sifriyat Ma'ariv, 1981.

Segev, Tom. *1949, The First Israelis*. In Hebrew, Jerusalem: Domino, 1984.

"Settlement of the Kurdish Problem." *Al-Thawra*, Thawra Publications, n.d., n.p.

Shemesh, Haim. *Soviet-Iraqi Relations, 1968–1988: In the Shadow of the Iraq-Iran Conflict*. Boulder: Lynne Rienner, 1992.

Short, Martin, and Anthony McDermott. "The Kurds." *Minority Rights Group* Paper no. 23. London: Minority Rights Group, February 1975.

Simons, Geoff. *Iraq: From Sumer to Saddam*. London: St. Martin's Press, 1994.

Smith, Anthony D. *Nations and Nationalism in a Global Era*. Cambridge UK: Polity Press, 1995.

Smith, Harvey Henry, and Richard F. Nyrop. *Area Handbook for Iraq*. Washington, DC: American University, 1971.

El-Solh, Camilia Fawaz. "Migration and the Selectivity of Change: Egyptian Peasant Women in Iraq." *Peuples Méditerranéens*, nos. 31–32 (1985): 243–258.

Sørli, Mirjam E., Nils Petter Gleditsch, and Håvard Strand. "Why Is There So Much Conflict in the Middle East?" *Journal of Conflict Resolution* 49, no. 1 (2005): 141–146.

Stansfield, Gareth R. V. *Crisis in Kirkuk: The Ethnopolitics of Conflict and Compromise*. Philadelphia: University of Pennsylvania Press, 2009.

———. "Finding a Dangerous Equilibrium: Internal Politics in Iraqi Kurdistan—Parties, Tribes and Ethnicity Reconsidered." In *The Kurds: Nationalism and Politics*, eds. Faleh A. Jabar and Dawod Hosham (London: Saqi, 2006), pp. 258–277.

———. "Governing Kurdistan: The Strengths of Division." In *The Future of Kurdistan in Iraq*, eds. Brendan O'Leary, John McGarry, and Khaled Salih (Philadelphia: University of Pennsylvania Press, 2005), pp. 195–219.

———. *Iraqi Kurdistan: Political Development and Emergent Democracy*. New York: Routledge Curzon, 2003.

Al-Tabari, Abu Ja'far Muhammad bin Jarir. *Ta'arikh al-Umam wal-Muluk*. Beirut: Dar al-Qamus al-Hadith, 1968.

Tahir-Kheli, Shirin, and Shaheen Ayubi, eds. *The Iran-Iraq War*. New York: Praeger, 1973.

Tahiri, Hussein. *The Structure of Kurdish Society and the Struggle for a Kurdish State*. Costa Mesa, CA: Mazda, 2007.

Talab Hilal, Muhammad. "A Study of Al-Jazeera Province from an Ethnic, Social and Political Aspect." In Jawad Mella, *Al-Siyasa al-Isti'mariyya li-Hizb al-Ba'th al-Suri fi Gharb Kurdistan* (London: Kurdistan National Congress, 2004), pp. 63–227.

Talabani, Jalal. *Kurdistan wal-Haraka al-Qawmiyya al-Kurdiyya*. Beirut: Dar al-Tali'a, 1971.

Teimourian, Hazir. "Turkey: The Challenge of the Kurdistan Workers' Party." *Jane's Intelligence Review* 5, no. 1 (1993): 29–32.

Tejel, Jordi. *Syria's Kurds: History, Politics and Society*. London: Routledge, 2009.

Al-Thawra Al-'Arabiyya, nos. 7–12 (1969).

Tilly, Charles. "War Making and State Making as Organized Crime." In *Bringing the State Back In*, eds. Peter B. Evans, Dietrich Rueschemeyer, and Theda Skocpol (Cambridge: Cambridge University Press, 1985), pp. 169–191.

Trabulsi, Fawwaz. "On Being Silent: A Response to Kanan Makiya." *Middle East Report*, nos. 187–188 (1994): 61–63.

Tripp, Charles. *A History of Iraq*. Cambridge: Cambridge University Press, 2002.

Tsafrir, Eliezer (Geizi). *Ana Kurdi*. In Hebrew, Or Yehuda: Hed Artzi, 1999.

US Senate Committee on Foreign Relations. *Civil War in Iraq* (Washington, DC, May 1991).

Vali, Abbas, ed. *Essays on the Origins of Kurdish Nationalism*. Costa Mesa, CA: Mazda, 2003.

———. "Genealogies of the Kurds: Constructions of Nation and National Identity in Kurdish Historical Writing." In *Essays on the Origins of Kurdish Nationalism*, ed. Abbas Vali (Costa Mesa, CA: Mazda, 2003), pp. 58–107.

———. "Introduction: Nationalism and the Question of Origins." In *Essays on the Origins of Kurdish Nationalism*, ed. Abbas Vali (Costa Mesa, CA: Mazda, 2003), pp. 1–14.

———. "The Kurds and Their 'Others': Fragmented Identity and Fragmented Politics." In *The Kurds: Nationalism and Politics*, eds. Faleh A. Jabar and Dawod Hosham (London: Saqi, 2006), pp. 49–79.

Van Bruinessen, Martin. *Agha, Shaikh and State: The Social and Political Structures of Kurdistan*. London: Zed Books, 1992.

———. "Ehmedi Xanî's Mem û Zîn and Its Role in the Emergence of Kurdish National Awareness." In *Essays on the Origins of Kurdish Nationalism*, ed. Abbas Vali (Costa Mesa, CA: Mazda, 2003), pp. 40–57.

———. "Kurdish Paths to Nation." In *The Kurds: Nationalism and Politics*, eds. Faleh A. Jabar and Dawod Hosham (London: Saqi, 2006), pp. 21–49.

———. "The Kurds Between Iran and Iraq." *Middle East Report*, no. 141 (1986): 14–27.

———. "The Kurds and Islam." Islamic Area Studies Project Working Paper no. 13 (Tokyo: 1999).

Vanly, Ismet Sheriff. "Hawla al-Istratijiyya al-Siyasiyya wal-'Askariyya lil-Haraka al-Wataniyya al-Kurdiyya." *Dirasat Kurdiyya*, nos. 1–2 (1985): 22–23.

———. *Le Kurdistan irakien entité nationale: Étude de la révolution de 1961*. Neuchâtel, Switzerland: Éditions de la Baconnière, 1970.

———. "Kurdistan in Iraq." In *A People Without a Country: The Kurds and Kurdistan*, ed. Gérard Chaliand (London: Zed Press, 1980), pp. 139–193.

Vernier, Bernard. *L'Iraq d'aujourd'hui*. Paris: Librarie Armand Colin, 1963.

Wahlbeck, Osten. *Kurdish Diasporas: A Comparative Study of Kurdish Refugee Communities*. London: Macmillan Press, 1999.

Watha'iq al-Idana. Damascus: Manshurat al-Ittihad al-Watani al-Kurdistani, 1994.

Wimmer, Andreas. *Nationalist Exclusion and Ethnic Conflict*. Cambridge: Cambridge University Press, 2002.

Yildiz, Kerim, *The Kurds in Iraq: The Past, Present and Future*. London: Pluto Press, 2004.

Zaken, Mordechai. *Jewish Subjects and Their Tribal Chieftains in Kurdistan*. Leiden: Brill, 2007.

Zaki, Muhammad Amin. *Ta'rikh al-Kurd wa Kurdistan*, vol. 1. In Kurdish, 1931; in Arabic, Cairo: Matba'at al-Sa'ada, 1939.

———. *Ta'rikh al-Kurd wa Kurdistan*, vol. 2. In Kurdish, 1939; in Arabic, Cairo: Matba'at al-Sa'ada, 1945.

Index

absence as military commander in
Kurdistan War, 126; attempts to
prevent deterioration of relations with
Kurds, 88, 93; awards general rank to
Saddam, 153; claims no knowledge of
attacks on Kurds, 59; coup attempts
against, 101; does not sign Algiers
Agreement, 140; political weakening
of, 137; refusal to negotiate with
Kurds 104, 145; Saddam seeks
counterweight to, 115; visits Soviet
Union, 88; warned by Soviet Union
of coup attempt, 101
Baliq, 134
Balisan, 178
Barwari, Nasrin, 288
Barwari, Zubeyda, 165*n14*
Barzani, Ahmad, 119
Barzani, Idris, 39, 50, 52; assassination
attempts on, 54, 58; chosen party
leader for KDP, 162; death of, 156,
162; meets with CIA 77; negotiates
with Saddam on Autonomy Law, 116;
position in guerrilla army, 33
"Barazaniland," 273
Barth, Frederic, 5
Barvari, 255
Barzan, 31, 92, 129, 156, 282
Barzani, Luqman, 156
Barzani, Mas'ud, 39, 50, 52, 213, 280,
281; assassination attempts on, 156;
command of Parastin by, 33, 43*n10*,
162; encourages dialogue with
regime, 250, 251; involvement in
reorganization of KDP, 162; meets
with CIA 77; in parastin 162; power
sharing with Talabani, 203, 209–213;
reconciliation with Talabani, 211–
212, 264, 275, 276; refuses then
accepts invitation to Washington, 262,
263; requests political solution with
regime, 233; requests regime
assistance, 236–238; president of
KRG, 299
Barzani, Mullah Mustafa: 11, 22*n99*, 17,
37, 41, 50–51, 66, 79, 199, 283, 285;
advises moving to Iran, 145; appeals
to United States , 70, 72, 119, 142–
143, 145, 146, 156; approves March
Declaration, 49; assassination
attempts on, 54, 59, 60, 85–88, 156;

attempts to protect civilians during
Kurdistan War, 130; brings Talabani's
group into KDP, 53; distrust of Iran,
69, 77, 79*n15*; exile in Iran, 156;
favors relations with Israel, 75;
hostility toward communism, 70;
initiates skirmishes with Iraqi army,
119; operation as tribal leader, 32;
opponents denounce as traitor in
Kurdistan War, 130, 131; as president
of Kurdistan Democratic Party, 31;
pressures Western governments for
support, 121; regime attempts to
destroy image 130, 131; rejects
mediation efforts by Soviet Union,
119, 120; relations with Talabani, 33;
requests direct help from Iran in
Kurdistan War, 133; return of remains
to Kurdistan, 210; role in Kurdistan
War, 126; role in negotiations with
Saddam, 27, 39, 40; in Soviet Union,
31; talks with central government on
autonomy, 199
Barzani, Nechirvan, 21*n71*, 22*n99*,
166*n36*, 216, 265, 283, 294*n83*
Barzani, Sabir, 156
Barzani, Saywan, 165*n11*
Barzani, Shaikh 'Uthman, 119, 130
Barzani, 'Ubaydullah, 122; death of, 156;
involvement in assassination attempt
on father, 60; ministerial appointment
from regime, 120; relations with
Saddam, 60; speaks against father in
Kurdistan War, 130, 131; support for
Autonomy Law, 119
Barzani clan 6, 16, 156, 194*n76*, 298,
299
Barzanji, Shaikh Mahmud, 14, 15
al-Barzanji, Ja'far 'Abd al-Karim, 188
Basra, 2, 83, 87, 174
Batatu, Hanna, 6, 55
al-Bazzaz, 'Abd-al-Raman, 17, 28, 34–
35, 42, 48, 63*n58*
Be'eri, Yedidya, 119
Begin, Menachem, 75
Bekas, Sherko, 285
Ben Yishay, Ron, 218
Biden, Joe, 303
al-Bidlisi, Emir Sharif Khan, 8
Boumédienne, Houari, 138, 139
Bozarslan, Hamit, 34, 246, 278

About the Book

Ofra Bengio explores the dynamics of relations between the Kurds of Iraq and the Iraqi state from the inception of the Baath regime to the present.

Bengio draws on a wealth of rich source materials to carefully trace the evolution of Kurdish national identity in Iraq. Dissecting the socioeconomic, political, and ideological transformations that Iraqi Kurdish society has undergone across some five decades, she focuses on the twin processes of nation building and state building. She also highlights the characteristics of the Kurdish movement in Iraq relative to Kurdish communities elsewhere in the region.

This narrative of the profound vicissitudes of Iraqi Kurdish fortunes illuminates not only the complexities of politics within Iraq today, but also the influence of Iraqi Kurdistan on the geostrategic map of the entire Middle East.

Ofra Bengio is lecturer in the Department of Middle East Studies at Tel Aviv University and senior research fellow at the university's Dayan Center for Middle Eastern and African Studies. Her previous publications in English include *Saddam's World: Political Discourse in Iraq*, the coedited *Minorities and the State in the Arab World,* and *The Sunna and Shi'a in History: Division and Ecumenism in the Muslim Middle East.*